Espionage/
Memoir

Secret Missions

Secret Missions

THE STORY
OF AN INTELLIGENCE OFFICER

By *Captain* ELLIS M. ZACHARIAS, USN

BLUEJACKET
BOOKS

Naval Institute Press
Annapolis, Maryland

Naval Institute Press
291 Wood Road
Annapolis, MD 21402

First Bluejacket Books printing, 2003

Library of Congress Cataloging-in-Publication Data
Zacharias, Ellis M., 1890–
    Secret missions : the story of an intelligence officer / by Ellis M. Zacharias.
    p. cm. — (Bluejacket books)
    Originally published: New York: G. P. Putnam, 1946.
    Includes bibliographical references and index.
    ISBN 1-59114-999-1 (alk. paper)
    1. Zacharias, Ellis M., 1890– 2. United States. Navy—Officers—Biography.
3. Admirals—United States—Biography. 4. World War, 1939–1945—Military intelligence. 5. World War, 1939–1945—Naval operations, American. 6. World War, 1939–1945—Campaigns—Pacific Area. I. Title. II. Series.
V63.Z33 A3 2003
940.54'8673'092—dc21
[B]

                                        2002041096

Printed in the United States of America on acid-free paper ∞
10 09 08 07 06 05 04 03   9 8 7 6 5 4 3 2 1

Frontispiece photo courtesy of Jerrold M. Zacharias

To My Wife

CONTENTS

FOREWORDS

ALTHOUGH AN INSTANT bestseller when it was first published during
the fall of 1946 and again when it briefly appeared in paperback after
the author's death in June 1961, *Secret Missions* nonetheless soon faded
from the public memory. Now, thanks to the Naval Institute Press and
its nonpareil Bluejacket Books series, the autobiography by Ellis M.
Zacharias, then a captain in the U.S. Navy, is rescued from an obscurity
it doesn't deserve.

Essentially a personal account of nearly forty years of service that
begins in 1908 and concludes in 1946 with the rank of rear admiral, the
astonishingly detailed memoir offers far, far more. Readers are not only
privy to the rare psychological profiles of pre–World War II Japanese
political and military leaders, such as Nomura, Suzuki, Takagi,
Yamamoto, Uyeda, and Yonai, that Zacharias prepared for the Office of
Naval Intelligence but also learn of the role he played in easing the
Japanese nation into surrender in 1945 by defining the term "unconditional surrender." Zacharias made one of our first ventures into the
realm of psychological warfare via a series of broadcasts beamed at
Japan, stressing in impeccable Japanese the futility of continued fighting and that submission didn't imply an overturning of the national system or traditional way of life.

With his acuity of judgment (all too lacking in today's assessments
of the Pacific war and its personalities), Zacharias writes in a style that
allows us to experience his story vicariously. For example, in 1912 we are
present on the Naval Academy field when he's commissioned an ensign
and then accompany him on his first assignment as an engineer officer
aboard the battleship *Virginia*. After service on several cruisers during
World War I, he is appointed assistant naval attaché to Japan. In late
1920, when he is dispatched to the U.S. Embassy in Tokyo by the Office
of Naval Intelligence "to acquire a further knowledge of the Japanese
language and the people of Japan," we learn that the young lieutenant
commander is the only officer in the entire U.S. fleet who can speak
and write a few words of Japanese.

Amid the delightful whirl of semidiplomatic parties and a naval attaché's social life, Zacharias goes to school and completely masters the language while diligently studying the people and their character. By 1922 he is convinced that the Japanese navy had begun thinking in terms of an intercontinental war with America but dreads the possibility for realistic reasons. Immediately, the lieutenant commander succeeds in gaining the confidence of several military leaders destined for dominating positions in the war to come. Zacharias's goal: gather as much information on the Japanese military as possible and somehow get it to the ONI with equal speed.

In 1967, almost half a century later, a very close colleague and personal friend, Rear Adm. Cecil H. Coggins (Ret.), recalled the lieutenant commander's determination to get crucial intelligence out of Japan during those troubling 1922–23 years.

> Zach was remarkable. Active, lean, alert, and full of energy, with bright eyes and a broad smile, he made friends with the Japanese naval officers and never forgot one of them. With his nimble mind and retentive memory went the prime quality of imagination. In a flash he could see the potentialities of an idea that would completely escape the average attaché officer. While his contemporaries were groping to grasp a concept, he had already understood it, developed a dozen possible corollaries, rejected some, and was always making plans to put the rest into effect. When it became obvious that even if the problem of retaining military information could be solved, getting it out of the country was a much bigger problem. After the Washington Naval Limitation Conference, held in 1921, which had established a 5:5:3 ratio of naval shipbuilding for the U.S., Great Britain, and Japan, Zach didn't trust the Japanese to stick to their side of the agreement. Soon he was in the thick of things.[1]

Although the lieutenant commander remained first and foremost an assistant naval attaché and language officer assigned to the U.S. Embassy in Tokyo until 1 November 1923, his first love was intelligence. Yet Zacharias was proud of his seamanship, and now that his tour of duty was about to end he sought the bridge of a ship to command.

Upon his return to Washington, D.C., Zacharias expected someone in the Office of Naval Intelligence to promote his perspective on the increasing Japanese effort to wage war in the Pacific. We read that although friends he encountered in the Army and Navy Club's grill sympathized with him, no one in the ONI gave a damn.

From 1924 onwards we follow the lieutenant commander's naval career as he alternates between sea duty and the intelligence service, specializing in Far Eastern affairs. We're there when Zacharias learns of each phase of Japanese aggression in the 1930s, tracks enemy spies on the West Coast, and listens politely as Adm. Husband E. Kimmel, then commander of the Pacific Fleet, rejects outright his prediction in March 1941 that the Japanese will undoubtedly attack Pearl Harbor with an air strike from the north on a Sunday morning in late November or early December.[2]

Three months later in June 1941, we join Zacharias as commanding officer of the cruiser USS *Salt Lake City*. In the Pacific his ship escapes the 7 December attack and for the next six months remains at sea, participating in the first U.S. counteroffensive strikes against Japanese-held territory—the Wake and the Marshall Islands. Later in September 1943 when he boards the battleship USS *New Mexico* as captain, we again engage in bitter naval campaigns, this time in the Gilberts, Marshalls, and Marianas.

Meanwhile, in June 1942 Zacharias receives new orders: report immediately to the chief of naval operations in Washington, D.C., for Duty in OP-16, the code name for the Office of Naval Intelligence. As much as he enjoyed commanding a cruiser in the thick of the early fighting, this new assignment is an even greater challenge—an opportunity he now relishes. Yet the captain now encounters his third major naval disappointment: after serving as acting chief for almost a year, he is passed over for the post of chief of naval intelligence—a position he had been led to believe was his by Adm. Ernest J. King, commander in chief of the U.S. Fleet—for a complete novice in intelligence work. Instead, Zacharias is confined to serving as assistant director.

But disappointment turns to elation when he is ordered back to sea in command of the powerful battleship *New Mexico,* berthed at the Navy Yard in Puget Sound. To captain a crew of more than seventeen hundred men is the greatest challenge he has yet faced. After a series of victories in the Marshall Islands, Kwajalein, New Ireland, the Marianas, Tinian, Rota, and Saipan, Zacharias is relieved of command of the *New Mexico* in September 1944 and becomes chief of staff of the 11th Naval District in San Diego.

It isn't long, however, before the U.S. Navy's Office of Public Information, recognizing his knowledge of the Japanese and their language, offers the captain to the Office of War Information as official spokesman of the U.S. government in making psychological warfare broadcasts to Japan. In May 1945 Zacharias begins a one-man radio campaign against the Japanese leaders. Fourteen psychological warfare broadcasts are made between V-E and V-J days. Aimed to clarify our surrender terms to the Japanese High Command, the work proves highly successful as evidenced when King congratulates the captain for his "good work in making the Japanese see the light and bringing about surrender."

Zacharias, who retired on 1 November 1945 as a rear admiral, was awarded the Legion of Merit with two gold stars. The first of these was for his liaison work between the Office of Naval Intelligence and the Office of Strategic Services in 1943. The second was for exceptionally meritorious conduct in the performance of outstanding services as a spokesman for the government's psychological warfare program during the summer of 1945. In that citation, it was recited that he "contributed materially to the reduction of Japanese morale toward the end of World War II." Zacharias's third Legion of Merit was awarded for exceptionally meritorious conduct commanding the *New Mexico*. He also received a letter of commendation with authorization to wear the commendation ribbon for his exploits as commanding officer of the *Salt Lake City*.

After his retirement, Zacharias wrote *Secret Missions* and later, in 1950, *Behind Closed Doors: The Secret History of the Cold War*. In addition, he began a new career lecturing on world situations and national security, critiquing U.S. intelligence and propaganda activities. In his lecture tours and magazine and newspaper articles, he campaigned for an independent and militant program of psychological warfare. Needless to say, many found his outspoken criticisms controversial, and he was often regarded as little more than a Cassandra or gadfly. Yet in spite of the skepticism he aroused with some of his sensational allegations during the early 1950s, he was considered by all an outspoken, pugnacious, and sometimes mistaken pioneer that America sorely needed at the time.

Don DeNevi

1. From *The Man Who Watched the Rising Sun: Admiral Ellis M. Zacharias* by Maria Wilhelm, published as a Ginger Book in association with Franklin Watts Inc. in 1967. The "M-Plan" and the "Colonel X Affair" are discussed in considerable detail in *Secret Missions*.

2. Zacharias never claimed to have predicted the exact date of Pearl Harbor— 7 December. In 1946 Kimmel testified before a Senate Committee investigating the attacks that he had no recollection of the conversation, adding, "Captain Zacharias had only warned me the Japanese would attack the fleet off Long Beach from an airfield in Mexico."

REAR ADM. Ellis M. Zacharias dedicated thirty-eight years of his life to a Navy that he loved. He proved his worth to this service and the nation in three distinctly different areas: first, as commanding officer of the heavy cruiser USS *Salt Lake City* and battleship USS *New Mexico* in battles of the Pacific war against Japan; second, as an intelligence officer, adept at counterintelligence and code breaking, who knew the Japanese character so well he warned naval commanders of the impending attack by Japan; and third, as a Japanese linguist, who in 1945 with the title of "official spokesman of the U.S. government" made broadcasts to the Japanese High Command explaining what unconditional surrender would mean to Japan, thereby hastening the day of surrender.

When Admiral Zacharias was sent to Japan in 1920 to study the country and the language, only one officer in the entire Navy could speak Japanese. Thrust into the world of naval rivalry that led up to the Washington Conference and into the prewar age of spies and counterspies, he found himself launched upon his life's work. He soon came to know Admirals Yamamoto, Nomura, Suzuki, and Yonai; Prince Takamatsu, brother of the emperor; and many other leading Japanese militarists. Admiral Zacharias was a keen student of the Japanese and through the years he maintained close touch with these leaders and other elements and obtained an unrivaled insight into their plans and thinking.

It was the realization of the importance of intelligence to the future security of the United States that prompted Admiral Zacharias to write *Secret Missions*. The title itself represents an unintentional dramatization, but it is accurate in every respect because the missions described in the book were secret at the time they were entrusted to him. Individually, they were colored stones of minor significance by themselves, but when fitted together they show a mosaic of the dramatic development through which intelligence passed from 1920 to 1945. Zacharias tried to describe in as great detail as possible the primitive gropings of our own intelligence effort as contrasted with the skill displayed by our adversaries who regarded intelligence as the "third oldest profession." He showed the growth in technique and principles as the years passed and the progress that made our own intelligence not only a match for that of our adversaries, but even their superior, especially insofar as regard for moral values is concerned.

My brother, Ellis Jr., and I often wondered where our father gleaned the information that enabled him to predict the attack on Pearl Harbor so accurately—even that it would come as an air attack on a Sunday morning. We knew that he clearly understood the Japanese character, but it was not until 2001 that we found the apparent answer we were looking for. While cataloging his many files and papers we found his Naval War College thesis, "The Relation Between Policy and Strategy in the Sino-Japanese War and the Russo-Japanese War," dated 1 February 1934. In the "Lessons For Us" section of this sixty-seven-year-old thesis, Admiral Zacharias (then a lieutenant commander) emphasized the great invitation presented by the weak U.S. position in the Philippines and the exposed position that our fleet occupied in the open roadstead on the West Coast. He wrote, "The Japanese are great students of history, particularly their own history and it is not to be expected that, in the event of strained relations, if they feel that war must come, they will overlook the opportunity to strike a tremendous blow in both of these positions without warning. The meager sources of information in Japan would make for the formation of such expeditions in secret." Admiral Zacharias's lone voice in the wilderness was not heard.

Capt. Jerrold M. Zacharias, USN (Ret.)

BOOK ONE

PRELUDE TO CONFLICT

1

ASSIGNMENT IN TOKYO

"When directed by the Director of Naval Intelligence you will regard yourself detached from present duty and will proceed to Tokyo, Japan, for the purpose of acquiring a knowledge of the Japanese language and the Japanese people.

"This employment on shore duty beyond the seas is required by the public interest."

THESE ORDERS, issued by Josephus Daniels, Secretary of the Navy, were handed to me on October 4, 1920, by Captain Andrew T. Long, USN, Director of Naval Intelligence, in his office in the Navy Department. It was obvious to me even then that the order sending me to "shore duty beyond the seas" was in reality my passport to adventure. With one stroke of his pen Mr. Daniels had opened a new world before me, so different from the monotony of routine and regulations which marks the career of a naval officer. There may be occasional thrills and excitements to punctuate the repetitious life in the Navy: cruises to faraway lands, maneuvers, ceremonies on gala occasions, parties, receptions, and pretty girls. But broad as the oceans are, the life of a naval officer is narrowed to the bridge of his ship, to the room where the engines pant, to the gun rooms and turrets, to the wardroom with its stereotyped discussions of the drills of the day, and the cook's gastronomic imagination.

There in Captain Long's office the memories of a long-forgotten day returned to me, the day when I first decided to enter upon a naval career. I was then eight years old, a fascinated witness to great events, as from the coast line of my native Florida I watched American warships deploy for the Spanish-American War. Enraptured, I stood watching the steaming parade, the battle-clad men on the decks, the guns elevated for the range. Then and there, the lure of the Navy, rather than the sea, gripped me—and it has held me captivated ever since.

3

4 Secret Missions

Since late August 1920 I had been attached to Naval Intelligence for temporary duty. I was quite hazy about the meaning of the word "intelligence" *; and I shared the indifference and even suspicion with which some of my fellow officers of the line habitually regarded intelligence work. With an attitude mixed of ignorance and mistrust, I had emphasized in my mind the temporary character of my intelligence duties rather than the duties themselves.

But standing in Captain Long's office, I suddenly realized the implications of the word. The Captain tried to discourage me from placing too much emphasis on my assignment to Naval Intelligence. "Although you are attached to Intelligence," he said, "you are going to Japan as a language student and not as an intelligence officer. In fact, I would advise you to keep away from intelligence work as far as possible. We expect you to bring back the most valuable information we now need: knowledge of the Japanese language and the Japanese people. We don't expect you to tie your hands with other activities. These are your orders."

But as he tried to minimize the importance of my connection with Intelligence, he merely opened my eyes wider to its manifold aspects and phases. I thought to myself: How can the knowledge of a foreign language and strange people be divorced from intelligence? How can I, even if I want to, refrain from learning Japan while studying its language and folkways? Indeed, my assignment is an intelligence mission in its most highly developed form, no matter how the Director of Naval Intelligence may regard it.

An incident which followed immediately my call on Captain Long served to reinforce this intuition. Quite abruptly and without warning I was introduced to the adversary: Japanese Intelligence, then trying its wings in Washington. It was suggested to me that while waiting for my travel orders I lease an apartment in the Benedict, a bachelor apartment house near the Army-Navy Club. I do not know whether it was only coincidence, but the apartment recommended to me was just above the quarters of Captain Uyeda, who was then Japan's naval attaché in Washington, and known to our own Naval Intelligence as a promising member of that

---

* "Intelligence," of course, is used here and throughout the book in its meaning of information and knowledge, and the activity of obtaining them. When capitalized, it refers to specific organizations engaged in that activity, such as Naval Intelligence. To avoid confusion, the word will be used *only* in those senses, not in the psychologists' sense (I.Q.) or the everyday usage meaning "brains."

country's budding espionage organization. Perfunctory and haphazard though our system of surveillance then was, we kept a watchful eye on Captain Uyeda, and I was to report any untoward incident observed during my stay over his head.

Impressed with my task, and following the urges of natural curiosity, I did a little investigating of my own and found that Captain Uyeda was a merry bachelor indeed, at least here in the United States, who made widespread use of the apartment's liberal rules regarding ladies. Night after night I could hear shrill Japanese laughter interspersed with feminine giggles. Patches of conversation floated through the open windows; and it did not take much effort to find out that these girls were secretaries in the Navy Department. This, of course, gave a new impetus to our interest in Captain Uyeda's parties, and soon we discovered that among his most frequent guests was a confidential stenographer in the office of the Secretary of the Navy. Soon after our discovery in the Benedict there were some sudden transfers in the secretarial staff of the Navy Department, which removed any danger of the "Arnold" having to be added to the name of the apartment house. However, we did not wish to be kill-joys and were happy to provide carefully briefed replacements. Captain Uyeda's social life then proceeded merrily both for him and for us.

The incident in the Benedict revealed to me the two fundamentally different aspects of intelligence. In Captain Long's office I was initiated into what the "lingo" of our profession calls *positive intelligence*. In the Benedict I was introduced to *negative intelligence*. Few people realize that in the broad field of activities which are usually classified as intelligence functions, a sharp distinction must be made between these two forms of operations. Positive intelligence may be defined as the collection of information regarding an enemy or a prospective enemy as to his intentions, strength, organizational structure, and deficiencies, to enable us to base our plans on the knowledge of these data. Intelligence material, then, is this information in its evaluated form.

Negative intelligence is the gathering of information regarding foreign agents to prevent them from obtaining the same type of information of our activities which we seek of theirs. Neither phase has much to do with the cloak-and-dagger work which receives widespread publicity in the wake of every war. The overwhelming majority of basic intelligence data is obtained by open observation, by studying reference books, consulting libraries, reading the newspapers of foreign countries, listening to their radios, interviewing bona fide travelers. The collection of information by surreptitious means is no longer intelligence. It is espionage. Both are closely related, but there are some crucial distinctions—as our Axis enemies discovered too late.

By the time my orders to proceed to Tokyo were handed to me in Washington, I knew as much about intelligence as it was possible to learn in two months of intensive study, seasoned with a dash of field experience as has just been related. Now everything was ready and waiting for me to turn my newly acquired knowledge to use.

"The War Department has been requested to furnish you transportation on the Army Transport 'Sherman,' sailing from San Francisco on or about 11 October 1920 for Japan."

At the time of my arrival in Japan, the country was in a peculiar ferment. The tide of militarism was ebbing in the wake of the Siberian expedition, which was turning out disastrously for Japan. It may be remembered that the turmoil which followed in Siberia subsequent to the Bolshevik revolution, and the presence there of certain Czech prisoners of war, induced the Allies to send an expeditionary force to Siberia, ostensibly for the purpose of enabling the escape of the Czech troops. Japan was invited by Great Britain and the United States to participate in the expedition and was asked to send a contingent of 7,000 men. The invitation was avidly accepted in Tokyo, where the militarists, still glorying in the defeat of Germany, to which they had contributed precious little, now hoped for an easy conquest across the sea on the Asiatic mainland. Instead of dispatching the contingent of 7,000 men, they sent 70,000—but even this force could not ultimately secure the Russian Far East for Japan.

The failure of the militarists encouraged the people to raise their voice against the clique of armed adventurers. Protest meetings were held in Hibiya Park, petitions were presented to the government, and speakers representing political groups and trade unions vociferously demanded the recall of the expeditionary force of Japan. By the time of my arrival in Tokyo in November 1920 I could see the backwash of these protests. I was told in the United States that militarists dominated Japan's political life and that they rode arrogantly high on the shoulders of the people. But when I made my first contacts in military and naval circles, I could not help noticing a subdued atmosphere in their midst. Indeed, they were bemoaning a lost opportunity and discounting the Siberian escapade as a dismal failure.

The people vented their anger in various forms. Soon it became quite dangerous for an officer to show himself in public wearing his uniform or to display his military rank on the name plates on his doors. The Chief of the Imperial General Staff was forced to resign, and military appropriations were cut in the budget, an unprecedented effrontery, my military contacts told me.

During the early part of my stay I did not quite grasp the political significance of these events and failed to discern the forces which boiled deep in Japan's imperialistic volcano. As usual with newcomers on a quasi-diplomatic mission, I was thrown into the whirlpool of diplomacy. Reporting to the Naval Attaché, Captain Edward Howe Watson, and striking up friendships with the younger set in the Embassy, I had gained access to that part of life in Tokyo which I was least eager to study. As I now turn back to the pages of my engagement book recording my early days in Japan, I find entries like these:

"February 7, 1921   Reception in the French Embassy
"February 8, 1921   Dinner at the house of Van Horn, Secretary
                      of the Dutch Embassy
"February 13, 1921   Luncheon with Captain Watson..."

I found it somewhat difficult to fit myself into the rigid social procedure which seemed to delight some of our younger diplomats. A newcomer to diplomatic etiquette, I committed a few *faux pas* and was promptly denounced for them to the counselor of our embassy, "Ned" Bell, a brilliant and energetic diplomat, who did not seem to be greatly disturbed by my first stumbling steps in the drawing rooms. When on one occasion a second secretary, who later rose to the rank of ambassador and became a most valuable member of our foreign service, reported to the Counselor that, *horribile dictu*, I had dared to take a picture at the Emperor's garden party, he just laughed and told his eager subordinate: "Forget about it!"

In Captain Watson I found a most gracious chief and an understanding guide to the scenes "backstage" of Japanese naval politics, or what Admiral Sato himself called "Japanese Navalism." Captain Watson was one of the most likable and dynamic, intelligent and alert naval attachés we have had in any country. He was extremely popular with the Japanese naval officers, who were mystified by his technique of telling them too much so that they could learn too little. On one occasion the chief of Japan's Naval Intelligence visited him to inquire about certain matters which required elucidation. Captain Watson erupted in his usual manner and went on talking about the matter for almost an hour, but as the dazed Japanese captain left his room, he frankly told Watson:

"Eddie, I don't think I have a right to complain. You certainly were not a bit taciturn. But frankly, I haven't the slightest idea what you are talking about."

To me, however, he confided that his loquaciousness was one of the many tricks he had up the sleeve of his uniform coat. He had an immense job in Japan and needed a whole set of similar tricks to cope with his task. When he had first arrived in Japan and inspected the files in the office of his predecessor, he was flabbergasted to find that they were almost empty. It was not his custom to swear, but on this occasion he broke his resolution, and he did it beautifully. And then continued to the officer he was relieving: "Is this all you've got?"

"That is all."

"You mean to tell me that these few sheets of paper represent all the information you have obtained during your three years in Tokyo?" he demanded.

"I couldn't take advantage of my peculiar position with an ally in time of war to extract information from their files," explained the other.

Watson was thus forced to start from scratch; but by the time he left, the files were bulging with reports and documents, and the Japanese Navy was accurately delineated in our office.

His first step when I arrived was to introduce me to the bigwigs of the Japanese Navy. To the Minister of the Navy and the chief of the Naval General Staff we paid merely a short courtesy call, but not so to the chief of the famous Joho Kyoku, Japan's Naval Intelligence. I had my first taste then and there of the seriousness with which the Japanese Navy regarded intelligence, far different from the haphazard improvisations and nonchalance with which we handled this important function.

We drove to the Navy Ministry building and entered through the main entrance, but that was as far as we were permitted to go. A guard conducted us to a waiting room, took our cards, and disappeared. Soon a junior officer accosted us, inquiring about the nature of our business, then bowed himself out only to disappear completely. Another aide finally came and conducted us up to the second floor, where was located the large but simple office of the Chief of Naval Intelligence.

A tall Japanese officer wearing the uniform of a Navy captain received us at the door, holding out his hand for a hearty handshake with Captain Watson: "I am glad to see you, Eddie," he greeted my chief in excellent English and with a smile which immediately put me at ease.

"Zacharias," Watson turned to me, "this is Captain Kichisaburo Nomura," then to Nomura: "This is Lieutenant Commander Zacharias, the new language student of whom I spoke."

The friendly atmosphere in which my first meeting with the later Ambassador Admiral Nomura took place persisted throughout my stay in Japan and even long after. Here again I found a Japanese to whom Westernism was no empty mode of manners. A man with a broad outlook and critical mind, Nomura was able to perceive the pros and cons in every argument and weigh against realities the chimerical plans which were then being woven in that same building.

We were on the eve of what Yamato Ichihashi, secretary to the Japanese delegation attending the Washington Naval Limitation Conference in 1921, later called the great diplomatic adventure. In London, Washington, and Tokyo the offices of naval intelligence were already maneuvering for position to learn about the proposals and schemes with which the others planned to go to the conference. Captain Watson's time was almost entirely taken up with study of possible Japanese plans, of which we happened to know more than most Japanese themselves, despite certain of our organizational deficiencies. The messages which passed between the Tokyo Foreign Office and its envoys in London and Washington were intercepted, decoded, and transcribed. The story of this has been told in full though somewhat exaggerated detail in Major Yardley's book, *The American Black Chamber*. I was amazed at these revelations; and I could never understand why the existence of this activity, much more the details of it, were permitted to be revealed. An irreparable harm was thereby done to our intelligence technique, a harm second only to the disclosures of a similar nature made before the Congressional Committee investigating the Pearl Harbor disaster. Furthermore, I could never understand the subsequent decision of the State Department to discontinue the activity, with so many other nations concentrating on it. Statecraft has many activities which, like the virtue of a lady, are better left undiscussed.

It was through Captain Watson that I gained my first insight into what may be called the Haute Ecole of international diplomacy. Although the intercepted and decoded cables told most of the story, there were innumerable little gaps which the naval attaché was expected to fill in. The cables dealt only with the overall diplomatic aspects of the complex problem; they contained but few references to naval details and the minutes of the proposals which the Japanese planned to place before the conference. Nor did they indicate how far the Japanese were willing to go in their claims and at what point they were ready for a compromise.

In long and serious discussions, Captain Watson explained to me the whole background of a then existing diplomatic triangle— United States, Great Britain, and Japan. In 1920 the Japanese Navy received its first major appropriation since 1912, when a corruption scandal within the Navy had undermined the admirals' prestige and enabled the Imperial Diet to withhold from them the appropriations for which they were always lobbying. The memories of that scandal were all forgotten and forgiven by 1920, and the Imperial Navy was permitted to embark upon an ambitious construction program envisaging the building of eight battleships and eight battle cruisers, known as the Eight-Eight Program. The strategists of the Kaigun-Sho, as the navy ministry is called in Japan, calculated that the possession of sixteen capital ships would provide them with a well-balanced fleet, at least for the time being.

In the middle of this program Lord Curzon's suggestions for a naval limitation conference reached Tokyo, threatening to cancel the whole construction schedule and relegate Japan to the role of an inferior sea power. The dilemma with which the admirals of the Kaigun-Sho were confronted was a difficult one indeed; but Captain Watson never doubted that they would solve it with a compromise.

"Japan," he told me, "knows well that the choice is between

armament limitation and an armament race. They know that we prefer a limitation agreement, but would not shrink from the race either. If it comes to a race, Japan will be far outdistanced and will remain a minor sea power if only by the comparative strengths of the American, British, and Japanese navies. They will try to take the bitter medicine with a pleasant smile and forget about the Eight-Eight Program if absolutely necessary." It was also clear that the British would abandon their alliance with Japan rather than antagonize the United States.

Captain Watson gained this accurate estimate of the situation during long and intimate meetings with Japanese naval officers who were destined to play an outstanding role in shaping Japan's destiny. Shortly after my return to Tokyo in September 1921, after a summer in the mountains, I was permitted to watch Captain Watson girding for battle and going into action. The locale of this first "naval battle" was not the ocean. It was a teashop in the Shimbashi district, one of the geisha houses where Nomura and his colleagues gathered frequently for business—and pleasure. As the preparations for the Washington Conference were now in full swing, these meetings became more frequent. Both Watson and Nomura were anxious to sound out each other, to pick up a remark inadvertently dropped during these intimate talks, and fit it like a colored stone into the mosaic of the whole.

The meeting to which I accompanied Captain Watson was well attended on both sides. In our corner sat the Captain; his assistant, Lieutenant Commander John Walter McClaran; and myself. Japan was represented by Captain Nomura, who brought with him Captain Nagano and Commander Yonai, two of the most promising men on the Naval General Staff. The significance of these meetings can be seen in the fact that all three of these Japanese officers attained top positions in their country's political line-up. Nomura became ambassador to the United States just when the long-strained relations flared into war; Nagano was at the head of the Naval General Staff at the outbreak of hostilities and during its early years; Yonai rose to the rank of navy minister, and held that position until just prior to the signing of the Tripartite Pact on September 27, 1940, and also at the time of Japan's surrender.

In those early days of our teashop meetings, however, Yonai was, like myself, a language student, oriented in another direction—*toward Russia*. At the time of our first meeting he, too, was a newcomer to Tokyo, freshly returned from an assignment in Moscow, where he was ostensibly studying the Russian language.

In September 1921 Captain Watson called me into his office for what turned out to be a momentous occasion in my life. It was to be my first "secret mission." It was evident from the Captain's opening remarks that I had earned my spurs in diplomacy and that he now regarded me as ready for the assignment.

"Zack," he started, "there is certain information I would like to send to Washington. It is vital information. We must know in as great detail as possible the extent to which the Japanese are willing to go in accepting a compromise solution in a projected naval limitation agreement. I have a lot of data myself, but I have to check and countercheck my information before I can vouch for its validity in a report to the Navy Department. I want you and McClaran to do the checking for me."

"I'll be happy to serve you, Captain," I responded eagerly as Watson outlined his little plot:

"You remember our Shimbashi meetings with Nomura and his crowd?"

"Yes, sir."

"Well, I want you and McClaran to make them as frequent as possible. I can no longer attend them myself. They have grown too intimate. Their frank exchange of opinion prevents the presence of an official of my position. As Nomura runs these meetings on a *quid pro quo* basis, I have outlived my usefulness from his point of view, since I can no longer oblige him with the tidbits of information he hopes to obtain from me. I am confined to official calls on top-ranking naval officers and parties where I can gather my stuff, but you and McClaran can go ahead freely, in your give and take."

"Have you any further orders, sir?"

"No, just go to Shimbashi with the Nomura crowd and try to find out from them what their plans are for the Washington Conference. Pick up whatever information you can, and keep me posted on what goes on behind the scenes."

Captain Nomura was to make my assignment rather simple for me, since it was he rather than we who initiated the next meeting after my conversation with Captain Watson. Apparently he did not share Watson's personal qualms about the dangers of the *quid pro quo* and was willing to continue our little Shimbashi game of give and take. Just as anxious to get an insight into American plans as we were to learn theirs, he called Captain Watson and asked him to the Shimbashi for cocktails and tea.

It was September 21 at the usual six o'clock of our meetings, with Nomura and Nagano already waiting for us, when our two jinrikisha boys pulled up with us in front of the teashop entrance. Sitting on the highly polished steps, we changed our street footwear to the slippers provided by the house and were escorted to the second floor to a private room to join Nomura and Nagano, alternately sipping Japanese tea and American Martinis.

"Captain Watson regrets," we said in the stiff words of diplomatic etiquette, "but he is unable to attend the party." Nomura did not seem to mind our captain's absence. He regarded him as a mute placed on our own youthful strings that toned down the information he was to gain from us. Without him, he hoped, we would open the floodgates of information and tell him all and more. But we had been carefully briefed, the information we were permitted to dole out carefully apportioned and weighed, leading questions rehearsed in advance, even the tone of our conversation, feigned surprises, the pauses between sentences practiced ahead of time so as to play our role as perfectly as possible when the performance came.

It turned out that we did not burn the midnight oil in vain. The meeting was to provide us with the exact information Captain Watson wanted to obtain: it gave us the clues to the Japanese plan which Baron Kato, the chief Japanese delegate to the Washington Conference, was eventually to take with him. Through leading questions in the course of the conversation we lured both Nomura and Nagano into conceding that there was a conciliatory attitude taking shape in Japanese councils and that a compromise would be possible, even on America's terms.

When we returned to Captain Watson's house he was waiting for us and hung upon every word. With his own information the picture was complete, and he was able to tell our Navy Department that Japan would eventually accede to the proposed 5:5:3 ratio. This prediction was borne out when the conference finally accepted the naval limitation program on this basis.

The value of the advance information thus gleaned was shown clearly. I saw how the course and results of a conference depended on it, and that the importance of such information could not be overemphasized. Even as early as 1921, the efforts of our intelligence officers enabled us to enter the conference with a knowledge of the problems with which we were to be confronted.

2

THE STRANGER IN ZUSHI

IT WAS April 1922. I stood on the long, curving sea wall in front of my house at Zushi, where I had taken up residence that day. Now, a year and a half after my arrival in Tokyo, I could survey the new vistas of my naval life and all its manifold implications. Tokyo with its cosmopolitan whirlpool and international intrigues was already behind me. I had had a taste of diplomatic life and made an excursion into secret diplomacy gathering confidential data in connection with the Washington Naval Limitation Conference. Now I was on the road to new undertakings. A milestone on the road was this tiny Japanese fishing village called Zushi, and there, standing in the fresh spring breeze that whipped the waves against the sea wall, I could survey the past and look straight into the future.

The contrasts which these months between October 1920 and April 1922 presented to me were striking. Far behind me was Captain Long's simple office in Washington, the fifty-day journey on the *Sherman* to Tokyo, my first visit to the closely guarded Navy Ministry of Japan, the dances, the dinners, the receptions of the capital and even the secretive little conclaves with Japanese naval officers in private rooms of fashionable geisha houses—they all belonged to the past. Zushi was like a serene but living hyphen between my memories and my plans and hopes.

There I stood, overlooking the grayish-green waters of this inlet of Tokyo Bay. Scores of little sampans were gently rocking in the swell. The afternoon's rapidly setting sun painted the dark red sails an uncanny crimson, a color which only nature can mix on its own palette. There was quiet around me; only a few of the home-coming fishermen remained squatting on the shore, discussing the catch of the day, the repairs which their overworked nets needed, or the local gossip of the village marriages.

From time to time the crisp breeze brought to me the boom of Japanese naval guns carrying out their customary practice. The huge Yokosuka naval base was to the north, just beyond the horizon. The sound of the guns faded into the silence that was settling on the bay of Zushi like the off-stage music that accompanies the action of an Oriental drama. Little heaps of whitebait were piled up on the shore, tiny silvery fish which the men of Zushi discover in their nets when the bigger haul is removed. A short, stocky fellow whose muscles revealed that his body was disciplined to the sea squatted over the heap and watched them with hungry eyes. Then he scooped his palms and lifted a mouthful of the wriggling bait for a strange hors d'oeuvre to the sukiyaki * which perhaps his wife had prepared as a luxury for him at home.

Soon the hungry little fisherman departed, and I was left alone on the beach to watch the Japanese sunset. The quiet which surrounded me was not matched by my emotions as I glanced backward over the eventful past which had brought me to this strange present. It was just ten years ago that I had graduated from Annapolis with the class of 1912, a proud class destined to provide scores of heroes for the war that was at this time still twenty years away.

As I reviewed the past on the screen of memory, a late sampan came in to Zushi, dragging its empty net behind. There must have been some disagreement on board, or perhaps her six-man crew was just discussing the weather in somewhat heated terms; but as the breeze brought their conversation to me with every syllable clear on the evening air, their chatter suddenly recalled vividly the moment on the other side of the world when I heard Japanese spoken for the first time. There was an immediate connection between that experience and my presence in Zushi. Without that conversation overheard ten years ago, my life would have taken a different turn.

It was long ago, in the fall of 1913, on board the battleship *Virginia*, where I served with my one lone stripe as senior assistant engineer officer. I was in the wardroom mess, sitting near the foot of the table, the forgotten man. We waited for lunch that was already some fifteen minutes late, the tenseness of the atmosphere growing more and more with the darkening scowls of some thirty hungry officers. The stillness was suddenly broken by an outburst from Lieutenant Fred F. Rogers, the mess treasurer for that month, sitting at the foot of the table where his duties had relegated him.

* Pronounced "Ske yakī." Thinly sliced beef cooked with vegetables and soy sauce.

"Steward! Send that steward in here!" yelled Rogers in a sharp, incisive voice.

In half a minute, a little old man, some five feet in height, shuffled through the wardroom door, adjusting his ill-fitting coat which he had evidently put on hurriedly, his deep-set eyes blinking as if he had come from darkness into sunlight, but with a smile on his face that was half inquiry and half guilt. And then, as he reached Lieutenant Rogers, the steward, clasping his hands in front of him, made a half bow and said through his teeth, which still showed through his disarming smile, *"Sayo de Gozaimas."*

Lieutenant Rogers, as if finding it difficult to put his American indignation into the language of a people who consider it the height of ill breeding to show one's feelings, suddenly took on that Oriental composure which he had learned through three years' close association with the Japanese. But to a careful observer his flashing eyes and the lack of the usual suave smile disclosed that he was highly peeved. I had seen the steward many times before and was accustomed to him as one of the fixtures of the wardroom as he efficiently supervised the serving of the meals. But today this little man in his blue petty officer trousers and white mess jacket now buttoned up to his chin attracted my attention. He was a Japanese. In those days, incredible though it may now seem, many alien Japanese served on our warships as mess stewards and cooks. Although we did not bother about their loyalties and extracurricular activities, I am certain that even then in their frequent conversations with their fellow countrymen they discussed the details of the U.S. Navy in knowing terms.

The little steward bowed to Rogers, who addressed him in what sounded like a very strange language to my inquisitive ears. I was certain that it was not the lingua franca of the mess, or some kitchen dialect of overworked American slang. There was no doubt, Rogers was talking to the steward in some foreign tongue.

"Hiru-han, mo ju-go fun osoi yo. Hayaku motte kitte koi," came the proper colloquial form for the master of the house when speaking to the head servant, as Rogers told the steward that lunch was already fifteen minutes late and to hurry up and get it served.

Ishiyama, apparently as unmoved as his name, "Stone Mountain," implied, made two little bows as he backed out, and without a change of expression repeated his only words, *"Sayo de Gozaimas,"* one of the most polite forms for "Yes, sir."

During this short but apparently comprehensive conversation, I looked from one to the other as many thoughts raced through my mind. Where does such perfect self-control come from? I tried to picture the East and Japan; but from what little I had read of it, all that passed before me was the rikisha man trotting down the street or the little women with the children lashed to their backs.

And then, as Rogers began an explanation of the Japanese mentality, I remembered that he had lived in Japan as a language student. I found myself asking innumerable questions about their customs, habits, and language, and wondering how anyone could master such sounds and speak without even separating the teeth.

From then on I attached myself to Rogers if only to hear him talk about his years in Japan. He told me in gruesome detail his struggle with this forbidding tongue; how he had to devote almost all his waking hours to classes with two teachers; how he had had to memorize the ideographs imported to Japan from China in the year 600 A.D. to provide a written language for the Japanese, each ideograph standing, like a picture, for a different sound and meaning a different word; how he watched the people and tried to understand their folkways; intimate little stories ranging from life in the Imperial Palace in which old Meiji still ruled supreme down to the geisha houses in Shimbashi where, he confided to me, he usually made the greatest progress, particularly in the study of Japanese character.

Like a *kakimono* * unrolled before my eyes, I saw the picture of a strange land with all its peculiarities and mysteries, the differences standing out in my mind in far stronger relief than the similarities. I began to read about Japan and occasionally tried to memorize a colloquial word which would come out in our discussions. I picked up a few words of everyday usage, like *machi* for street, *denwa* for telephone, and, of course, *beppin* for beautiful girl. They remained with me for years, just as my yearning to go to Japan persisted as I shifted from ship to ship, from assignment to assignment. I recall how overjoyed I was when I managed to memorize the phrase to be used when introduced to another: *"Hajimete O Me ni Kakarimashita"*—"For the first time I have hung myself on your honorable eyes." Then I found the game turning into a real purpose to learn this language.

---

* Translated "hanging thing." A water color on silk in scroll make-up.

But how and where was anyone to begin? It seemed such a hopeless jumble of sounds—half muffled, half exploded—but still there was a subtle fascination in those sounds, like the dangling prize jerked from beyond one's reach when almost within his grasp, or the vivid dream that is still heavy in the dimness of incomprehension. The little mannerisms, almost perfect in their significance, immediately tempt one to imitate them. And then I began to drift back to my boyhood days when in the center of an admiring and amused circle I used to repeat with almost perfect tones the sounds of the steamboat, the train, the woodcutter, the scissors-grinder, and what not; and later at the Naval Academy, where in the period of relaxation after study hours these same sounds gained for me in the graduation yearbook the title of "the Man of Funny Noises."

Suddenly it dawned upon me that here was an opportunity for the application of these funny noises. It has been said that there is a place in the world for everything, so why not my little power of imitation in this language where everything seemed to depend so much on intonation? Day by day my enthusiasm increased, and even later when it had apparently subsided, it seems that its full force had remained latent in the subconscious.

I realized that Japan was beyond my reach. It might be possible to visit some of her ports on courtesy calls which our ships made in return for the frequent visits of Japanese vessels to American bases. But those days are usually crowded with the ceremonial of international naval etiquette, and one has to spend more time with American diplomats than with his native hosts, continuing the American way of life in the midst of a strange environment. These trips, even if I were privileged to participate in one or two of them, would show me only the contours of Japan. What I wanted was to penetrate the shell of international etiquette, to divorce myself from the routine duties on shipboard, and to devote months or, if possible, years to the study of the Japanese language and people.

I inquired casually as to whether there was a chance of sending more language students to Japan and if volunteers were needed for such a detail. But the Navy seemed to be satisfied with just one officer in the whole naval service who was capable of speaking Japanese. Previously there had been two; but the other had resigned by then, and no plans were afoot to enlarge this one-man task force; so it seemed that my hopes would remain forever unfulfilled.

Then suddenly there came one of those strange turns of life which change everything. I was accompanying the midshipmen on their 1920 practice cruise and not even contemplating more than a possible routine trip to Japan some day. While we were in Honolulu, a dispatch reached me from Rogers, who was then a commander attached to the Office of Naval Intelligence in Washington. It read:

"The Navy has decided to send two language officers to Japan. Do you still desire to go?"

My reply was prompt and unequivocal.

"Your message, affirmative."

Another dispatch from Rogers arrived next day:

"You will be detached and ordered to Japan as soon as the practice squadron returns to the United States. Your running mate will be designated later."

Immediately I was looked upon by my shipmates as some strange being. "Think of going out there to study Japanese." "Will you go to school?" "Will you wear Japanese clothes?" "What kind of food will you eat?" A thousand and one foolish questions were shot at me as I tried to digest the possibilities and realize that this was just the thing for which I had been waiting.

After what seemed an unending voyage, at last we dropped anchor in Annapolis and I hurried to Washington to get the details. Rogers told me that Lieutenant Commander Hartwell C. Davis would go with me to Japan. Then he took me to the office of Captain Long, Director of Naval Intelligence, who provided the necessary confirmation and instruction. And thus intelligence, a new interest which captivated me from the start, and which has never lost its fascination for me in all the years since then, became a vital part of my life. Intelligence, the core of national defense was not then—nor is it now—adequately appreciated. The whole Far Eastern Section of ONI (the Office of Naval Intelligence) occupied just one room, holding one officer and one stenographer. ONI itself comprised a handful of officers and a few yeomen, filing the occasional reports of naval attachés about naval appropriations of the countries to which they were attached, a few notes on vessels building or projected, most of them clipped from local newspapers, and descriptions of parties given in honor of some visiting American celebrity. The last-named usually represented the most illuminating and comprehensive of these so-called intelligence reports.

It was not the fault of Intelligence that it had to play the role of a naval Cinderella, still waiting for someone to turn up with the legendary slipper. The world had just gone through a devastating war and yearned for lasting peace. Armaments were derided, and disarmament was the slogan of the day. Most of our ships were already collecting barnacles in ports, and so were our statesmen who mobilized to conduct their private war against the U.S. Navy which, they felt, was blocking our return to peacetime normalcy. In other countries, too, anti-naval campaigns were in full swing, even in Britain where the Royal Navy is the untouchable senior service. There was but little an office of naval intelligence could record or a naval attaché could report, unless he joined in the hysterical clamor against his own service.

Even so, I felt that there was much Intelligence could do in support of the statesmen's work for peace. As is only natural with a continental power like the United States, the vast resources and territories of which make it self-sufficient and, psychologically at least, isolated between two oceans, we knew but little about the lives and ways of other peoples, real friends or potential foes. Whatever knowledge we had was haphazard and colored by sympathies or antipathies, and by that sterile intellectual pacifism which followed in the wake of the last war. Although not generally recognized, it is nevertheless a truism that professional soldiers and sailors hate war. True, the legendary Russian grand duke hated war because, in his own words, it usually spoiled the Czar's armies, and the witty French general opposed war only because it interrupted spirited conversation. But deep down in the heart of the professional officer is a hatred of war, for he knows better than anyone else what it costs in life and blood.

In all my years in the Navy I have heard more pacifist talk among naval officers than among the ill-advised civilians who persist in accusing the professional soldiers and sailors of being warmongers. I know that I express a general opinion when I say that the personnel of the U.S. Navy fully realize the implications of war and do not glory in the temporary glamour of battle. We regard our ships and our bases as the guarantors of peace, the symbols of security, and look to the diplomats and statesmen to maintain them moored to safe anchorages. This does not mean, however, that we are unaware of the true meaning of the term "security." To us, the term has a broad meaning. It rests in physical force embodied as it is in the ships and their bases, but also in intellectual factors among which Intelligence plays an outstanding role. To *know* what the others think and how their actions are stimulated by their thinking processes; to *know* what they have and what they intend to do with their forces; to *know* our opponents and partners in the international chess game lends immense strength to ourselves and should save us from unpleasant surprises.

In 1920, when I stood in front of Captain Long's desk in his Office of Naval Intelligence, we lacked much of this essential knowledge and had no means of filling the gaps. The small force of the office with its mechanical routine, the ephemeral reports of the attachés and the general reluctance on the part of the high command to assign to Intelligence the place it fully deserved, were accepted by me as a challenge. I was standing at the crossroads of my life and determined to go the way of my inclinations. Japan and Intelligence stood written on one road sign, and I eagerly chose the road to which they pointed.

My memories thus caught up with me as I stood alone staring out to the sea. I hardly noticed the fading of the day and the swiftly encroaching darkness which embraced me like an invisible giant. Suddenly the coast was ablaze with little lights, merging into a yellowish patch to the north where Hayama and the summer palace of the Emperor were situated. Across the peninsula at Yokosuka the batteries were still firing intermittently, and now I could see the flash stabbing through the blackness. It was cold and quiet, and I felt alone. Alone with a host of ideas and tasks which had accumulated in my mind ever since I settled down in Japan.

I turned around and returned to my house which bordered on the sea wall. My two servants, who were named O Haru-San (Miss Spring) and O Natsu-San (Miss Summer) waited for me, squatting on the doorstep as Japanese women usually do while awaiting the return of their master. They rose and bowed deeply as I approached and Miss Spring announced:

"Sato-San awaits you in the living room, Zakurai-San."

3

SATO-SAN MAKES A VISIT

IF I were writing an intelligence report, I would now in retrospect describe Kishiro Sato as an "A-1 contact." For the next year and a half he was my best source of information, my guide into the intricate web of Japanese politics and aspirations, a man whose statements I could trust implicitly. He was my neighbor and first visitor in Zushi. But his first call on that spring night in 1922, motivated by the insatiable curiosity which drives the Japanese to innumerable little adventures, was followed by many visits. When I left Zushi eighteen months later, Sato was the last of my newly won friends to grasp my hand in a final handshake.

By then he was risking much with this friendship, since he was closely watched by the police and suspected of disclosing to me certain information which the Black Dragon Society regarded as best kept from foreigners in general and from an officer of American Naval Intelligence in particular. But Sato-San had a mind of his own, and then shaping in that mind was a plan. He assigned to me an important role in his scheme.

Now, however, he was still groping his way toward my confidence and friendship in that peculiar mixture of shy reserve and brutal frankness which characterizes human relations in Japan, even among the closest friends. As I entered the room, I saw him standing in front of a *kakimono* which adorned a niche in the wall. In deference to Japanese custom which prescribes a change of these hanging scrolls with every change of the season, I displayed a spring scene in Kyushu dominated by a branch of the cherry tree, its blossoms painted in mellow pastel. Framed by the pink colors of the tree, in the background, was a bluish lake whose waters carried a raft with a maiden on it, looking toward the grayish contours of a majestic peak which gave the picture both force and balance, despite the gentle strokes with which it was drawn. It was painted on silk, and a broad silk ribbon provided a fitting frame In front of the scroll to the right stood a vase with just one branch of a cherry tree in it. I designed the whole arrangement with the help of Miss Spring as my own little shrine to the Muse of Art.

Sato turned around when he heard me enter, and even before he introduced himself, he complimented me on the selection of the picture and the arrangement of the niche. "I feel," he said, "you understand Japan."

I had been in Japan long enough then to know that this was a unique compliment; but Sato was a unique Japanese, not blinded by the ethnocentrism which characterized the majority of his countrymen. He bowed, and as I returned his ceremonial greeting, he said: "*Watakushi wa, O tonari de Gozaimas.*" Then he continued: "I am your neighbor, and my name is Sato. From the window of my house I watched you this afternoon, standing alone on the sea wall and absorbed in thoughts. I was sorry for you because I felt that the loneliness of this place must be a burden on your mind. My wife suggested that I pay you this call so that you can share your thoughts with me."

Here again Sato revealed a different slant in the uniform Japanese character. His average countryman would not give credit to his wife for a pleasant thought. In fact, he would not have mentioned her at all.

We sat down on the *tatami* * which formed a square around the charcoal burner on which tea was now boiling. As if he had run out of the few English words of his limited vocabulary, Sato sat quietly, but watching me with curious eyes, perhaps waiting for me to start the conversation, or trying to penetrate my thoughts. Then and without transition, in a tone which was almost hostile in its bluntness, he asked:

"Why did you come to Zushi?"

So Sato-San isn't different after all, I thought. Did his nonchalant Western approach conceal the mission of a policeman? Or was his suspicion generated by the jealousy which motivates Japanese hatred of foreigners? But his question echoed in my mind. Indeed, why had I come to Zushi? There it was, just off Tokyo Bay with a view of the surroundings of the Yokosuka naval base and neighboring airfields—certainly a logical hide-out for an intelligence officer to do a bit of observation. Could I blame Sato for being suspicious? But I had no such sinister plans in Zushi and answered Sato's inquiry with his own bluntness:

* The thick padded mats (3' x 6') fitting into the floor.

"I am a student of the Japanese language, Sato-San, and found that the urban hustle and bustle of metropolitan Tokyo deprived me of the opportunity of making rapid progress. Here in Zushi I hope to be able to concentrate on my studies and also to gain an insight into the real Japanese way of life."

This truly *was* my motive in coming to this pleasant fishing village of a little over four hundred families. It was recommended to me as a place where I could see Japanese rural life at its naked best. Most of its people were simple fishermen, whole families providing the crews for the sampans, fathers and sons, mothers and daughters rigging the sails, attending to the primitive little engines, throwing the nets and dragging in the catch, then preparing it for the near-by markets. The contrast with the city was quite remarkable even on my first day in Zushi. There was no Western dress in sight, and the manners of the people were free of that cosmopolitan hodgepodge of Hollywood modernism and native etiquette which was marked in the conduct of the Tokyoite. As far as I then knew, Sato was the sole link between the world of Zushi and the turmoil I had left behind in Tokyo. It turned out that he, too, was an escapist in Zushi, but for different reasons. His health was failing, and he sought to restore it here in the salty air of the village. It seems that he sensed my own suspicion and hastened to dispel my doubts:

"Perhaps you think I am too inquisitive. In a sense I am, but only because I am conducting a peculiar search. Please do not misunderstand me," he added when he saw that I looked up to him in vexed astonishment, "I am not a policeman. What I am looking for is a tiny gap through which I could slip out of the narrow confines of our Japanese life."

The expression with which I followed his words now changed to one of surprise; it was a sympathetic though confused surprise. Before I could ask him to clarify his words, he said to me:

"What is your conception of a friend, sir?"

"Well," I answered somewhat taken aback by such a big order for a definition, "we think of a friend as one who is very close to us both in our joys and our sorrows, to whom we can turn for advice and aid, and who shares with us the pleasures of our pastime. A friend," I hesitated, "is a . . . *friend*, Sato-San," accentuating the word in the hope that it would carry its full connotation.

"You see," Sato said, "this is the object of my search—a friend. We in Japan have no friends in your sense of the word, since we feel that it would be an imposition to burden an acquaintance close to us with our own petty troubles and worries. I have no friend, Zacharias-San," he said in a plaintive tone that was both amusing and pathetic and brought a faint smile into my eyes.

This was the outset of our friendship, and soon enough Sato-San had his friend to whom he could confide his troubles and worries. They were not of a personal nature and were very far from being petty. He was one of those farseeing Japanese who somehow sensed that the old order had outlived its usefulness and Japan had to reorient herself toward more modern and progressive ideas if she was to become a truly modern nation in the philosophical sense and not merely in a superficial display of chromium, glass—and guns. He was a well-educated man although he had never been out of Japan. He was, however, what in the United States would be called a politician. He was confidential adviser to the mayor of Tokyo, and did important political errands for his boss and received small favors in return. He was privy to many Japanese secrets and watched from close quarters the development of a plan that was to receive its final shape in the notorious Tanaka Memorial of July 25, 1927.

The Washington Conference was now a matter of the past, and I had been somewhat initiated into Japanese politics by the time Sato visited me. Still, in our first conversation the conference was reviewed. By then the "5:5:3" had become the most popular slogan of Japanese jingoes. They chalked these three figures on walls, printed them on posters—blackboards; and they were on the lips of most Japanese.

"You make a lion yearn for the miseries of the desert when you lock it in a cage," Sato said. "By imposing a limitation on the Japanese you have played into the hands of the militarists. They can now go to the ignorant masses and say to them: 'You see, America and Britain refuse to accept us as their equals, and worse than that, they try to keep us inferior forever.'" I tried to reason with the same rational arguments which had impressed Nomura and Nagano some months before, but Sato protested:

"These things have nothing to do with reason. Those jingoes whose aims they serve are peculiar creatures. They reason against reason, because they know that if once they stop to think, their whole scheme will be revealed as a preposterous fraud and like a bubble will burst in their faces."

"What is their scheme, Sato-San?" I asked, but Sato rose from the mat and, without answering my point-blank question, bowed deeply to take his leave. I showed or felt no impatience when my question remained unanswered. It was premature at best. So I, too, jumped from the *tatami* and, towering over the little figure of my guest, held out my hand for a parting handshake.

"*Sayonara*," Sato said crisply, then added with a smile: "So-o-o long."

"Let us meet again," I said, and he repeated the words in that plaintive tone which sometimes crept into his conversation:

"Let us meet again."

I watched him hurrying home, his fragile figure just a shadow under the frugal street light that barely illuminated the narrow passage between our two houses. Then I turned to the right where another house marked the end of Zushi. It was dark and uninhabited at this time of the year. Its owners came down for the summers. But just as I looked toward the deserted house, I saw a man almost jumping through its door, then abruptly slowing down his motions and casually walking past my house, as if returning from a stroll to the end of the sea wall.

I was to see that man again. He was to become my shadow in Zushi.

4

JAPAN FACES NORTH AND SOUTH

ON THE second morning after Sato's visit I was forcefully reminded of the powers of the Japanese police, and also of my own
isolation at Zushi, when quite early, at around six-thirty, Miss
Summer stormed into my bedroom. She was obviously quite excited although trying to restrain herself as she said:

"Zack-San, there is a policeman outside to talk to you!"

In Japan the policemen were the most common symbols of
authority, the omniscient and omnipotent arm of the government.
Standing in their wooden booths at street corners or occasionally
walking their near-by beats in slow, measured steps, their actions
suggested a shepherd dog keeping the flock in check. They were
quick with their swords, which they used with little provocation,
and, in common with primitive men when placed in a position
of authority, they made an elaborate show of their powers whenever they could. That being well known to the Japanese, the
necessity for using it seldom arose. I was fully aware of the popular
Japanese attitude toward these whimsical, swaggering policemen
when in my broadcasts in 1945 I promised the Japanese people
that these remnants of the Samurai past, left over from the oppressive Shogunate, would be removed once we could do something about them.

In 1922, however, the appearance of one of them at my house
was quite a shock to my two servants. While donning my light
kimono, I was turning over in my mind the possible errand of
the policeman—so soon after Sato's call on me. I had no doubt that
it was in connection with his visit. So I prepared myself for the
explanation I would provide, not to apologize for my visitor, but
to save Sato from embarrassment.

As I stepped out into the little garden behind my house to
face this guardian of the minatory law, I saw a rather shabby-
looking little man in his dust-covered blue uniform, his hand
firmly planted on his sword, and almost visibly swelling with

pride. It was obvious that the nature of his mission increased his pride even beyond the customary conceit of his caste.

The deep bow with which he greeted me and the reverence with which he addressed me revealed at once that he did not come as an investigator. It turned out that he was carrying a message for me, and it was the status of the person who sent him on this errand that made him so proud so early in the morning. The message was from the Navy Ministry, and it sounded quite harmless when the policeman conveyed it to me in the most flowery terms at his command. The role of the police in this capacity was quite natural. I had no telephone in Zushi since I did not want to pay the exorbitant sum of three thousand yen to buy one. In fact, the only telephone in the village was installed in the police station. When my friends in Tokyo wanted to get in touch with me they called the police and asked them to convey their message. I was to see this blue-coated messenger quite often during my stay at Zushi.

"The Junior Aide of the Navy Minister," he now said, "phoned a short while ago and asked me to read this message to you." He fumbled in his pocket and brought out a piece of paper from which he read: "If you are to be in Tokyo tomorrow, please come to the Navy Department at eleven o'clock in the morning." Then he bowed again, said, "Thank you," and, like a peacock, marched away. The Junior Aide had been a convivial partner at many informal parties in Tokyo; so I was not greatly surprised over his call. But the Japanese knew our habits. This was the day the language officers customarily dropped in to see the Naval Attaché —payday. I decided I would answer the call. I took the electric train to Tokyo, and at eleven o'clock sharp I was sitting in front of the desk of the Junior Aide.

At another desk which seemed to be improvised was another Japanese officer, to whom I was introduced. From his uneasiness I gathered that he was there for a specific purpose; so I watched his actions carefully.

"Why did you bury yourself in a little hole like Zushi?" jokingly began the Aide.

"Well, the big hole of Tokyo was not too conducive to concentrating on your difficult language," I replied. "There are too many parties."

"Do you know Commander Yamaguchi, Tamon Yamaguchi,

who is now studying English in your country?" asked the other officer.

"No, I do not know him," I replied.

Thus I heard for the first time the name of Yamaguchi, a name that I was to encounter often for the next twenty years.

Here, then, was the motif. My presence in Zushi reflected something which had to do with Yamaguchi in the United States. At this time Yamaguchi was a language officer like myself and was registered at Princeton University. But judging from later Japanese language officers, he, too, must have been engaged in activities extraneous to those of learning English. Their concern must have been great, as the officer stumbled right to the point and said quite abruptly:

"Your stay in Zushi raises no objection, Commander Zacharias, as long as you confine yourself to the study of the language. You now live among simple people who see strangers but rarely. They are blessed, or cursed, with a vivid imagination and see shadows in many a corner. They will naturally attribute many foolish things to your stay among them; so please keep this in your mind when you move among them in Zushi."

He paused for a moment, looked down on a sheet of paper in front of him, then turned to me again and said:

"Your neighbor, Mr. Sato, is a cultured and educated man, but he is given to extreme ideas and hallucinations. I thought you might want me to tell you this, since I understand he has been calling upon you."

I was annoyed, and following him on his own road of bluntness, I said:

"Do you think it is courteous to check on the visitors I receive?" But he now forced a smile onto his broad face and said in a voice which would have been disarming had it not betrayed just a touch of sarcasm:

"We are not checking on you, Commander. But you cannot prevent these things from getting around." He leaned over his desk toward me and in the friendly way of a sight-seeing guide said:

"We Japanese are inquisitive people, interested in even the most minute details around us. Have you never been accosted by strangers on a train or in a restaurant, asking you many little questions which sound like an intrusion on your privacy? We mean it well. It is our way of striking up friendship. As far as your visitor is concerned, it was your own maid who told about him to the butcher boy, who in turn carried the gossip to his employer, who told it to Madame Fujisawa's maid; the maid told it to her lady, the lady to her husband, and, since Fujisawa happens to be a colleague of mine here in the Navy Department, this is how we learned about it."

The slight tension that kept me sitting forward on my chair dissolved into hearty laughter. The Aide smiled but his comrade laughed in a shrill pitch, resembling the forced laughter of a stage "ham" who does his best to carry out the playwright's instructions. The scene called for a laugh, and he laughed. But he was not the laughing type of man.

"Incidentally," the Aide interjected, "how long do you intend to stay in Zushi?"

"I really don't know. You see, I arrived there only recently. Everything depends on how conducive seclusion will be to my studies."

"Well, I wish you a pleasant time and hope you will benefit by your stay." He rose and the audience was over. I thought it strange that he requested me to come all the way from Zushi just to hear that Mr. Sato suffered from hallucinations. But I knew enough of the practice of Japanese Naval Intelligence to sense that my acquaintance with Sato bothered them a bit. So I spent the early afternoon in Tokyo checking up on my new friend. I spoke to a correspondent of a Japanese daily whom I knew and to an American who was very close to the mayor and knew his aide Sato. They agreed that Sato was a levelheaded liberal who also had the courage of his convictions. At that time it was not quite so risky to harbor dangerous thoughts as it became some years later when the so-called Peace Preservation Law was introduced. In 1922 the Japanese felt free to express libertarian ideas even to strangers, and the general trend was slightly toward those things which democracy had to offer.

As I now think back on my many long talks with Kishiro Sato, I am inclined to sympathize with the Japanese Navy, who disliked the idea of Sato having me for a neighbor. It was, indeed, this unobtrusive intellectual who first outlined for me those grandiose plans which later formed part of Japan's grand strategy for conquest and domination. Without him I would have realized too late that the program embodied in Japan's so-called Fundamental

Policy was an aggressive scheme which would inevitably engulf the whole Pacific world in war. The picture which emerged from my conversations with Sato presented to me the whole Fundamental Policy in all its arrogant details and prepared me for a life devoted to fighting against it.

The contact which was thus established, and shadowed by Tokyo, had to be placed on a more plausible basis than just a mere friendship between neighbors. My preoccupation with the language studies gave me the opportunity to do this. In Tokyo I had had two teachers with whom I spent as many as three or four hours a day, studying the language and learning the ideographs. One of them accompanied me to Zushi, and so I decided to hire Sato to take the place of the other. Now, whenever he came, he carried a book on grammar, and those who wanted to eavesdrop on our conversations could hear only his efforts to acquaint me with the tricks of the language. Our political talks were conducted in English, and there was nobody else in the house who could understand us.

With Sato there flooded into my house a whole tidal wave of gossip which he picked up in the mayor's office in Tokyo. It supplemented all that was in the newspapers and compensated for the frequent omissions. He recalled when Prince Yamagata resigned as elder statesman in February 1921, and caused a nationwide sensation with his retirement. Sato told me the reason: the Marshal's opposition to the then Crown Prince's trip to Great Britain. When the Crown Prince was about to take a bride, Sato reported the gossip attending this important step. Princess Kuni was chosen to become Japan's future empress; but although *raison d'état* approved of the match, the Princess bolted. Through Sato I was able to follow events in the Palace from day to day—and I learned of the decision of the Princess to marry the Crown Prince, after all, long before it was officially and joyfully announced in the press.

The gossip which Sato supplied in abundance was just the side show, like the funny page of a newspaper. He had far more important things to tell which filled in many a gap and completed the picture. Japan was facing both south and north as she struggled to burst the narrow confines of her island empire. There were cliques and cabals in every official building in Tokyo, pulling the nation now to the right, now to the left—but always toward expansion. All eyes were strained to the west, across the sea, toward the Asiatic continent, where white spots on the map of China marked the steppingstones of this plan.

The picture which Sato presented to me and which I had ample opportunity to confirm from other sources was vastly different from the conception which prevailed in the mind of the American public and different even from the accepted view of most observers on the spot. The gulf that separated the Army from the Navy in Japan was far deeper than mere rivalry between two politically minded factions of the armed forces. The Army and the Navy represented two planets which have their own courses in the firmament and are destined never to meet. The Navy was ocean-minded and internationalist. It was brought up in the admiration and envy of British sea power, and looked to distant lands for conquest, easy conquest as far as it was possible, since it recognized that the naval forces at Japan's disposal were inadequate for a major war. Most of the high-ranking naval officers knew the world from personal observation. They had been to the United States, to England and Germany, and had many friends the world over. Their horizon did not end at the coast line of Japan; in fact it began where the coast line ended.

The Army, on the other hand, was land-minded and, more than that, fascinated by land masses across the sea. While the Navy was thinking in terms of an intercontinental war and, in 1922 at least, dreaded its possibility, the Army thought in terms of a continental war and was impatient to move, since it could see no obstacle to the Japanese steam roller in territories which it had singled out for easy conquest.

The Army regarded the Navy as merely a transporter of Army troops. It needed the Navy so that the troops could get to their destination, but once the troops were put ashore, the Army could see no other use for the Navy. In fact the Army regarded the Navy as a potential competitor who might contest the loot which the Army expected to find overseas. Most of the Army officers, even the highest-ranking of them who did the scheming and plotting in the Rikugun-Sho, or War Ministry, had never been outside of Japan. Since they did not belong to the aristocracy, their imperialism did not have the philosophy and sweep of real empire-builders. They were petty men, coarse in their likes and cruel in their dislikes, sons of the lower middle classes whose children now replaced the ancient Samurai, the professional warrior of Japan's chivalrous past. This interesting historical change which portended even more significant developments in the future was explained to me by Sato in one of his first conversations. "Foreigners," he said, "usually think of Japanese militarism in terms of the Prussian military system. Nothing could be more erroneous. It is true that our Army was patterned after the Prussian Army much as our Navy was patterned after the British Royal Navy. The Army was first trained by French officers; but success is a heady wine in Japan, and when we watched the Prussian Army conquer half of Europe between 1860 and 1871, we decided to entrust our military training to Prussian officers. They were excellent drillmasters and made good soldiers of Japanese peasants, but they did not transplant to Japan the Prussian military philosophy. Japan developed herself a military philosophy which is as confusing as the ideographs in which it is put to paper."

"Where is it put to paper?" I asked.

Sato suddenly grew silent and looked in a different direction, as if regretting that he had uttered the words. "Well," he said at last, "it was just a figure of speech, you know, just words. They have no meaning." He hesitated for a few minutes, then said in a hasty voice: "It is not put to paper, it was just a figure of speech."

I did not press the point, since it was obvious to me that Sato was speaking of a definite document filed in some secret safe, while I was thinking of published books and articles. I had hit upon one of Sato's closely guarded secrets, and I decided to bide my time. To relieve him of suspicion, I shifted the conversation by asking him to outline for me the development of the Army caste in Japan since the Meiji Restoration. He obliged by giving me a good insight into the development of the military hierarchy from 1868, the year of the restoration, to 1922. He also outlined the forces which were at work behind the scenes. It was the skillfully drawn picture of a military proletariat with all the obnoxious shortcomings of the parvenu.

"You must realize," I interjected assuringly, "that I am here as a guest of the country, and it is not my intention to snoop into the secrets of Japan." Sato smiled approvingly. "But what is the name of the group who guide the military objectives?" I asked. He hesitated, throwing his head back in characteristic Japanese fashion, staring at the ceiling and exhaling a long "*Sa-a-a,*" the typical Japanese play for time and thought. Then he suddenly exclaimed, "The Koku-Ryu-Dan"—the Black Dragon Society.

When he mentioned these magic words, the whole story assumed a different complexion. As far back as 1915 the Koku-Ryu-Dan was behind Japanese expansionist demands, which were delivered in the so-called Twenty-one Demands to China. If accepted, the demands would have given Japan political, economic, and military control of all China. Although preliminary moves were made to translate those demands into practice, Japan was prevented by foreign pressure, largely from the United States, from consolidating her gains on the Continent. Here was the proof that the plan persisted in the minds of its original plotters and that it was still the fundamental policy of Japanese militarism.

Now the whole story made sense to me. From information I obtained from Sato and a few others over a considerable period of time I was able to construct a fairly comprehensive picture of a plan that was then being prepared in what was called the research department of this political-action committee of Japanese jingoism. It was in its earliest stages; the draft was just that—a draft, and did not as yet contain the specific points which it later acquired. But even then snatches of pronouncements necessarily passed along between Japanese on high levels indicated their significance. Although Sato was not a member of this society, he was in a position to glean much information that leaked out from high levels.

It spoke of the necessity of colonizing the Far East and of the development of the Japanese Empire in the direction of Manchuria and Mongolia. What struck me as the most significant was the contention that it was not Russia but the United States which was regarded as the major obstacle blocking the road which would lead to the accomplishment of the Japanese plan. Even now, I remember in detail the part of Sato's conversation which criticized the United States for its role behind the scenes that resulted in the Nine-Power Treaty and which interfered with Japanese expansion in Manchuria and Mongolia. The implication that "in order to control China, we must crush the United States" was to appear as plain statement five years later in a memorandum prepared for the Emperor of Japan which became notorious as the Tanaka Memorial. This document is too well known and was discussed often in such minute detail that I will not devote much time to its description. In 1922, when I discussed with Sato the ideas which contributed to its subsequent formulation, it was still floating nebulously in the minds of its authors, although its principles had been applied previously. But when the memorial was published in China a few years later and provoked indignant denials from the Japanese, there was no doubt in *my* mind that it was the genuine transcript of a real document and not the forgery the Japanese authorities said it was. Step by step and stone by stone, Sato provided for me the details of which the Tanaka Memorial was built.

Future plans projected on the screen of the present may lose much of their interest to the casual observer. But shortly after Sato left my house I was forcefully reminded of the fact that I had become privy to a top Japanese secret. The shadow which I noticed after Sato's first visit had grown larger. There were now several shabby-looking characters loafing around my house at odd hours. And I could no longer regard myself as a casual observer. The future had already assumed an ominous reality.

A few days later a man presented himself at the office of the U. S. Naval Attaché and indicated that he had a personal matter to take up with Captain Watson. In a moment the Captain sensed the unusual situation and keyed himself up to his usual affable manner of penetrating curiosity. Mr. Yoshimoto, as the man introduced himself, was a poorly dressed elderly Japanese in his late forties, wearing glasses and bearing himself in that typical manner which characterizes the Japanese when he feels that he is carrying out an important mission. He was short, and his skin was dark, but his eyes radiated alertness of mind as well as fanaticism and contradicted the insignificance of his appearance.

Mr. Yoshimoto represented himself as an employee of the Hydrographic Office. In recent years family troubles and unusual expenses had caused him to fall upon evil days. He had brought with him some important strategic charts of a secret nature which he would like to dispose of for a worth-while consideration.

Only those who knew Captain Watson intimately could appreciate the disarming appeal in his "Why, my good man, how nice of you to come to me." A little obvious conversation followed this remark, and the Captain added, "Now of course you realize that I could not pay out a large sum of money before I had an opportunity to examine carefully the thing I was buying. My government would cut off my head in a jiffy," he added significantly. Mr. Yoshimoto nodded assent. Then Captain Watson continued plausibly, "You know it would not be well for you to remain here too long. I would suggest that you come back in two hours and I will give you my decision." This was quite agreeable, and Mr. Yoshimoto cockily took his departure.

Hardly had he passed from view down the street before Captain Watson called for his car and proceeded immediately to the Kaigun-Sho, to see Captain Nomura, the director of Naval Intelligence. He was shown up to the office in short order—a roll of charts under his arm.

As Nomura greeted him in the usual cordial manner, Captain Watson, after shaking hands, held Nomura at arm's length and regarded him with patronizing study. "Nomura," he began, "you ought to know better than to send one of your amateurs to sell secret papers to me." He paused, and added: "At least you might have sent something good."

Nomura laughed in artificial amazement and said, taking Captain Watson by the arm, "Come over here; let's sit down and be comfortable."

"No, I can stay only a few minutes. Your man might come back, and I don't want to disappoint him. Now just look at these charts you want me to pay good money for."

Nomura feigned surprise and interest with much indrawing of breath as Captain Watson told the complete story and concluded, "Nomura, my friend, they are now safely returned to your hands."

"But Eddie, this is serious."

"You're darned right, it's serious. You are setting me up to get my head cut right off. Well, anyhow, we know how we stand." With that and with Nomura apologizing for dishonest Japanese, Captain Watson hurried back to his office.

As expected, Mr. Yoshimoto did *not* return. However, a few months later the Japanese translator in our naval attaché's office significantly pointed out to Captain Watson a small news item on an inside page of a newspaper. It was strange that the translator should pick this out, as Captain Watson had avoided discussing the matter with anyone but his close assistants. The news item read: "Mr. Yoshimoto, a former employee of the Hydrographic Office has just been given a long term in prison for attempting to sell secret papers to a certain foreign government." They had even used the name Yoshimoto, which was obviously fictitious.

The import of this whole occurrence became evident a few months later, when the same procedure was tried on our military attaché. In this case the Attaché retained the papers for about eight hours, not reporting the matter to anyone. At the end of this time he received a call and was questioned by Japanese Military Intelligence about a certain suspected individual who had visited the Attaché on that day. When these officers were shown the papers which had been left by the visitor, they became very indignant and the incident almost resulted in the serious involvement of the Military Attaché.

These events were typical of attempts on the part of the Japanese to discredit the United States and, thereby, not only to further but also justify Japanese military expansion—with an eye to ultimate empire expansion to the north and south.

5

THE STRANGE CASE OF "COLONEL X"

THE GATHERING shadows around my house, the increasingly frequent visits of pseudo traitors to Captain Watson's office and also to that of Colonel Charles Burnett, our military attaché, and clumsy snares prepared for every one of us by the Joho Kyoku revealed that the Japanese recognized us as open adversaries in the game of intelligence. They were obviously attempting to discredit our activities or nullify them before they could become truly disadvantageous for Japan. Our meetings in Captain Watson's office had, indeed, become more frequent and had also grown in length as the task before us became more serious. The Washington Naval Limitation Conference might have settled the question of a makeshift disarmament of a distinctly temporary character, with the Japanese acquiescing only because they had no alternative in view of the lack of development of the economic and industrial bases on which a modern naval power is founded. But it did not make intelligence unnecessary. This was pointed out to us by Captain Watson, who was keenly alert to the new tasks which the Washington Conference placed as an added burden on our intelligence work.

"We now have," he said, "three major problems to solve, and the solution of each one is by itself a full-time job. The first problem, of course, is to observe the Japanese in their adherence to the Washington agreement. In brief, we have to find out whether they are going to do what they promised in Washington: to scrap their quota of supernumerary vessels. The second problem is to find out whether the Japanese are going to observe the conditions under which the League of Nations assigned to them the mandate over several islands in the Pacific. The third problem is to find out the intentions of the Japanese naval high command, their geographical orientation, and especially how they intend to implement in practice the chauvinistic policy of the Black Dragon hotheads."

Captain Watson was a farseeing officer who regarded his mission to Japan as one that might secure the peace, if only by acquiring comprehensive knowledge of Japanese plans for war. "If we know," he used to say, "the minute details of Japanese plans for aggression, we are in a position to thwart them while they are still in the planning stage. Only knowledge of their moves well ahead of time can enable us to counteract those moves. Otherwise we shall one day be confronted with a surprise that will hit us right between the eyes."

We realized during those conferences in the Captain's office that our intelligence organization as it was maintained under Watson in Tokyo was quite adequate to cope with problem number one— the observance of the naval limitation treaty. According to its Chapter II, Part 3, Section II, the Japanese were required to scrap ten capital ships at once and ten others between 1934 and 1942. They were also required to discontinue their building program which involved some of the aircraft carriers that were later effectively scrapped, not by them but by us, in the course of the Pacific war.

Japan's naval strength in the categories of escort vessels and screening craft was not affected by the treaty, a provision which was accepted with relief in the Japanese Navy. In our conversations with members of the Naval General Staff we learned that particular hopes were placed in light cruisers, destroyers, and other types of escorts. Our attention called to these vessels, we made an extensive study of Japanese destroyer tactics and found that this type was to be conserved and used for night actions, for which the Japanese had prepared truly ingenious plans. The Washington treaty did not interfere with these plans in any way whatever (a fact which we regarded as one of its major deficiencies, especially in view of the information at our disposal).

Problems two and three, however, required special attention and, indeed, special personnel. The limited means at our disposal prevented us from observing the Japanese in their administration of the mandated islands. Neither did we have means or men to find out Japanese intentions and aggressive plans beyond what we could pick up in the open market of peacetime intelligence. Captain Watson was concerned about these mandated islands, where the Japanese were reliably reported to be going about merrily violating the mandate which prohibited their fortification. The few reports which reached us from these Pacific islands indicated feverish activities: merchantmen discharging material obviously designed for the building of gun emplacements, bunkers, and underground passages; naval vessels calling at those islands and delivering heavy-caliber coast guns and other equipment—all contraband according to the provisions of the mandate. Although greatly concerned, Watson could not obtain permission to establish an effective check on these activities or to ascertain the accuracy of the numerous reports coming to his ears.

Several involved plans on a rather ambitious scale were then considered in the Captain's office. They included the landing of secret agents from submarines, the smuggling of observers to the mandated islands in the guise of commercial travelers and missionaries, and similar schemes; but they were all discouraged by higher authority or dropped by us as impracticable. Finally we hit upon the solution which we felt would bring us the desired information. It was customary in times of peace to send naval vessels on courtesy calls to foreign naval bases. So we suggested that some of our cruisers, particularly those ships going to and returning from China (with alert intelligence officers on board), call at the Japanese mandates on such courtesy calls and make the best of the time which they would be permitted to spend at these bases. While our military and naval authorities regarded the plan as admirable and supported it with considerable vigor, our diplomatic authorities discouraged the idea. They felt that requests for such visits might lead to troublesome complications of diplomacy; and they were, therefore, reluctant to permit any disturbance within their circles jealously preserved in the drawing rooms of Tokyo and Washington.

A few halfhearted efforts were made in the form of meaninglessly polite diplomatic notes, suggesting to the Japanese the "advisability" of the proposed courtesy calls in the central Pacific. But the Japanese hardly bothered to answer these suggestions, or answered them in the same indirect manner in which our own notes were drafted. I felt that some of our diplomats were relieved when the Japanese refused to accept our suggestions, since it saved them from what they regarded as unnecessary diplomatic complications.

When the idea of the courtesy calls appeared to us as definitely eliminated, we returned to our original plans in the stronger category of intelligence. More and more, as time passed, we came to believe in the immediate necessity of sending an observer to the mandated islands whether the Japanese liked it or not. It was obvious that no observer would be permitted to go once his identity was revealed and his mission openly stated. The alternative was a secret agent, an observer traveling in some plausible guise but capable of surveying the field in a professional way. While we in Tokyo were still considering the advisability and practicability of such a move, Washington authorities apparently decided to act—and their action led to one of the strangest incidents I was privileged to witness in my long career in Naval Intelligence.

In the spring of 1923, by which time Captain Watson had been relieved by Captain Lyman H. Cotten, USN, the attention of our naval attaché was directed to an American who had just arrived in Yokohama and who was seen frequently in rather shabby drinking places and geisha houses. The "system" which had been established by Captain Watson had been working effectively, and we ascertained that this American was in reality a retired officer, purportedly on a secret mission. As he told it during his "lighter" moments in Yokohama, he was selected by Washington to go to the mandated islands in the guise of an innocuous traveler "to find out what the hell was going on down there."

The American Naval Attaché was not privy to this typical Washington secret but was left in complete darkness about the scheme. Captain Cotten was not the type who grows sulky when overlooked by bureaucracy. He realized at once that, whether or not he was officially informed, the officer's mission was his immediate concern, and that now, added to his already complex duties, he had the task of shadowing this American stranger in the bars of Yokohama.

It was not very difficult to establish the stranger's identity and also his intentions. We could never understand how such an irresponsible individual, who violated every rule and principle of proper intelligence, could be entrusted with a mission of this serious nature. But though we were alarmed and somewhat scandalized, it was difficult to do anything about the mysterious stranger in his capacity as a retired officer, or if he were in fact under secret orders from higher authority.

For several days we maintained our surveillance over the "agent" and watched him toboggan rapidly in the Yokohama bars. Every one of his appearances there revealed more data on his proposed trip, not only to us but obviously to Japanese counter-intelligence as well; and we realized that this "secret agent" had outlived his usefulness long before he could embark on his actual mission.

It was not long after the first news reached the Naval Attaché about "Colonel X," as we now called him, that I was privileged to participate in some emergency conversations. I found the Attaché in a rather agitated mood:

"We are having real trouble with 'Colonel X,' " he said.

"Drinking again, I know," I remarked.

"Not again," the Captain answered. "He is now in a permanent state of protracted inebriation." Even in such an emergency Captain Cotten maintained his sense of humor.

"What can we do?" I asked, and the Captain said:

"Well, I have a plan. The Colonel is obviously in bad physical shape and requires immediate medical attention. I propose to have him delivered to our naval hospital in Yokohama, have him certified as sick by Captain Webb (Medical Corps, USN, the commanding officer), and ship him back to the States as fast as we can."

The plan was generally accepted as admirable, and next morning an ambulance picked up the Colonel, then soundly preparing himself in prolonged sleep for the inevitable hang-over. When he awoke, he found himself in sober surroundings in a private room of our naval hospital, attended by Chief Pharmacist Zembsch, who acted as his confidant and jailer rather than as his nurse. Although originally motivated by security considerations, Cotten's concern about the Colonel's physical condition appeared fully justified after Dr. Webb's first examination. Here was a typical case of "the Lost Weekend" with a touch of secret service. The Colonel was in no shape even for transportation back home, so we were advised to permit him to regain at least some of his strength in his private ward before sending him on a strenuous journey by transport. Captain Cotten was reluctant to accept the delay but finally agreed, and the Colonel was left under the care of the hospital and Zembsch.

About a week later I had another call from the Captain's office for still another emergency conference. "Zacharias," he greeted me, "it is our friend 'X' again!"

"What now, sir?"

"Damn it all," the Captain exclaimed, "he is A.W.O.L. from the hospital."

"Escaped?"

"I don't know. Webb has just called to tell me that they can't find the Colonel anywhere. Zembsch has spent a whole day looking in the favorite hangouts, but he can find no trace of him."

In our amusing though discomforting plight, we enlisted the aid of the Japanese Missing Persons Bureau and other local authorities. The cities of Tokyo and Yokohama were searched both by us and the Japanese, all without success. For two long months the "Colonel" remained on the list of lost articles, but at the end of this period the Attaché was called to the Japanese Navy Ministry to receive certain information. Colonel X had been located on the Island of Jaluit, one of the mandated islands—at last at his destination, so loudly proclaimed by him in Yokohama. Nobody could deny that the Colonel was a man of great ingenuity and determination despite the tragic shortcomings of his character. The news from Jaluit was alarming for more reasons than one. The Colonel was sick. "In fact," the official in the Navy Ministry informed the Captain, "the doctors don't expect him to live much longer."

"How about getting him back to Tokyo at once?" the Captain asked, and received the promise of quick action, which made him immediately suspicious. "You'll see," he told me when he returned from the Embassy, to which the international aspects had already carried the problem, "they have something up their sleeves. I don't expect 'Colonel X' back here alive—ever."

The Navy Ministry assured us that the details would be arranged within twenty-four hours and that the Colonel would be brought back at once. But next morning a telephone call from the Kaigun-Sho informed the Attaché that no transportation plans were necessary. "The Colonel passed away the night before. His body was cremated at once," the Japanese informed us, "and the ashes are at your disposal if you care to take possession of them."

These circumstances further aroused our suspicion, since they had all the earmarks of prearranged play. Rumors were numerous, and the Captain bluntly told the Japanese that he expected them to give him the exact circumstances under which the Colonel died. An autopsy was out of the question, for all that was left of "X" was his ashes. But this situation presented the opportunity to conduct certain investigations on the spot and Cotten was quick to seize it.

"I will send a representative to take charge of the ashes," he informed the Japanese. "This gentleman was an important personality in the United States, and we wish to bury him with the ceremony due his status."

Captain Cotten's request caught the spokesman by surprise, and as is usual with the Japanese when the unexpected happens, they had no prearranged plan to meet the situation. They had hoped that the strange case of "Colonel X" would be closed forever and that no further thought would be given to his ashes. The Japanese always require considerable time to reorient themselves in such a contingency. Many persons have to be consulted; responsibilities have to be divided and subdivided, and reluctance to assume authority has to be overcome—the Japanese dreading nothing more than the necessity of making a decision on the spot. In the confusion which followed Captain Cotten's blunt and unexpected decision, the Japanese interposed no objection to sending Chief Pharmacist Zembsch to Jaluit. The barrier was down. An American was traveling to the mandated islands openly, with the *laissez-passer* of the Japanese Navy Ministry. In his death, we felt, "Colonel X" had rendered a greater service to his country than he had been able to render in life.

Zembsch was carefully and minutely prepared for the trip in the Naval Attaché's office. He was instructed in detail how to conduct himself and what to look for. In the limited time available for this indoctrination, we imparted to him as much intelligence technique as was possible under the circumstances without making him too conscious of the intelligence aspects of his trip.

Then followed the long period of waiting. Zembsch traveled both ways on Japanese ships which consumed about two weeks on each leg of the journey. The Japanese kept us advised of his progress and informed us of his arrival; but after that, news from Zembsch abruptly ceased for about two weeks, until one day during the seventh week of his absence the announcement came from the Kaigun-Sho that Zembsch was expected to land in Yokohama the next morning. Our curiosity, denied satisfaction for seven long weeks, was now expressed in the excitement with which we all awaited the Chief Pharmacist's return. Several of us went down to the pier to meet him, traveling in the ambulance which our naval hospital used as its means of transportation. In this case it was sorely needed.

After the Japanese ship was secured to the pier we waited in vain for the appearance of Zembsch. As there was no sign of him we finally went aboard ourselves to locate him and determine the cause of delay. We were received politely by the skipper of the ship, who had been eying us from the bridge and came down to meet us at the gangway. He conducted us to a cabin below decks which was occupied by Zembsch. As we opened the door we saw the Chief Pharmacist sitting on his bunk with eyes aimlessly gazing into space. He was unshaved, unkempt, deranged in mind as well as physical appearance. He was completely unmoved by our entrance; failed to rise to greet us. In fact, he did not seem to recognize us at all, but continually muttered incoherent words from which we could gather no clue to his amazing condition. He was clasping a white box in his folded arms like one protecting a priceless treasure. It was the typical white box which is used by the Japanese to transport the simple urn in which the ashes of cremated bodies are preserved.

The driver of our ambulance was the first in the group to recover from the state of astonishment which gripped us. With appropriate conversation, he bent over Zembsch and patted his shoulder, then gently forced him to stand up so that we could carry him to the ambulance. The car carefully snaked its way off the pier and through crowded Yokohama streets up to the U. S. Naval Hospital, which occupied a commanding position on the bluff overlooking the bay. We realized that the man who had just returned from his strange mission to Jaluit was hardly more useful to us than the ashes which he continued to clutch tenaciously.

Captain Webb was summoned at once, but there was little he could do. The catatonic stupor which held Zembsch a senseless captive persisted for days, and despite the most attentive mental treatment we failed to break through the impenetrable wall which some strange occurrence had erected between Zembsch and the outer world.

For four days Captain Webb remained at his bedside applying all methods known to mental therapy to snap him back to coherent consciousness. At last, on the fifth day, reason seemed to be returning to the deranged mind of the unfortunate man. His talk became more articulate; there seemed to be some co-ordination between his thoughts and actions; but while he became aware of the present, an acute case of amnesia prevented him from remembering anything of the immediate past. We, too, returned to his bedside day after day, now attracted by his strange condition rather than by the hope of obtaining an immediate explanation of its causes. Daily Captain Webb received us with the discouraging words: "No use. He is still in bad shape."

"What do you think caused his collapse?" I asked. "Was he unstable at all before he left?"

"No, he was not," the Captain said. "He was a fine man, energetic and enthusiastic, and nothing was wrong with him so far as I could see. There must have been some shock which unbalanced his mind between his departure and return. You know," he added in thoughtful words, "I think our Japanese friends are the only ones who could give the proper explanation for his present condition."

"You mean, Captain, they did something to him?" I said.

"I have no other solution to the mystery," he answered. "They must have slipped powerful drugs into his meals to dull his senses —morphine or overdoses of opium—and obviously the man who was in charge of the operation did his job somewhat too well. There is nothing we can do. Zembsch is in a bad mental state, and it will be some time before he regains his former self."

The double mystery of "Colonel X" and Chief Pharmacist Zembsch was never completely solved. Before Zembsch had completely regained his health, he and his wife both perished in that same hospital in the great Japanese earthquake of September 1, 1923; and most of the secrets of the Colonel's death remained interred in the little urn which contained his ashes. We, however, persisted in trying to obtain at least some information of the circumstances under which the Colonel died, and were successful in finding a missionary who had stood at the unfortunate man's bedside when he was drawing his last breath. It seems that the Japanese themselves helped the Colonel to reach Jaluit, since they planned to get rid of him there rather than in Japan proper. A passage was arranged for him with mysterious ease, and his journey was made as pleasant for him as he could desire, for there was plenty of strong liquor at the ship captain's table during the voyage and convivial "friends" awaiting him at Jaluit. His short stay at this strategic point was a continual round of drinking parties, and undoubtedly lethal drugs were slipped into every glass the Colonel lifted to his lips. During this period he was visited by one of the missionaries who had been on Jaluit since the time of German occupancy, but by then there was nothing that could be done for him. A Japanese made frequent inquiries about the Colonel's condition and was at the hospital when he died. Shortly after, his body was removed by another Japanese and was immediately cremated before the missionaries could voice a protest against this arbitrary action.

Thus ended the strange case of "Colonel X" and our first attempt to seek information on Japan's mandated islands. The Japanese obviously designed this incident as a warning to us. They clearly intended to demonstrate that they would tolerate no interference with their plans for the islands and were willing to go to any length to discourage our curiosity. With the exception of a few foreigners, undoubtedly believed innocuous, who were allowed to touch at certain "open ports," no stranger ever set foot on any of these mandated islands to report back the status of their defenses and their offensive strength.

Japanese secrecy in which these islands were shrouded was explained to us only many years later when we at last decided to inspect them—this time in force. When we occupied Truk, Jaluit, and the other so-called strong points of the Pacific in the course of the recent war, we discovered that it was their weakness rather than strength that the Japanese were so anxious to conceal. Admiral Murray, who took possession of Truk, once called an impregnable bastion and the Gibraltar of the Pacific, found the major Japanese base hardly more than an empty shell when measured by standards. Jaluit, advertised by clever Japanese propaganda as an "unsinkable aircraft carrier," was an antiquated defense post with overage guns and primitive landing strips—facts which the Japs were eager to keep from reaching us via "Colonel X" and Chief Pharmacist Zembsch. It was the very difficult nature of amphibious operations rather than the prepared defensive strength of these islands which made their occupation so difficult. And it will remain an everlasting credit to the strategic genius of Fleet Admiral Nimitz and other planners that the decision was made to by-pass Truk and Jaluit despite the forbidding odds advertised by Japanese propaganda and without proper advance intelligence of the true status of these islands. The entire course of the Pacific war might have been altered and victory speeded up had we known through peacetime observations the potential role these outposts might play in a wartime emergency. But the hands of American

Intelligence were tied even when it was confronted with its most legitimate tasks.

As much as twelve years later, 1935, when the situation in the Pacific had deteriorated to the point where war between Japan and the United States was not remote, we tried in vain to obtain an insight into Japanese conditions. At that time I was in charge of the Far Eastern Division of the Office of Naval Intelligence in Washington, D.C. I tried to revive the idea of the courtesy calls by our naval vessels, recommended more than a decade before by the naval attaché's office in Tokyo. The proposal was carried to the State Department and discussed in its Far Eastern Division. It was received with the same bewilderment and reluctance with which Captain Watson's and Captain Cotten's original suggestions were met. Eugene Dooman, who was then chief of the State Department's Japanese section, bluntly advised against even attempting to obtain permission from the Japanese for such courtesy calls.

"I do not think," he said in effect, "that a pressing of this issue can serve any useful purpose at this time."

"Even if they refuse," I countered, "we should compel them to communicate their refusal in writing. We would then have an opportunity to present the case to the League of Nations and demand action one way or the other."

Of course Japan was then no longer a member of the League, but her commitment concerning the mandated islands still continued unchanged. But I could not move Mr. Dooman. "This is a controversial issue," he merely said. "I am against an attempt to bring it up." I have a full understanding of the difficulties under which our diplomats work, and also of the etiquette in international relations which commits burning issues to pallid diplomatic notes. I could even sympathize with Mr. Dooman's point of view—not entirely shared by others in the State Department's Japanese section but habitually maintained in our Tokyo embassy—since I knew that Japan was working itself into a high state of emotional tension and was willing to take risks which could not be settled by diplomacy. What I resented was the bluntness of the refusal and the unwillingness of Dooman to endeavor to reach a compromise whereby both diplomatic etiquette and national security could have been preserved. It was largely the shackles which our prewar diplomacy placed on our peacetime intelligence that forced us to embark on a difficult total war without even elemental data on the enemy.

We had foreseen this development long before 1935 when I tried to break down diplomatic opposition to our plans and needs. Even in 1922, when Captain Watson was still holding the post of naval attaché in Tokyo, we realized that we should have to intensify our intelligence work if we were to dispel the artificial fog with which the Japanese tried to conceal their secrets from us.

6

THE "M-PLAN"

THE VITAL question in 1921 was: how can we penetrate Japanese obstructions in times of peace so that we may have at least a working organization available for immediate application if war comes? What we needed and hoped to organize was an information service similar to those maintained by other nations who have traditionally regarded their own national security as the first concern of statesmanship. We needed such a service in Japan, and Captain Watson reported to Washington that he intended to organize one before relinquishing his post.

To stimulate thought on this subject, the Captain confided in his close associates in Tokyo, but he failed to gain the necessary support his sound suggestion deserved.

"What you have in mind, Eddie, is an impossibility," he was usually told by the old-timers. What seemed impossible to others was only a challenge to Watson. Still he was stymied, since he could find no one available with sufficient technical knowledge to draw up the details of the plan which he had so clearly outlined in his own mind. His enthusiasm was contagious, and I, too, became concerned about the need of an information service. But I felt that as a newcomer to Intelligence and to Japan I was inadequately acquainted with conditions there and should not try my own hand at drafting a plan for Watson. So I carried the Captain's ideas to a fellow countryman of ours, a long-time resident of Japan whom I knew to be thoroughly grounded in the psychology and practical behavior of the Japanese people and who was vitally interested in American prestige.

"Tom," I said to him, "you ought to know the best way to obtain information in the various parts of this secretive country."

He amazed me with his answer: "There are no secrets in Japan," he said. When he saw my astonishment, he elaborated on his unorthodox statement. "Do you remember the grapevine process in connection with Sato's visit to your house? Well, all you have to do is to tap the grapevine and you will learn everything that is taking place anywhere in Japan." Incredible as it was to me then, I later had ample opportunity to verify the truth of this statement. As I am writing these lines, still another confirmation has just reached the newspapers. Certain Japanese Army officers, refusing to regard their recent defeat as final, concealed a reported two billion dollars' worth of gold and platinum in shallow waters off Tokyo for "the Day" when they could turn their attention to the rebuilding of Japan's armed forces. But recently, although the treasure was thought to be safely hidden, an American raiding party surrounded its watery hiding place and the hoard was confiscated. The information which led the American authorities to the treasure was supplied by a geisha who picked it up while listening to conversations of her guests and transmitted it to our counter-intelligence authorities. When I read of this incident, I recalled Tom's words of twenty-five years ago: "There are no secrets in Japan."

The conversation with Tom solved in my mind only half of our basic problem. I was now convinced that information could be obtained by eavesdropping along the grapevine, but information is useless unless it can be transmitted to a collecting agency by some quick method.

"Tom," I asked, "how do you think the information could be sent out of the country once it is obtained?" To this question he only smiled and slowly moved his head from side to side. He had no solution for that question, and for a time I, too, felt baffled. I reported the discussion in detail to Captain Watson, but he refused to share my discouragement.

"Your friend may know the Japanese," he said, "but obviously he knows very little about intelligence. Why don't we talk to somebody who knows both?" He thought for a moment, then said: "I think I'll talk things over with Sid Mashbir," which he proceeded to do.

Sidney F. Mashbir was a captain in the United States Army and also a Japanese language officer. In 1916 he had worked for General Funston over the Mexican border on things Japanese, and in World War I he engaged in much counter-intelligence work. I have always thought of him as my counterpart in the Army, where officers with an interest in intelligence could be counted on the fingers of one hand. His accomplishments wherever he has been allowed to function have been unsurpassed.

"Sid," the Captain asked him, "do you think you could draw up a plan for getting information out of Japan in time of war?" The question amazed our friend. He had been long convinced of such a need but had been discouraged by the indifference of his own superiors. Here at last was a senior officer who, like himself, was keenly conscious of our own intelligence needs and determined to do something about them.

"Yes, sir," he replied, "I certainly could."

"How long do you think you would need to draft such a plan?"

"Not more than two weeks, if I work day and night."

"Well, start at once! Write down your plan and give it to me. I'll see to it that it reaches the proper hands in Washington."

"I'd be delighted, sir, if it is made available to both departments," Sid replied.

In just two weeks Sid returned to Captain Watson's office with a folder which contained the neatly typed copy of what we came to call our "M-Plan." Captain Watson, sensing the drama of the occasion, inspected the outer office to ascertain that all doors were closed before he started the perusal of the plan. Quickly he went through page after page, alternately pursing his lips or nodding his head to give emphasis to the thoughts as they raced through his mind. Occasionally he paused to look up at Captain Mashbir or myself, and with a smile he would exclaim "Splendid!" in sincere admiration. Mashbir's face glowed in appreciation of the words and the recognition of his work. When Watson finished the last page and slowly closed the folder, he turned to Mashbir and said:

"This is perfectly marvelous. How on earth did you do this so quickly and so well?"

"Well, Captain," he answered, "I have been thinking of this problem for a long time, and I am very grateful to you for the opportunity to put it in this concrete form." His memorandum demonstrated his keen knowledge of Japan and also his long and fruitful preoccupation with intelligence. He was an expert in both; but, perhaps because of his outstanding qualifications, he was hampered in his own activities by the barbed jealousies within his own circle. He was an Army officer, responsible to the Military Attaché in Tokyo. The fact that he was now working for the Naval Attaché did not promise to enhance his standing with his superior. Captain Watson was well aware of the little bickerings and departmental jealousies within the services, but expected that the high quality of

Mashbir's memorandum would aid in making the Military Attaché forget the semideparture from the old-fashioned chain-of-command principle.

"You know what I'm going to do right now?" Watson asked Mashbir. "I am going over to see your boss and show him your splendid work. I know he has been skeptical about the whole thing, but I don't think he will persist in his doubts when he sees this plan."

The striking part of Captain Mashbir's clever scheme was its utter simplicity. It listed the points at which the Japanese grapevine could be tapped, and, more important than that, it outlined the system whereby the information thus obtained could be transmitted out of Japan. It involved the organization of a few strategic personalities who were expected not to be affected by the emergency for which the plan was prepared. It described in great detail the means of communication which could be placed at the disposal of these agents. The imagination which he manifested was evident on every page. He recalled, for example, after a discussion we had, that a diplomatic custom in Japan enabled departing diplomats to dispose of their superfluous properties in public auctions. By this means we envisaged the transfer of certain communication equipment to the agents left behind. One of the proposals involved the auctioning of an attaché's motorcar with the prospective agent winning it in open bidding. This, however, was not to be an ordinary automobile. It was to be equipped with a double gasoline tank, the inside tank holding a small radio transmitter for the agent to communicate with friendly submarines approaching the Japanese coast for reception of the messages. The idea was truly ingenious, since the car could be moved from spot to spot for the purpose of transmitting, thereby defying detection by the most sensitive radio-locating devices.

But no matter how good the plan appeared to us, its acceptance and implementation eventually depended upon mutual acceptance by Mashbir's own superiors in the Military Attaché's office. Captain Watson did not waste time in acquainting his opposite number in the Army with the proposal. He called his car and drove to the Hikawa-cho district, where the Military Attaché had his combination house and office. The Attaché glanced through the folder and then, before he had time either to absorb or consider the outline, he said:

"I can't see anything new in this. It's merely the adaptation of the old German system."

"That may be," Captain Watson countered. "But do you have anything better? In fact, do you have anything?"

"Well. . . . No-o-o."

"That settles it. I am sending this plan on to the Navy Department. You may keep this copy. Send it on to your people in Washington, or do with it as you please, but I would appreciate it greatly if you would give your young man appropriate credit for the splendid work he did for me." The answer to this last request was noncommittal. The "credit" Mashbir was to receive later assumed the form of increased jealousies and attack which eventually led to obstructions when he served as a Military Intelligence reserve officer subsequent to his resignation from the Regular Army in 1923 for a specific vital purpose connected with intelligence work in Japan. These intentions were known only to the Military Attaché, Colonel Burnett; Colonel (then Captain) Warren G. Clear, and myself, and are still today in a secret category.

Caught in this cross fire of contrary views, our M-Plan went the way of all unorthodox proposals advanced within a bureaucracy. Watson did send it to Washington, but we could never ascertain what happened to it after it had been taken from the pouch and sent around the department with a limited distribution list attached to it. Captain Watson was detached soon after Mashbir submitted his plan, and his new duties prevented him from pursuing its progress after he left Tokyo. When the plan thus lost its greatest advocate, it also lost its effectiveness, since from then on it became merely one of the innumerable memoranda in all government offices. The rest of us were too young and too junior in rank to support the plan with the effectiveness of a senior proponent. In the files it remained, until I dug it out in 1936 and took steps to put it in operation. But inability to visualize the vital necessity for such a concrete intelligence plan by those in a position to initiate it completed its final doom.

As I now look back on the M-Plan and view it in the light of subsequent events, my regret increases a hundredfold that it was permitted to be pigeonholed between Tokyo and Washington. The war which Captain Watson could foresee even in 1921 did come less than twenty years later. But the organization plan to meet this emergency was gathering dust in the "Finished File," where it rested in a back room safe, and eventually was sent with other papers to a shelf in the government archives.

When war came we had nobody in Tokyo to tap the grapevine of Japanese gossip and information, and nobody to send information out of Japan to us. Our ignorance of conditions within Japan was so complete that in 1942 the Chief of Naval Operations was obliged to confess publicly that he did not know whether or not Japan was building monster battleships of 45,000 tons' displacement. This situation exhausted the energy and ingenuity of men to build up a system as best they could in a country closed to us by the often impenetrable barriers of war. We did succeed in organizing a rudimentary information service within Japan, but it proved far too inadequate to collect the vital political information which Mashbir's plan would have secured for us had it been adopted. In the full knowledge of all facts, I feel confident that the war could have been shortened by at least six months had we had available the system envisaged by him. Many lives might have been saved and the world returned to peace so much faster, escaping the agony of those last six months which included the bloody battles of Iwo Jima and Okinawa.

In 1923, as the days passed in Tokyo and no word of approval of our M-Plan reached us from Washington, our enthusiasm subsided somewhat, and we went about the habitual procedure of life during the summer months in Japan. Mashbir and others went to Oiso to relax in the quiet surroundings and cool climate of this delightful seashore resort, while I stayed on at Zushi to finish my studies. My tour of duty was drawing to a close, and there were numerous final arrangements to be made for my return home two months hence.

The first of September 1923 dawned as one of the typically delightful days of the Japanese autumn. I arose before daylight. In the suspended silence of the early morning I watched the speckled dawn stirring gently like a slumbering animal of the jungle. A silvery quarter moon looked down upon the placid waters which moved almost imperceptibly. In the half-light, where distant objects were accentuated by the lambent air, I was served my usual breakfast of "hamon" and eggs. Then I hastened to catch the "Businessman's Special," an early train with an extra coach for the businessmen commuting from Kamakura, the village resort next to Zushi. I was still following my monthly routine, which included a trip to Yokohama, then to Tokyo to pick up my pay check. Today friends were to sail for home on the *Empress of Australia,* and I was to see them off. Completing my business in Tokyo, I returned to Yokohama, where I devoted some time to shopping, and at eleven o'clock I proceeded to the pier where the big liner was making ready for departure exactly at noon. There seemed to be an unusually large crowd departing and a correspondingly larger crowd to bid them farewell. The pier, about a thousand feet long and quite wide, was built largely of reinforced concrete piles and steel girders. It was the center of feverish activity. Astern of the *Empress* and moored alongside the end of this pier was the *Steel Navigator,* a small freighter of the U.S. Steel Corporation. On the other side of the pier was a large French steamer, the *André Lebon,* with engines disabled and under repair.

At one minute to twelve the pier had taken on a festive appearance, with a maze of multicolored streamers fluttering in the breeze which came in occasional gusts along the dock. Finally, down came the gangway; up went hands clasping handkerchiefs for a last farewell, faces wreathed in smiles or expressions of sorrow.

Suddenly, the smiles vanished, and for an appreciable instant everyone stood transfixed as the sound of unearthly thunder, that peculiar subterranean roar which precedes an earthquake, signalized to the paralyzed minds the catastrophe that was already engulfing them. The huge pier became an undulating sea, with a strong lateral motion that made standing impossible. People scrambled to their feet only to be thrown down again, while the cries of terror-stricken men and women were drowned by the din of falling structures and the roar of the earth. It was as though one were riding inside the large wheel of a steam roller over the rockiest road.

Acting instinctively, I tried to leave the pier, but a second shock came with renewed force. Once again the structure began to writhe and groan under the stresses that were tearing it apart. I felt myself falling through space, as the wooden section of the pier collapsed into the water. I grasped a section of an accommodation ladder near by and struggled to the top, jumping to a portion of the pier which still stood. As I glanced toward Yokohama, the whole view was cut off by an opaque screen of dust which hung low over the city and came drifting toward us. I realized that the terrible roar which had followed the first shock was the sudden destruction of a great city. The dust was followed by billowing seas of smoke. Explosions sent columns of black smoke and flame high into the air. Fanned by the rising winds, the fires spread rapidly, and the burning embers passed over our heads, warning us that the flames soon would reach the water front.

The force of the heated air rapidly increased until it reached such strength that no movement was possible, but by that time I was in a sampan between the *Empress* and the *André Lebon*, assisting in the rescue work which foreigners on the pier began with the first destructive quake.

From the first moment of crisis and horror it was the foreigners among the crowd on the pier who recovered from panic and started rescue efforts. The Japanese were captives of an amazing psychic inertia, completely incapable of grasping the situation or of opposing the elements either by saving themselves or by rushing to the aid of others. They seemed struck to absolute helplessness.

Minute by minute the wind increased in force, whipping up the sea until it began to break over the bow of our sampan. The whole water front became a solid wall of flame, and it was quite apparent that landing was impossible. We were forced to haul alongside the gangway of a steamer anchored offshore and wait.

The fire on shore spread with amazing swiftness and increased to a degree that is difficult to describe. Approaching the warehouses along the embankment, the flames appeared to pounce upon them as a tiger on its prey and with a loud crackling roar burst from the buildings, spiraling high into the air and crying out with a morbid joy of destruction. The wind rose to a sixty-mile gale. Burning cargo lighters were drifting aimlessly in the harbor, carrying destruction wherever they went.

The heat from the fire on shore made our position alongside the huge steamer almost untenable, but we feared that we might run into greater danger should we cast off. The tension increased as the seconds passed and we were condemned to inaction.

Finally, as the flaming water front burned to blackened, smoking embers, we ventured ashore. It was five o'clock, five hours after the earthquake. The rest of the day and night was spent in rescue work, helping women and children to safety; freeing men imprisoned under fallen debris; reviving the unconscious; giving first aid to the injured, and calming, as far as it was possible, those who harbored the worst fears for their loved ones left behind in the city.

What only a few hours ago had been a busy metropolis was now hardly more than a gigantic heap of glowing rubble.

The night was painted by the terrific fires raging in the city, turning the landscape into a terrifying crimson nightmare. The sea was shrouded in impenetrable darkness; and this contrast between fire and dark gnawed at the nerves of those on board the ships in the harbor. The early rays of the sun revealed the sea: angry waters, soiled by the thick oil which flowed out from shore and covered the surface with a heavy film as far as the eye could see.

No further useful work on shore being immediately necessary, I returned to the *Empress* at four o'clock in the morning, taking with me Major William C. Crane, U.S. Army, who had been searching Yokohama for his wife whom I knew was on board the ship, safe, but greatly shocked from a harrowing experience. It was a joyful reunion. But now back aboard the *Empress,* my second thought was that this oil film on the water was a great potential hazard and could bring the peril of the shore to us at sea. Tensely I viewed the dangerous situation about which nothing could be done and awaited the moment when the oil would become ignited by the fire that was still burning on shore. I did not have long to wait.

About seven o'clock in the morning, a new fire started in the water near the middle of the bund, just off the Standard Oil Company's office. It was first believed to be paint, but as the fire continued to grow, it became evident that it was being fed from underground tanks which had exploded. There was no wind now, and the ship was in no immediate danger, but as the flames climbed higher and the black smoke became thicker, the people on board grew more nervous. In this tense atmosphere, women would come to the rail alongside of me, gaze toward the shore a moment, and then ask in frightened voices: "How long do you think it's going to burn?"

Each time I tried to cheer them by saying: "It seems to be burning out now and the smoke isn't so thick," but I am afraid my voice did not carry the necessary conviction, and they would walk away only half satisfied with my answer. In half an hour a light breeze came up, nudging the fire at leisurely pace along the water front to the corner of our pier. The danger to the *Empress* had now become real and imminent. The crew got all lifeboats ready, lowered them to the rail, and ran out all fire hoses. Captain Robertson of the *Empress* held an emergency meeting with the first mate of the *Steel Navigator* astern of us, whose skipper had been killed in the city. It was decided that we should lash our stern to the bow of the *Steel Navigator* and they would slip the anchor cable that was around our port propeller. She would then endeavor to back out and tow us with her.

Just as the work was begun, the most terrifying sight I was ever to witness was revealed to my incredulous eyes. The fire, now at the corner of the pier and engulfing the bund, burned fiercely, the heat reaching to the ship. Suddenly the fire began to whirl. Faster and faster it turned; higher and higher it spread; until it took the cyclonic form of a waterspout at sea. As those on board watched it, panic-stricken, praying that it would subside, the huge mass, now roaring like a thousand furnaces, started to move, driven by the force of its own whirling in our direction. The crowd on the deck surged back and forth in uncontrolled panic. We all knew that if this fire, now a hundred feet in diameter and reaching five hundred feet into the air, were to pass over the ship it would strip her clean.

For a moment it seemed to hesitate; and then, as the dark line at the base of the cone widened, it suddenly exploded and settled down to a normal burning mass. The suction of the whirl had become so great that a large quantity of water had been taken up, turned into steam, and had extinguished the upper flame. In the meantime, the lines to the *Steel Navigator* had been made fast and all moorings to the dock thrown off. The ship astern began to back her engines. For a while we did not move, while the fire still edged in our direction. Then we seemed to tremble, move an inch, then another; and to those like myself who had taken a bearing on distant objects it was evident that we were now moving out steadily. As the motion become perceptible, a huge sigh of relief issued forth from the crowd; we had won.

With a prayer of thanksgiving on our lips, we looked back at the pier which had been our prison just a moment ago. The fire was now completely engulfing it, wiping out everything that was left behind.

This was the climax of those first two harrowing days. In comparison, our other tragic adventures and rescue efforts seemed to be minor incidents. That they were not minor incidents was demonstrated when the American authorities awarded the Congressional Medal of Honor to Ensign Tommy Ryan (now a captain) for his rescue work.

It was not until three days later that I, by chance, was able to see my house at Zushi. I was en route with a rescue party proceeding by water and land to Kamakura, where the families of many foreigners greeted us as the first arrivals from Yokohama or Tokyo with news of their husbands and friends. Both little villages had been visited by a twin disaster. A tidal wave, which did not reach Yokohama, had hit Zushi and Kamakura in full force. Though my house was in its path, it had withstood the tremendous wave which covered the floors with four feet of water.

As I approached through debris-covered streets and over the sea wall broken in many places, I saw the servants drying my things in the bright sunshine of the Monday morning. Life was returning to normal, and the day's work had to be done. As I watched the old cook and his daughter, who had replaced Miss Spring and Miss Summer, going about their work with an impassive indifference in the face of the destruction which surrounded them and must have still harrowed their minds, I suddenly recalled the strange behavior of the Japanese masses throughout the catastrophe. Their peculiar conduct in the face of disaster was a revelation more forceful and illuminating than all the experiences of my three busy years in Japan. For the first time I felt that I had gained a real insight into the character structure of the Japanese people, penetrating the thick wall which only few strangers can break down, no matter how long they may stay in Japan. The wall was now broken before my eyes. It had required an earthquake to collapse it.

7

JAPANESE CHARACTER

WHENEVER I inquired in Japan about the characteristics, habits, and customs of the people, and whenever I tried to discover the inner thoughts which motivated them, I always found a hazy, over-all vagueness in the explanations offered. I turned to friends, both foreigners and Japanese, and searched books both ancient and modern, for a comprehensive answer. But wherever I turned, the same generalization confronted my question. It was obvious to me, as it was to many, that Japanese character or personality, or what-ever scientific name we might ascribe to that strange, inscrutable, and peculiar phenomenon, always defied, like electricity, a proper scholarly definition. Even Lafcadio Hearn, widely recognized as one of the outstanding authorities on Japan, and Basil Hall Cham-berlain, undoubtedly the best guide to things Japanese, seemed to be stumped when it came to an explanation of Japanese character.

The Japanese themselves seemed to be fascinated by their own national character; but they too, seemed incapable of explaining Japanese personality in simple and logical terms. "It is difficult for us Japanese," Masanori Oshima once wrote, "to find out our own mental characteristics, as our old proverb says: 'At the foot of the lighthouse it is darker than a far-off place.'"

The Japanese preoccupation with their personality induced D. C. Holtom, still another authority on Japan, to write: "There is probably no nation on earth today more conscious of itself, its psychological and institutional characteristics, its problems and tensions, than is the Japanese." Japanese writings on all subjects abound in lengthy disquisitions on the possession of unique and superior racial qualities and character traits. Holtom added, "To enumerate these qualities, count them over and over, analyze and describe them, and proclaim them as the basis of unparalleled achievement, has become almost a national obsession." This Hol-tom called *Japanese ethnocentrism*.

If the average intelligent Japanese is asked how the Japanese people acquired their "unique personality," he will usually say that it was inherited *in toto* from divine ancestors whose innate personality it embraced. In this sense I am tempted to agree with Cervantes that the Japanese are as God made them, and often a great deal worse. But the Japanese habitually frown upon such petulance. To them the divine inheritance of a cut-and-dried personality was a sacrosanct dogma which no cultural anthropologist could shake. Even today in the face of defeat and gradual enlightenment the old notions persist, especially in the rural areas where, after all, the majority of the Japanese live. I have no doubt that the promotion of ancient beliefs and superstitions—the theory of the divine origin and manifestation of Japanese character—will be powerful instruments in the hand of Japanese underground organizers.

In the early twenties I set out to make my own study of Japanese character, first by reading up on the subject as much as possible and comparing the findings of those whom I regarded as unquestioned authorities, and then by going out among the people like a collector of butterflies with a little green net, to gather my own samples to complete the analysis. In this latter excursion I had the advantage of splendid guides in several old residents, some of whom were in fact among the first Americans to knock on the closed door of Japan. But much useful, though naturally biased information was provided by Japanese observers as well, who were stimulated by the rather ostentatious Western interest in the Japanese character and decided to make their own native studies if only as a defensive measure against the adverse findings of Europeans and Americans.

I found that the first Japanese and Western observations along scientific lines were made almost simultaneously in 1890–91 by a Japanese school principal named Nose, and a European writer, Walter Dening, who later became well known as the biographer of Toyotomi Hideyoshi. Nose's catalogue of character traits was naturally all favorable to the Japanese, while Dening's appraisal was far more objective and may be regarded even today as a sound and sober assessment. Nose found eight purely national elements predominating in the Japanese character and enumerated them as: extreme aversion to disgrace, high regard for unspotted honor, loyalty to superiors, dutiful feeling toward parents, straightforwardness, cleanliness, chastity, and a tendency to controversy.

Dening, on the other hand, listed four outstanding traits as basic to the Japanese character, namely: precocity leading to overbearingness and conceit, unpracticality, levity, and fickleness. Another Western observer whose observations I regard as both satisfactory and reliable, Captain Frank Brinkley, a retired British naval officer, added to these traits: frugality, obedience, altruism, a genius for detail, imperturbability, and stoic endurance.

My first three years in Japan convinced me that both Nose and Dening were correct in their appraisals, and Brinkley's additional list was also justified. But not until 1943 did I find a fully satisfactory presentation of the Japanese character in any one of the books to which I turned. Then, however, Dr. Holtom succeeded even in the midst of war in drawing up an unbiased and truthful picture of the Japanese character. The objectivity of many modern writers was often clouded by their own prognostic ability to foresee the goal toward which Japan as a nation, rather than the Japanese as individuals, were relentlessly moving. These books succeeded in analyzing the Japanese character only in part. As an obvious reaction to the obnoxious Japanese ethnocentrism they usually stressed only the negative character traits, often, as in the case of Dr. O'Conroy and others, to the complete exclusion of positive ones.

Dr. Holtom, however, freed himself of the emotional bias which is nearly inevitable in time of war and presented this picture of the Japanese character: "A general list of those primary national psychological qualities," he wrote, "that are emphasized in present-day discussions would have to include a unique loyalty and patriotism, a special endowment of assimilative power which can take in the best foreign culture and yet remain forever Japanese, unusual powers of organization, an unrivaled capacity for expansion and achievement, reverence for ancestors, and regard for family name, a this-worldly and practical nature, love of natural beauty, an artistic and refined skill (particularly manual skill), candor and open heartedness, optimism, unique regard for purity and cleanliness, propriety and orderliness, and, finally, a gentle and forebearing disposition." Those who read Dr. Holtom's blistering *Modern Japan and Shinto Nationalism,* in which he outlined the religious motivations of Japanese aggression, must admire him for the objectivity which he succeeded in preserving and expressing in the face of Japanese provocations in the political field which he so convincingly described.

Even though the Japanese preferred to represent their character as unique and peerless, there were a few agnostics who dared to swim against the current and present a more objective picture of the nation's collective personality. If Carlyle is right that the greatest fault is to be conscious of none, then the fact that these native writers, and especially Nitobe, succeeded best in describing some of the deficiencies of the Japanese character may augur well for the future rehabilitation of the people of Japan. It was, indeed, a Japanese who once said: "Time may come soon for me to choose hell rather than life in a Japanese community." And in 1930 Nitobe declared: "About twenty years ago my mischievous mind was tempted to write a book called *A Humorous State* by which I meant, a country where the government and the people talk big and do little, where the art of governing is a ridiculous farce and a lie. How little did I then dream that I should but wait a score of years—until the year 1930—when I might select good illustrations nearer by."

It so happened that during my research in Tokyo I discovered that Nitobe actually wrote such a book. He wrote it at the turn of this century when Japanese books on the national character were not yet by necessity confined to the propagation of virtues only, but occasionally exposed national weaknesses as well. Such a book was Dr. Nitobe's *The Way of Life,* which he published in 1903. It has come to occupy a place by itself, since it remains the only work by a Japanese author devoted entirely to the deficiencies of the Japanese character.

Nitobe gave national conceit the first place on his list of deficiencies. Second place he gave to coercive etiquette and formal politeness, then in third place he listed an innate hostility to strangers, and finally, incapacity for fair and friendly competition. All these traits were evident to me as I watched the Japanese character in action, revealed in stark reality in their daily life, and then again on a gigantic scale at the time of the earthquake of 1923. The earthquake itself provided me with the answer to the most debated aspect of Japanese character and revealed the background of the proverbial Japanese imperturbability. Whole volumes have been written on this subject, and I myself accepted most of their findings, viewing the Japanese as a stoic and phlegmatic race by nature.

Chamberlain, for example, regarded their imperturbability as so ingrained that he listed it among the physical, rather than mental, characteristics of the race. But Dening, on the basis of historical examples, called attention to the fact that this almost deadly impassivity and equanimity was not among the original endowments of the Japanese but was a quality developed through centuries of rigid training and indoctrination. "It savors more of the nature of etiquette," he wrote, "than of actual lack of emotional feeling." But just as custom in time becomes accepted law, I feel that so does etiquette evolve as a characteristic.

Brinkley, too, although inclined to overstress the importance of imperturbability in the Japanese, agreed that this stoicism was effected by education at the expense of the feeling it sought to conceal: "Feelings cannot be habitually hidden," he wrote, "without being more or less blunted."

It was quite common in Japan to meet a friend just bereaved by the loss of a loved one, and to find him or her smiling. Nitobe asks in this connection, "Isn't it the smile of the Japanese that requires profound study? The hidden meaning of the smile is differently understood by different people." One immediately wonders about their emotions. The first conclusive answer to the question of whether the Japanese are emotional I found in a book written by a German physician, Dr. Erwin Baelz, who was invited to Japan late in the nineteenth century to modernize their medical system. He rose to considerable prominence in Japan and married the daughter of a respected aristocrat. His diary is one of the best guides to Japan as it was under Emperor Meiji. However, it was not in his voluminous diary that the answer to the question was found. It was contained in a little brochure in which he discussed the proverbial Japanese imperturbability in the face of death; and he finally called it: contempt for death.

Dr. Baelz's analysis was scientific in approach and detail. He attributed the apparent imperturbability of the Japanese in the face of disaster, first, to rigid regimentation and habituation, then to a combination of psychic inertia and catalepsy. The impact of earthquakes and other national catastrophes is not absorbed in an emotional vacuum. It merely causes a delayed reaction in the Japanese. The failure to respond to the overwhelming stimulus is caused not by a lack but by a blocking of emotions. Baelz himself experienced such an emotional blocking during a severe earthquake at the turn of the century. Its sudden impact caused in him, as it caused in the Japanese whom I watched during the earthquake of 1923, a catatonic stupor which was sustained until his servant awakened him.

A graphic demonstration of Dr. Baelz's theory was now provided during the earthquake. I suddenly realized that Dr. Baelz was right: the greatest weakness of the Japanese was their inherent psychic inertia in the face of disaster. It so happened that the cabinet had fallen two days previously; the government was not functioning when it was most needed, and without orders from above no one knew what to do. This was no accident. It was the pattern of Japanese action or inaction. As I watched this stupor which had every individual Japanese in its grip, I visualized that this would also be the pattern of Japanese behavior in a supreme crisis of war when the unexpected happened. This experience of complete inactivity for ten full days following the earthquake left a deep impression on my mind. It helped me in my later evaluation of the whole Japanese psychological structure, and it was the memory of 1923 which outlined for me the pattern I was to follow in 1945.

Although my own observations confirmed most of the analyses of these highly qualified Western judges of the Japanese character, I felt that mine went somewhat beyond their findings, chiefly because I made the most of an opportunity to observe separately the urban and the rural Japanese and their "character in action." It was my opinion that a distinction between city dwellers and the rural population was absolutely essential, both in a qualitative and a quantitative sense. Such a crucial distinction was regrettably disregarded by most analysts until 1937 when Dr. John F. Embree made his admirable comprehensive survey of Japanese village life and succeeded in bringing out many character traits which are native to the masses of Japanese villagers but can no longer be found in city dwellers.

The urban population of Japan has acquired many of our characteristics through such superficial influences as, for example, our motion pictures, which are extremely popular in Japan and provoke considerable attempts at emulation. But villagers retained much of what may be called aboriginal traits of the Japanese character. Considering both groups, I found that the Japanese, like all human beings and social groups, have both saints and sinners among them, and that the individual Japanese has both good and bad characteristics whether we consider these traits absolutely or relatively, using their own or our own moral standards as yard-sticks. Among the "good character traits" one can find physical cleanliness, a certain inherent kindliness, and refined artistic taste in every Japanese no matter how low he may stand on the social or educational ladder. But they also have negative traits in abundance, among which conceit or vanity, and an almost utter failure to appreciate abstract ideas, stand out as most prominent. The absence of a philosophical approach increases Japanese empiricism and slows down their action in the face of new experiences and unexpected situations. It also develops in them a certain life nega-tion and indifference which is characterized in their shoulder-shrugging attitude to natural catastrophes and overwhelming odds, and is expressed in their favorite solution to difficult problems: *"shikata ga nai"*—it cannot be helped.

Probably my most important discovery was that the Japanese character must be viewed in its moral habitat and ethical milieu and cannot be divorced either from the ethical indoctrination or strict regimentation to etiquette to which the whole nation has been subjected through centuries. Because their moral standards are different from our moral principles, we must regard their moral actions according to their, and not our, moral standards. If viewed in the light of Christian morals, the Japanese are deficient in their conception of sin, but merely because the conception of sin was provided with a different interpretation in Japan.

The Japanese woman is among the most moral in the world. Possibly this is affected somewhat by Japanese law, which made an unfaithful wife liable to two years in prison on complaint of the husband; while the husband had complete freedom in this respect, even to bringing a concubine into the home. But these condi-tions did not prevent community bathing, which we look upon as improper. It is the only method of bathing provided at the fashion-able and popular Japanese hot springs resorts. My investigative in-stincts caused me to inquire into this, too, and with many amusing results, one of which I shall relate. I must say, however, that it tends to prove the saying: We can get used to anything.

Having heard of the popularity of these hot springs resorts which afforded a splendid opportunity to study at close range Japanese life as well as anthropological aspects known as physique, I de-cided to spend the New Year's holiday at Izu San, a hot spring popular with the elite of Tokyo and noted for its *sen-nin-buro* (thousand-person bath) maintained in the leading Japanese hotel. So with Toyoda-San, a Japanese student of Waseda University, I set out for Izu San.

Upon arrival, after discarding the street clothes and donning the cotton kimono provided by the hotel as a bathrobe, sleeping gown, or street clothing, we had the customary pot of tea. The next step in the regulated procedure was a trip to the *sen-nin-buro*. This bathhouse was a part of the hotel near the end of a long corridor open to the then January weather, which was quite cold. As we arrived at the first door of the bathhouse I pushed it open energetically and jumped in. My astonishment, as Toyoda crashed into me because of my sudden halt, was because I saw before me mostly women in various stages of bath and in striking attitudes. Hurriedly I backed out, and, once more outside, I said to Toyoda, "We don't go in there, do we?" In his desire not to be mistaken, he quickly replied. "Oh, no. We go in the next door." Outside of the next door was a line of hooks on some of which kimonos were hanging. Upon the advice of Toyoda, we denuded ourselves of our kimonos, and urged on by the cold of the corridor I pushed open the door and dashed in, holding my washcloth in one hand and my soap in the other.

To my utter amazement we were in the same room from which a few minutes before I had beat a hasty retreat, only a bit farther along, and from the snickers which came forth from the giggling females, it was obvious that they were amused at the apparent embarrassment of the foreigner who had backed out of the other door so hurriedly. All eyes were now turned upon me as I entered the second door.

There was no alternative now except to conceal my embarrassment as best I could; so I proceeded with as much nonchalance as I could muster to one of the smaller tile tubs sunk into the floor alongside the wall opposite the door, and began my ablutions.

This experience revealed one fact: that the vast majority of so-called typical Japanese character traits are the products of cultural influences, most of them Chinese which have been skillfully adapted to Japanese conditions and requirements. Different cultural influences may produce different character traits, such as, indeed, the adaptability and susceptibility of the Japanese to extraneous influences, and makes it comparatively easy to mold or change what to the casual observer appears an ancient and inflexible character.

I could never bring myself to join either in the blanket condemnation or uncritical admiration of the Japanese character which was so typical of many observers who were either fascinated by the many positive traits or repelled by the innumerable negative characteristics of the average Japanese. I always strove for objectivity in my appraisals and excluded all preconceived notions and prejudices from my own interpretation of the Japanese character structure.

Most important of all, I viewed the Japanese character in the light of their moral standards and succeeded thereby in understanding many of the motivations which were behind their acts both in war and in peace. It seemed that the Japanese with whom I came in contact realized or sensed this objectivity and showed greater confidence and sincerity in their dealings with me than was usual in the ordinary contacts with other foreigners.

More than twenty years later when I had to devise a campaign directed to the Japanese character, these early observations served me well and brought forth a response to my efforts which was fully satisfactory. After my fourth broadcast the Japanese accepted my words as trustworthy, despite the fact that they came over the radio that was then an enemy transmitter. Thus did I go through a school of character studies, the field work of which included the agony of a major disaster and the pastoral quiet of a sojourn in a Japanese fishing village. I am now convinced that without the anguish of the 1923 earthquake much of the Japanese character would have remained concealed from me, just as my education would have remained incomplete without my stay in Zushi.

EPISODE "FIGARO"

EXACTLY THREE YEARS and six months after my departure from Washington, I was back again in the Navy Department standing in the familiar office of the director of Naval Intelligence. Captain Long was no longer there. He had been transferred to the Bureau of Navigation, which in those day also handled all personnel matters. In fact, he had signed the orders which brought me back to the United States.

During the last forty-two months so many things had occurred to give me greater insight into Japanese plans and aspirations that I naturally had to reorient my thoughts and ambitions. We were confronted by a scheming imperialistic power bent upon pursuing its plan: "The United States must be crushed." It was organizing a network of political and military agents both within our borders and beyond them, deploying its secret forces well in advance of the day when it would be in a position to deal the opening blow. My return to Washington, I had hoped, would give me an opportunity to organize countermeasures, to utilize my newly acquired knowledge in the deployment of our own forces to nullify Japanese moves.

The attitude with which I was confronted upon my return was like cold water thrown upon the fire that burned within me. The new director of Naval Intelligence was learning his job. The Office of Naval Intelligence continued its protracted hibernations, and nobody in the Navy Department showed other than slightly amused interest in my experiences and ideas. There was no one to take up seriously the question of my assignment to a post which would best utilize and justify the three years in Japan. There was little more than passing interest in the reports of my observations, and by calling attention to certain undeniable facts which I felt at least demanded consideration I risked being called a daydreamer who sees ghosts at high noon.

The director listened to my report with gentlemanly boredom

and evident condescension and then suddenly closed the discussion without any indication of a follow-up job for me. I soon found out that no one had given it the slightest thought. It was not in the routine. I had spent three years studying a forbidding language, penetrating the mind of a strange people, gathering data of vital importance, participating in secret missions—and now it was my turn for sea duty. To put it bluntly, I was to forget all extraneous matters and refit myself into the general routine of a naval career. I went to the Far Eastern Section of Naval Intelligence, but there, too, I found but yawning indifference and complacency, regardless of the hostile attitudes then displayed by the Japanese in their vitriolic press. My reports were gratifyingly acknowledged but completely overlooked. I was concerned and frustrated, a state of mind which was hardly conducive to ingratiating myself to my superiors, but I could not arouse them to the dangers of the day. The tensions in Japanese-American relations of 1907 and 1912 were all forgotten, as was the 1907 cruise of our battleships around the world, with the implications of its dramatic demonstration of American naval strength.

It was obvious that I would have to plan my own future if I wanted to continue what I then considered a vital intelligence work, and would have to pursue my investigations as a free lance during the spare time which a naval career abundantly provides. The alternative was to drift with the current and forget what I had learned in the past three years. Needless to say, I was not prepared to do this. Rather, I was willing to risk everything to further intelligence even if the disinterested ones felt that I was stepping on their toes. And step on innumerable complacent toes I did during those days, but even that failed to awaken them.

With a few sympathetic friends, I discussed my concern and desires in the grill of the Army and Navy Club. One of them had recently returned from duty in the Panama Canal Zone and was relating some of his experiences. Then suddenly he suggested:

"Why don't you look into the Panama situation? The place is full of Japs. You could continue your Japanese studies to your heart's content in that hotbed of intrigue."

Panama, indeed! During my stay in Japan hadn't I discerned a burning interest in the canal throughout the Japanese naval service? Wasn't it evident to me as well as to every other observer who had the slightest contact with reality that the canal was one of the major objectives of Japanese Intelligence?

I had visted there in 1912 while serving in the new battleship *Arkansas,* which carried President Taft to the Canal Zone to inspect this gigantic undertaking before opening it to sea-borne traffic. Even then the first Japanese agents made their appearance in the territory bordering the forbidden ten-mile zone which snaked its forty-six-mile way between the two American terminals, Cristobal on the Atlantic side and Balboa on the Pacific, each of which was separated by an imaginary dividing line from the Panamanian jurisdiction in the cities of Colón and Panama City. There were unobtrusive but alert Japanese waiters in the Tivoli Hotel, a few barbers in the newly opened shops, dentists scattered over the town, and of course fishing vessels manned by Japanese crews. Superimposed on these scattered activities was the beehive of the Japanese Consulate, working virtually day and night protecting, as they said, the interests of Japan.

We had a nebulous and condescending attitude toward these busy little men from Nippon who seemed to have an insatiable curiosity and a passion for photography. They rushed to Panama with the first water to wet the locks. We suspected that some of them were spies, but the general attitude was: "So what!" The whole idea of espionage and secret service was so remote that its main coverage was relegated to the pulp magazines where the descriptions of a skillful espionage ring merely amused us.

But a decade later, with my newly acquired knowledge of secret things Japanese, I had an entirely different appreciation of these activities. I did not regard them as characters in an Oriental Keystone comedy but as adversaries who required imagination, energy, and courage to combat their well-planned schemes.

The morning after Panama was suggested to me as a future billet, I was in the Bureau of Navigation welcoming an assignment to the area of the Canal Zone. I had hoped to go there as an intelligence officer, but that inflexible table of organization was saturated, and I was informed that my services could not be utilized in that capacity.

"What could you give me?" I asked the detail officer.

"Well," he said, "I have already assigned you to the cruiser *Rochester,* flagship of the Special Service Squadron, as navigator. I thought you would like that."

It sounded good, since the squadron was assigned as a quasi-protective fleet to the Canal Zone, and in addition the navigator had collateral duties as ship's intelligence officer. So in due time I received my orders to the U.S.S. *Rochester,* then anchored at Balboa, and was to steer her through many interesting situations, even to discovering a periodic freak of nature—the Gulf Stream traveling in the wrong direction.

My hope that duty on the *Rochester* would leave me with enough time to devote to a survey of the Japanese situation soon abated when I found myself extremely busy, both on board ship and ashore. The delay in approaching the task for which I was most eager to go to Panama is forgivable, if events are now viewed in their perspective of 1924. A gradual calm had returned to the world after five hectic and chaotic postwar years. There was still trouble in England, and in other European and Latin American countries, too. But for the first time since the termination of hostilities, domestic issues seemed to replace the international ones. Even to the most pessimistic observer the world had become a peaceful place compared to the war-ridden planet to which we had been accustomed.

As the international tensions subsided, the enthusiasm in such by-products of tension as intelligence also decreased. Instead of chasing Japanese spies in Panama, I found myself devoting my time to milder but more pleasant pursuits. If Panama was crowded with Japanese agents, it was also amply supplied with attractive young ladies, enhancing its charm with their presence as we lounged in the Century Club or in the lobby of the Tivoli Hotel.

It was in the Tivoli's lobby that shipmates from the *Rochester* first saw a certain young American girl whose arrival in Balboa caused quite a furore. The news of this young lady's arrival having spread on board the ship, plans were being made for a special expedition to the Tivoli. Unfortunately, I could not participate in the excursion, but a shipmate of mine, Jimmy Bain, agreed to report on his observations in objective detail. When Jimmy returned from shore, he was more excited than becomes a burly Marine Corps captain under peacetime conditions.

"I walked into the lobby with Bill, looked around, and Bill says suddenly, 'There she goes,' " related in characteristic Marine oratory. "I looked, and I'll be darned if it wasn't Claire Miller, the girl I introduced to Dinks Randall, the Marine flyer who was killed in an air crash some time ago. They were engaged, and it was a heavy blow to Claire and to their big group of friends. You can imagine it.... And I'm telling you, Zack, she is more beautiful than ever!"

I let Jim ramble without interruption until he said:

"I asked her to have dinner with us on board."

"When?" I inquired with what must have sounded like justified impatience to Bain, since he answered with a straight face:

"Tomorrow night, if it's okay with you."

Next day as I was finishing my usual late-afternoon stroll on the quarter-deck she came on board. A slender young woman of exquisite charm, her face radiating beauty and intelligence, an inimitable grace in her movements and a worldly amiability in her gestures—this was Claire Miller arriving for her dinner date with the wardroom officers of the *Rochester*.

At dinner she sat at my right, while Jimmy Bain, seated on her right, vainly struggled to edge in on our conversation. It was not difficult for me to discover that Claire was an exceptional person— and that I was in love. She told me all about the crowded schedule of her past seven years, and I drank in her words with eagerness. It turned out that Claire was a pioneer as well as a veteran in American aviation who had participated in the trial-and-error years which saw our Air Corps become an important instrument of our armed strength. At the beginning of World War I, swayed by that urge which gripped the country to do something useful, she went to Washington and took a job in the photographic section of the U.S. Army Signal Corps. Soon afterward this activity was absorbed by the new U.S. Air Service. She then became interested in photo-interpretation, which, I was happy to discover, was itself a form of intelligence work, providing through microscopic analysis of photos taken from the air the best means of determining ground targets.

During her association with the original setup which later became the Army Air Corps she was able to watch the parade of officers destined to become big names across the stage of American aviation. In the front office General Patrick and his assistant, Billy Mitchell, held forth. The aide was Burdette Wright. Down the hall frequently passed; with the characteristic flamboyance of the Air Corps, Hap Arnold, Harmon, Spaatz, Brett, Frank, and many others, as well as those gallant men who have since given their lives in the service of their country: Hickham, Dargue, and Tinker—all members of an enthusiastic group with vision. She watched their parade, some moving with busy inconsequence, others with the easy flippancy of aviators, and still others with the precision of the newly learned drill, their expressions abrupt with authority. And soon back from the war to advise them on features of great practical value for photo-interpretation was the famous artist Steichen, who, as General Pershing's photographic officer, instituted the first aerial photographs.

Claire's experience in aerial photography and photo-interpretation focused her interest on the world's most vital target for attacking aircraft, the Panama Canal; and as the dinner progressed, our conversation became quite professional, enhancing the unusual charm of this clever young lady even to a man far less in love than I was at first sight.

"Don't you think," she asked, "that the Panama Canal is exposed as an easy target to any hostile plane that dares to make the run?"

"It undoubtedly is," I answered with an air of importance. "True, the locks on both ends of the canal are provided with safety gates. They can be swung into place when necessary, but they can be effective only in case of minor damage to the locks. They are not intended to cover the destructive force of an aerial bomb." We agreed that something ought to be done.

Just when my life was enriched by my love for Claire, I was reminded of my first love—intelligence. The morning after my meeting with Claire I had to go to Panama on business. I was walking down Avenida Central, the busy downtown street of the town, when I saw a Japanese who seemed to turn his head somewhat too abruptly in the other direction. The man was wearing civilian clothes and was not particularly well groomed, but there was something unconcealable in his bearing that revealed him to me as a naval officer in mufti, and I turned almost instinctively to follow him as he increased his pace, obviously trying to evade my pursuit. He went to Calle Carlos A Mendoza, another downtown street, and disappeared at number 58, a house inhabited by the many Japanese fishermen who at that time were still permitted to catch fish as well as intelligence around the canal. Inquiries revealed that on the second floor of this house a pseudo trade union of Japanese barbers had its offices. At that time we were not particularly interested in the accumulation of Japanese barbershops around the

Canal Zone, but this directed my attention to them, and as I walked down Avenida Central and Calle Mendoza I began looking into these little shops; watching the four or five barbers sitting unemployed in the chairs waiting for customers with complete indifference. The shops seemed to be so numerous that I started counting them. There were many, with four or five barbers sitting in every one. Quite a force of barbers, I had to admit, especially in view of the scarcity of faces in need of a shave. Occasionally I saw an American sailor sitting in one of the chairs. I stopped for a moment to make a more detailed inspection and saw the barber losing his reserve and indifference and engaging his customer in lively conversation as is the custom of barbers all over the world.

Unlike the Barber of Seville, these "Figaros" of Japanese extraction were engaged in more serious matters than the trimming of beards or making of love matches. It was quite obvious from this first cursory inspection of a strange situation that these barbershops were tiny outposts of Japanese intelligence. The Japanese and other foreigners were barred from the "sensitive zone" of the canal itself, but they had no difficulty in picking up tidbits of valuable information from the many sailors and minority nationals who regularly crossed the dividing line from the Canal Zone into Panama.

I tried to establish the identity of the man who had passed me on Avenida Central, but all I was able to learn was that he was a Japanese merchant in transit in Panama by the name of Tetsuo Matsuoka and traveling on a legitimate passport issued by Tokyo a few months before. I never saw him again.

When later I met Claire I told her about my strange experience, and she listened to the description of my discoveries with avid interest. From then on we spent much time strolling along Avenida Central and Calle Mendoza, watching activities in the barbershops. We saw Japanese apparently in no need of a shave or haircut disappear in these shops. Occasionally a member of other minority groups also paid a visit. Most of these men were not customers, for they usually went to the room in the rear of the shop and came out again a few minutes later.

Claire called my attention to the great number of barbers lingering in these shops for the comparatively small trade there was to be divided among them. It was obvious that their number was a form of camouflage. If there were four or five barbers in a shop, nobody would ever notice the absence of one or two away on some intelligence mission or picking up some information and acting as a "mailbox." We also discovered that the Japanese consul was a frequent visitor at number 58 Calle Mendoza and regularly attended the Sunday meeting of this Barbers' Association with its totally Japanese membership. Another feature along these avenues of espionage was the presence of an unusually great number of Japanese dentists. Obviously, they too acted as mailboxes, since it would be difficult to detect whether a man calling on a dentist of this kind had a toothache or a message for transmission to Tokyo.

It was strange to watch these harbingers of war in the midst of the calm of peace. A war with Japan appeared more than remote, and the presence of these Japanese agents did not seem to bother our authorities, who felt safe within the "sensitive zone" guarded by efficient members of the Military Police.

I later learned that the Canal Zone played an important role in Japanese plans against the United States. From a German document prepared by a staff officer of the German Air Force named von Bülow we ascertained that an attack was seriously considered against the canal to begin an aggressive war against the United States. At that time the canal had espionage priority over the west coast and Pearl Harbor, and the numerous agents maintained there reflected the importance that was assigned to this spot on the map of Central America in the books of Japanese Intelligence. Considering the effort that was wasted on the Canal Zone, I could never fully explain why no attempt was made later to interfere with operations there as the Germans did, in a perfunctory manner, interfere with traffic through the Suez Canal. It was a matter decided in far higher echelons. The stage was perfectly set for it insofar as intelligence was concerned, for the secret war against the United States reached its first stage as early as 1925, when I first had an opportunity to view Japanese Intelligence doing its field work.

My investigations were made in a vacuum and, looking at them in retrospect, were somewhat premature. Japanese espionage in Panama as it existed in 1925 was not a hostile act against a country with which Japan maintained friendly relations. It was a permanent fixture of Japanese power politics which had its beginning in 1868 together with the Meiji Restoration. It would be wrong to criticize Japan for trying to implement its brawn with brain; for intelligence is, indeed, a natural means to supplement the purely physical strength of a country.

Even then in 1925 I recognized the shallowness of arguments (advanced by certain observers) against the United States engaging in intelligence work. Could modern firms exist without proper market analysis? Do we not inspect a house before we buy it? The contempt with which General Sweeney, author of *Military Intelligence: A New Weapon of War*, and himself a pioneer in American Intelligence during World War I, settled the question of applied intelligence in support of our foreign policy and legitimate aspirations always impressed me as an abdication of rights inherent in our position as a world power. In Britain, Intelligence plays as great a role in the conduct of international relations as any division in the Foreign Office. The result is that wherever another power has to send soldiers to gain its ends, Britain sends one or two of her brilliant operatives.

Frederick the Great, discussing his opponent General Soubise, once said: "He is preceded by a hundred cooks. I am preceded by a hundred spies." It was his superior intelligence setup, and definitely not his distinctly inferior armed strength, which enabled Frederick to survive the Seven Years' War despite the many setbacks he suffered in the purely military sphere. In Europe, where the value of intelligence has been recognized ever since Montaigne paid the most eloquent tribute to its operatives, agents are highly regarded and amply rewarded. The best brains of all countries aid in collecting vital political information which any great power needs for a proper conduct of its foreign affairs. Somerset Maugham has proudly described the role he so skillfully played as a British intelligence operative, as have many lesser writers but greater agents. The knighthood is frequently conferred upon outstanding British agents, diplomatic and otherwise. I need to cite only Sir R. H. Bruce Lockhart and Sir Paul Dukes to emphasize my point. It was with justifiable pride that Bruce Lockhart entitled the account of his activities in Russia *British Agent*—and he was not ostracized during the years which followed the publication of his book. The history of the British Empire is resplendent with great deeds and heroic accomplishments of remarkable men whose contributions as empire-builders were made in the field of intelligence. In the final analysis, empire-builders like Clive or Rhodes were "intelligence agents" in the highest echelon; today their statues adorn British squares and memorials in Westminster Abbey.

America, now rushing to its rendezvous with destiny, has much to learn in this field. Above all, it must learn to distinguish between the subversive espionage work which we may well leave to authoritarian regimes as their self-defeating pastime, and legitimate intelligence which every country vitally needs and is fully entitled to. The secret operative working with Mata Haris in fashionable hotel lobbies is not my ideal of the intelligence agent. In fact, from experience I find that only infinitesimal information of real value can be gathered by these pulp-magazine heroes, whose only recognition comes from exaggerated performances in B pictures. Throughout my association with Intelligence I have always refused to deal with professional spies who were ready to serve any master and two masters at once if possible. The epitome of the good intelligence agent is the patriotic citizen with open eyes who can do his intelligence work in the normal pursuit of his main occupation. An American businessman, traveling on a commercial mission for his firm to faraway lands, could submit a report on his observations without violating the hospitality enjoyed during his stay in the country. Americans are the most traveled people on earth. Every month hundreds of them are participating in cruises around the world and thousands are called to distant lands on business and other transactions. American newspapers maintain correspondents everywhere in the world. But even with this veritable army of globe-trotters, we know very little of what is going on in foreign lands. I remember an incident which occurred sometime in 1940. We needed some material on a German intelligence organization called the German Foreign Institute and asked for its file. We had none, despite the fact that every year scores of Americans going to Stuttgart dropped in to see this institute, which in fact was one of the sights of the Swabian capital.

In 1925 at Panama as I watched the activities of Japanese Intelligence, these thoughts were rather uncorrelated in my mind. I did not realize then the complex problem in its manifold implications, but already felt that our approach to the question was not necessarily the best one. During the ten years which followed my sojourn in Panama I devoted much time and unending thought to the problem, and the conclusions which I reached were evident in my actions of later years. They become the incentives for my secret missions.

In this work of study and implementation I found a companion of wisdom, understanding, and energy in Claire, who, six months after our first meeting in the wardroom of the *Rochester,* became my wife. If ever two people were destined for each other, we were. We both had to make the detour to Panama to meet in the most unexpected manner, but from then on we have traveled together on roads which often have led to disappointments and frustrations, but never to a dead end. In this co-operative effort of ours, I have been usually the tactician while Claire has stood by with splendid strategic advice.

In Panama, too, she aided me during my first steps toward positive intelligence work until duty again called me away from what then was merely a hobby with me. The *Rochester* was suddenly assigned to an important mission. She was to take General John J. Pershing to Chile, where he was to mediate and settle the Tacna-Arica dispute between Peru and Chile. We expected to be away only ten days, but we made our calculations in ignorance of Latin American disputes. The element of *mañana* entered into these international negotiations, and even efficient General Pershing needed six months to settle the argument. At last we were ready to return to the United States with Pershing. Just two days before Christmas we entered New York harbor, where the long-awaited and hoped for order reached me. I was ordered to proceed to Washington for temporary duty with the Chief of Naval Operations. All signs indicated that I was back in Intelligence, this time for good.

9

TOP-SECRET INTERLUDE

EVEN THOSE who agree with the Greek philosopher that in this world of ours all is change must feel that our directors of Naval Intelligence change somewhat too often. There seems to be even today no system for the selection of officers for this all-important post, and no specific qualifications are required to make a man eligible for the office. In recent years, between 1940 and 1945, our Naval Intelligence had no less than seven directors, while the British Navy changed its director of Naval Intelligence only once.

Of the seven directors (they are now called Chief of Naval Intelligence) only one was qualified by previous training, intellectual interest, and personal disposition to fill this particular job. Characteristically, his tenure was the shortest. The others were naval officers some of whom had distinguished themselves as administrators or as leaders in combat, but none had the specific qualifications which would have recommended him for this particular work. Furthermore, some of them had no desire whatever for the job. At a time of the greatest emergency a brilliant officer was made director over his protestations that he wanted to go to sea rather than be "completely submerged" behind this desk in the Navy Department. Another stipulated that he would spend only a limited time in Naval Intelligence in work for which he had little interest and for the problems of which he had no understanding. A third liked the job but regarded it as a sinecure and burdened Intelligence work with an inborn timidity which would have been contagious had this director been permitted to have everything his own way. The continuity of leadership in British Naval Intelligence was guaranteed when the brilliant Admiral Godfrey, destined for far bigger assignments, was replaced by Commodore Rushbrook, a congenial officer sincerely believing in the mission of Intelligence and inspiring his subordinates with the same faith. In World War I a single director, then Captain Reginald Hall, served throughout the war effectively. However, it was fortunate that once in a while chance placed an officer at the top who tried, in the predetermin-edly limited time at his disposal, to improve the office which was so haphazardly entrusted to his care.

One of these was Captain William W. Galbraith, USN, who in 1925 was made acting director—probably to fill the gap until a far less qualified man could be shifted to the job. Captain Galbraith took up his duties with great energy and contributed several in-novations and organizational changes at a time when many of our naval policies, principles, and techniques were themselves under-going fundamental changes. At my post off Panama I could not know that Captain Galbraith had become interested in me. He had been one of my instructors in the Naval Academy when I was a midshipman, and later I had met him upon my return from Japan. It seems that my Japanese experiences remained imprinted upon his memory, since he now felt that my specialist knowledge was being wasted needlessly in Panama in a job for which I needed pre-cious little of it.

At this time a change in command was contemplated in our Asiatic fleet, and Admiral Clarence S. Williams, USN, was chosen as its new commander in chief. Admiral Williams was one of the outstanding flag officers of the United States Navy, a naval scientist as well as a brilliant tactician. He was just completing a term as president of our foremost naval educational institution, the Naval War College at Newport, R. I. It was to Admiral Williams that Captain Galbraith made a suggestion involving my future. In cor-respondence which continued for some time the Captain suggested that I be attached to the Asiatic fleet in an intelligence capacity, to take care of a special problem which was just beginning to occupy a prominent place in our considerations. Of course, I knew little of the plans thus being prepared for me until January 1926, when I was suddenly detached from the U.S.S. *Rochester* and ordered once more to proceed to Washington, to report to the Chief of Naval Operations for temporary duty. Intelligence was a subdivision of CNO.

Certain minor mysteries surrounded my new assignment. I was not told immediately what I was supposed to do, but the location of my new office, Room 2646 in the Navy Department, indicated in itself that it was a top-secret assignment. I found my room at the very end of a long corridor on the second floor's sixth wing, hidden away from the rest of the offices and requiring special permission for entry. The few persons who were assigned to this section of the Navy Department were taciturn, secretive people who refused to discuss their jobs or to reveal details of their assignment. For the next six months I was part of this phantom outfit, myself a cog in the hidden wheel which was then just beginning to turn. It was to be a top-secret interlude, opening up before me new vistas of modern intelligence.

The office was in charge of one of the most delicate, intricate, and challenging aspects of intelligence: cryptanalysis. Talleyrand once said that language merely serves to conceal one's thoughts. Intelligence, however, is not satisfied with this means of concealment; and like adolescents who use newly phrased slang in words and phrases to hide or emphasize the meaning of their conversation, it has its own language to conceal its messages from those who are anxious to determine their content. The language of intelligence is expressed in cryptography, the codes and ciphers, a science highly developed in modern times but retaining much of the secretive mystery of the old Egyptian hieroglyphics.

Codes and ciphers were really developed by modern diplomacy as it grew, itself, from primitive beginnings toward the end of the eighteenth century. Events in France, first the revolution and then the Napoleonic era with its contrasting interests dominating the sphere of international politics, revived on a large and Europe-wide scale the secret diplomacy once practiced with great skill and gusto by the Italian principalities and the Papacy. Intelligence formed part of the game. In all European capitals the powers of the day maintained their agents, often disguised as diplomats.

According to Walter Alison Phillips, one of the great historians of diplomacy, the ambassadors of the seventeenth and eighteenth centuries were "honorable spies." And in the words of François de Callières, himself an ambassador of Louis XIV, "the two principal functions of an envoy were: first to look after the affairs of his own prince; second to discover the affairs of the other." A clever ambassador, he maintained, will know how to keep himself informed of all that goes on in the mind of the sovereign, in the councils of ministers, and in the country; and for this end "good cheer and the warming effect of wine" are excellent allies. These ideas survived in the system which Nazi Germany dumped on the world when it turned its genuine spies into pseudo diplomats. The Nazis were quite candid about representing their envoys as diplomatic agents interested in the secrets of the countries to which they were accredited. Even their official manual of military science and politics described intelligence work as the primary function of diplomats; and General Haushofer, the late geopolitician of Hitlerism, insisted that a good diplomat must have "a sense of anticipation aided by elaborate intelligence."

But it was really the nineteenth century which expected diplomats to be "honorable spies," with Napoleon's perambulations, the Holy Alliance, and the Congresses of Vienna and Aix-la-Chapelle, and other power-political maneuvers going on under the skilled guidance of Talleyrand and Metternich.

The reports which these diplomatists were sending to London, Paris, Vienna, and St. Petersburg were entrusted to couriers whose travels were fraught with danger. One could never know whether the dispatch would reach its proper destination or would fall into unauthorized hands, providing the opponent with the intelligence which his adversary needed most. As a safeguard against this unpleasant development, codes and ciphers were invented and used with considerable skill even in those early days of secret diplomacy. They were to remain a permanent fixture of diplomacy and its instrument—intelligence.

Alert as Americans usually are, we recognized the value of cryptography quite early in the game and used its methods with great dexterity both in 1776 and also during the War between the States in 1860–65. The widespread use of cryptography by the British during World War I, and the successes which its proper exploitation brought to our allies, suggested to us that we, too, make use of this important instrument. Our participation in the First World War was too short to permit a proper development of an American system, and the British, far more advanced than we were then, provided us with most that we needed in this field. They had several of the enemy's codes and were reading his messages, forwarding to us copies of the decoded transcripts. However, when peace dissolved our wartime alliance and the co-operation with British Intelligence ended at the crossroads of postwar diplomacy, we were left to our own devices and had to shift for ourselves.

The feeling was general that the armed services were in the greatest need of this secret language, but they were not provided with necessary funds for the development of this important weapon. In the wake of the victorious World War I, the contributions of the armed forces were as completely forgotten as their new needs were overlooked. Cryptography was one of those essentials which were withheld from them in the curtailed appropriations. It was, however, recognized as an important weapon of modern diplomacy, and the Department of State was given appropriations to develop a small cryptographic staff chiefly to compete, as well as it could, with the ambitious cryptographic divisions of foreign chancelleries. What was needed in organization was compensated for in the energy, ingenuity, and skill of the few persons who were assigned to this task. Although our cryptographic organization was probably the smallest maintained by any great power, it turned out to be one of the best, providing the most useful data for the makers of our foreign policy.

The development of modern communications was accompanied by the development of cryptography in both its positive and negative aspects. The codes and ciphers have become ever more intricate, just as the means for their solution have advanced well beyond all expectations. The Pearl Harbor investigation, which revealed far too much of our own efforts in this field, has given the impression that only we have this important weapon at our disposal. The fact is, however, that all belligerents had excellent and uncannily efficient cryptographic services. But certain of our officials, unaccountably blinded and lulled into complacency by our own successes, were inclined to rest on our oars and stagnate while others were progressing. The codes used by our diplomatic agencies, hardly changed throughout the years, and obviously antiquated by modern standards of cryptography, were subjected to cryptanalysis with comparative ease. It was well known to me that considerable progress had been made in this field by Japanese and other intelligence services, and I had frequently advised our authorities to change their codes from time to time, particularly during international conferences, to prevent our potential enemies from gaining an insight into our secrets. But for fifteen years our diplomatic codes remained the same, making the work of foreign cryptanalysts child's play.

Frequent changes of codes and ciphers are essential if cryptography is to be maintained at a high level of efficiency. Twice in World War II such changes led to developments which may now be regarded as of decisive importance. One of them, I believe, had an immediate influence upon the outcome of the war. After the fall of France, the Germans began preparations for the invasion of England, then stripped of its armed strength by the losses she had suffered in Europe, and exposed to enemy onslaught all along her coast. There were a few German agents reconnoitering the ground within the United Kingdom preparatory to invasion, but their task was merely secondary to the high-class intelligence the Germans had at their disposal through the reading of British codes. In fact, the Germans had throughout the war as efficient a crytographic service as any belligerent can desire, and the greatest triumphs of their own intelligence work were due to the efficiency of their crypt-analytical staff.

The operation which the Germans designed to subdue England went under the code name "Sealion" and was prepared quite thoroughly and feverishly along the occupied channel coast with a knowledge of British countermeasures, which became known to Hitler and his planners by reading British codes. The enterprise was scheduled to start in August 1940 with an all-out attack against England, to reach its climax by September 15, to be followed immediately by an invasion in two waves accompanied by a feint toward the north to draw off the British fleet. In fact, the German fleet was not committed to the main invasion effort at all but was to be used as a decoy to lure the British fleet away from their job of protecting the vital invasion-zone coast line. All these plans were made on the basis of intelligence provided almost exclusively by deciphered British messages. But just when the Germans felt safest in their apparent knowledge of British secrets, a development upset all their calculations. It was not the massing of British forces or any physical measures of defense. It was an abstract move that cost Britain little but saved everything. On the eve of the German invasion *all* British codes and ciphers were changed. The panic in the German high command was overwhelming. As if his eyes and ears had suddenly been destroyed, Adolf Hitler was groping in complete darkness, not knowing what was going on inside Britain. Above all, he had hoped to discover the extent of damage caused by his air attacks through the reading of British codes, but now his cryptanalysts could advise him only that they were incapable of solving the new ones. The artificial fog which thus enshrouded the British islands remained for months; and Hitler, deprived of one of his most vital weapons, did not dare to act without penetrating it. By the time the new codes were deciphered in Germany, it was too late.

for the invasion. Britain had gained a vital breathing spell, and more than that, she had nullified the greatest threat that confronted her throughout the war.

The other incident was detrimental to us and delayed some of our preparations for the liberation of Europe. An unauthorized raid on the office of the Japanese military attaché in Lisbon, Portugal, alerted our enemies and caused them to change their codes which we were reading with gratifying regularity. Suddenly this vital source of information was withheld from us, and it required months of hard work to get back on the beam by solving the new Japanese codes.

In 1926 when I was first introduced to this fascinating phase of modern intelligence, cryptanalysis was at the beginning of the great progress it was to make in subsequent years. My assignment was confined to Japan, to design ways and means by which we could listen in on Japanese conversations and pick up Japanese messages, and to learn what they were all about. I would like to emphasize here that, regardless of its significance, cryptanalysis is only one part of intelligence. No one can discover everything that is taking place within the enemy camp by concentrating alone on the decoding and deciphering of his messages. Only part of the data needed by intelligence can be gathered in this manner. Even the most comprehensive and efficient cryptanalysis leaves many gaps unfilled and many of the problems unsolved. The messages which pass between various agencies of a belligerent are never by themselves comprehensive. They often contain subcodes within themselves, oblique references to facts the knowledge of which is presupposed or short cuts to previously given oral instructions. It is left to other means of intelligence to obtain these additional data. Cryptanalysis is supplemental; it may be considered as filling the gaps left by other intelligence. It would be fatal indeed if a great power with international commitments should attempt to satisfy its needs by concentrating on cryptanalysis alone. All this is part of the great and complex intelligence setup, one supplementing the other rather than making it superfluous.

A newcomer to cryptanalysis and code work, I required much time to familiarize myself with this delicate science. My top-secret interlude was to consume about seven months in Washington, D.C. My friends, though curious and questioning, knew nothing of my latest pursuits. Neither did the watchful Japanese, however anxious they were to learn about it. To all, I was only "reading up" on various situations preparatory to a new job. I fitted myself unobtrusively into the leisurely pace of peaceful Washington, which was then far from being the world metropolis and busy crowded international hub that it is today. It was not difficult to find quarters, and preoccupied then as I was with applied numerology, I selected 1616 16th Street, an apartment house on Washington's embassy row. My days were spent in study and work among people with whom security had become second nature. Hours went by without any of us saying a word, just sitting in front of piles of indexed sheets on which a mumbo jumbo of figures or letters was displayed in chaotic disorder, trying to solve the puzzle bit by bit like fitting together the pieces of a jigsaw puzzle. We were just a few then in Room 2646, young people who gave ourselves to cryptography with the same ascetic devotion with which young men enter a monastery. It was known to everyone that the secrecy of our work would prevent the ordinary recognition accorded to other accomplishments. It was then that I first learned that intelligence work, like virtue, is its own reward. Even today the pioneers of those early days of American cryptography are unknown to the American public, although some of them have become veterans responsible for many a victory during the Pacific war. The young Air Force officer who shot down the plane carrying the Japanese fleet admiral Yamamoto received the highest decorations his country had to offer, but the men who provided him with the vital information that made possible his routine operation, the cryptanalysts working in their secret rooms, remain unrecognized and unrewarded. The ships and men who turned the tide of the Battle of Midway by intercepting and defeating a mighty Japanese invasion fleet received the nation's gratitude. Their names are carved in the war memorial erected to the heroes of America. But the quiet men and women whose unrecognized but spectacular work made such victories possible by reading Japanese codes and ciphers, remain anonymous and undecorated. It requires a true passion for anonymity to become wed to cryptography. In a sense, the people employed in Room 2646 in the Navy Department were the Trappist monks of Intelligence, who said nothing but knew and saw all.

My colleagues seemed to be singularly unaware of the romance which was inherently attached to their work. They were simple and unspectacular people, completely absorbed in their work and interested in nothing beyond it. They were hard workers keeping long hours, forgetting meals and Sundays when engaged in the solution of an enigma. Often they hit upon the solution after midnight while pondering the problem in bed. They would leave home as soon as possible, rush to their offices, and continue their work without interruption until assured of solution or the fact that they were again up a blind alley. It was an inspiration to watch these people work, week after week, month after month, year after year, for decades, training themselves and improving their art in the secrecy which is part of their craft. I hope that these lines will be recognized as my own modest tribute to these forgotten men and women of secret intelligence, if only by calling the nation's attention to their anonymous accomplishments, now that these activities have been disclosed in the press and by investigations.

I was now part of this secret order and immensely proud to belong to the small group of nameless people. But my return to Washington did not go unnoticed by the man who watched every move I was to make. The Japanese were quick to learn of my new assignment in Washington and tried hard to find out the nature of my new duties. They had little success in their attempts, since not even my wife, privy to most of my secrets, knew of the work in which I was so completely absorbed. If they shadowed me, as they undoubtedly did, they could see me early in the morning leaving the apartment house on 16th Street, going down to the Navy Department, and disappearing there with the hundreds of fellow officers who hurried to work. I made certain that nobody ever followed me to Room 2646, since my intelligence training had taught me well how to shake off, like Chamisso's Peter Schlemihl, an unpleasant shadow.

When they failed to obtain information about my work by indirect methods, the Japanese tried the direct approach. I began to receive invitations to parties given by them in Washington, and often my wife and I were the only Occidentals present. We went through the usual long, general conversations; and then the Japanese, clumsy actors that they were, would proceed with pertinent interrogations, every move rehearsed in advance, with naïve sentences, each one prepared as a little trap calculated to be inviting. In another corner my wife smiled pleasantly while being "grilled" —but nothing was revealed to our Japanese inquisitors. I do not doubt that the failure to learn about my activities in Washington merely served to increase their curiosity. The invitations to Japanese parties became ever more frequent, the conversations became more pointed, until I felt like the unconcerned witness sitting in the dock, undergoing energetic cross-examination by some ambitious but not very skillful prosecuting attorney. It was fun.

At that time in 1926 a new Japanese naval attaché was sent to Washington, and his selection in itself indicated the growing significance attributed to this outpost of Japanese Intelligence. He was Captain Isoroku Yamamoto, destined to become the commander in chief of Japan's combined fleet, and the man who drove Japan to war. I had known Yamamoto in Japan only slightly, although he was pointed out to me as a coming man of the Naval General Staff. He was an air enthusiast and a brilliant tactician keenly interested in the operational problems of naval strategy. His arrival in Washington represented a significant change in Japanese intelligence methods and also in the subject which most interested our Japanese friends. Until Yamamoto's arrival, his predecessors had concentrated on information of a tactical nature: problems and techniques of gunnery, technological details of our vessels; battle order and detailed data on technical progress in our fleet. Now, it seemed, the naval attaché's office in Washington was no longer interested in these tactical and technical data. Suddenly operational problems within the framework of highest strategy shifted to the forefront of the subjects on the Japanese shopping list.

We recognized this change and endeavored to find out what caused the Japanese to shift from tactics to strategy. We concluded eventually that it was due largely to the sweep of Yamamoto's own intellect and the scope of his own interest, which now dominated Japanese intelligence work in the United States. Tactical matters were assigned to intelligence agents in somewhat lower echelons. The Naval Attaché was interested in greater things; he was interested in war.

I always felt, after Yamamoto was appointed commander in chief of the combined fleet and wartime leader of Japan's navy, that the first plans for the Pearl Harbor attack originated in his restless brain right here in Washington. He belonged to that small group of Japanese naval officers who opposed the Washington Naval Limitation agreement to the very end. His opposition was motivated by the attempts to scrap the aircraft carriers. Part 4 of the treaty defined aircraft carriers as vessels of war with "a displacement in excess of 10,000 tons (10,160 metric tons) standard displacement designed for the specific and exclusive purpose of carrying aircraft." Japan had a number of ships built or building just above this category, and Yamamoto was the driving force behind increasing appropriations to enlarge the number of Japan's fleet of aircraft carriers. Being the great naval strategist that he was, he recognized even at that early stage of sea air power development the significance of carriers, and it was with chagrin that he saw his fondest dreams rudely interrupted in the agreement of the Washington treaty. He never forgave our insistence that the four Japanese carriers be scrapped. It was on these carriers that he had based his hopes and on which he had focused his ambitious plans.

Although he was assigned to the command of cruisers and served a term of shore duty, he remained in close contact with the Japanese naval air arm throughout his career. In the United States, too, he was to preoccupy himself with matters which linked air power to sea power on a high operational level. When he first arrived in Washington, I looked up his biographical card, compiled through the years by the Office of Naval Intelligence, and found that he was born April 4, 1884, at Nagaoka city in Saga prefecture, the sixth son of Teikichi Takano, probably an adopted son, the custom of adoption being common in Japan. He entered the Navy in 1901 and graduated in 1904. By 1915 he was a lieutenant commander and aide to the Navy Minister. He was, like myself, a language student, spending several years in the United States and England and now speaking the language with fluency. His card described him as "Exceptionally able, forceful, and a man of quick thinking." I did not have to wait long to confirm the accuracy of this analysis.

One night on returning home from my arduous work of the day my wife received me with news which indicated that the big fish was after me. After the small fry had failed to learn the nature of my duties, and interest was accentuated by the fact that the Japanese could not reach me by phone at the Navy Department, Yamamoto had called my apartment and had spoken at length with my wife. He had invited me to a party at his own quarters which served as his office as well. Although he was married and had a daughter, he had left wife and daughter behind in Tokyo and did his entertaining without the benefit of a hostess. He did not follow the technique of his predecessors who used feminine means of penetration.

His parties were usually stag affairs with only moderate drinking, dignified, but always including a suggestion for card playing, in which he indulged with complete abandon and considerable skill. The party to which he asked me was also confined to male guests and a card game. Poker was his favorite, and he played it with an unreserved and unconcealed determination, as if he must defeat us at this game before he could defeat us in war. I knew his reputation as the Go champion (Japanese chess) of the Japanese Navy and also as a habitual winner at poker. My classmates will admit with regret that I was no slouch at the game myself. In this game, which provides ample time and opportunity for character analysis, I was most interested in his reactions when trying to bluff or when bluffing was tried against him. Unlike most Japanese, who feel that they lose face when defeated even in a harmless card game and are usually embarrassed, Yamamoto appreciated my attempts to beat him. I found him a man of open challenge and a lover of combat.

When I entered his apartment, I encountered the same stocky, black-browed man of years before. He wore his hair cut short. He smiled broadly but in a rather condescending manner, his aggressive nature unconcealed even in his smile. Almost immediately cocktails were served and then dinner, a mixture of Japanese and foreign dishes. It was obvious that he loved his game, this combination of intelligence and cards, since the dinner was hardly over when the table was cleared and set up for poker, he inviting us to indulge in a game. He was soon interspersing his bids and bluffs with slightly concealed inquiries of a distinctly naval character.

In our subsequent meetings, too, he tried to combine his two favorite pastimes, and it needed considerable effort to beat him at both games. Yamamoto had only three fingers on his right hand, the result of an explosion on board ship during the Battle of Tsushima while he was serving on Admiral Togo's flagship *Mikasa* as an ensign. I found it very distracting to watch him manipulate his cards with unusual dexterity with those three remaining fingers. I felt that he was aware of his trick and emphasized it by using his three fingers in a wizardly manner, laughing out loud whenever we complimented him on his skill.

A man who did not believe in attacking points of least resistance, he invited people to his house who confronted him with a difficult task both in intelligence and poker. I don't know how much he was able to learn from us, but I do know that we often defeated him in poker and learned considerable from him, if only about his ideas on naval strategy. It was during these meetings that I first recognized the direction Japan was taking in her naval development. The aircraft carrier, the combination of sea power and air power, was an obsession with Yamamoto.

His almost complete preoccupation with operational questions might have aroused our interest in the individuals to whom he had entrusted the other task of tactical intelligence, had we not followed the activities of many of his subordinates. It was not unduly difficult to locate the agents to whom Yamamoto delegated this task. Shortly after the war, when Japan embarked upon its naval construction program, offices were opened in New York to purchase new designs, patents, and manufacturing licenses from our factories to speed up the building program through the acquisition of American inventions on the open market. It was the custom of these purchasing commissions to buy only one sample of everything, be it a plane or a range-finder or a fire control apparatus. It was this frugality in their purchases which directed my attention to this phase, and I personally tried to persuade our manufacturers to refrain from selling them just one of everything.

"If we are willing to sell at all," I told them, "let's make them pay as much as possible for every new device. Make it a condition that they must buy a hundred if they want it at all." But I am not aware that I ever succeeded in convincing our manufacturers of the wisdom of controlling Japanese technique by heavy drains upon their limited funds. Even on the eve of the Pacific war they displayed their misplaced zeal for business by selling the Japanese one of everything, including our latest airplane designs soon to fly in combat under some Japanese name against our own boys.

Yamamoto's aloofness from tactical intelligence increased the potential significance of these purchasing agencies in New York in my calculations; and our interest led us to others of a similar character: the Army Inspector's Office, the Silk Intelligence Bureau, and the Japan Tourist Bureau. Naval Intelligence remained on the trail of these and knew quite a lot that was going on inside them. In fact, when I first discussed them in the office, I was told that plans were being made by our high command to close these offices as hotbeds of Japanese espionage. Amazed and greatly concerned over this proposal, I asked permission to discuss this with an officer of high rank.

"These Japs think they can get away with anything," I was told by the officer in the "front office." "They use these offices not only as 'mailboxes' [by which miscellaneous agents send in their reports] but also as centers for their technological intelligence activities."

"How do you know?" I asked.

"Well," he answered, "I know. And I am not going to stand for this monkey business any longer. We are going to clamp down on them now, before they become too hot to handle." It was a fact that we had a fairly efficient system to check on the business of visitors to these offices as well as on the personnel employed in them. There was very little taking place in their spacious rooms that was unknown to our own counter-intelligence.

"You don't really mean," I said when the details of his precautions were outlined to me, "that you are going to destroy your best sources of information on their activities! That is not counter-intelligence. That is a last resort. As long as they think that we are dopes and they can get away with their clumsy techniques of well-nigh open intelligence, we are pretty safe, aren't we? Let them play their little game. After all, they can do nothing that harms us—as long as we know in detail what they are doing. And we seem to know pretty much about it."

It is a truism in intelligence that if you give the opponent enough rope he is sure to hang himself. Often an agent is permitted to continue his work seemingly without interference for as long as five to ten years. All the time he is under surveillance and his information checked and counterchecked, every one of his moves observed and recorded. By this method foreign agents, particularly key men and even entire organizations, can be identified. As long as an agent supplies the material his bosses expect of him, he is usually left at his post and the surveillance is facilitated by the permanence of his assignment. Once he is withdrawn and a new man appointed in his place, counter-intelligence has the difficult task of determining the new agent and then establishing the same surveillance that existed over his predecessor. Ten old agents are usually less dangerous, regardless of how much they may seemingly know, than one new man whose identity and activities are unknown to our counter-intelligence.

After lengthy arguments and logical presentations, the high command was persuaded of the advisability of not disturbing the pretty circles drawn in these pseudo purchasing missions. Instead we made plans to "supply" them with information they vitally needed and sought so avidly, by preparing ourselves for that fascinating game of "double agent" which we were to play extensively in the battle of wits.

10

AMBUSH BY RADIO

BY MIDSUMMER OF 1926 I had acquired a sufficiency of both the secrets of cryptography and Yamamoto's system of poker to enable me to end my top-secret interlude in Washington and to apply my newly won knowledge in a practical way. In fact, I was anxious to go. The sedate Washington atmosphere with its routine of leisurely work and constant parties was becoming monotonous, and there was little in the way of Japanese activities to alleviate the boredom. About this time Yamamoto himself underwent a period of contemplation. It was obvious that he was at the crossroads of his life and trying to decide which road to travel. One of these roads led to peace, relegating the Japanese Navy to enforced idleness while Japanese diplomacy maneuvered for position. The other road was a difficult one, full of detours and warnings and eventually leading to inevitable war. In several conversations I had with Yamamoto I learned from him that he was keenly aware of the choice Japan should make. He was inclined to give diplomacy a chance and see what it could accomplish without the application of force. But he was restless and impatient. He wanted too much too soon, and was disinclined to wait for the settlement of issues by the normal exchange of polite diplomatic notes.

It was the question of peace or war which occupied his alert mind during his first tour in Washington, but by the time he had concluded his duty as naval attaché he seemed to lean toward war rather than peace. He knew that he was still far from the top position where he could influence policy and impose his own ideas on the upper layer of Japanese power politics. And he made the decision that he would hasten his own rise, thereby furthering the realization of his plans, the unfolding of which we shall see later.

In the summer of 1926 the decision was definitely made to assign me to the Asiatic station as an intelligence officer specializing in cryptographic research. The assignment represented a long step forward in our positive intelligence against Japan. It was the first attempt to penetrate the screen with which Japan hoped to shield from us the secrets of her fleets. We decided that the penetration could be made from a distance, by listening to conversations conducted on the radios of Japanese ships and by trying to establish certain patterns from decoded messages. We hesitated to attract Japanese attention to our activities by giving me a blanket assignment or ordering me to a duty for which, on the surface at least, there seemed no justification. With the approval of Admiral Hepburn, who was then chief of Naval Intelligence, Captain Galbraith picked a cover assignment for me. I was detailed to command the destroyer *McCormick* if only for a few months while I was preparing myself for my real work.

I joined my new ship in Chefoo and took her down through the China Sea to Hong Kong. Many Japanese were already entrenched wherever we stopped. They had gone to China in the course of normal immigration to relieve what the Japanese called the population congestion of their small islands. In reality they were spearheads of the invaders who were soon to follow them across the sea. In Hong Kong for a few days, I was again with my wife and son and then continued to Manila. Shortly after my arrival there a trip to the southern Philippines provided an opportunity to inspect those places which were later so vital in our return invasion. The presence of the Japanese in the Philippines was too evident for comfort. They seemed to be doing everything to ingratiate themselves with local populations, and in those days the friendship was returned by many Filipinos. The casual observer would never have expected that the day would come when the friendly atmosphere would turn to bitter hostility and that the Filipino admirers of things Japanese would fight their former guests in innumerable guerrilla bands.

Japan's design in the Philippines as it first manifested itself to me had been accentuated shortly after my first arrival in Manila three years before. A Japanese training squadron under the command of Vice Admiral S. Saito had arrived there on a courtesy visit, and we were busy giving our guests the usual reception prescribed by international naval etiquette. On November 30, at eight o'clock in the morning, Saito's flagship, the *Yakumo*, steamed into the harbor and was saluted by the boom of our guns. The day was spent in formal ceremonies, our own General Read and Admiral Marvell calling on Saito, and the Japanese admiral calling on the Governor-General and Admiral Washington. Calls were made and returned the whole day as well as on December 1, followed by receptions, dinners, smokers, and drives to the country, including a visit to the Yahagi Monument at San Pedro Macati. Throughout their stay I watched the Japanese with rather inquisitive eyes, noting especially their relations with the local authorities. I felt somehow that the friendship shown to Manuel Quezon was somewhat too lavish, as if they were making a deliberate attempt to impress him, and through him the Filipino people, with their importance and power.

I had been appointed aide to Admiral Saito and thus was enabled to observe the proceedings from the Japanese side. Admiral Saito was a mild individual, obviously enjoying the ceremony and pomp which surrounded him, and seemingly content with using navies merely for courtesy calls rather than for wars. But even in this friendly atmosphere I detected a distinct design, and I planned to make a report on my observations. I remembered, however, the usual fate of premature reports and recognized that no purpose could be served by giving a warning when minds were not yet receptive enough to appreciate its potential implications. But something had to be done to arouse at least a feeling of suspicion in the midst of Japanese scheming. Instead of writing a factual report then, when I returned in 1926 I prepared a story setting forth my opinion of the shape of things to come. It was entitled "Governor-General Yamanaka of the Philippines." It viewed the moves I expected to be made by the Japanese for seizing control of the islands and placing their own man in charge when our governor-general was ousted.

The scene I visualized in 1926, a great part of which was borne out subsequently, was a series of events to follow one after another with gunfire rapidity. The Filipino yearning for independence was the center of all motivations. In my essay I indicated that immediate independence would be granted the Philippines after a crash of the stock market which resulted in a depression of unprecedented proportions. This independence was to bring the inevitable isolation of the Philippines which were so dependent on overseas trade. It was at this stage that I expected an intensification of Japanese activities: fishing in troubled waters, as aggressors usually do in order to deepen the chaos to further their own machinations. I described this legendary Yamanaka as the head of a Japanese fifth column in the Philippines, exploiting existing situations and creating new ones until the Philippines fell like a ripe apple into Japan's lap. Nobody can say that the Japanese did not try to carry out what I envisaged in 1926. If they failed, it was not due to their own inactivity but rather to the wisdom with which President Roosevelt later handled the Philippine situation, and the decision of the Filipinos themselves to stick by the United States in bad days as well as good.

I sent the story to my brother for consideration and possible use by the *Atlantic Monthly,* but his legal mind detected the manifold implications which, while based on fact, would prejudice the position of a naval officer regardless of extreme dangers to our national security then existing. As I reread this story now, many thoughts race through my mind. The attitude of the visiting Japanese toward the Philippines was only thinly concealed by the amenities of the occasion. To some of us their visit had the earmarks of an inspection trip, surveying the ground to which they intended to return in force in a not-too-distant future. The Japanese of Manila flocked to greet their compatriots and in their boundless enthusiasm revealed themselves as "quartermasters" of a future invasion. During the five days of the squadron's visit they were like the prospective customer examining the property he intends to buy even while the old tenant is still in possession. Their exuberance produced a feeling of discomfort although the feeling was by no means articulate. It was rather an instinctive anticipation, a mixture of apprehension and annoyance.

My presence with the Asiatic fleet was now sufficiently justified, and there was no longer any need to camouflage my assignment. I was therefore transferred to the flagship in a move that appeared to be normal procedure. I was to advise the Commander in Chief on special activities and supervise certain ones on shore. But the Japanese whom I saw were led to believe that my duty was largely in the social sphere, like my previous assignment as aide to the Japanese admiral.

However, I was to begin in earnest the work for which I was minutely trained during the seven months in Room 2646 Navy Building, Washington. The political situation in the Far East emphasized the urgency. General Chiang Kai-shek, then still in alliance with the Russians, had begun his drive to the north, advancing as far as Hankow with their help. He had fifty Russian advisers on his staff, including such top-ranking Soviet leaders as Borodin and Blücher. The success of his drive appeared to fill the Chinese leader with self-confidence, convincing him that he could continue his progress without Russian aid. In a sudden move which was to upset Russian plans in the Far East for decades to come and disorganize Lenin's old and carefully prepared timetable, Chiang Kai-shek broke with the Russians and in addition expelled the Russian advisers and aides quite unceremoniously overnight. The Far Eastern situation was tense, and we were suddenly ordered from Manila to Shanghai to stand by for whatever developments might result from the General's bold move. This trip did not represent a serious interference with my own plans, for which the ground-work was completely prepared in Manila. On the contrary, I welcomed the shift to the focus of all political and military moves and was enabled thereby to begin my work right at the center of gravity, Shanghai. My assignment was to supervise the listening post in an American radio station at Shanghai; to monitor Japanese radio communications passing between headquarters in Tokyo and the fleet at sea; to evaluate whatever open information became available by these means and to decode or decipher the concealed messages.

The radio station needed for the job was immediately available. It was located on the fourth floor of the American Consulate building just opposite the Astor House, the most fashionable hotel in downtown Shanghai. There was nothing secret about the station itself. It was openly maintained by the Navy so that the Commander in Chief and the Consul-General could keep in touch with their respective departments at all times. All other powers with concessions in Shanghai had their own radio stations—and undoubtedly their own monitors as well.

It was immediately evident to me on the day of my first inspection that it was an open station indeed. Visitors were never barred from the fourth floor of the building, and many Japanese used to come and go, doing little personal services for the radiomen, or just looking them up on a friendly visit. It was not regarded as judicious to interfere with this stream of visitors at once, since it would have attracted attention to the sudden change from open activities to secret ones. But when I became a regular "visitor" myself, the character of the station's Japanese visitors suddenly changed. Clever and pretty Japanese girls made a habit of calling on their boy friends during working hours, but they seemed to confine their selection to men engaged in my radio work. Alarmed by this abrupt increase of amorous interest around the radio station, I made discreet inquiries about these girls and confirmed their connection with Japanese Intelligence as well as their pastimes with our radiomen. Therefore one of my first jobs was a thorough lecture on security for the men, which resulted in gradual and automatic severance of relations with the girls and other visitors. The men were taught the virtues of an intelligence cog, and their interests were shifted without too much difficulty. We devised a tactful plan to screen the station from unwelcome guests, especially when the time arrived to go into action.

Both from published reports and intercepted messages as well as from the dispatches of our naval attaché in Tokyo we learned that Japan was planning to increase her naval activities from routine drill to broadened fleet problems. The gradually increasing volume of message traffic which we intercepted and decoded in Shanghai indicated that the time for the annual Japanese fleet maneuvers was rapidly approaching, and all signs indicated that it was to be an ambitious affair in 1927. My listening post was too distant from the scene of events, and I could not hope to obtain much information from the snatches of messages which drifted toward our aerials in Shanghai. It was considered essential that the earphones and reference books be moved to the center of the Japanese beehive afloat. We hoped thereby to establish a pattern of Japanese naval tactics by following their secret exercises from an ambush by radio. The plan for this operation was prepared in great detail. We hoped to pick up all orders and instructions, as well as the reports radioed back to the flagship on which the umpires were reaching their conclusions. From this information we expected to gain sufficient data from which to draw up the complete and accurate plan of the Japanese operations; to find out what they themselves were trying to learn; to establish their methods of practice together with their own confidential findings not available to their own observers who were permitted just a modicum of insight into real events from the narrow bridge of the Japanese flagship.

It was evident that we would have to move right into the radio center of the deployed Japanese fleet to gain all this information. But how? After long conferences a plan was drawn up. I was to transfer to one of our ships and sail straight into Japanese waters as if participating on a routine cruise unaware of the activities taking place. My presence on the ship was to be kept secret, as, indeed, was my whole mission, which was known only to the Commander in Chief, our naval attaché in Tokyo, and myself. The ship chosen for this operation was the same *Marblehead* which a little less than twenty years later so gallantly withstood the ferocious attack of a superior Japanese armada and returned with almost fatal wounds after combat. When I read of the *Marblehead*'s heroic fight and her arrival in the Philadelphia Navy Yard in 1943, I recalled the days in 1927 when she carried me on her first encounter with the Japanese fleet. I could not avoid becoming somewhat sentimental and grateful that she survived her second encounter with the same skill and devotion to duty with which she carried out her first.

We had no qualms about the intrusion of our ships upon Japanese privacy. We regarded it as a return call for the sudden appearances of many Japanese oil tankers wherever and whenever one of our own fleet problems was in progress. Even in the immediate vicinity of Hawaii, where most of our exercises were held, we found these Japanese tankers turning up when and where they were least expected. We could picture the surprise and chagrin of our Japanese friends when they suddenly discovered foreign ships through their binoculars. But even so, they would not know that interested personnel were sitting in the radio room, listening to their messages and conversations.

However, on the eve of my departure this closely held secret was almost published to the world. Claire was attending the Shanghai version of a ladies' tea party at the French Club when the wife of a fellow officer turned to her with the question:

"Are you going to accompany Zack to Japan?"

Claire evinced genuine surprise, since she had no idea that I would be going to Japan—or anywhere for that matter. My assignment was a top secret, and naturally I would not discuss it with anyone. I had even postponed revealing my prospective departure to Claire, and intended to tell her only that I was going on a short routine cruise. So she answered the sudden inquiry in good faith:

"But Zack isn't going away, and certainly not to Japan."

Her friend was quite insistent that I was going on a trip and that Japan was included in my itinerary. This was too much for Claire. She left the party and hurried home to call me on the carpet for keeping my news from her "while the whole town knew it."

"Zack," she asked in a tone as if she had found scented letters in my pocket, "what is this about your going to Japan?"

"I am going where?" I asked in feigned surprise.

"To Japan. Marjorie told me all about it, and, whatever your little secret was, there is no point in keeping it from me any longer."

I exploded. "Marjorie told you all about it, eh? Well, this is serious, Claire; and we have to do something about it. I must stop the wagging of Marjorie's tongue right now."

I immediately began an investigation of the leak to stop it before it could interfere with my mission. It was not difficult to find out how Marjorie had obtained her information. I surmised that during one of the inactive periods which sometimes bored the members of communication offices of the ships on this station her husband's ship had decoded the messages which passed between Tokyo and Shanghai regarding my prospective mission. He had then in his efforts to keep his wife current on the news of the day revealed their content to her. I called the officer responsible for this most flagrant breach of security and after a short conversation determined that I had surmised correctly. I then cautioned him of the possible consequences of his indiscretion.

"I would advise you," I said, "to be more careful in your conversations with your wife. You must now do everything you can to discredit anything already told her and say no more, or we shall have to take different measures." I do not know what happened that night in the officer's house, but the leak was definitely stopped before the nature of my mission and my ultimate destination could reach the oversized ears of Japanese listening posts.

My departure on the *Marblehead* on October 17, 1927, was quite an exciting affair. There was smuggled on board certain necessary equipment, and care was taken that nobody might witness my boarding the ship as a passenger. There was nothing secret about the *Marblehead*'s itinerary. She was due at Nagasaki and Kobe on routine courtesy calls, and the Japanese were fully advised of the forthcoming visit. What was secret was the route we were to take and my presence on board. We reached the area of the Japanese fleet maneuvers on the third day at sea. All the time we were listening in and making transcripts of the messages passing to and from the Japanese flagship and established that it was a combined maneuver destined to test co-operation between sea power and air power, the latter represented by carrier-borne planes. We wanted to time our arrival in the middle of the fleet to witness activities such as the recovery of planes by carriers, since the Japanese seemed to have difficulties with this phase of the operations and we wanted to see how they were solving the problem.

We did not encounter the Japanese fleet but later a squadron of our destroyers did; and with seeming nonchalance they steamed on while intercepted messages indicated that they were detected by the Japanese. There was excitement and annoyance evident in these messages; and as our ships watched the carrier recovering her planes, fast Japanese destroyers wedged themselves between the carrier and our force, laying down a thick smoke screen to shield the operation from our eyes. But no smoke screen could interfere with the radio waves, and we learned much that we wanted to know by reading their messages, even if we could no longer observe the action through our binoculars. It was evident that the Japanese had considerable difficulty in landing on the narrow decks of their carriers, a fact which later intelligence confirmed and which caused them to continue their interest in our landing procedures and equipment right up to the day of Pearl Harbor. It was an important phase, and special study was made of the subject, revealing to us considerable data on this aspect of Japanese naval air tactics.

We arrived in Kobe on October 28 and were met by our naval attaché, who came from Tokyo for this purpose. I told him of my observations, showed him my notes, and the preliminary draft of a report I was already preparing. As is usual with this type of information, there were certain important gaps which needed to be filled in, so it was suggested that I accompany the naval attaché for a conference in Tokyo, during which time I could outline the additional data needed to make the report complete.

My arrival in Tokyo coincided with a Japanese fleet parade in Tokyo Bay. For several miles Japan's battleships and smaller vessels were lined up just outside the breakwater of Yokohama for inspection by Hirohito, who then was still acting for his demented father as prince regent. No outsiders were invited to this fleet review, and the ships were kept at a safe distance from the inquisitive eyes of foreign observers. Such precautions are justified, since a trained observer can gain considerable intelligence even by outside inspection of a vessel. I remember the interest shown by certain German and Japanese intelligence agents in ordinary news pictures offered for sale to newspapers by our picture agencies. They were only too glad to pay the usual five dollars for a seemingly innocuous picture of an American or British cruiser visiting a foreign port. All they had to do was to compare the picture with one previously taken to discover certain structural changes, new characteristics, the possible addition of antiaircraft guns, changes in armament, and other important details. Indeed, a news picture costing only five dollars in original or obtainable for three cents when printed in a daily paper reveals much of the data intelligence services would have to pay for dearly were they to obtain them through agents or other means.

We planned to exploit the opportunity provided us by the presence of the Japanese fleet in Tokyo Bay to do a little observing of our own. But putting our plan into operation was not so simple. Finally we decided on what appeared the simplest and most straightforward but also the most risky solution. I decided to obtain a small motorboat and go out to the spot where the fleet was anchored. Captain Eddie Pearce, one of our present outstanding Japan experts, was then a lieutenant studying the language in Japan. We hatched our little plot together with the blessing of the naval attaché. Using certain old connections of mine, we obtained the boat without attracting attention, and, lavishly supplied with notebooks and pencils, embarked on our little adventure under the noses of the ever-suspicious Japanese.

We got into our boat at one of the landings in Yokohama late in the morning. We waited for the best opportunity to time our departure, and when certain that nobody could observe us, we cast off and went as fast as our little motorboat could take us, but slow enough to avoid attracting attention. We were soon in the midst of this accumulation of Japanese sea power. Eddie and I were not visible to our specially selected Japanese helmsman, who was not aware of our mission and could be counted upon to keep our secret at least until we were back in Tokyo and divested of our notes. Concealed behind the side curtains of the boat, we could observe everything that was exposed to view without ourselves being observed from the outside. It was our intention to dispose of our notes if detected, but nobody seemed to suspect that two American intelligence officers were behind the drawn curtains of the little boat, if the boat attracted any attention at all, as it went unostentatiously up one line of ships and down the other. I believe that the idea of two American naval officers flouting Japanese security measures in such an inspection trip never even entered Japanese minds. We could return unmolested and as far as we knew, even undetected, with voluminous notes on all the construction and other features of modern Japanese vessels that could be obtained by means of observation. It was a highly successful "fishing" trip, and our catch satisfied us as well as the naval attaché. This work completed, I now telephoned to several of my Japanese acquaintances to remove any impression that my trip to Japan had been made secretly. I advised these listening posts that I had taken advantage of the *Marblehead* trip to visit Japan again.

Immediately after completing this detour to Tokyo and Tokyo Bay, I returned to Kobe and rejoined the cruiser, which was preparing for a full-power run to Shanghai. There was nothing sinister about the speed. It was one of our routine practices, testing the engines and gauging the time one needed to make the run under full power. But when we moored in Shanghai a day and a half later, the Japanese received us with open consternation. The speed itself was inconceivable to them, but even more puzzling was the motive which induced us to make this top speed. What was the *Marblehead* up to? Why was it necessary to return to Shanghai so fast? What secrets did Zacharias have which needed such a rapid transportation? When they could provide no answers to these questions, they openly approached us and asked:

"Why did you make this full-power run from Kobe to Shanghai?"

"Full-power run?" we asked with feigned incredulity. "Well, it was just our normal cruising speed." Whether they believed us or not, the answer certainly failed to put their minds at ease. The *Marblehead* mystery, from her leisurely departure from Shanghai with her secret passenger on board to her full-power return only seventeen days later, remained unsolved by Japanese Intelligence.

On November 4 I returned to the flagship to prepare a detailed report on my observations during the mission. It was a long and carefully documented paper, giving in minute detail the secrets of the fleet maneuvers and much supplementary information which together presented a complete picture. We had used a comparatively cheap but immensely effective means of participating in a Japanese fleet practice, and it seemed that the pioneering venture fully justified itself by the information it yielded. When my report reached Washington, the Director of Naval Communications expressed himself in a letter which was most encouraging for the future.

MY DEAR ZACHARIAS [it read]:

I have just read with interest a very excellent report you submitted some time ago with regard to certain maneuvers which you had an opportunity of observing in a communication sense.

I thought I would drop you a line and tell you that I consider this report excellent, as it covers a line of Naval information which is very important for us to get hold of and the value of which we so far have failed to appreciate.

With congratulations and best wishes,

Sincerely yours,
T. T. CRAVEN
Captain, U. S. Navy,
Director Naval Communications.

Here then was the appreciation of a pioneering venture and the encouragement needed to continue the development of an idea which had proved itself practicable and valuable, although never tried before. With the mission on the *Marblehead* a pattern was created for the gathering of this type of information, using radio waves where other means of intelligence are of no avail. We used the method in afteryears and scored our greatest success with it a few years later when we charted the entire grand maneuvers of the Japanese combined fleet in a far more ambitious but equally successful effort. The smoke screen which Japan perpetually maintained around her naval activities was effectively penetrated, and Intelligence again scored a significant victory.

11

JAPAN REVISITED

My INITIATION into intelligence now belonged to the past. I was no longer a neophyte but an experienced hand, devising ways and means by which both the quality and quantity of vital information could be improved through the introduction of new methods and the opening up of new avenues. I was given adequate scope for my pioneering work, although the initiative remained with me most of the time. Often I had to combat incompetence, indifference, and ignorance. I was opposed by men who had a negative approach to everything and whose life philosophy was that the best way to get along was to do nothing. My fingers were occasionally burned, and at times my ears were "pinned back." But frequently I was supported by enthusiastic and forward-looking superiors who were at least willing to provide me with the rope on which I could do a bit of dangerous tightrope walking or with which I might hang myself.

What began as an inarticulate and rather vague hobby enlivening my imagination with its inherent romance now appeared to me in all its seriousness as a sober business requiring my full time, energy, attention, and devotion. At last I was an intelligence officer in name as well as in fact, one of the very few who regarded intelligence as a permanent assignment and career. Wherever I was and whatever I was doing, I continued my intelligence studies, however remote they were from the duties of the day. In command of a destroyer, cruiser, or battleship, I spent my spare time reading anything which bore on the subject or listening to foreign radio broadcasts trying to cull from them anything of an information nature. In distant lands I tried to penetrate the national characteristics of the people, or pick up whatever information the means at my disposal provided. In my associations I cultivated people who could implement or supplement my own knowledge or interest, and also utilized my entree to drawing rooms to gather information of many shadings and varieties.

As early as fifteen years ago I developed the idea that intelligence officers should be regarded as specialists within the naval service, as are medical and engineering officers, who are specially trained for their craft and retained in categories of their own throughout their careers. I revolted at times against the chance assignment of untrained line officers to difficult intelligence duties. I became convinced that the routine training of a run-of-the-mill naval officer, regardless of his mentality, does not qualify him for intelligence work. On the contrary, I felt that it somehow disqualified him. There is a certain uniformity in the naval training procedure, a deliberate co-ordination of outlook and inevitable regimentation of ideas not at all conducive to turning a man into an intelligence officer, an individual who must have endless flexibility. I have seen and worked with many naval officers who could be made into excellent intelligence officers if given the training and sufficient recognition to ensure security in the competitive promotions; but the majority of the men who are either semipermanently or temporarily assigned to this specialist task have proved unsuited for the work. There is no scientific test devised for the selection and classification of men for intelligence duties. But the urgency of our situation impelled me to set forth in concrete form my ideas of the qualifications necessary. As early as 1940 while I was district intelligence officer at San Diego, these qualifications were reduced to concrete terms after consultation with two capable colleagues and were incorporated in letter form awaiting the opportunity when its presentation would meet with receptive consideration. Immediately after Pearl Harbor (when I was filling my routine sea assignment as captain of a heavy cruiser), chagrined at what had been allowed to come to pass, I forwarded the letter to the Chief of Naval Operations with high hopes for its acceptance even at that late date. This letter was subsequently made a part of the record by the Congressional Pearl Harbor Committee.

Even today the true significance of intelligence is still not realized. Only a few years ago I asked a flag officer:

"How is the intelligence work in your force, sir?" And he answered with a straight face, convinced he was giving the proper answer:

"We don't need any intelligence work. There are no Communists in our ships."

His answer went far to reveal how little even a man with three or four stars understood the true meaning of the word and the task of intelligence. To him it was confined to one minor phase of counter-intelligence and investigation. The positive sides of the art did not occur to him even though he was a strong advocate of the War College and was fully aware of the fact that orders usually begin with a review of the information available on the enemy's moves, strength, and intentions. How this information is gathered and evaluated seemed to be a secondary consideration. And remarkably little is done to improve the facilities or provide the men needed for the gathering of this vital and accurate information.

Even by 1928 I was determined to do whatever I could to remedy a situation which I felt was a threat to national security. As usual, I made plans for approval, but they were found to be too ambitious. So I shifted for myself as best I could. I did obtain permission to return to Tokyo on my way to Washington from China for what officially was described as a refresher course. I felt the need of brushing up on my Japanese, renewing contacts, and making further observations on the spot.

In July 1928 I again arrived in Tokyo to find most of my friends and acquaintances absent from the city seeking refuge from the perniciously humid heat of the Japanese summer in the delightful mountain resort of Karuizawa. Seventeen years later Karuizawa served as the haven for high Japanese officials who went there to escape our insistent bombing raids. In 1928 it was an international playground, about five hours from Tokyo to the northwest, high up in the mountains but nestling near the foot of the smoking volcano Asama Yama. However cool the breezes of Karuizawa, there was little this mountain retreat could offer me, so I decided to stay in Tokyo throughout the summer and renew my contacts established five years before. I visited Sato-San and found him far more taciturn than during my first visit. It was no longer permissible to harbor dangerous thoughts, and the *gendarmerie,* or military police, was already at work to read the minds of dangerous thinkers. But the boisterous and self-confident talk of other acquaintances, which revealed to me what I regarded as truly dangerous thoughts, compensated for the sudden taciturnity of Sato-San. The liberalism of the early twenties now belonged to history. It was not regarded as good form to talk of those days of political freedom, and even friends who appeared truly liberal now spoke of those benighted days with a self-righteousness that was astounding.

The swagger of the military men, formerly curtailed by postwar events and the failure of the Siberian adventure, was now fully evident in talk and action. I learned that the Japanese military and naval structure was undergoing a radical and highly significant reorganization, shedding its enforced timidity as the years passed. It may be remembered that in the wake of the 1912 corruption scandal within the Navy, and then again after the Siberian adventure of the early twenties, the armed forces had suffered a serious loss of prestige, enabling the civilians to assert themselves against these boisterous heirs to the worst that was in the Samurai tradition. The spirit of liberalism, not confined to dissident groups, swept the whole country and enabled casual observers to speak of a decline or even the twilight of Japanese militarism. The new spirit swept even to the barracks and the lower decks, and soldiers and sailors expressed open opposition to the inhuman drills prescribed by their manuals. The opposition was particularly vociferous against General Mizaki, who, as head of the omnipotent Inspectorate of Military Education, was responsible for the indoctrination and morale training of the men.

In the face of this opposition Mizaki had to resign, and his successor was obliged to rewrite the manuals and to provide more humane living quarters for the men. But when I returned in 1928 I was told that the manuals were being revised once again, restoring to them all the severe aspects which had had to be eliminated a few years before. The entire military organization was undergoing a large-scale tightening, and it was evident that the men responsible for the reorganization were preparing Japan's armed strength for some definite purpose.

Although my interest in the Japanese Army was only secondary, I could not but notice that all Army heads were turned to the north, eying with unconcealed greed the Manchurian spaces across the waters. There was open talk resembling the vocabulary of the pro-Japanese German general Haushofer, who coined the phrase "living space." Living space it was these men clamored for, and they expressed their desires in no uncertain terms. I realized that it was merely a question of time until Japan would spring its unpleasant surprise on an unsuspecting world by moving to the north, with destination Manchuria.

In the naval sphere an interesting development was just about to begin. Still in its earliest stages and largely in the blueprint phase, it was nevertheless a development which filled me with apprehension. Circumstances of my stay enabled me to gain a deeper insight into developments than I had hoped when returning to Tokyo. Shortly after my arrival the naval attaché had fallen ill, and our chargé d'affaires suggested that I take his place as acting naval attaché. For a variety of reasons I preferred not to assume the title, so I advised him to request Washington that I be made assistant naval attaché while taking actual charge of the office.

Considerable opportunities for observation were soon to be offered by events which crowded the Japanese calendar. Emperor Taisho had died, and the Prince Regent was to be enthroned as the new emperor. The enthronement ceremonies were to be followed by a grand fleet review in Yokohama, at which Admiral Mark L. Bristol, USN, an outstanding naval diplomat and then the commander in chief of the Asiatic fleet, was to represent the United States. It was fully realized by all concerned that little information can usually be derived from such official functions; so we made plans to organize our own efforts unofficially. However, because of certain influences and little understanding of my plans, petty unconcealed hostility and opposition developed within the Embassy which caused me to give up all work in this direction and shortly return to Washington.

At this time Japan was concentrating on the development of her fleet air arm and training her carrier fliers along purely aggressive lines. But with our facilities handicapped we did not learn that a Japanese island was to be evacuated and turned into a full-scale target for these aircraft practices or that this target was to be a replica of Oahu. It was obvious, however, that in the training methods of the Japanese fleet air arm the notorious Tanaka Memorial was on the eve of implementation. Commander Minobi, one of the officers closely connected with these secret activities, was an acquaintance of mine, but I was unable to contact him during these days in Tokyo.

By a coincidence, however, I learned almost fifteen years later what had been taking place and that Minobi was deep in a plot which reached its climax in the attack against Pearl Harbor. He was one of Yamamoto's closest friends and professional intimates; and in 1942, flushed by the early success of their plan in actual practice, he revealed in a book all that had been kept a secret for more than a decade. I was then in Washington as deputy director of

Naval Intelligence, and a copy of Minobi's book in German translation was obtained when our censorship intercepted it being sent
to a German prisoner of war in the United States.

According to Minobi's belated revelation, the island which was
converted into a target area for carrier bombers was Shioku Island,
deliberately rebuilt to resemble Oahu even to the addition of full-
scale model buildings and imitations of the harbor area. He revealed the early anguish which accompanied these preparations for
Pearl Harbor, how 300 planes were lost in two years, partly due to
unfavorable weather conditions and partly to the inexperience of
the aviators. He described how Yamamoto continued the trials despite the serious losses, and how the skill of carrier-borne fliers was
gradually improved as the years went by—all the details of the plot,
until that fateful autumn day in 1941 when the pilots, making
their last practice run prior to their trip to Pearl Harbor, were
frankly told that they were now prepared for the Greater East Asia
war against the United States. Minobi was an admiral by then, and
he prided himself on the fact that he was the one designated to reveal to the unsuspecting aviators that the target island on which
they were dropping their bombs was in reality modeled after Pearl
Harbor.

If we had possessed an adequate intelligence organization in
1928–30; if we could have followed up and enlarged upon the
tidbits of premature information which one was then able to pick
up but could fit into no existing patterns; if we had been permitted
to carry out our plans, or had the "M-Plan" never been pigeonholed between Tokyo and Washington, we could have watched
these secret maneuvers of the Japanese Navy instead of listening to
their siren songs and believing their protestations that they were
in favor of peace. We would have known that while they courted
American friendship and protested their peaceful intentions, they
were making practice runs with heavily loaded carrier planes on
an island which even then in confidential conversations with his
closest associates and conspirators Yamamoto called "Pearl
Harbor."

BOOK TWO

THE WAR BETWEEN THE WARS

12

COLONEL WASHIZU SHOWS HIS HAND

The disappointments of my Tokyo trip were offset by a new assignment—I was ordered to take charge of the Far Eastern Section of the Office of Naval Intelligence. Many people know this office only from overseasoned mystery yarns or through "Admiral Warburton" in the famous Don Winslow comic strip. In fact, I had an opportunity to learn that a certain director of Naval Intelligence began the day's work by first turning to Don Winslow's adventures in the *Washington Post,* and not until he had absorbed the adventure of the day did he devote his attention to the far less romantic pursuits of his own intelligence officers.

I wish to emphasize that the available sources of information to which the public at large has easy access provide a somewhat distorted picture of the organizational structure and functions of Naval Intelligence—even to our own officers. My close and long association with it provided me with many adventures, exciting problems, and fascinating tasks; but on the whole, the Office of Naval Intelligence was a businesslike organization, not very different from any research agency doing scientific investigation.

Naval Intelligence is organized and equipped to exercise the dual functions it embraces automatically: intelligence and counterintelligence. The first task, entrusted to several geographical research sections, involves the collection of information on foreign navies and the naval policies of foreign countries. The other task is assigned to a branch which has the responsibility of watching over the security of our own navy by denying access of foreign espionage agents and saboteurs to activities vital to our national security.

Approximately 95 per cent of our peacetime intelligence comes to us from open sources: from books published abroad; from the reports of observing travelers; from newspaper articles or surveys in professional magazines; from foreign radio broadcasts and similar sources. An additional 4 per cent comes from semi-open sources:

reports of naval attachés or informants who gather their data in the normal pursuit of their everyday business. Only 1 per cent, and often less than that, is derived from truly secret sources: agent reports and the information obtained from certain confidants and contacts. There is very little these confidential agents can tell that is not accessible to an alert analyst who knows what he is looking for and knows how to find it in open sources.

Very often foreign countries set up barriers and thereby compel intelligence agencies to expend their energy in snooping where no actual necessity exists for undercover work. Comparison of the American and Japanese Navies as they existed prior to World War II will illustrate this point. Aside from certain construction secrets, which, however, were largely perceptible to a well-trained agent, most of the data concerning our peacetime navy were easily available to Japanese observers. Debates on Capitol Hill, discussions of appropriation bills, articles in technical magazines, and similar open sources provided most of the material needed. Our naval bases and other shore establishments were open to visitors. Our combatant ships were easily accessible after working hours, and during fleet reviews visitors were welcomed on board. The identity of the guests was never questioned, and intercepted agents' reports sometimes indicated that they had penetrated forbidden zones aboard ships. The size of our navy, the strength and armament of our ships, their movements, maneuvers, and other details, were all revealed in *Jane's Fighting Ships* and other annuals.

How different was the Japanese Navy! There, nothing was revealed to public gaze; ships were usually kept from view; naval bases were declared restricted or forbidden zones; appropriations were discussed little if at all in the Imperial Diet; the whole setup was shrouded in secrecy, and even misleading data were circulated to baffle the observer. The task with which we were then faced in Naval Intelligence was to get around this confusing curtain to see the stage prepared behind it. Frequently this task presented only minor difficulties, since it proceeded from a comparative analysis on the basis of generally known standards. Once in a while certain questions had to be answered. Is it true that Japan is building 45,000-ton battleships with 18-inch guns? Is it a fact that certain naval bases have new coastal fortifications? What is the actual manpower situation in the Japanese Navy or in their navy yards? Research and investigation usually provided the answers to these questions even without the employment of secret agents. But the major problems to be solved were the intentions behind the fleet, the use to which the ships and bases were to be put at some future date. These required real intelligence work; and, even there, common sense combined with mental capacity uncovered more clues than secret intelligence work.

Another aspect of the complex problem which should be emphasized is the practice of intensifying our intelligence activities *after* the outbreak of hostilities, while allowing them to languish during times of peace. This fundamentally wrong approach inevitably leads to serious deficiencies in our entire national-security structure. The fact must be realized that intelligence is as important a function in peacetime as it is during war. The better a nation is prepared by its intelligence agencies for any eventualities in times of real or nominal peace, the better chance it has to maintain that peace or to shorten the war. The methodology of peacetime intelligence is carried over on a larger scale in wartime. Then, instead of occasional monitoring of foreign broadcasts, all radio channels of the enemy are regularly watched; trained agents are at large, documents are captured, data virtually flood the desks of intelligence officers. What is brought to those desks in bales during wartime must be gathered piecemeal in times of peace.

But what is peace? From the viewpoint of an intelligence officer "peace" is a misleading term devised by man yearning for eternal tranquillity merely to deceive himself. The realists of international relations know well that no such thing as absolute peace exists. When the so-called shooting war is over, wars continue under the surface of a deceptive peace. They are continued by diplomatic, economic, and psychological means by both the victors and the vanquished, occasionally reaching peaks of tension and depths of baseness which shooting wars can hardly ever duplicate. The realization of the fact that wars by other means continue even after the formal cessation of open hostilities suggested the title of this Book Two. It was my own experience, shared by many fellow officers, that we were engaged in a war soon after the First World War ended and long before the second started. The totality of modern life and the complexity of modern society condemn us to eternal war even while we try to calm our disturbed consciences by remorsefully speaking of eternal peace as the panacea just around the corner. We do not want war; and more than that, our whole moral being revolts against war. But we are confronted with realities, and only a somnambulist can walk along the edges of rooftops without being aware of the danger momentarily confronting him.

It was in such an atmosphere of nominal peace fraught with the realities of the ever-continuing war that I assumed my duties as head of the Far Eastern Section in the Office of Naval Intelligence. The limitations imposed upon our work in those years bore heavily upon us, and there was little we could do to break out of the narrow confines of our restricted task. So in carefully kept files we collected the routine data. The staff available for this work was hopelessly inadequate in size to make an ambitious effort. In fact, I was myself half of the whole staff in the Far Eastern Section, the other half being Miss Sublett, my secretary. This at a time when our potential adversary, the Japanese, had scores of people assigned to their oversized North American desk. Later, one additional officer was assigned. He was one of our Chinese language officers detailed to me to handle Chinese matters.

While we struggled against misguided parsimony and short-sighted restrictions, events were moving fast toward the onset of climactic years, beginning in 1931. The turn of the year was already heavy with apprehension. There were certain unmistakable indications that Japan was ready to translate her Tanaka Memorial into action and move across the water toward her Manchurian "living space." By March 1931 the situation became sufficiently serious to suggest conversations with two friends, both intensely interested in the Far East. They were Lieutenant Colonel Sidney F. Mashbir, U.S. Army (G-2) (Reserve), a Japanese language officer like myself, and Major James F. Moriarty, U.S. Marine Corps, a good soldier, an aviator, and a fluent Russian linguist. Our thoughts were crystallized by the appearance in early 1931 of a magazine article on Henry Pu-yi, the ex-emperor of China. The article indicated that he was being sued for divorce by his number one concubine for impotency. Pu-yi was then living in seclusion in Shanghai. To anyone familiar with the Far East the situation described in the article was humorous and unlikely. But to intelligence officers it savored of something of international import. The ludicrous report about Pu-yi was clearly intended to make him "lose face" and to place him in a position to be approached for "saving" and used for an ulterior motive. The only possible use at that time would be as a puppet ruler if the Japanese were on the verge of moving into Manchuria. We decided to make an effort to find out, and we proceeded to plot in our own minds the possible course of the Japanese. We also felt that we should try to test our apprehensions by gaining whatever information we could straight from the horse's mouth, Japan's military attaché in Washington, Colonel Shohei Washizu of the Imperial Army. We frequently played golf with him and maintained very friendly relations. Often we ended the golf game up in his apartment for the nineteenth hole, which was doubly welcome during the prohibition era. I was commissioned to make the first move toward transforming our golfing into serious business. I called him up on the telephone, with a "Good afternoon, Colonel, how is your golf these days?"

"Eh, *Domo,* not so good," Washizu moaned.

"How about a game sometime in the near future?"

"That will be fine. Why don't you come around for a drink this afternoon?"

This was too good to be true. Our little colonel was falling into the trap.

"I would be delighted. I'll try to arrange it after I meet Mashbir and Moriarty as I have promised to do."

"Why don't you bring them along?" the Colonel asked.

"I'm sure they would be delighted. These are dry days, you know. What time?" I asked.

"Any time," Washizu said. "How about five o'clock?"

"We will be there," I replied, scarcely able to repress a chuckle as I replaced the receiver. At five P.M. sharp to the half minute according to Japanese custom we rang the bell to Washizu's quarters on the third floor of the Portland Apartments, one of the older buildings at the corner of 14th Street and Thomas Circle. It was a drab, poorly furnished apartment but served the purpose of Washizu's office and living quarters as well—Japanese military and naval attachés usually lived where they worked.

Colonel Washizu had already assembled his two assistants, Lieutenant Colonel K. Teramoto (air attaché) and Major Yutaka Hirota. After the usual greetings we were soon holding pleasing glasses of Old Parr Scotch and soda. The drinks were normal, not heavily loaded, a clear indication that Washizu did not have any vital questions to propound to us. He planned it as one of those ephemeral sociable evenings. In 1931 there was much to talk about in general terms, and we were in no haste to get around to our mission immediately. But there was a feeling of crisis in the air nevertheless.

For this was the year in which the tide turned; and the trend of events and the deterioration of the world situation made the rush toward war inevitable and unmistakable. The Seventy-first Congress struggled with problems of wages, price levels, and tariffs, trying to stem the onrushing depression while believing that prosperity lay in a monopoly of the home market. There were uprisings in Bolivia, Peru, Argentina, Brazil, Chile, and Cuba, critical developments in central Europe, with political extremists gaining strength in Germany. There was crisis in Britain, too, her Labour government split over the problem of balancing the budget and safeguarding sterling by the reduction of the "dole." Gold poured from London in large volumes, and the cabinet decided to suspend the gold standard.

And then, almost at the precise moment when the President of the Twelfth Assembly of the League of Nations invited the United States to take part in discussions about a proposed truce in armaments, Japan gave indications of having decided to embark upon a military adventure in some direction. The questions foremost in our minds were: first, In what direction are they going to move? and second, Is it going to be an Army show, a Navy show, or a combined operation with both the Army and Navy co-operating? To these questions we hoped to obtain an answer by using Washizu and his little group of assistants as guinea pigs. But in the pleasant atmosphere of this late-afternoon party, we bided our time.

Washizu suggested that we have dinner sent up from the restaurant below, and we accepted with thanks.

"What will our wives say about such a sudden announcement that we shall not be home for dinner?" I asked jestingly, which provoked good-natured jibes about the women controlling our lives and movements in America. I had to admit that the training of Japanese women, which required that the wives wait up for their husbands at night to put their clothes away no matter how late the hour of their return, possibly had its merits.

Our small talk continued. We discussed Washizu's imminent promotion because he had broken 100 at golf. And when Colonel Teramoto entered with another drink we inquired about his frequent trips to New York to attend certain burlesque shows. Major Hirota was questioned about his well-known and widely advertised feminine conquests in Washington. But throughout the banter and easy conversation the party was maintained on a level of dignity. Colonel Washizu was typical of the Japanese officer of his rank. Of moderate height, he had a small face with finely chiseled features. He wore glasses, and his general appearance greatly resembled that of Heinrich Himmler. He was inclined to be uncommunicative, but he was always precise.

Lieutenant Colonel Teramoto represented a somewhat different type. He had the rounded face of the average Japanese, further accentuated by his closely cropped hair. He was rather quiet for an aviator; however, he did have that particular broadness in the chin often found in the good flier.

Major Hirota, the assistant military attaché, had the rugged confidence and simplicity typical of the foot soldier. He had been in the United States for almost four years, the permanent fixture and driving force in the military attaché's office. He was brawny, with oversized features which just missed making him the grotesque Japanese of caricature. This effect, however, was softened by a twinkle in his eye which revealed his buoyant nature, his flamboyance emphasized after a few drinks by volubility and loud laughter which he felt was "typically American."

I describe these men at some length because in them I see the typical crew of a typical Japanese military mission abroad. Contrary to common belief, the choice of Japanese officers for the delicate functions of military and naval attachés was not always the result of careful selection. At times I have been greatly surprised by the intellectual shallowness and ineptitude of some of the men sent on these important missions. The men we met in the diplomatic drawing rooms in Washington were products of a definite system. The Tokyo clique picked these men when they were still young and full of promise and showed signs that they would make good military diplomats. They were minutely trained for their jobs, enjoyed certain privileges, and were given many advantages not generally provided their fellow officers. But not all justified the confidence placed in them. On the other hand, this system of cliques and cabals resulted in the ascendency of a definite group of mediocre but insatiably ambitious men. I was closely acquainted with many of them and knew their strength and weakness intimately. It was my knowledge of this group at the apex of Japan's military hierarchy which convinced me that Japan was by no means impervious to psychological attack. I anticipated their reactions to this type of assault and felt confident that sooner or later they would succumb to it. This was the kernel of the plan which motivated my later psychological-warfare campaign.

Indeed, the Washington representatives of Japan showed a wide variety in ability and temperament. Captain Sakano, a former naval attaché, a man of great discernment and personal charm, agreed with our contentions regarding the 5:5:3 ratio of naval strength and saw no reasons for Japan fearing us, but lost much of his astuteness after his return to Tokyo. As vice-minister of the Imperial Navy, he was suddenly removed from office for a *faux pas* in a domestic conflict between the Army and the Navy. He was asked if the Navy had any objection to the appointment of General Umezu as premier of Japan over the Army's violent opposition, and he naïvely answered in the negative. This was the wrong answer. He was expected to join the Army in its opposition to Umezu. For his mistake he was thrown out of office and forced into obscurity. On the other hand, Admiral Nomura, generally regarded in Japan as genuinely pro-American, remained in favor because he towered above all other Japanese in ability and temperament, as well as in stature. He was always sure of himself and dependent on his own opinions; he had the courage of his convictions, the only Japanese I have met who was willing and able to discuss any subject in detail at any time without the halting embarrassment and bewildered chuckle which characterized his mediocre fellows.

The three Japanese we were facing on that early spring day in 1931 were of three distinctly different types. Because of this fact we expected entirely different reactions from each of them when we were ready to spring our surprise on them during this "cooked-up" gathering. We distributed roles as observers among ourselves. I was to observe Washizu, Mashbir was to watch Teramoto, and Moriarty to watch Hirota at the moment that I was to propound the question with which we were to confront them. Their reactions to the question rather than their words were to be the clues.

Toward the close of the dinner our conversation with seeming casualness drifted to the situation and attitude of the Chinese. The situation in north China and Manchuria was chaotic indeed under the war lord Chang So-ling. I professed sympathy for Japan and showed full understanding for the difficulties they were encountering in the face of events in Manchuria. The beatific smiles on the faces of our three adversaries assured me that the bait was tempting. Finally, at what we felt was the psychological moment, I turned to Colonel Washizu and asked in a most serious tone:

"Colonel, do you think Japan can exist against a boycott of the rest of China if you should invade Manchuria?" Although pronounced casually, without the emphasis the words now may have, the question was carefully prepared in advance and rehearsed before we went to Washizu's quarters. It was the sixty-four-dollar question, the provocative query which we hoped would yield us the needed clues. We were not disappointed, since their reactions were fully revealing. The Colonel colored a deep red, put his hand to his mouth, and cleared his throat with apparent difficulty; Colonel Teramoto, who was in the process of sipping his drink, choked on it and had to leave the room in obvious panic; Major Hirota burst out in drowning laughter and fell over backward in his chair as he lost control of himself. Mashbir, Moriarty, and I looked at each other and winked. We had rung the bell. Although the question never received an answer, we had the clue we needed.

But as soon as calm was once more restored and Teramoto returned to the room, we followed up with two other leading questions which we had decided to propound. This time it was Mashbir who addressed a question to the Colonel by designation but also to the group in general by looking from one to the other quickly as he finished speaking.

"Colonel, what do you think the League of Nations would do in the event of such a move by Japan?"

Major Hirota was the first to pick up the ball. He answered quickly and in a derisive tone: "Oh, the League. All they can do is talk!"

Moriarty was quick to follow with his question: "Colonel, would you set up Pu-yi as a puppet in Manchuria such as General Merkuloff was in Siberia?"

Hirota was again the one who answered, showing that he was the driving force of the group:

"That may be," he said now in very solemn tones.

If we had stumbled upon something, it was Colonel Washizu who, through the medium of strict Japanese courtesy, gave us a clue to timing. Just before we prepared to leave, the conversation drifted to the question of Moriarty's length of duty in Washington, and it was stated that he expected to be detached in November. As we reached the front door, Colonel Washizu (whose strict Japanese mind was working efficiently insofar as speed was concerned but not so well as to judgment) suddenly said:

"Major Moriarty, I would like to give you a farewell party before you leave. It will have to be in September because I shall be very busy in October!" This was in *March* 1931.

As the three of us walked home together, we assembled our observations into one solid piece. It was obvious to us that: *the Japanese Army had plans for the invasion of Manchuria to be executed in the near future.* We had uncovered one of the greatest secrets of the Japanese Army.

Before making a report of our conclusions to our superiors we decided to seek an answer to our second question: Was the Japanese Navy also involved in the plot? So we decided to repeat the exact performance with the naval attaché and his staff, all of whom we knew through golf and other activities. We felt certain that by rigging up such a call with Captain Shimomura, the naval attaché, we would have a similar number of assistants present, because the Japanese always made it a point to match the number of foreigners present.

When I called Captain Shimomura to ask about his golf, there was an identical response, the same cordiality, and the same invitation. "How about a drink?" There was the same doubt on my part, the subterfuge of a previous engagement with Mashbir and Moriarty, and then the suggestion that they should come along. Everything moved 'according to plan and schedule, the only difference being in the quarters occupied by the Naval Attaché and that there was no invitation to dinner. The Imperial Navy provided him with two apartments in Alban Towers, a fashionable apartment house at Massachusetts Avenue and Wisconsin. It was handed down from naval attaché to naval attaché and served as living quarters and offices. During those days, wives and families did not yet accompany them to the United States chiefly because it would have meant according them a social position to which they were not accustomed at home.

This time the Scotch was of a different brand but equally good. The conversation was guided along from here to there. Finally, after a bit of horseplay about our sympathies for Japan's difficulties in China, the big question was popped. We waited. There could be detected not even the slightest reaction, except a mild, slowly drawn-out: "Well, I really don't know," from Captain Shimomura.

Again Mashbir, Moriarty, and I looked at each other. Our looks had a different significance.

This time as we walked home there was little debate. But here again was confirmation of the fact that the Japanese Army was facing north while their navy looked to the south. We no longer had any doubt in our minds; both questions were unequivocally answered. When next day I drafted my report for the Director of Naval Intelligence, giving an estimate of the situation with prognostic conclusions, I stated in no uncertain terms that the Japanese Army was on the eve of moving against Manchuria without the knowledge or support of the Japanese Navy. This was March 1931. During the night of September 18-19, 1931, "trouble" between China and Japan developed in Manchuria.

But when the news was flashed by the radio on a quiet Saturday afternoon, I was no longer in Naval Intelligence. Shortly after my meeting with Washizu, Shimomura, and their assistants, I was transferred in that routine cycle of ship-and-shore duty to the command of the destroyer *Dorsey*.

But as I left Washington it was to accompany Prince Takamatsu, the second brother of the Emperor, and Princess Takamatsu on a tour of the United States. This gave me the unusual opportunity for studying constantly and at close range a group of ten highly placed Japanese who constituted the party. It later gave me, in my psychological warfare against the Japanese High Command, an entree into Japanese confidence not possible by any other means.

13

FLEET PROBLEM 14

WHEN THE NEWS of the Manchuria incident reached me on shipboard on September 19, 1931, I was unable to obtain an authoritative account of what had taken place the night before. I am inclined to agree with Walter Lippmann, who wrote that "there is good reason to think that the Japanese Foreign Office and also the Japanese Ambassadors at Geneva and at Washington were without complete and accurate information." They even hinted that the Army was staging a coup and acting without the knowledge, and much more without the approval, of the Foreign Office. The administration in the United States accepted in general this disclaimer and based its subsequent policy "on the assumption that the civilian government in Tokyo had been surprised by the Army's action." Secretary of State Henry L. Stimson, one of our great statesmen, did not share this belief. He was in agreement with those who felt that while the Tokyo Foreign Office was probably without information about the details of the attack, it did possess general knowledge that the Army had been planning some such coup.

The League of Nations was informed of the incident on September 19 by Japanese Ambassador Yoshizawa and Dr. Alfred Kao Sze, the Chinese delegate to the League of Nations. The following Monday, China appealed formally to the League, invoking Article XI of the Covenant. On Tuesday, Secretary Stimson told Mr. Debuchi, the Japanese ambassador in Washington, about the profound concern of the American government in the face of what he regarded as the flagrant violation of the Nine-Power Treaty and of the Pact of Paris. The policy of the American government was gradually shaping up under the adroit and courageous leadership of Mr. Stimson, whose activities during those days remain forever impressed upon my memory with a feeling of admiration and gratitude. But events were moving with uncanny rapidity. On November 27 I heard on the radio that Japanese troops were moving in force from Mukden toward Chinchow to obtain full control of the Peking-Mukden railway. The move was stopped when Mr. Stimson made firm representations to Baron Shidehara, the same Shidehara who assumed the premiership fifteen years later in a Japan prostrated by defeat. It was not expected, however, that the sudden change of Japanese tactics would mean the abandonment of the project. In fact, the clash between Mr. Stimson and the Japanese was just about to take shape. The Secretary of State made a guarded statement about difficulties in crediting the Japanese version of the incident, but his remark became garbled or deliberately distorted in transmission and was presented in Japan to read that "the Japanese Army in Manchuria was running amuck." Whatever consternation the Japanese feigned to discredit this statement, I agreed with Mr. Stimson that Japan was bent upon absorbing Manchuria completely. The Japanese Army was no longer merely facing the north. It was swallowing it with unchecked speed.

The Japanese Foreign Office was quick to accept the distorted version of Mr. Stimson's statement and now joined the Army in running amuck—even if only in the diplomatic sphere. In language rarely employed by diplomats when making a public statement, a spokesman of the Foreign Office rejected the Stimson statement in its garbled version. This contributed to the generation of intense resentment in Japan over what was represented as American interference in affairs regarded as essentially domestic.

The "war" between the State Department and the Tokyo Foreign Office was waged in the diplomatic sphere, and the tension mounted as the weeks passed, but in the fleet there was no evidence of a changing relation between the United States and Japan. Our days passed with routine matters: inspections, drills, practices, as if the world were still at peace. As one looks back on those days, the truism inherent in the saying that "peace is indivisible" appears in stark reality. There can be no isolated war waged by a major power. It is bound, sooner or later, to lead to world-wide conflagration. But even wars were then still assigned to the care of diplomats. If one could have judged the condition of the world by looking at the American Navy on the west coast, he would have thought that there was no trouble brewing anywhere.

This does not mean, however, that there were not farsighted men in our naval service who envisaged in startling detail the road which Japan was to take from her conquest in Manchuria. Admiral Joseph

K. Taussig, USN, was one of these men, and was among the first Americans to warn against Japanese imperialism, not in the terms of superficial publicists but with the undeniable facts and figures of the naval scientist. The late Admiral Frank H. Schofield, USN, was another such man of outstanding vision. He was then commander in chief of the United States fleet, stationed in the Pacific. It was largely due to his foresight and initiative that our navy made a first significant move to prepare for Japanese moves in the Pacific. The visible symbol of his apprehension was Fleet Problem 14.

A fleet problem is a basis for realistic naval maneuvers. In a fleet problem the naval officer has the best opportunity to reveal himself as a leader qualified to command his ship or his forces in actual combat. Or he may be revealed as unfit to be entrusted with the great responsibilities of battle.

The fleet problem has a very real significance in the training of naval officers and in the study of the possible actual problems that may confront the fleet. It is a most important check on the potential power and efficiency of the fleet as a whole. It tests the officers' knowledge of their ships. It tests the imagination and foresight of every command. It provides in peacetime the nearest possible approach to war conditions, and it anticipates what may conceivably occur.

The fleet problem is constructed in three stages: The commander in chief states an imaginary political or war crisis, listing the number and strength of United States and enemy naval forces in operation in the area concerned. Our own forces are usually given a certain color designation (Blue) while the imaginary enemy is given another (Black). This is all the information placed at the disposal of commanders on lower echelons including commanders of battleships, carriers, cruisers, and destroyers. Having received the commander in chief's scant statement as raw material, they must make an estimate of the situation and arrive at a decision with all the details necessary to meet and repel the onslaught of Black through a most propitious application of the forces available to Blue. This estimate includes: (a) courses of action open to the enemy, (b) most probable course the enemy will take, (c) how to frustrate and destroy the enemy. All the material thus submitted by the various commands is studied by the commander in chief, careful analysis and selection are made, and the best resulting features combined into a plan for maneuvers on the part of the entire fleet.

The fleet problem is traditionally the "swan song" of a retiring commander in chief, its execution left as an intellectual legacy to his successor. The practice of the fleet problem was started in 1920, so it was the fourteenth problem for which we received our raw material late in 1932 to be worked up for practical exercise in February 1933.

Fleet Problem 14 was destined to become one of the most famous of all fleet problems. It was designed by Admiral Schofield, one of the most brilliant strategists the Navy has ever produced, a tremendous brain housed in a fragile body. Even in 1932 Admiral Schofield perceived the situation clearly and faced it courageously, displaying a vision that appeared to be lacking in some of his successors in far more acute situations of real emergency.

Obviously, then, a familiarity with existing and past fleet problems is a vital and indispensable part of every naval officer's equipment in the field of naval strategy and tactics. No responsible officer should dare ignore the lessons of fleet problems.

What was the significance of Fleet Problem 14? Here are five of Admiral Schofield's prerequisites:

1. An acute situation exists in the Pacific; *war is imminent but not declared*.

2. The enemy will strike *where the fleet is concentrated*. (In 1932 the Pacific fleet was not yet based at Pearl Harbor but at west coast ports, at Puget Sound, San Francisco, San Pedro, and San Diego. Major forces were held in the Atlantic, including a scouting force and carriers. Pearl Harbor was a secondary base from the viewpoint of the fleet, harboring submarines which needed this advance base.)

3. The enemy will use *carriers as the basis of a striking force*. (Another significant point, especially important in the historical perspective. The concentration of six carriers, as it came to pass in 1941, was properly regarded as premature in 1932. So it was estimated that the enemy would strike with two large carriers, escorted by six heavy cruisers, a squadron of destroyers, and fuel ships.)

4. The enemy may make raids on Hawaiian Islands or west coast *prior to declaration of war*.

5. *Consider any Black forces east of 180th meridian as hostile*. (Prophetic words indeed! The 180th meridian was to become the

crucial spot in the Pacific almost exactly ten years later when in its immediate vicinity the Battle of Midway was fought and the outcome of World War II decided in its Pacific phase.)

The emphasis on air power in a naval war at such an early date may now well be regarded as great foresight on the part of the commander in chief. If Fleet Problem 14 proved nothing else, it certainly established the fact on a historical scale that the United States Navy was not behind the times in its estimation of a situation and its vision of the future's potentialities.

It was not hard for subordinate commanders to follow Admiral Schofield's farsighted lead in making their estimates; and I wrote in my own estimate of the situation:

"1. Enemy will try to delay the departure and advance of the overseas expeditionary force by sudden aircraft raids on the forces fitting out, critical areas, and basing facilities as may be accomplished in one dash to or from home territory." The nature of this imaginary first raid was never doubted in my mind. Even at that time, nine years prior to Pearl Harbor, we expected an outbreak of hostilities with Japan in the form of an air raid, and it is regrettable that this fixed notion, long regarded as the only natural course open to the enemy, was not sufficiently appreciated by the commander in chief who in 1941 was in charge of the most serious fleet problem the United States was ever made to face.

"2. Enemy has accurate information as to the location and strength of our forces. He is kept informed of departures of our forces from port." This estimate was fully borne out in unlimited testimony before the Roberts Commission and the Joint Congressional Committee investigating Pearl Harbor.

"3. Enemy's exact location is unknown, and must remain unknown in order to launch a successful raid before being attacked by an equal or superior force. All his forces except the tankers are capable of high maintained speed. Destroyers may be refueled from carriers or cruisers, thereby giving all an unlimited cruising radius, except during prolonged flight at full speed.

"It appears then that the enemy has the following specific courses open to him:

    (a) To make an air raid on basing facilities Pearl Harbor unopposed except by aircraft and return to own waters.

    (b) To make an air raid on forces fitting out at Bremerton

and upon basing and other facilities in that area, returning direct to own waters.

(c) Same as (b) but with the San Pedro–San Diego area as the objective.

(d) Same as (b) but with San Francisco area as the objective.

(e) Dividing forces to carry out both (c) and (d).

(f) Same as (d) but conducting another air raid on Pearl Harbor returning to own waters."

At that time course (d) seemed the most likely because our strength was concentrated in that coastal area.

But conditions had changed in 1941. The west coast had but little, and Pearl Harbor had all. Pearl Harbor in 1941 was an oversized bait luring the Japanese into what could have become a gigantic trap had Fleet Problem 14 been given the study and consideration it so fully deserved, and had the ideas propounded in it prevailed in the minds of responsible commanders. Even the sixth course estimated to be open to an enemy contained a direct reference to the vulnerability of the Hawaiian area.

Whatever was to occur, my estimate proposed, there would be an air raid on Pearl Harbor prior to the enemy's return to his own waters. Pearl Harbor was the chief motif, the recurring theme of the estimate, but I placed what later appeared an unjustified faith in our defenses. "The raiding force," I wrote, "would undoubtedly be hotly pursued beyond the Hawaiian area. At the same time the strong defenses, in this area, both aircraft and antiaircraft, have already demonstrated the hazard to and ineffectiveness of invading aircraft. The force of Blue patrol planes in that area is easily sufficient to detect the approach of a raiding force twenty-four hours before reaching the launching radius of their aircraft. It is assumed, therefore, that course (f) would not be adopted, *unless the initial raid were highly successful, the Black planes returned to carriers, and pursuit is abandoned early.*"

When I prepared my estimate in 1932 there was only thirty-eight shore-based aircraft in Pearl Harbor, but this force was then regarded as sufficient "to detect the approach of a raiding force twenty-four hours before reaching the launching radius of their aircraft." This is an important point in evaluating the responsibilities as they existed in 1941 and the failures accruing from an improper appraisal of these responsibilities.

So the significance of Fleet Problem 14 is obvious. It showed that one of the defending forces of Blue had failed in its mission and permitted the imaginary enemy to break through to the coast however small his forces might have been. The vulnerability of our west coast was revealed in glaring light. It furnished the U.S. Navy in 1933 (when it was actually put into practice) a blueprint of the action of the Japanese Navy in the Pearl Harbor attack of December 7, 1941. It was a clear warning based on the prescience and skill of a great naval fleet commander who had studied the Japanese and the Pacific situation. It clearly envisaged every probability and possibility of the attack which really came.

At the critique held in the Auditorium at Long Beach, California, the lessons were so apparent that it was not considered necessary to carry the analysis beyond the usual peacetime discussions.

I have no way of knowing how far the lessons of fleet problems influenced strategic thinking throughout the Navy. These problems are studied and are replayed at the Naval War College, and the conclusions are made available to those officers who are interested in reading them.

In 1933-34 when I attended the War College, immediately after Fleet Problem 14, two of the officers in the same class were Captain (later Admiral) J. O. Richardson and Commander (later Vice Admiral) W. W. Smith. On the closing day of this course when every officer is given an opportunity to express himself in any manner I was favorably and deeply impressed by the remarks of Captain Richardson when he said:

"I have been trying to come to the War College for the past fifteen years and I finally made it. Upon leaving I just want to say that I think a good officer coming to the War College will leave here a damned good officer. But I also want to say that a fool coming to the War College will leave here a damned fool."

When we concentrated our fleet at Pearl Harbor at the moment of most intense Pacific crisis in 1941, we repeated the very conditions of Fleet Problem 14. How it happened that the lessons taught by that problem were disregarded is not known. It is not the fault of the organization. The cause must be sought and can be found easily in individuals who are inclined to shrug shoulders and dismiss warnings when they are made in the intellectual sphere. With Fleet Problem 14 easily available to the man truly on the spot, there can be no excuse that the worst fears expressed in an early estimate became realities largely or almost exclusively due to the fact that the preconditions for success outlined in the fleet problem and practically tested in an exercise were disregarded. This is the major lesson of Fleet Problem 14 in its relation to the events on December 7, 1941.

In retrospect I visualize Fleet Problem 14 as an unwitting rehearsal for Pearl Harbor. It is regretted that while the stage was set in 1933, the script prepared, and everything ready for the *première,* the leading man in the show and the supporting cast forgot their lines and spoiled the actual performance just a little over eight years later.

14

COMMANDER YOKOYAMA
GOES TO NEWPORT

IF I were asked to fix the date when Japanese espionage was started in the United States on an impressive scale, I would say it began between April 19 and 23, 1933. We had just completed Fleet Problem 14, and the outcome was by no means entirely satisfactory. Considerable shoptalk attended this incident; and although certain details of the problem were kept confidential, several phases were disclosed through the press, representatives of which were present at the exercise itself.

There was no doubt in my mind that the Japanese attached significance to the problem, as indeed all navies watch closely the exercises of their opposite numbers. It was impossible to ascertain how much the Japanese knew or were anxious to learn; but certainly because of the almost negative nature of our security precautions, considerable data could have been pasted into Japanese Intelligence scrapbooks from articles published in the press. In fact, as I shall relate on a later page, one of our major fleet problems of 1937 provided the Japanese with much of the data they still needed for the completion of their plans for the attack on Pearl Harbor.

The situation in the Far East continued to be serious, and Mr. Stimson was singled out by Japanese propaganda as the scapegoat, blamed for the mounting tension in international relations. Japan was definitely on the warpath, and I knew enough of intelligence to realize that an aggressor starts his wars by increasing his espionage activities.

It was in the midst of these and similar considerations in the field of peacetime intelligence that I was advised of the imminent visit of a Japanese training squadron under the command of Vice Admiral Gengo Hyakutake flying his flag on the old cruiser *Yakumo*. On the surface there was nothing unusual about the visit. The clouds which darkened our diplomatic relations and made us view with alarm the activities of the Japanese Army did not disturb the cordiality of our relations with the Japanese Navy, which we then regarded as innocent of Tokyo's imperialistic plans. It is a fact, however, that because of the situation then existing, Admiral Hyakutake showed considerable nervousness on his arrival. A stiffness of attitude was noticeable not only in him but also among most of the officers of the squadron. A fine reception was prepared for them, and I was detailed by Admiral Leigh, our commander in chief, to act again as an aide to the visiting admiral.

I was thus one of the first American officers to board the *Yakumo* when she moored to Pier 60 in San Pedro just ahead of my destroyer, and I was in a position to watch Japanese skepticism melt as the days passed and cordiality greeted them everywhere instead of rebuffs as they had expected.

I was introduced to the Admiral, who greeted me in good English. I found him a pleasant man of scholarly appearance and great dignity, a jovial and sociable officer who would nevertheless maintain a reserve in his personal relations. He was primarily a strategist, well read on general naval matters and particularly well versed in the problems of American naval policy. He seemed to be positively inclined to the West, which he frankly admired, especially for its music. Admiral Hyakutake was soon to retire to become president of Tokyo Imperial University, the first naval officer to be so honored in Japan's scholastic history.

I performed my duties as aide to the Admiral with the usual careful regard for naval protocol, while keeping my eyes open as much as possible under the circumstances.

The round of entertainment was exacting and interesting. At a luncheon given at MGM Studio by Louis Mayer, I sat next to the well-chiseled features of pretty Jean Parker, then a starlet of eighteen, who succumbed to curiosity as I read character from her handwriting and indicated she would have to watch the self-determination of those backhand strokes if she were not to interfere with a promising career. Across from me sat the gorgeous Jean Harlow and a little farther the beautiful eyes of Irene Dunne were filled with merriment. It was a perfect day and the scenery was wonderful.

But it did not prevent me from adding to my analysis of Japanese character and procedure. In the cavalcade which took us to Hollywood were cars loaned and driven by prominent individuals of Los Angeles. I sat on the front seat of one of these. Behind us in the long column was a car driven by one of the members of the Japanese Consulate. We were late, and the emphasis was on speed. In Tokyo I had had ample opportunity to watch the antics of speeding Japanese drivers, who were inveterate dreamers. I had even realized my worst fears in Japan while driving with one of them to Yokohama—he plowed into and upset a "salad cart," one of those long oxcarts, loaded with barrels used to collect night soil from the houses, a method of disposal made necessary by the lack of sewerage facilities.

So today, as we speeded toward Los Angeles, I explained to my host-driver the unpredictability of Japanese chauffeurs and added with careful emphasis that when he had occasion to stop he must *not* do so suddenly and must be sure to give ample arm signals to the Japanese driver behind us. He listened carefully and acknowledged everything I had to say. Then, as we neared a corner, a traffic light quickly changed to red. My driver as suddenly stepped on his brakes. I closed my eyes, stiffened, and waited in apprehension, counting the seconds I knew it would take for our follower to close the normal distance. Then—Crash! as he hit the back of our car.

I looked at my surprised driver and said lightly:

"See what I mean?" He blinked and muttered acknowledgment.

The damage was not great; so we hurried on again. This time as I had advised, the driver behind us took double distance.

Behind these cordial relations, however, lurked the first signs of future Japanese aggression. It had been suspected for some time that Japan was preparing for the dispatch of secret agents to the United States, and I was particularly eager to discover whether the visit of the training squadron was being used by them to put a few major agents ashore. No identification cards were needed by Japanese, particularly those aboard a man-of-war, to visit our cities along the coast, and therefore nobody could determine whether all those who left their ships in uniform and ostensibly on temporary shore liberty were actually returning to them. It was comparatively simple even for an officer to leave his ship, obtain civilian clothes in town, and submerge himself in the Japanese colony on the west coast.

I focused my attention on as many Japanese officers as I could under the circumstances to check their numbers, departure, and return, but it was impossible to ascertain singlehanded any facts regarding the goings and comings. But I felt that my suspicions were confirmed a few years later when I learned of the intelligence activities on the west coast and was certain that some of the Japanese who arrived with the training squadron had preferred the balmy climate of California to the long voyage home. We were then, and remained for some time to come, rather hospitable to foreign operatives; whereas a checkup for illegal entrants would have disclosed illuminating numbers.

Shortly after Admiral Hyakutake's departure I was transferred from the *Dorsey* and ordered to proceed to the Naval War College at Newport, R.I., for my postgraduate training in strategy as a member of the senior class. I looked forward with eager anticipation to my year in Newport because of the great admiration I had for this fine educational institution, the highest and best in our naval service. Admiral Sims, when president of the Naval War College, had succeeded in introducing there many of the reforms which obstructionists prevented him from making more widespread throughout the Navy. By imposing on the college his own high intellectual standards this famous naval scientist raised the educational level of the institution to unprecedented heights, just as he had, in a sense, "made" the modern American Navy through bold reforms in our gunnery, which he had forced through in spite of the strongest opposition and with only the aid of his little group called "ASIA"—the Association for the Suppression of Ignorant Assumption—and the active interest of President Theodore Roosevelt himself.

I reported for duty in the Naval War College on June 26, 1933, for the course that was to begin on July 1. I anticipated a complete and pleasant interlude from all other types of activity. Fitting myself into the routine of the Naval War College was easy, but at times I found my duties somewhat crowding me. I was called upon to give a lecture on Japan, and considering the analytical qualities of this most critical audience, I spent about three months suitably preparing my lecture. This was in addition to the full-time work of the course itself.

Then suddenly on September 26 I was brought back to my main interest, Japanese-American relations, by the arrival of a visitor who traveled several hundred miles from Washington to Newport just to have a friendly chat with me. My visitor was Lieutenant Commander Ichiro Yokoyama of the Imperial Japanese Navy, assistant naval attaché to the embassy in Washington. I did not regret that the routine was interrupted by the visit of Yokoyama, and events made me feel that it was beneficial, because he continued to remain conservative throughout the war. I never missed an opportunity to present concrete arguments to Japanese of the levelheaded type to take back home in the hope that some good would come of it. Japanese who were not influenced by self-interest, and who spent enough time in this country to get an idea of its magnitude and potential strength, generally arrived at the intelligent conclusion that Japan would be ruined by war with the United States. They usually tried to put this idea across at home with a view to resolving the controversies between the two countries in some way short of war. This was done not because of any particular love for the United States but because they considered it good judgment. Some of them were later mistreated because they tried to use their influence in this direction.

There existed a pleasant relationship between Commander Yokoyama and me, and he represented his journey as a pleasure trip prior to his return to Japan, but I doubted the professed motive.

I arranged a cocktail party in his honor, and Yokoyama proved an amiable and pleasant guest. I paved the way for a frank talk with him next day by inviting him for a long drive. He accepted the opportunity quickly, and when we were driving along the deserted ocean front, he turned to me and asked:

"What do you think is to be done in order to create a more friendly feeling between Japan and America?"

I drove the car to a small clearing on the seashore and stopped. There in the open air began a conversation which was to have considerable significance twelve years later. In 1945 this same Yokoyama, with the rank of rear admiral, acted as the representative of the Japanese Navy Minister during the days which led to Japan's surrender, and he was the senior naval officer present in Manila for preliminary surrender formalities. On June 16, 1945, I had used him as the focal point around which to build my seventh broadcast to the Japanese, which evidently created the impression that he would be *persona grata* to us.

Sitting in our car in Newport in 1933, I felt, and I told Yokoyama, that there was a great need for frank discussion to enable the Japanese to arrive at a proper understanding of America.

"The United States," I replied, "has no designs in the Far East,

Our people are inclined to be outspoken and frank. They always want to help the man who is down, and they have no hostile thoughts whatever toward Japan. Can the same be said of the Japanese, Yokoyama-San?"

"Well," he answered in obvious embarrassment, "what do you think Japan ought to do?"

"To begin with," I said firmly, "the anti-American propaganda campaign of Japan ought to be stopped immediately. That is the thing which I am most concerned about. Some of your so-called young patriots might do some foolish thing like the Inukai affair which would embroil the United States and Japan. You know certainly, Yokoyama-San, that there is no real conflict between Japan and America. You know that a war between our two nations would lead to the ruin of Japan. Nothing pleased me more than to see this very fact stated in your most jingoist newspaper, the *Kokumin Shimbun,* when it said that a war between Japan and the United States would be a foolish thing. 'It would be ruinous to both,' it wrote in effect if I remember correctly, 'particularly to Japan. We must watch carefully other nations who would benefit from a war between our two countries.' "

"Yes," Yokoyama interrupted me, "I remember the article."

"Now if that is the real feeling in Japan," I asked, "why do you keep up that anti-American talk in your papers? You know as well as I do that your government controls the press and can stop this sort of thing whenever it wants to."

"Yes," he said with what appeared to be a sigh. "Our navy is trying to hold the reins on the Army. It's the Army which promotes the press campaign."

"There is yet another thing. Japan ought to give up the idea of trying to increase the capital-ship ratio. The American people feel that the ratio as it now stands is the result of a long study of the defense problems of our country, and that a great deal was sacrificed to get a limitation of arms. What possible objection could Japan have to letting the ratio stand?"

There was a moment's silence, and Yokoyama looked out toward the open sea, as if seeking prompting from the sea gulls circling at some distance. Then he turned back to me and said:

"At the present time, Japan fears America!"

"Japan fears America!" I repeated the words in genuine astonishment. "Now let's see what those fears are, and let us analyze each one separately. What is the first one?"

"Japan sees the United States demanding a bigger ratio than Japan," Yokoyama said, "and can't see any reason for it other than that the United States wants to be in a position to attack Japan."

I tried to explain to him the reasons for the United States' decision to establish the ratio.

"Do you remember," I asked, "during the World War when there was a time when it looked as if the United States might get into the war against England? That was because the United States never has and never will tolerate restriction of movement of her merchant marine—her freedom of the seas. At that time we learned our lesson, and you must recall that nearly every war in which we have engaged has been over this same point. It was during the World War that we decided against limiting our defense to such a point that another state could deprive us of our freedom of the seas. Now with all the trouble we took just for the sake of this principle, do you expect us to sign a treaty which would return us to the point where we started?"

"No," Yokoyama answered, "but why should the United States have a ratio of ten when Japan is limited to the ratio of six?" This was an important question, and I recognized it at once as a product of Japanese propaganda. It was not hatched in Yokoyama's brain but only planted there. In my answer I was trying not only to enlighten Yokoyama but also to answer Japanese propaganda, hoping that he would carry my answer back to Japan to the proper circles. So my reply, carefully calculated to serve this purpose, had to be circumstantial, adapted to the workings of the Japanese mind.

"Let us see," I said. "What have Japan and the United States to protect? The United States, at the time the last treaty was signed, had about two billion dollars' worth of trade in the Far East, including Australasia. Since that time this trade has decreased much less than trade in the other parts of the world. Japan had and still has very little trade outside of that with the United States which would require protection on this side of the Pacific. Now, you as a naval strategist will surely realize that a naval force, to protect its lines of communications seven thousand miles from home, could not possibly afford the protection unless she starts out with a force at least ten to six in ratio to that of the country which represents a menace to her commerce, however remote the menace now appears to be. The United States has two billions to protect in the Far East, while Japan has nothing to protect on this side of the Pacific. Isn't it reasonable that we ask that ratio necessary for our own protection?"

Yokoyama was far from convinced. He demanded:

"But why do you not ask a greater ratio than England? Why do you ask a greater ratio than Japan only?"

"Because England has just as much trade to lose on this side of the Atlantic as the United States has on the other side. The Royal Navy is in fact very small in relation to the sea lanes it has to protect. And you will agree with me that fleets have to be computed in relative figures—I mean, in relation to their commitments in terms of miles of their sea-borne interests."

"Well," Yokoyama asked, "would the United States be satisfied with the ratios as they now stand in the other categories?"

"I should think so," I answered, then added after a pause: "Well, what is Japan's second fear?"

"You have suddenly begun a big building program. Why?"

"I don't believe any would deny that the treaty gives us, you, or anybody a moral right to build up to it when they so desire. Is that not right?"

"Yes."

"Japan and England have been building ships ever since the treaty," I continued, "but the United States has done practically no building, perhaps for the purpose of setting an example for other nations. Suddenly we find our country in a depression, and several industries can be greatly assisted by shipbuilding; so we decide to build some of the ships we are entitled to under the treaty. Now this causes a howl in England and in Japan, despite the fact that they were both busy building ships while we left our shipyards idle. Is there any justification for their complaint? As it is, even by 1935 the United States will be far behind her allotment of one hundred and one ships, while England will be behind by only sixty-four and Japan by only eight ships. Is that not so?"

"I guess that's right," Yokoyama said, obviously impressed with my facts and figures. He forgot that I was in the midst of a tour of duty in the Naval War College where we study naval diplomacy.

"Well, if you agree with me, do you still think that there are any grounds for fear on this score?"

"No," he said. "But you have your fleet in the Pacific, and people in Japan think it is concentrated there against Japan."

"Yes, our fleet is in the Pacific. But let me tell you the reason. For years the Navy has been trying to get the fleet together in order to do some proper training, but certain individuals in the country have overcome these efforts and have kept our fleet split up so that their own districts and ports would benefit. You don't have this system to contend with in Japan. But what would your professional pride do if you did have that condition? You'd work just as we have to get your fleet together so that you could make something out of it. That is your profession and your life's work; so would you stand by idly and look on while selfish interests make your fleet impotent? I should say you would not. And now that we have got out fleet together for the first time in our history, Japan tries to separate it again, by asking that part of it be sent back to the east coast. You saw today the kind of weather we have in Newport. It is the same and worse all along the coast. Since I've been here we have had nothing but rain and fog. How far could you see over the water today? And this is one of our "splendid" east coast bases. Down on the Virginia capes you have much the same condition: fog, rough weather, and haze. So where could our fleet go to get any training?"

"To Guantánamo," Yokoyama said promptly.

"Yes, but how many of our officers and men would be content to stay down there more than three months out of the year? Most of them have families, and they demand more home life than some other nationalities. So with three months in Guantánamo we would have nine months of idleness. Could you ask us to do that?" I paused for a moment, waiting for the ideas to sink into Yokoyama's thoughts, then asked: "Are there any other fears?" The question was asked half jokingly, but Yokoyama took it seriously.

He said: "History shows that the United States has been advancing steadily westward. Doesn't that show that Japan has something to fear?"

"Why, no, not at all," I answered. "Let us analyze our so-called advances westward. We were involved in the war with Spain, and one day we woke up and had the Philippines on our hands. If it had not been the oppressive policies of Spain which forced us into the war, we would have given the Philippines back to her at once. But we preferred to think of the Filipinos and pave their way toward self-government. Even so, we gave Spain twenty million dollars. Then there's Guam. I think you know as well as I do that it's good for nothing."

For the first time the slight tension was broken as Yokoyama burst out in laughter.

"Yes," he said. "It's worth nothing."

"Then we get to Hawaii. Our advance there was at the real request of the people of Hawaii. They have prospered and have been happy ever since. So, you see, our advance was really a push from behind."

"This is all very interesting," Yokoyama said with visible relief. "But how could these things you have just told me be best conveyed to the people of Japan? You see, their fears are very real and are being fanned every day by so-called patriotic speakers and the newspapers."

"It has to be done gradually," I answered, "because with the present state of mind of your people it might have no effect if it is done too quickly. I think a great many of your statesmen and politicians themselves realize the situation but are reluctant to take the people into their confidence."

"Do you think," Yokoyama asked, "that to have some prominent people of ours come over to the United States before the next disarmament conference to talk about these things and then go back and tell the Japanese people about their conversations would help?"

"A man like Admiral Nomura?" I asked.

"Yes, a man like Admiral Nomura," Yokoyama answered with enthusiasm.

"I think it would be splendid if he and others could come over here to talk, but he musn't talk about armaments. He must stick to the things that we have talked about, frankly and without reserve."

For a few moments Yokoyama remained thoughtfully silent, then he turned to me and said with genuine feeling:

"This talk has been very interesting and beneficial. I would like to have more talks like this before I return to Japan next month, because I want to do what I can to create a more friendly feeling between Japan and the United States."

"That is the only way it can be done," I said. "I'm sure that you noticed the friendly feeling that all the people here had for you yesterday afternoon, both the men and the women. They were delighted to meet and talk to you. Some of them had been in Japan and some had not, but all felt the same way. You know well that the feelings of the west coast are the result of purely economic problems, which you handle in exactly the same way in Japan, especially in your attitude toward Korean and Chinese laborers. So those of you who know the problem and found a way for its solution ought to prevent such questions from being put in other lights, arousing hatred between the peoples of our two countries."

We drove back to Newport, and Yokoyama took his leave. I had noticed a slight tension in his bearing and attitude upon his arrival. It was all gone now. He was friendly, relaxed, almost buoyant. Above all, he seemed convinced. But Yokoyama was only one Japanese; and although he might have had some influence, as one who had spent some time in the United States and was intelligent enough to review the situation with an open mind, he did not have much success in the face of the odds he encountered upon his return to Japan.

Nevertheless, he attached himself to a group within the Japanese Navy which shared his thoughts and convictions. This group was led by Admiral Yonai, the same Yonai who used to sit in on our conferences during the early twenties in the Shimbashi tearoom, when we discussed identical problems with Nomura and Nagano. Of the three men, two retained their original convictions and their opposition to war against the United States. The third man, Admiral Nagano, joined the rabble-rousers and became, next to Yamamoto, the most rabid advocate of war against us. But Yonai retained his influence; and although he had lost most of his battles for peace, he did win the last one when he became influential in paving the way for Japan's surrender. In that very moment, Yokoyama was at his side, perhaps repeating to him fragments of our conversation on the seashore in Newport—so many years before.

15

IN THE PINCER OF SPIES

I REALIZE THAT this chapter head sounds somewhat loaded with melodrama—words borrowed from those same pulp magazines which I have derided on another page. But if the chapter head now appears a bit melodramatic, so were the years just ahead of me when for the first time since World War I the United States was again caught in a pincer of spies. The sudden arrival of enemy operatives in a peaceful country is a sign, only too often disregarded, that the country has been singled out as a military objective in the plans of aggressor nations. Spies precede invading armies and air fleets, and their appearance should reveal to the watchful observer the plans made in foreign countries behind closed doors of operations sections of busy general staffs. France was infested with German spies in the 1860's in preparation for the campaign of 1870-71. Belgium was crowded with German agents in 1912-13. There were many Austrian operatives in Serbia in 1913. As it was then obvious that these countries were singled out for conquest by the Prussians, the German Reich, and the Austro-Hungarian monarchy, so it was obvious to me in 1934-35 that the United States was moving into the forefront of German and Japanese aspirations as I watched the sudden influx of their operatives into this country and the increase of subversive activities.

After an absence of almost three years, spent at sea and in the Naval War College, I was now back in what I like to call my natural habitat. Waiting for me in Washington was my old job at the head of the Far Eastern Section of the Office of Naval Intelligence.

When I departed in 1931 I had left a section still understaffed and overworked, woefully inadequate as a truly effective part of our defense system. But now in 1934 there was a different atmosphere, a refreshing breeze filling for the first time the sails of Naval Intelligence. The effects of withdrawal from our commitments as a great sea power no longer existed. The Navy Department was wide awake to its responsibilities as the nation's first line of defense. Still hampered by certain defeatist influences, especially in our diplomatic circles, and by isolationist indifference pervading some sections of Capitol Hill, the Navy was nevertheless going ahead full speed, bolstered by the support it received from the White House and its Navy-minded occupant.

The change was evident in every bureau in the Navy, but it was particularly gratifying in Intelligence. At the head of Naval Intelligence now was a man who was the ideal planner, who, though always intolerant of stupidity and inaction, inspired his subordinates with the enthusiasm which filled him too, and showed the way to considerable achievement by his own ingenuity, energy, and devotion to duty. He was Captain William Dillworth Puleston, USN, one of the few great directors of Naval Intelligence we have had. The progress which our office made under his leadership is even today visible in every phase of our intelligence activities, since he understood how to activate on a practical basis many of the tasks which had remained dormant under his predecessors. He enabled us to carry out our ideas as long as they were constructive, and he was willing to shoulder the responsibilities when and if some of us stepped out of line in the course of investigations. During those years Naval Intelligence was happy in the increased activity; and they were, indeed, probably the greatest years of development in our intelligence field.

There was work aplenty when I reoccupied my Far Eastern desk with an adequate staff at my disposal to carry out the tasks. A short survey of activities in which the section was engaged convinced me that we were on the receiving end of the battle of espionage. During previous years I had concentrated on intelligence in its positive aspects; but now that the "enemy" had deployed his secret services against us, my assistants and I became counter-intelligence men; that is, instead of seeking primarily to gather information about the "enemy," we sought to prevent his gathering information about us.

Shortly after my arrival in Washington an informant sent to us a Japanese book which provided convincing evidence that the United States was now in the path of Japanese expansion. At first sight the book seemed innocuous enough, just a child's book prepared for Japan's boys and girls to entertain and amuse them as our own children enjoy the adventures of the Wizard of Oz. But a closer scrutiny of this book for children revealed that here we had to do with a different kind of entertainment. The book was the most candid revelation of Japanese plans for the future we had seen up to that time. Especially so was one of the crude little illustrations which betrayed the ambitions of our adversaries. It showed two Japanese boys standing on what the caption called "the New Map of the Empire." The boys themselves were martial enough, one dressed in the Army uniform with steel helmet, the other wearing the Navy uniform, banzai-ing to their hearts' content, with arms lifted and mouths wide open in their unrestrained enthusiasm. The map itself on which they were standing encompassed the whole Pacific from the Philippine Islands to San Francisco and Mare Island. Little Japanese flags with the rising sun on them indicated the steppingstones of Japanese conquest. One was flying from the spot marking the Philippines, another on Guam, a third on Hawaii, and a fourth on San Francisco. The Army boy stood on the Philippines and Hawaii, while the Navy lad had one foot on Guam and the other on Mare Island, symbolically assigning different tasks to the Japanese Army and Navy.

After I had studied this book and come to realize its significance, I recommended that we send the original with complete translation to the White House. This was done, and the data were immediately brought to the attention of President Roosevelt. If there was hope that the Japanese still had only peaceful aims, or any illusion left anywhere along the line, I felt that this picture would serve to dispel it. It was received by the President with amazement and interest and undoubtedly had a bearing on the shaping of our future policy which led up to his famous Quarantine Speech in Chicago when he suggested that we isolate the aggressors.

To us in the Far Eastern Section of Naval Intelligence the picture was the bugle call to general quarters. It emphasized the danger we were facing even then and outlined for us the task just ahead. But while we were thus concentrating on the menace from the Far East, we were made to realize in a forceful manner that a pincer was being prepared for the United States by subversive forces deployed from the other side as well. Hitler's Germany had joined with Japan in the secret war against the United States.

In a book autographed and sent to me with the words: "To Captain Ellis M. Zacharias, USN; if you like this, it will be the highest praise of all," I now have just reread the following passage: "At the time no one in the United States Government knew that a

Nazi spy ring was in existence here. No one even suspected it, not even the Federal Bureau of Investigation, or G-2, the United States Military Intelligence. The idea would have seemed too preposterous. Why should Nazi Germany conspire against our national defense?"

These lines were written by one of the best G-men that that exceptional investigation and law-enforcement agency, the FBI, has ever employed—Leon G. Turrou. It is possible that in 1935 these authorities did not "even suspect" the existence of a Nazi spy ring in the United States. If his account is correct, and the FBI and G-2 were not aware of the beginnings made, it is a significant revelation of the complacency with which we defended ourselves against these Nazi agents. As for our own organization, Naval Intelligence *did* suspect the existence of the Nazi spy ring, as indeed the Nazis rather than the Japs provided us with our most important assignment in 1935.

On September 25, 1935, the motor ship *Europa,* pride of the German merchant marine, was about to sail for Bremen. Her pier in New York was crowded with passengers, relatives and friends, officials and inspectors, as is usual with every departure. Flowers were delivered to staterooms, parcels arrived for departing passengers, little farewell parties were in full swing in the cabins, and acquaintances were boarding the ship to say *bon voyage.* Among the visitors, just prior to her departure, was a lean, bespectacled man carrying a violin case as he boarded the ship. A member of one of our most efficient agencies, the U.S. Customs Service, always alert in these contingencies, stopped the man on deck with the question:

"What kind of violin have you in that case, mister?"

The little man took the inquiry lightly, used as he was to the leniency of the inspection on such festive occasions.

"Oh, just an ordinary violin," he answered nonchalantly.

"Is that so? I am greatly interested in violins. Would you mind letting me see it?" the guard asked, still in a casual way.

Nervously the little man opened the violin case, and there was his violin. But as the guard lifted the violin from its berth, he saw beneath it a collection of pictures all showing American planes, some of them in the experimental stage. The guard assumed a serious attitude, since it was obvious to this minor guardian of the law that fate had confronted him with a spy. He replaced the violin, closed the lid, and quietly beckoned the man to come along with him. They left the ship and went to the office at the head of the pier. The guard called in his superior, the man was detained, and contact was established with the Army Intelligence office at Governor's Island.

The head of the G-2 office was not available, but a subordinate came immediately to the pier to inspect the spy and his pictures. He was a private and not particularly impressed with the importance of his job; he was sufficiently aroused, however, to call in an officer from G-2 before he made his decision. The situation became tense, and the man with the violin case visualized himself in great difficulties as his little game was rapidly drawing to its ignoble close revealing him as an espionage agent. His dejection now indicated there was little hope left in him, especially when he saw the American officer entering the customs office to decide the case. The newcomer turned to the man.

"What's your name?" he asked.

The little man hesitated for a moment considering the advantage of giving an alias; but realizing that the game was over, he decided to be as co-operative as possible, hoping thereby to save his skin.

"William Lonkowski," he said. His accent revealed him as a German.

"Well, Mr. Lonkowski, what have you there?" The officer looked at the pictures of the planes, considered the case for a moment, then turned to the guards with a statement which flabbergasted everyone present:

"I don't see anything wrong with these pictures. Anybody might have them. You may go," he said as he turned to Lonkowski.

Lonkowski did not know what to make of the situation. He was suspicious that they were playing some trick on him. Possibly they wanted him to depart so that they could shoot him and then explain that he was shot while trying to escape, the favorite mode of execution employed by the German secret police. He did not move but remained there staring at the officer with incredulous eyes, refusing to believe his own ears. The officer grew somewhat impatient and repeated his words:

"Didn't you hear me?" he asked. "You may go!"

"I can go?" Lonkowski repeated. "I am free?" he asked slowly and uncomprehendingly.

That was the end of the inquiry. Lonkowski did not try to recover the photographs. He just put the violin back into the case and hurried away. The case was closed insofar as G-2 was concerned. A notation in the G-2 files on Governor's Island, in a folder labeled "Spies," was all that remained of the incident in official records: "William Lonkowski," it read; "suspected spy; reported 9/25/35 by U.S. Customs and United States Military Intelligence." That was all, the barest outline of a major incident which minor officials permitted to slip through their hands.

But even while G-2 was satisfied with the solution of the case, the customs guard was not. On the following Monday morning when Naval Intelligence operatives were making their routine rounds on the water front, one of them was told of the occurrence the previous Saturday. The pictures were still in the office and were shown to the naval investigator.

"Holy smoke!" the man exclaimed. "These are naval experimental planes. What happened to the guy who had them?"

The customs guard just shrugged his shoulders. "G-two let him go," he said.

The naval investigator broke into language which will not bear reproduction. When he recovered from his fit of anger he called his office to report the incident. Washington was called at once; Captain Puleston was advised and asked for instructions. A few minutes later I was called to the Director's office, where he related the details of the case to me and then ordered me to "jump into a plane for New York immediately and see what this mess is all about."

Within two hours I was sitting in the office of our district intelligence officer listening to a tale that was almost impossible to believe. What could still be done to save the situation? It was immediately obvious to us in Naval Intelligence that we had stumbled upon a major lead. I decided to proceed to Governor's Island to contact the head of G-2 of the Second Corps Area, whom I found in his office. He was Major Joseph N. Dalton, an officer generally respected as an able intelligence man. But regardless of the fact that he was handicapped by having only two assistants, I could not be tolerant about the handling of this particular case.

"Major," I said to him, "to me this is a pure case of espionage, and I feel that your people should have communicated immediately with Naval Intelligence, especially since the pictures involved are experimental naval planes."

Major Dalton was still not convinced. In an offhand way, he just said:

"Well, it did not seem like much to us."

I wasted no further time in argument but hurried back to the district intelligence office to start the ball rolling at once. It was evident that anything we could do was too late. Even so, we rushed an investigation which led to the Long Island house where Lonkowski and his wife boarded. As expected, the birds had flown. A bewildered landlady told us that Lonkowski's wife, after a phone call from him, had left hurriedly for an unknown destination and for an indefinite period. There was no forwarding address, although they had left behind all their scant furnishings.

It was no longer a case for counter-intelligence. From now on it was a case of investigation. We determined that Lonkowski had made only one stop in his flight at a house, not on 92nd Street, but actually at 56 East 87th Street, in which a certain Dr. Ignaz T. Griebl had an apartment. We succeeded in establishing Lonkowski's itinerary by rushing to his home address provided during his interrogation. There a patriotic landlady helped us with all the information needed to retrace his movements to the Canadian border. We had the help of others who observed Lonkowski during his flight, including an omniscient elevator man. And at that time it was possible to trace the numbers used in numerous telephone calls made from his home. Further investigation developed that Dr. Griebl was a key man in the Lonkowski group, despite the fact that he was a reserve officer in the Medical Corps of the United States Army. Lonkowski warned Griebl that the group was uncovered. Then he proceeded to call his wife by phone and told her to draw all money out of the bank and leave by ship the next day. Lonkowski then went to Canada in Dr. Griebl's car and was never heard of again, having sailed for Germany on the first ship out.

The incident was not quite closed insofar as the Germans were concerned. When the *Europa* returned next time, the steward whom Lonkowski had tried to see was no longer on board, but somebody with a heavy German accent went to the office where Lonkowski had been detained.

"Is this the office," the man asked, "where a certain William Lonkowski was detained some time ago?"

"Yes," the guard answered. The man started a conversation in the course of which he tried to ascertain the circumstances of Lonkowski's escape, especially to find out whether it was true that Lonkowski had paid $1,000 for his release. When the inquiry had ended, the man was thoroughly convinced that no money was involved in Lonkowski's release, and we had no doubt that the Gestapo would take good care of Herr Lonkowski for fraudulent claims on the German treasury.

I hurried back to Washington and reported to Captain Puleston. It was evident to us all that the improper initial handling of the case had destroyed a major lead and thereby deprived the United States of the opportunity of quickly smashing an important Nazi spy ring. Even before we learned that Lonkowski had been able to warn Griebl, it was fully expected that the original detention and subsequent release would cause the whole group to become inactive for an indefinite period, which is what happened.

When I told the story to Captain Puleston, he could not repress his feelings. He immediately proceeded to write a letter to General Knight, the head of Military Intelligence, expressing his opinion in no uncertain terms. His letter was not a funeral oration over spilt milk. It had a constructive purpose. Captain Puleston tried to impress upon the Army the necessity for a unification of effort, the activating of Army intelligence resources and pooling them with the Navy so that a similar slip would never happen again. For the time being the case had to be ended in this unsatisfactory manner, with an opportunity slipping out of our hands through blunders over which we had no control. Three years later headlines announced the disclosure of this Nazi spy ring, but they were just three years behind schedule. During that period Dr. Griebl and his crowd were living on borrowed time—but they could not escape their eventual fate.

It was in 1937 that Leon G. Turrou actually succeeded in cracking the German spy ring. It may be remembered that at that time the stupidity of German Intelligence and the low quality of their agents enabled American investigative agencies to follow important leads given them by British Intelligence and subsequently destroy a dangerous Nazi spy ring recently reactivated in the United States. Working on a tip from a postman in Dundee, Scotland, they picked up a woman, Mrs. Jessie Jordan, an elderly hairdresser, who was being used as a "mailbox" for the German Intelligence. By then German Intelligence in the United States had been revived by employing Günter Gustav Rumrich, a deserter from the United States Army, whose activities were disclosed by MI-5, the counter-intelligence section of the British War Office.

The spy ring was again made inactive—two years after Lonkowski's adventure in New York, and two years after Naval Intelligence had succeeded in determining the identity of the group. Even so, it was a considerable accomplishment for which well-deserved gratitude was widely given to those involved in the solution of the Nazi scheme. What happened in 1937, however, had its overture in 1935, and in fact could have been concluded then had all been fully aware of the dangers we were facing at the time.

16

THE BATTLE OF ESPIONAGE BEGINS

THE SIGNIFICANCE of the Lonkowski case of 1935 cannot be exaggerated. It was the first sign that Germany was back in the espionage business after seventeen years of hibernation. Prior to World War I, German espionage was a truly formidable weapon in the hands of the Prussian empire-builders. Bismarck prepared for the Franco-Prussian War by hiring the mysterious master spy Dr. Stieber and giving him full powers to prepare for the war by moving a whole army of spies into France to pave the way for Moltke's invading armies. Between 1868 and 1870, Stieber moved no less than 30,000 spies into France in a move which, in the words of Georges Bourgin, of the French National Archives, was similar to the "softening-up" campaign preceding both world wars.

"Germany took as careful precautions for the World War of 1914-1918 as for that of 1870," Bourgin wrote in his description of the German pattern of espionage. "Espionage was facilitated by the large number of German nationals who were settled in foreign countries, and by the wide extension of German trade. The eastern areas of France in particular were riddled with German agents—agricultural workers, domestic servants, hairdressers, commercial travelers, German teachers, many of whom posed as Belgians, Swiss, or Luxembourgians."

Stieber's successor in preparation for World War I was a Machiavelli in the uniform of the German General Staff, a personal confidant of the notorious General Ludendorff, a colonel named Walter Nicolai, chief of Section III-B of the operations division headed by Ludendorff himself. World War I found Nicolai in sole dictatorial charge of the German spy system, although some of the overseas espionage was done by a woefully inefficient group within the German Admiralty. They were by no means a match for those under Sir Reginald Hall, chief of the British Naval Intelligence, who was fully justified in describing his German opponents in words which are even today quoted with approval by all intelligence experts. "The German Intelligence Service," Sir Reginald said, "is as superficially clever as it is fundamentally stupid." Nicolai's activities provided the confirmation to this statement.

But Nicolai was a ruthless and unscrupulous spy master who was devoted to secret service work with the unconditional devotion of an ascetic monk. When in 1918 Germany's defeat became final, he retired from active duty, but he did not retire from secret service work. In his opinion the Armistice of 1918 did not put an end to World War I. He implored the Germans to remain in the ring and continue the struggle with the subversive means of a secret service. "War in peace," he wrote in a book entitled *Secret Powers:* "that is the proper definition of the present role of the intelligence service. Intelligence service cannot be hit by disarmament, because propaganda, its positive side, would displace military operations and become more than ever a political weapon. For this reason," he wrote in 1921, "the intelligence service stands on the threshold of new tasks." In the same book he provided the basic principle by which German espionage is always guided: "Intensified espionage," he wrote, "must precede intensified armament for war."

The democratic Weimar Republic of postwar Germany was in no mood to translate Nicolai's principles into action. In fact, the Versailles Treaty prohibited the maintenance of a German intelligence service; but as with every other provision and stipulation, this one also was flagrantly violated by the Germans. Within a camouflaged general staff, also prohibited by the peace treaty, a concealed secret service was maintained, called Section of Foreign Armies and Statistical Bureau, the former maintained for military and political, the latter for economical espionage work. But it was a far cry from Germany's aggressive espionage system under Nicolai. The head of the German intelligence service during the Weimar Republic was a gentlemanly officer of high ethics—Colonel Fritz Bredow, who refused to conduct aggressive espionage activities and confined the activities of his organization to the collection of information available in public or semipublic sources. Although there were a few operatives maintained in neighboring countries, especially in Poland, no agents were sent by Bredow to France or Britain or the United States. It was evident to those of us who checked up on the intelligence activities of all of our potential adversaries and watched rather carefully the espionage work of the Germans that, except for sporadic activities, German intelligence work was more or less dormant as the Reich tried to fit herself into the family of civilized nations.

Hitler's seizure of power in 1933 brought a fundamental change. Like Bismarck before him, Hitler was a firm believer in secret service work. His whole character and psychological make-up guided him in this direction; and he practiced espionage and fifth-column methods on an unprecedented scale even during his Nazi party's struggle for power between 1926 and 1933. When later he was in control of the Reich, he tried to force his ideas on a reluctant German General Staff. But Colonel Bredow resisted the pressure and incurred the wrath of Hitler and Nicolai, who was himself back in the saddle acting as Hitler's chief adviser on all espionage and secret service matters.

Colonel Bredow was in their way. He refused to carry out Hitler's instructions and was even more reluctant to work with Nicolai. It was evident to both Hitler and Nicolai that they could not carry out their secret service plans as long as Bredow was in charge of German Intelligence. But Bredow had the backing of the German General Staff and especially that of General Kurt von Schleicher, a powerful force within the German armed forces, himself a chancellor just prior to Hitler's own seizure of power. The blood purge of 1934 provided the long-sought opportunity to get rid of both Schleicher and Bredow. On June 30, 1934, a special squad of SS men went to Schleicher's home in a suburb of Berlin and killed him with five shots fired point-blank. They then rushed to Bredow's office in the Bendlerstrasse, dragged him from his desk in the War Ministry, and "liquidated" him in the courtyard. The day after Schleicher's and Bredow's elimination Nicolai moved in and, acting upon Hitler's authority, started the establishment of an aggressive German intelligence service to operate in France, Britain, and the United States.

The comeback of German espionage in the unmistakable Nicolai manner was first detected by MI-5 of the British War Office, which was fortunate indeed to have in the person of Colonel Cox a most ingenious and skillful counter-intelligence officer at its head. Early in 1935 a German agent named Hermann Goertz was arrested in England. He was mapping the airfields in Kent which provided a defense ring in front of London, the first German spy to appear on the scene since 1918. Simultaneously a German spy ring was uncovered in Czechoslovakia, and another in Belgium, the latter working under an agent named Leo Pees, who was trying to obtain the fortification plans of the Liége military zone. By early 1935 the French Deuxième Bureau estimated that five hundred German agents were active in France. Among them was an agent named Otto Baltes, who obtained plans of the Metz fortification system controlling the entrance to Alsace-Lorraine, and also a French officer, Captain Georges Froge, who sold detailed plans of the Belfort fortifications to other German agents.

It was clear that German agents would soon arrive in the United States as well, and the Lonkowski case proved to us in 1935 that Nicolai had extended his activities to the Western Hemisphere with the establishment of a haphazard and inferior spy ring, but a spy ring nevertheless.

Colonel Nicolai had still another plan and obtained for it Hitler's wholehearted support. He worked on the establishment of a German-Japanese spy alliance partly to benefit from the information at the disposal of the Japanese intelligence services and partly to speed up the establishment of a huge German espionage network by obtaining for it financial support from the Japanese. His idea was simple enough. He tried to convince the Japanese that only Caucasians could do effective espionage work for them, since Japanese agents are easily detected by their appearance. He also argued that the White Russian operatives, widely employed by the Japanese, no longer provided all the data needed and were in the long run unreliable since they worked independently in an unco-ordinated effort and without the backing of a sovereign state.

German Intelligence made a formal offer to the Japanese to pool their resources and employ German agents wherever Japanese could not work. Nicolai also offered to place at the disposal of the Japanese all data obtained in their European theater of operations and to organize a network in the United States, if only to supplement the material obtained by Japan's own agents. The proposition seemed fair enough to the Japanese, and the decision was reached to implement the plan by action. A Nazi spy named Eugen Ott, later German ambassador to Japan, was Hitler's own agent in General Schleicher's circle and provided information even while he served Schleicher as a confidential aide. He was entrusted with the task of liaison between the German and Japanese intelligence services. Another experienced spy, Von der Osten, known to Allied counter-intelligence agencies from World War I (and later killed by a taxicab in New York while on a secret mission but not connected with the atom bomb), was also sent to the Far East to prepare the ground for the co-operation. In 1935 the agreement was definitely reached; and even while the Axis pact was several years in coming, the German-Japanese spy alliance became reality, German spies working for the Japs, and Japanese agents working for the Germans. The meeting place of the two systems was the United States.

Although these facts are now confirmed history, in 1935 the agreement between Germany and Japan was for a long time a suspicion only, and it was vitally necessary to secure confirmation.

I confirmed it to my own satisfaction in the fall of 1935 during a party given by the Japanese naval attaché in the Mayflower Hotel. This naval attaché was Captain Tamon Yamaguchi, whose suave manner and broad knowledge of the United States, gained during his long period as a "language officer," made us feel that he would bear watching. He was not so tall as Admiral Nomura, but still he was large for a Japanese and impressed one at first sight. Although his eyes indicated acuity, they nested in an impassive face that reflected a quiet, cold, efficient determination. There was a general cleanliness about him.

When the Japanese decided to intensify their espionage activities in the United States, they made him the center of their activities and established him with all the paraphernalia of secret service work in an office at the Alban Towers, a fashionable apartment house in Washington's residential section. If evidence was needed to confirm the intensification of Japanese espionage work in the United States, Yamaguchi's arrival in Washington provided it. I for one had no doubt that his transfer to Washington was of the greatest significance, and Captain Puleston shared fully my apprehension. Yamaguchi's appearance on the Washington scene was a storm warning and alerted us fully to our responsibilities and immediate duties. I made occasions to see Yamaguchi as often as possible, both officially and socially, and Yamaguchi did not try to avoid me. I became a permanent fixture at all his parties and was of course one of the guests at the Mayflower party as well.

The future Axis was well represented at this affair. The Italians were present, and so were the Germans in the persons of their military attaché, a smooth operative named Lieutenant General Friedrich von Boetticher, and their naval attaché, Vice Admiral Witthoft-Emden, an old-timer who had been the gunnery officer of the World War I cruiser *Emden,* a somewhat more noble representative of the ignoble Nazi game. That afternoon I was struck by the changed relationship between the Japanese and German attachés. During previous get-togethers their relationship had been casual, formal, almost cool. But now there were apparent closeness and warmth in their contact, completely missing before. The Germans now felt at home at Yamaguchi's party.

The Mayflower party was held in the Chinese Room of the hotel, an unwitting but grim little gesture these Japanese often used to make. At these Japanese parties I always made it a point to stay until all the other guests had departed, both as a mark of appreciation to my host and also to take every advantage of the opportunity to practice my Japanese. I noted that on this occasion Yamaguchi's newly won German friends tried to outstay me. General Boetticher and Admiral Witthoft-Emden remained close to Yamaguchi even while most of the other guests were departing. On previous occasions they had been among the first to leave.

As soon as I noted this unusual occurrence I sought my wife and advised her that something was afoot, explained what I had observed, and said that we must stay to the end to see what was going to happen. I advised her of my plans not only in order to forestall pressure from her that we, too, go home but also to utilize her keen powers of observation to supplement my opinions. The guests were by then rapidly thinning out; and as we observed from across the large room, the two Germans again went over to Yamaguchi's side and fawned upon him in a manner that was too noticeable. I tried unobtrusively to find out what was behind this sudden friendship, but nothing was volunteered by the other Japanese. I therefore reached the conclusion that some kind of agreement had been formed or was in the making between the Nazis and the Japs, and that it was the friendship based on this alliance which made Boetticher and Witthoft-Emden glue themselves to their new ally even at this seemingly social function. I told my wife: "I am certain that there is a new development in German-Japanese relations. Watch those two Nazis clinging to Yamaguchi. They have never acted like that before. The fools are too obvious in their suddenly found love for the Japanese."

It was soon evident that the Germans were irked by our presence at a time when everybody else had departed. Our little game of staying to the end was getting on their nerves, especially when the waiters gave unmistakable signs that insofar as they were concerned the party was over. At last, when Yamaguchi took notice and all of us left the Chinese Room together, I had the satisfaction that it was my wife and I who left with Yamaguchi, while the Germans departed just ahead of us.

Next morning I went to the Director and told him of my observations. He agreed with my conclusions. We were all certain that from now on we should have to contend with the Japanese working in close alliance with the Germans, injecting a new element of danger. The battle of espionage now was fully joined, and events were moving into high gear. We were still on the eve of developments in this combined espionage, but they were gradually expanding into all spheres of our national security, to reach their climax in the attack against Pearl Harbor.

There was no doubt in my mind that the party in the Chinese Room of the Mayflower Hotel would have its continuation in China itself, since I remembered the plan provided by Sato-San in the early twenties which marked out China as the first step of Japanese aggression. But beyond China loomed the greater adventure: the war against the United States, blocking by its moral indignation the road to conquest.

As I prepared to leave Captain Puleston's office, I said to him: "There are busy days ahead for us, sir."

"I would not be surprised," he answered, his eyes focused on the open window but his facile mind looking into the immediate future beyond the narrow confines of his simple office. "But they'll find us ready, won't they?" he asked.

"We are ready now, sir!"

17

THE DOCTOR TAKES OVER THE CASE

WHILE OUR activities were necessarily transferred to counter-intelligence to an ever increasing degree, our intelligence work continued in the field for which a pattern was established in 1927. In that year, watching the Japanese fleet exercise from our ambush by radio, we had succeeded in gaining considerable valuable information on their tactics; and radio intercepts had ever since remained an important means of our intelligence work; but it was not until 1933 that the technique developed six years before was used again, now on an unprecedented scale.

In 1933 the whole Japanese fleet was assembled for grand maneuvers, providing us with a unique opportunity to eavesdrop on their communications and find out what they were trying to ascertain from their gigantic exercises. By then the system so primitively tested in 1927 was highly improved, and several radio stations were picking up the messages passing between Japanese ships participating in the fleet problem. Reams of paper poured into our offices giving data and details, and we worked hard and long to put together the innumerable little pieces of information obtained on so many different receivers to form a complete picture of the whole. In 1935 the great work of analysis was completed and the purpose of the grand maneuvers revealed to us. It was a game of war, somewhat in the defensive field, since the Japanese assumed for the sake of this exercise that in a war of the Pacific an enemy would gradually approach Japanese shores. The features of the problem simulated wartime conditions in that phase of the war which was to take place close to Japan proper, an event that came to pass in reality several years later when Admiral Halsey's Third Fleet did steam up to the very coast line of Japan in the crescendo of the closing months of our war against Nippon.

The Japanese strategy prepared for this eventuality was revealed in their games and was now typed out on neatly prepared sheets before us. Their plan was to lure an attacking force into a gigantic trap prepared of coastal submarines and shore-based aircraft, to hold back all defensive forces for a huge last operation in which they planned to open up everything they had and annihilate the attacking force in one single effort, just as they did with the help of a divine wind (Kamikaze) centuries before with the invading armada of Kublai Khan's Mongolian forces. Their confidence this time did not rest in supernatural forces. They planned that their air forces should substitute for the divine wind, delivering the decisive blow at the decisive moment.

We outlined in specific detail the whole Japanese plan, and as our analysis was distributed to higher echelons it brought understanding praise and commendation for Naval Intelligence. Only one officer, interested in ship movements but not in the movement of Japanese ships, showed remarkably little interest in this shape of things to come. When the plan and analysis was shown to him, he just shrugged his shoulders as if to say: "Those impertinent little Japs!"

I recalled this significant little incident a few years later when I heard that this same officer was given a responsible command where the defense of the United States depended on him. And when those impertinent little Japs confronted him with a ship movement in dead earnest, he revealed, to the detriment of the whole nation, that he would have been better prepared psychologically for his overwhelming task had he devoted greater attention to the analytical activities of Naval Intelligence.

While we were thus parading our analysis of the 1933 Japanese grand maneuvers with justifiable pride, marking another milestone in the work of Naval Intelligence, our attention was by necessity focused on events much closer to home. Captain Yamaguchi was about to come up to bat, and we were ready to pitch the first ball.

The district intelligence officer of the 11th Naval District reported to Washington an espionage case of considerable proportions, the first big case of counter-espionage since the end of World War I. All hands in Naval Intelligence and especially in the Far Eastern Section were assigned to help in the investigation, since the case threatened to have repercussions on the highest diplomatic level, including our relations with Japan. At the apex of the pyramid of spies was Yamaguchi himself, master-minding this particular case, although there was still another spy master over him whose existence at this stage was not yet known to us. It was left to later counter-intelligence work to uncover the chief of all Japanese espionage in the Western Hemisphere, the most efficient and powerful spy ever to work in this country on behalf of a foreign power. For the time being, however, Yamaguchi was in command in the center of a web which extended from Washington to the west coast. His immediate representative on the coast was a Japanese language officer, Lieutenant Commander Toshio Miyazaki of the Imperial Japanese Navy attending the University of California, where he majored in English. It was known to us that he was interested in many things only remotely connected with our tongue, and we had him under general surveillance. This was a difficult task, since Miyazaki was a highly skilled intelligence officer, a man of considerable personal initiative and ingenuity who understood how to camouflage his extracurricular activities at the university. But he was tripped up by the vigilance of an ordinary American citizen.

Indeed, the co-operation of the public is one of the greatest props of an intelligence service as long as no spy scare is created and the persecution of aliens as alleged spies does not become a national psychosis. The American people have always shown not only great ingenuity in spotting malefactors but also admirable restraint in confining their own activities as amateur sleuths to cases where their suspicion proved justified. Some of the greatest catches in the field of espionage have been made on tips received from the public. Their observations reflect credit on the intelligence and enlightened patriotism of the American people. It is usually a simple person, a janitor, a housewife, or a bus conductor, who provides the most valuable tip, never expecting reward beyond the satisfaction that he has performed his patriotic duty. These unknown heroes of our counter-intelligence work fully deserve a part of the recognition which the nation so generously and lavishly extends to law-enforcement agents and intelligence investigators when the arrest is made public in glaring headlines.

In the Miyazaki case a beachcomber in the San Pedro area named William Turrentine was the first to give us a lead and helped us follow through. He appeared one day on the deck of the flagship of the Commander in Chief of the Pacific fleet and demanded to see the Admiral at once.

"I have something important to tell him," he said.

"How about telling it to me?" the officer of the deck asked in a semijocular way.

"You ain't high enough," Turrentine answered. "I wanna see the big boss." He was escorted to the executive officer, but Turrentine insisted: "You ain't high enough either. Take me to the big boss." The Admiral's aide was summoned but was greeted by Turrentine's stereotyped: "You ain't high enough, I wanna see your boss."

"What is the nature of your business?" the aide inquired. "I'll have to tell the Admiral what you want to see him about." This sounded reasonable to Bill Turrentine; so he said: "I wanna tell him about some Jap spies I know."

A few minutes later the simple California beachcomber was in the presence of Admiral Joseph M. Reeves, USN, Commander in Chief, United States Fleet.

"I understand you have information about certain spies, Mr. Turrentine," the bearded admiral said to the beachcomber, who was not unduly impressed by the dignity of the occasion.

Turrentine replied: "Yes, sir. I'm living with one of them."

"Well, tell us all about it," Admiral Reeves encouraged him as they sat down to discuss the case.

"I am living with a man named Bill Thompson, Admiral. He is a bum seaman, was once an enlisted man in the Navy but got kicked out—I dunno for what. Well, I see this Bill Thompson getting into uniform again, going to the ships in the harbor, picking up some papers, coming home, and hiding them in his room. So I get suspicious and keep watching him. And I'll be darned, Admiral, if he doesn't slip those papers to some Jap I see him meeting in town. Now this Bill Thompson is a faker from top to bottom, Admiral. He was only an enlisted man, but whenever he now goes to one of our ships to pick up those papers he wears a chief petty officer's uniform. He must be up to somethin' no good, Admiral."

"It seems he is, Mr. Turrentine," the Admiral answered, "and I want to thank you not only for myself but in the name of the United States Government for your patriotic conduct in this case. I can assure you that we will take good care of your friend; but of course, we shall not be able to tell you the details of our investigations. You would greatly help our work if you would keep quiet about the whole affair and leave the rest to us. You have done more than your duty, Mr. Turrentine, and the nation is grateful to you." The beachcomber was quite moved when he heard these dignified words and merely said: "That will be fine, Admiral. So long, sir."

The moment Turrentine closed the door, Admiral Reeves called for his aide.

"Get that man Coggins," he said. "Let us see if he can handle the case." This was an unorthodox decision, for "that man Coggins" officially was no intelligence officer, no investigator, no detective, but a naval surgeon specializing in obstetrics in the Long Beach Dispensary of the United States Navy. He delivered from thirty to sixty babies per month and saw innumerable out-patients every day; but somehow he still found time to read all books published on espionage and intelligence, and had become an expert on intelligence. He had written reports about the dangers of the Japanese fishing fleets off the west coast and similar items which had come to the attention of Admiral Reeves. It was natural, then, that when a real case was brought to the Admiral's attention his first thought was to let the Doctor handle it. "I have a hunch he'll get us results," the Admiral said.

Coggins was overwhelmed with joy when he was thus permitted to turn his hobby into reality. In a sense, the case was a simple one. Thompson was a typical victim of foreign intelligence agents, a former Navy man going downhill after his discharge, getting drunk more often than he could afford, in need of money, and gradually drifting toward the net thrown out for his type by the Japanese then operating on the west coast. Finally, he had met Miyazaki and made the momentous deal. He would put on a chief petty officer's uniform, go on board a strange ship, go down to the gunnery office, and introducing himself as the gunnery yeoman from another ship in port, obtain classified material not otherwise accessible.

Coggins had a fine grasp of counter-intelligence methods and fully appreciated their difference from pure investigation, a technique with which it is so often confused. He went to work. By careful "shadowing" and close observation by himself and his assistants, the patterns of Thompson's daily life and that of the Japanese suspects were established.

Thompson would return from the ships, go to his apartment, hide the documents under the carpet, change to mufti, then go into Los Angeles for a meeting with Miyazaki, when he turned over whatever he had obtained, or made arrangements for delivery by mail to the Japanese operative. They usually met in or near Pershing Square in Los Angeles; and it was there that Lieutenant Coggins watched a transaction take place—the last he was to permit Thompson to carry out.

All the evidence was now collected. Coggins had examined stolen documents under the carpet in Thompson's apartment and, through other extensive means of investigation, established an unbroken chain of evidence which was turned over to the United States attorney for prosecution.

But just before the arrest could be made, Coggins lost sight of Thompson for a day and was considerably worried. He met Turrentine again and learned from him that the fake yeoman had mentioned something about going to see the Japanese naval attaché in Washington. We were immediately notified of this turn of events, but Thompson did not leave Los Angeles. His absence was due merely to his participation in a drinking bout.

Until then the office of Naval Intelligence had only indirect control over the Thompson case, since Coggins had completed the investigation for the Commander in Chief and had turned all his evidence over to the United States authorities for prosecution. At that time Naval Intelligence was, and it still is, without the vital power of arrest, although it is the most interested party in investigations involving naval security. Coggins was therefore in no position to make the arrest himself. He could make only a "citizen's arrest," which is permissible under the law when a crime is evident. But means were found to have Thompson expediently detained until the proper papers were prepared and competent authority could come in on the case to take the accused off Dr. Coggins' hands.

It soon developed that those in authority were reluctant to prosecute Thompson, despite the evidence on hand. Washington feared international complications because high Japanese naval officers were directly involved in the case, and the line of espionage led into the rarefied air of international diplomacy. Even in the face of incriminating evidence, with Thompson actually dangling in the net, the United States attorney was told by higher authorities not to prosecute unless he could guarantee a conviction. But who can guarantee a conviction without specific laws against espionage? We were up against the usual impediments which in the past did so much to undermine the ultimate effectiveness of our work: loopholes in our statutes against the secret armies which try to learn our national secrets. It was one of our first espionage cases.

Title 50 of the U.S. Code involves "intent" and other hampering phrases. It was now our task to convince the U.S. attorney that he could get a conviction. At this stage I was assigned to assist, and I flew to Los Angeles for a conference with Mr. Pierson Hall, then United States attorney and now a federal judge. I assured him that a California jury would certainly not be prejudiced in favor of a spy for Japan and urged him to go ahead with the prosecution, but he still needed the green light from Washington.

Almost changing from plane to plane, I hurried back to Washington for a meeting with the assistant attorney-general, Mr. Brian McMahon (now U.S. senator from Connecticut), who was in charge of the case at the Washington end. He was sympathetic but said that the authorities needed five more pieces of evidence before they could prosecute.

"What are they?" I asked, and he named them one by one. "Assuming we provide you with these additional pieces of evidence, can you then prosecute?" I asked.

"Yes, we can," Mr. McMahon said.

I had the evidence required by the Department of Justice on Mr. McMahon's desk by nine o'clock next morning, and the prosecution of William Thompson could begin. They were simple facts already a part of the evidence but they were submerged in voluminous data and not yet arranged to the satisfaction of the legal mind. By then, Commander Miyazaki had left the scene. He suddenly took a ship for Tokyo and departed from our jurisdiction, a relief to many as it might have been considered injudicious to involve him directly in the proceedings. But Thompson received fifteen years at the McNeil Island Penitentiary and is still there, paying for his crime, at the time of this writing.

The Thompson case concluded, we still had Captain Yamaguchi on hand. His apartment-office was now under constant surveillance. Again patriotic Americans in the vicinity were our greatest source of information and help. The few agents available to us were sufficient only to guide them properly in their observations. Yamaguchi's visitors were checked and rechecked. He himself was considered *persona non grata*, although we persuaded the higher authorities not to act upon this designation and send him back to Tokyo. We felt that such an action would destroy our leads, which were rapidly developing evidence against him, and would cause us to start our investigations from scratch with a new man coming in and spinning his own web. Also, we were in the midst of another investigation closely connected with Yamaguchi himself. Our investigations during the Thompson case had revealed that a white man was among his regular visitors, arriving in a car bearing a Maryland license plate. The car was registered in the name of "Barrett," and a further checkup revealed that the owner of the car was the divorced wife of John S. Farnsworth, a former lieutenant commander dismissed from the United States Navy.

Farnsworth was already under suspicion, but now we became convinced that our suspicions were justified. Over a considerable period he made visits to the Navy Department and asked many questions of acquaintances. One alert individual who thought this strange in view of the past bad record of Farnsworth made a report of it to ONI. Our investigation took note of the people visited and the questions asked, which were mainly technical in nature. It was evident to us that there was something behind Farnsworth's activities. But most of his former friends with whom he was in contact ridiculed the idea. One of these I had to caution that he might be sorry if he were careless in what he disclosed to Farnsworth. This individual was greatly surprised one day later when he was ordered back to Washington from the west coast to testify in this case.

Our suspicions regarding Farnsworth were fully confirmed when he made a visit to a destroyer in Annapolis. He was in civilian clothes and when met at the gangway by the officer of the deck, a young ensign, Farnsworth said: "I'm Farnsworth, class of 1915. I would like to check something in your book on ——," referring to a book with a confidential classification. The officer of the deck had the foresight to ask: "Are you still in the Navy?" Farnsworth knew the implications of misrepresentation and replied in the negative. He was not allowed to see the book. But later in the Navy Department he did extract another one from the desk of an old friend when the latter was momentarily called out of the room. The loss was discovered shortly thereafter and Farnsworth was apprehended —with the book. This was his undoing. We covered him completely, closed in, and obtained all the evidence that was needed for his arrest. I need not delay this narrative by outlining the Farnsworth case in detail. That unpleasant incident has already received more publicity than it deserved. From our point of view,

Yamaguchi rather than Farnsworth was the real villain of the case, and when the ex-officer was out of the way, safely locked up so that he could do no more harm, we turned our undivided attention to Captain Yamaguchi, preparing a trap for him into which he was obliging enough to fall.

18

DOUBLE AGENTS AND DIPLOMATS

It was now evident to all of us engaged in the maintenance of our national security that the Japanese campaign of espionage was in full swing, but it was not yet clear what the Japanese were after. The Thompson case revealed that our adversaries were interested in details of American gunnery. Farnsworth was a general handyman supplying the Japanese with all kinds of odds and ends, whatever he could pick up through his contacts around Washington.

These two cases, important though they were, provided no clues to the real interests of the Japanese secret service in the United States. From the point of view of counter-intelligence and also for a variety of operational reasons it is always of vital importance for us to know what we call the "shopping list" of prospective enemy intelligence services. With that we can better safeguard those particular secrets which we know interested aliens or their agents are anxious to obtain. Secondly, the knowledge of the enemy's intelligence objectives reveals to our operational agencies the orientation of the enemy's high command and permits an estimate of their intentions, the most difficult part of intelligence work. And finally, the opponent usually reveals his own deficiencies by seeking to obtain the secrets of other nations in order to compensate for his own shortcomings.

In the past, and chiefly in European espionage of the so-called classical school, practiced in the secret war between Germany and her neighbors to the east and west, the so-called *Aufmarschplan,* or deployment plan, was the prize objective of secret service agents. This was a part of the whole operational plan prepared by general staffs, revealing the opening moves of a war in considerable detail. The possession of this *Aufmarschplan* enabled the prospective victim to make his own dispositions, not merely in anticipation, but in actual knowledge of his opponent's moves, thereby enabling him to frustrate these at the outbreak of hostilities.

In view of their great actual and potential value, the deployment plans are the most carefully guarded secrets of all war offices and admiralties in Europe. But it has happened occasionally in the history of espionage that a major power has succeeded in obtaining the deployment plan of its future opponent—although it is possible to obtain these plans by means other than espionage: by observing the fortification system of a prospective enemy; by watching changes in his battle order insofar as it concerns the distribution of his military and naval personnel, and by observing the trend of the annual maneuvers. The French thus learned the first version of the Schlieffen plan in 1905; while Moltke gained knowledge of the French deployment plan in 1870 partly through the so-called General Staff trips to the future Franco-Prussian battlefields, during which the necessary observations were made, and partly through the activities of his brilliant master spy, Dr. Stieber, who worked in France with thousands of agents prior to the outbreak of hostilities.

The outstanding example of one major power obtaining the deployment plan of another through pure espionage was the case of Colonel Alfred Redl of the Austro-Hungarian Army. Colonel Redl was chief of the Austrian secret service and had access to all military documents, including the famous deployment plan which Field Marshal Conrad von Hötzendorf designed for a future war against Russia and on which the entire fortress system in Austrian Poland was based. It was not known to his superiors that he had certain personal weaknesses which made him susceptible to blackmail. This fact, however, became known to the Russian military attaché, Colonel Zubowitz, who approached Redl through a young man who he knew had been intimate with Redl. Zubowitz confronted Redl with the alternative: "You either work for us or we will expose your personal life." But at the same time Zubowitz offered to pay him well.

As a result of the treasonable activities of Redl the Austrian chances for success against Russia in the war of 1914 were greatly impaired, because it was found impossible to make radical changes in the fortress system on which their deployment plan was based.

The United States has been handicapped in the preparation of its plans since we, as a democracy, are habitually *not* stimulated for war. Our plan for the so-called M-Day was the subject of many newspaper articles; and although not all of its details were made public, so much was revealed that our prospective opponents directed their energies from this particular subject to something else, especially so when a certain Midwestern newspaper revealed its final version in great detail on the eve of Pearl Harbor.

Enemy agents working in and against the United States were chiefly interested in technical and tactical data, in the details of our technological progress, especially in naval designs. Since our army's real development must always wait for the war itself, our geopolitical situation requires that the Navy continually advance as the nation's only standing force in defensive strength. This was the main reason why the Japanese concentrated on our naval secrets rather than the negligible ones of our small peacetime army, thereby making the counter-espionage work of Naval Intelligence far more complicated than that of G-2.

Quite aside from this fact, G-2 was handicapped by a policy which has always prevented during peacetime the development of reserve officers who would contribute to proper expansion prior to the outbreak of actual hostilities. For some reason never clear to me there was a departmental order which prohibited Military Intelligence officers from requesting a reserve officer on inactive duty to obtain information or to check on a case in any manner whatsoever. This, regardless of how vital the need might be or how favorable the position of the reserve officer for such work. I often provided G-2 with evidence on which to base a request for such implementation; but whenever a G-2 plan was forwarded to higher echelons seeking peacetime provisions, it was invariably returned with the endorsement: "Nothing will be done until M-Day."

We were speculating about the Japanese intelligence objectives and preparing our own countermeasures when Lady Luck, the most important confidential agent of any intelligence service, provided us with an original document prepared by the Japanese themselves. Through the ingenuity and skill of an undercover operative we succeeded in luring an important Japanese agent, Lieutenant Ohmai, into a momentary diversion. Since our own officers have occasionally encountered such disagreeable experiences, it might be of advantage to indicate the dangers to which the traveler carrying confidential or secret documents is exposed. One of these officers "lost" his brief case from a hotel room in Davenport, Iowa, not long after he had told an inquisitive Japanese female, Miss Sakanishi, the route he was taking to the west coast. She was one of Japan's best operatives in the United States, screening her activities as an employee of the Congressional Library.

In the case of the Japanese intelligence agent Ohmai, it was not too difficult to take advantage of his susceptibility to feminine beauty and entice him from his own hotel room to another for a period of fifteen minutes. We felt repaid in full for the previous loss of the brief case. When Lieutenant Ohmai had extricated himself from the baited trap, he had left behind a document of the greatest significance. It was the "shopping list" of the Japanese intelligence service. It was an exceptionally long list, marked "Most Secret" by its authors in Tokyo, and contained in its various extensive sections details for procuring practically all the secrets of our military and naval establishments. One part was devoted to an outline of tactical information needed by the Japanese, including tactics in night combat. Another was devoted to means of identification and recognition signals; others to education and training, ability of our battleships and heavy cruisers in combat, and our fleet movements.

Just as our psychological warfare later envisaged the use of known characteristics of individual leaders, the Japanese then had an intense interest in the various outstanding men in the U.S. Navy who they felt would be in positions of leadership in the Navy in tomorrow's war; their life histories, character and conduct, peculiarities, special abilities, ideas regarding the art of war, career records, records of promotions, duties, and articles published by them. Japanese agents were instructed to determine the organization of our intelligence services, and the instructions indicated the means by which espionage should be conducted.

This was an extremely comprehensive list, in which, by enumerating individual items, the Japanese made significant comments on their own deficiencies, permitting us to draw up our own ideas of their shortcomings and, to a certain extent, their intentions. The great emphasis on night tactics and night actions indicated to us that they were counting heavily upon combat after dark, but while they were putting most of their eggs into this one basket, we were busy developing our own countermeasure—radar.

While we were exploiting this significant document and tightening our security measures to block the avenues leading to the secrets listed in the intercepted list, another document falling into our hands revealed in even greater detail the primary interest of Japanese Intelligence. It became known that the Japanese had managed to obtain access to one of our 8-inch turrets and that they were particularly eager to get as much data as possible on our new 8-inch projectile. With this information at our disposal and Captain Yamaguchi's activities under surveillance, Japanese Intelligence had few secrets concealed from us. The question now was how could we best exploit the material in our hands to the detriment of our adversaries by turning their own secrets against them?

We decided to employ a device well known in intelligence, requiring exceptional skill and caution to make it effective: the system of *double agent*.

This, indeed, is a time-dishonored by-product of intelligence, usually practiced by unscrupulous agents who are willing to serve two or more masters as long as they are willing to pay. The famous Mata Hari was such a double agent, and similar double agents can be found among professional spies whose motivation is their own self-interest rather than patriotism. But the best double agent is the individual whom the enemy or prospective enemy has approached to do espionage work for them but who reports the fact to us and subsequently agrees to work for us instead.

In this case which I relate, the Japanese had approached our man after lengthy observation of his meager circumstances and the fact that he worked in an important activity of the Naval Gun Factory. Such facts are easily ascertained by enemy agents, and that is why in my lectures to interested groups on "plant security" I advised them to "be careful of the company they keep during social hours."

As soon as our man, whom we will call Jones, was approached by the Japanese, he proceeded immediately to the Office of Naval Intelligence, where, after hearing his story, he was fully instructed how to "play ball" with them.

Thus we did not take risks in selecting our own double agents because we exercised great care in picking men whose patriotism was beyond the shadow of a doubt and whose integrity could be relied upon implicitly despite the involved nature of the work in which they were engaged.

The plan was simplicity itself. We knew exactly the items which the Japanese were keen to obtain, these details being confirmed by inadvertent references in conversation designed to extract information from unsuspecting and gullible personnel whom they met at social functions. So we decided to make these items available to them—but in slightly altered form, the one element which usually made the item a guarded secret either changed or removed. The material prepared was then to be given to a quasi operative who had been approached by Captain Yamaguchi or one of his underlings. The flow of information to the Japanese secret service would thereby be fully controlled by us. They would obtain only what we decided to give them—de-secretized "secrets."

It was a juggled blueprint of the new 8-inch projectile which was first given for delivery to Captain Yamaguchi. It was real in outward appearance, but the blueprint was prepared under the supervision of proper naval authorities who determined that all the improved data were carefully removed. When the double agent reported to Captain Yamaguchi, with his precious commodity, he was received with open arms and an open purse. After the Captain had made a cursory examination on the papers he handed Jones $500 in crisp notes for his services, an exceptionally high price in the business and paid only for scoops.

We were awaiting our double agent's return from his first excursion to Captain Yamaguchi with considerable anticipation; and he, too, was greatly excited when he reported back with his mission successfully accomplished.

"Here," he said, "he gave me five hundred bucks for the blueprints."

He was told to keep the money as a just reward for his services, and we permitted him to retain whatever funds the Japanese were willing to pay for his later deliveries. One condition was that he must keep us advised of every cent he received from any Japanese. However, it needed quite a bit of persuasion to convince him that he was entitled to the money and that it would not be held against him. The play progressed as planned, and money originally set aside for the "Manchurian Incident" found its way into bottomless wells.

But we counted without the lady in the game. The wife of our double agent became suspicious of his sudden affluence and began to ask embarrassing questions. We advised him to start a separate bank account and resume his regular style of life, for the present at least.

I hope that if the good wife reads this account she will recognize and appreciate the situation of over ten years ago, about which we had to keep her in the dark.

Since our double agents were active not merely in Washington but elsewhere, we received from one of our confidential informants in Detroit still another clue revealing particular subjects in which the Japanese showed intense interest. An exhibition of military aircraft was arranged in Detroit by an Army Air Corps group from Wright Field, Dayton, Ohio, displaying among others a radio direction finder which was high on the Navy classified list of secret devices. The Army had an adaptation of it, and though Naval Intelligence had worked long and hard to keep it secure, it was suddenly opened to public view by courtesy of a few overzealous public relations officers.

The attention of our confidential agent was attracted to the instrument when he watched a single Japanese who displayed unusual curiosity, then left immediately to put in a long-distance call to the "'inspector" of the Japanese Naval Purchasing Office in New York. Next morning our man was not surprised by the sudden appearance of several other Japanese visitors showing unconcealed interest in the exhibition. They were armed with cameras, notebooks, and blueprints. Our man in Detroit did not, of course, know the particular secrets of the device, but he was satisfied that when a Japanese displayed such an obvious interest, it must be of great importance indeed. Accordingly he phoned us in Washington and told his story. We got in touch with Army Intelligence and requested withdrawal of the instrument from the show. This was done immediately; and when the officials of the Japanese Purchasing and Intelligence Bureaus in New York City arrived by plane in Detroit the next day, July 26, 1935, in response to the summons of their local agent, this particular secret commodity had disappeared from the open market. So great was the significance of the device to them that the Japanese officers had flown to Detroit in a chartered plane; and when the big boss, Captain Sakurai, arrived from New York and found only the empty spot where the instrument had been, he was so violently indignant that he began to use abusive language to one of the guards when the instrument could not be located.

We now had a fair idea of the scope of Japanese Intelligence in the United States: we knew the layout and the particular subjects and objects in which they were interested. But we still did not know the means by which this information was sent out of the country. We did not know the machinery of Japanese Intelligence headquarters. So we sought additional information on the working methods of Captain Yamaguchi.

As I have already mentioned, the Captain lived and worked in two adjoining apartments at the Alban Towers, situated at the corner of Massachusetts and Wisconsin Avenues. The patriotism of certain other individuals in that apartment was fully established through their willing and comprehensive co-operation with our efforts to determine and follow up clues which the Japanese intelligence officers provided quite abundantly. It was now essential to make the most of these contacts in order to close in on Japanese Intelligence headquarters. We hoped that a simple method of surveillance would provide us with most of the information we needed, and planned to have an apartment occupied across the narrow court so that we could watch the goings-on in the Japanese office. It being summer, we expected that the shades and windows would be raised occasionally; but we were sorely disappointed when, armed with powerful binoculars, we occupied our battle stations behind the curtained windows of our own apartment. We waited patiently for days, then weeks, but the windows across the court were never opened, not even for a breath of fresh air which must have been badly needed. This reluctance to raise the shades served to increase our suspicions. In fact it convinced us that something very mysterious was going on behind them.

We became determined to make an inspection of these rooms, and finally a plan was drawn up in considerable detail requiring the co-operation of several operatives and even disguise, a method rarely used but usually effective when employed. The plan contemplated the removal of all key personalities from the two apartments—Yamaguchi and his aides—leaving only a subordinate staff on the premises such as a clerk and probably the chauffeur, who might be a bodyguard as well as a petty officer in the Japanese Navy. We realized that it would be impossible to empty the apartments entirely because our previous observations had revealed that the apartments were never left unattended. But we calculated that with the "big shots" safely diverted, it would be easy to deal with the "small fry." Opportunity was to be provided by the occasion of a dinner party given by me at my house on Porter Street in honor of Captain Yamaguchi and his staff, with attendance quite obligatory by the provisions of our strict Washington etiquette. The dinner, however, was but one phase of our little plot.

The second phase was to take place in the apartment house itself in two distinctly separate but nevertheless interconnected sub-phases. One of these provided for the lights to go out. It had been arranged previously for the lights in the Japanese apartments to go out periodically but to return almost immediately so that the temporary failures would appear to be due to some minor disturbance such as the installation of a new fuse. This had been repeated on several occasions to make it appear normal when the lights went out the night of my party.

The dinner party was held on schedule, Captain Yamaguchi and his aides bowing themselves into our house and making themselves comfortable around the improvised bar at which cocktails were carefully prepared to match their tastes—and to make them forgetful of the cares of the office. As I poured the refills, their contented smiles assured me of their unconcern as well as their genuine pleasure at the informality. The attendance at the dinner surpassed my expectations. Yamaguchi's whole office staff was present, and at my suggestion they had brought along their out-of-town guests, some language students from various universities. I had made a careful check to determine who might be in Washington on this particular evening so that they might be included, and now as I made a mental roll call I felt sure that only the clerk and chauffeur were absent. The stage was set.

I calculated that just about when the third round of cocktails was being handed to my guests, the lights in Yamaguchi's apartment would start to flicker, become dimmer and dimmer, and after a short show of electrical caprice would go out altogether, leaving the two attendants in darkness. I was aware of the timing of the show and kept myself close to the telephone to answer any possible calls from the Japanese clerk who might want to ask his captain for instructions. My plan was to advise him to call the desk in the lobby and ask the attendant there to do something about the lights. But he was an ingenious fellow and needed no advice. He phoned the desk himself, just as we anticipated.

The night clerk was full of apologies, went up to the apartments himself to survey the situation, and then announced regretfully that this was a job for professional electricians. He would send up a couple to restore the lights. A few minutes later two workmen dressed in the overalls of the trade and loaded with handbags full of the instruments of their craft knocked at the door.

"What's the trouble, Bud?" they asked and were told:

"Many weeks these lights too bad, go out, hope you fix good this time."

"We'll sure fix'em all right," one of the workmen answered.

"What's back here in this room?" His extra-powerful flashlight was sweeping the apartment from corner to corner, knowingly and expertly, since the layout of the rooms had been carefully studied by him prior to his entry into the apartment. He knew that the room to which he referred was Yamaguchi's inner sanctum, the actual objective of his penetration. It was his mission to get into that particular room, to survey its contents, and to find out what the Japanese were concealing in it. In the broad beam of the flashlight he now saw the open door leading into the inner sanctum; so he beckoned to his colleague and said:

"Come on, Jim, we'll look at these ceiling sockets in here."

Thus began a most minute inspection of all electrical equipment, walls, and *everything* in each room. The search was designed to reveal whether the Japanese operated their own radio transmitters and whether they had a mechanical coding machine. For both, they needed power. The survey of their coding machines would have provided us with important data, and we hoped to pick up tidbits of incidental intelligence once we were inside their camp. Now we were there, and the powerful flashlight traced the contours of the safe and other paraphernalia of intelligence techniques so long and so carefully protected from our eyes.

The men had to work expertly and fast if they wanted to escape suspicion, and they were fully up to standards both as investigators and electricians. By the time we were settling down to our soup, served in Japanese lacquered bowls which were calculated to provoke conversation on Japan and relieve any possible tension, back in the apartments one of the men exclaimed: "Here's the trouble, Bill! We've got a short right here."

After several minutes of tinkering, tape-winding, and other show of diligence, the men retired to the basement to finish their job—to put back the fuses which had been judiciously blown for the occasion. The lights flared in the apartments; but when the men returned to check on their success and started into the inner sanctum again just to make sure that everything was all right, the clerk stopped them on the threshold in a friendly tone which carried finality: "Thank you very much, you no can go in there."

"O.K., Bud," the electrician answered. "I'm sure everything will be all right from now on."

Their inspection by flashlight had covered everything we desired, so there was no point in pressing the survey further. The two electricians packed their bags and made ready to go when the clerk pulled two shiny twenty-five-cent pieces from his pocket and slipped the tips into the palms of the men. These two coins are still interesting souvenirs, as is the memory of an amusing little incident which took place in my house while the inspection was in progress.

We were assembled in my living room in animated predinner mood when I observed Commander Jo, an aviator and one of Yamaguchi's assistants, sitting next to a little table which held a silver cigarette box embossed with the crest of the imperial family, a cluster of fourteen chrysanthemum petals around a circle symbolizing the rising sun. The emperor himself has a crest of sixteen petals, but other members of the family are limited to fourteen. I saw Commander Jo's eyes wander to the handsome silver box, and he became transfixed looking at the crest. A sudden tension gripped him as he straightened up in his seat, and his face suddenly turned from jovial indulgence into solemn attention, almost devotion. For a moment he seemed to disbelieve his eyes. Then, using his index finger he started to count the petals, one, two, three . . . twelve, thirteen, fourteen. The Imperial Crest! As he reached the fourteenth petal a look of incredible solemnity came over his face, his hands dropped to his lap, and, sitting up straight, he made a deep bow to the cigarette box.

The dinner party was a great success, and the result of the examination conducted by the "electricians" was most satisfactory, for it revealed that there were no provisions for a short-wave or other type of radio sending set. And secondly the fact was confirmed that the safe was so small it could not house a coding machine of any consequence. It further assured us that all work of this nature was being done in the embassy on Massachusetts Avenue. If Yamaguchi was suspicious, he was discreet or shrewd enough never to mention anything to me beyond praising the delicacies and our hospitality, which were especially lavish on this particular occasion. I am recalling this incident in the hope that our own people will be made aware of the pitfalls in the game and will show a better consideration for security when exposed to the pretense of similar inspections. Lest some parsimonious reader complain about the waste of government funds on dinners and disguises, I might add that these activities were carried on at my own initiative and at my own expense. No reimbursement was requested by me or offered by the United States government when the final report of these activities was submitted.

While the sudden caprice of electric installations was by no means a common phenomenon, such dinners were quite regular occurrences behind the Washington scene. It was nevertheless surprising when, shortly after my own expedient party, I received an invitation to attend an intimate little dinner in the home of Takemi Miura, first secretary of the Japanese Embassy. We had frequently been invited to the houses of Japanese, but the invitations were usually given at least two weeks in advance; and unless it was otherwise indicated, it could be assumed that other nationalities would also attend. This time, however, the invitation came on the shortest notice, asking us to dinner for the next night, and we were told that we (Claire and I) would be the only ones other than Japanese present. These two indices were sufficient to assure us that it was to be a dinner for a purpose other than a merely culinary one. And so it turned out.

When we arrived at the apartment on upper Connecticut Avenue and Tilden Street, the guests were already assembled. The first to greet us was Miura himself; then Colonel Matsumoto, the military attaché, shook hands, and Army and Navy officers came up one by one. Captain Yamaguchi was the only individual of importance who could not be present, and when I first noticed his absence, I smiled at the coincidence. Otherwise the cream of the Japanese Embassy staff and service attachés were all in attendance. We were the only Americans. This occasion was to present another opportunity for intelligence to co-ordinate its efforts with diplomacy.

The dinner proceeded as is usual for these Washington gatherings, with the conventional chatter in an atmosphere heavy with the aroma of savory dishes. Finally we were escorted to an adjoining room where the coffee was served together with a dish of strawberries, causing me to remark to Claire in a muted voice: "Is this a straw in the wind?" Her glance convinced me that she too suspected something important coming up for service after the strawberries.

The cups were no sooner removed and cigars lighted than there settled an anticipatory quiet over the small but tidy room, interrupted by the coughing of Miura, who cleared his throat for a statement. His eagerness caused him to utter a betraying "Now!" before he launched into a little speech:

"Zacharias-San," he said, "we would like to discuss this evening Japanese-American relations."

The memories of Yokoyama's visit to Newport came flashing back to my mind, and I prepared myself for a similar *quid pro quo* of arguments in a strangely different setting.

"I would be delighted, Mr. Miura," I answered casually. "What is on your mind?"

The opening sentences of this discussion duplicated almost word for word my conversation with Ichiro Yokoyama, but then the conversation drifted back to history and the Russo-Japanese War, which revealed a different aspect of our relations.

"Let us go back to 1904," I said, "since I am certain you know that at the time there was the most friendly feeling in the United States toward Japan."

"Yes," Miura said, "that is correct."

"I wonder if you know that this friendly feeling once saved Japan from a most serious embarrassment, and more than that, from a considerable material loss?"

"Oh-o-o, that is astonishing!" Miura exclaimed. "How could that be so?"

"Well," I said, "as the Russo-Japanese War progressed, President Theodore Roosevelt realized that Japan had miscalculated the risks involved, not expecting a prolongation of the war beyond a few months; and since she was unprepared for a protracted campaign, she could not last very long, despite the splendid fight she was putting up." All those in attendance listened with exceptional eagerness. "Your military advisers realized themselves that the war had reached a critical stage for Japan. Were it to last for three or four months, Japan would exhaust her resources, and she would be defeated. Colonel Matsumoto"—I turned to the Military Attaché —"you remember the situation, don't you? Is that not correct?"

"That is quite correct," the Colonel answered with unexpected emphasis and finality. It was obvious to all in the room that I had won a great point. Although this version of the Russo-Japanese War was generally accepted by us, it was the first time that I had been able to obtain an admission from any Japanese, and particularly a military man, that it was an accurate appraisal of the situation. Only those who know Japan intimately can appreciate what an admission of this kind before a group of Japanese really signified. It meant that the Japanese themselves had never doubted the accuracy of that statement although heretofore they had avoided open admission of the fact.

I seized the opportunity which had thus opened up before me: "As you know, President Roosevelt stepped in and offered his services to bring about peace. The offer, previously encouraged by certain Japanese sources, was eagerly accepted by both parties. Then came the negotiations at Portsmouth and a peace treaty was finally signed. Japan asked an indemnity of two billion yen from Russia. President Roosevelt was fully aware of Japan's motives for starting the war; and knowing Japan's military situation at that particular stage of the conflict, he recognized that Japan was not entitled to the indemnity. Then what happened? Instead of being grateful to the American President for his intervention, the whole of Japan, led by a vicious press, turned against the United States. The propaganda disseminated in your country was readily believed by your people, and a resentment against the United States was artificially generated. Mind you, it was a one-sided resentment. Despite all the mud thrown at us we continued to harbor the kindest feelings toward Japan. But, although you realized that those artificial ill feelings could lead to no good, you have permitted them to rankle and continue throughout the years. Here, then, in undeniable detail, is the origin of present strained relations between Japan and the United States."

There was general agreement, and it was not motivated solely by politeness. I could see in the faces that a deep impression had been created by citing this historical example, an impression which was strengthened when I recalled other examples of more recent history, coming eventually to the Immigration Bill which excluded Japanese immigrants from the United States and resulted in still another anti-American campaign in Japan.

"You know as well as I do," I said, "that the bill was inspired purely by economic and not by racial considerations. The basic fault lies with the Japanese government, which permitted thousands of Japanese to emigrate but failed to inform them that as immigrants they would have to conform to the standards of the people among whom they planned to settle. When Japanese immigrants arrived in the United States, they proceeded to disregard all our living standards and way of life and continued the daily practices to which they were accustomed at home. They worked sixteen hours a day and were soon underselling our west coast farmers with whom they were competing. This was bound to bring conflict of interest."

"This is a very interesting new point of view," Miura interrupted. "Please go on, Commander."

"I would like to ask you a question, Mr. Miura. How does Japan handle such an economic situation?"

"I am really not aware that a similar economic situation exists in Japan," Miura answered.

"But it does exist," I answered. "I was on a ship once returning to Japan from China. When we arrived at the pier, all the passengers were lined up on the deck. The Chinese were separated from all other passengers. After a careful examination of all passports, a different group of your officials went to work on the Chinese, and I watched the procedure most carefully. First they asked each one of the Chinese if he had one hundred yen. This was known to be a requirement, and all of them had it. Then they started at the head of the line again and asked each one why he was coming to Japan. Everyone who stated that he was coming to Japan to engage in an activity competitive with Japanese labor was told to move to the other side of the deck. When they had finished with the hundred Chinese originally lined up, eighty-five had been told to go to the other side of the deck. The next step was to collect fifteen yen from each of the eighty-five Chinese. An official then said: 'Follow me!'; and he did not say it in the customary polite tone of the educated Japanese. The Chinese went with him; and as I followed them with my eyes, I saw them file down the pier to another ship which was tied up there. In fifteen minutes they were aboard that other ship; she sailed—for China, to return this competitive group to its point of origin. Now you must realize that we have never practiced such an extensive and inhuman form of exclusion."

There were sheepish looks as my Japanese hosts glanced at each other, but the tension was suddenly eased when Miura rose, came over to me, and in a friendly gesture put his arm on my shoulder. "You should have been a diplomat, Zacharias-San," he said, his words releasing general laughter in the rest of the group, who had been silently attentive all through my little lecture. The "discussion" was over. It was clear, frank talk designed to carry far. It was intended to go from this group to their superiors both here in the United States and in Japan. Japan was already far advanced on the road of aggression, but it was still hoped that she might be stopped before she went too far.

19

AN ANTHROPOLOGIST
TURNS STRATEGIST

THE JAPANESE and German friendship, first made evident at the love feast which we had witnessed at Yamaguchi's party at the Mayflower, had now assumed the proportions of an "engagement," encouraging a stream of German visitors to Japan. This initial infiltration became an influx of students and advisers, and in return an increasing number of Japanese military experts went to Germany to return the courtesy, to study the growing military might of the Third Reich, and to buy from the Nazis those implements of war which they could not obtain in the United States either by purchase or by stealth.

We had adequate information on the increasing influence of the Nazis in Japan but regarded their influence as confined to the Army alone. The Japanese military attaché in Berlin and the German military attaché in Tokyo were the two heads of the axis around which this new courtship revolved. General Hiroshi Oshima, who had gone to Germany by 1936 and established himself in his luxurious offices in the Tiergartenstrasse of Berlin, was the chief plotter. We had a good pen picture of this ambitious Japanese officer who was close to General Doihara and other notorious backers of Japan's plans for world domination. We knew, from reports of our military and naval attachés in Berlin, as well as from other sources, that Oshima was motivated in his pro-German orientation by an almost morbid infatuation for Adolf Hitler. He was under the spell of the Führer and completely absorbed by his admiration for the so-called accomplishments of Nazism; in fact, he became a Nazi himself, more Nazi than Japanese. In him the Germans had a willing tool to promote their aims in Tokyo. In lengthy reports, to which we obtained occasional access by effective intelligence, he outlined the progress of Germany under Nazism, emphasizing the military and naval developments and stressing the ultimate aim of these advances—war!

At the Tokyo end the Nazis built up a network of agents composed of their best operatives working under the guise of diplomats. Eugen Ott, the Nazi spy, had by then become a general and was named ambassador to Japan, the first time that an agent was given this high diplomatic rank in Japan. Assisting him were two outstanding men of the German air and naval establishments. The air attaché was General Gronau, pioneer in trans-Atlantic aviation and the man whose duty it was to survey the air route to the United States from a military point of view. The naval attaché was Admiral Paul Wennecker, a slippery Junker, who would profess his anti-Nazi feelings today but would be completely devoted to Nazism tomorrow. Behind them was a whole hierarchy of Nazi officials working feverishly to establish contacts, to place them on a firmer basis, and to gain support for the Nazi plan which was then prepared for Japan. They were all extremely well supplied with money, and when the wheels of treachery were slow in turning, they used these funds to oil the machinery. This was later confirmed by Admiral Nomura in my conversations with him and also by an editor of the newspaper *Osaka Asahi*.

Ever since our first suspicion of the formation of the German-Japanese spy alliance we had watched developments at both ends of the axis and expected that co-operation between Germany and Japan would be carried from the field of espionage to that of diplomacy and politics. What was the plan? It was a grandiose scheme for world domination in which Germany and Japan would divide the spoils between them. Hitler dreamed of building his by localized wars, and then a simultaneous conflagration at both ends of the earth, Germany attacking in the west and Japan attacking in the east. He planned to engulf the whole world in one single conflict to which Ludendorff gave the name of total war. It was to be a New Order, as the Germans called their system, replacing the Old Order which, Rudolf Hess said in 1937, had outlived its usefulness.

With all their efforts and bribes, however, the Germans were still on the fringes, and their influence did not penetrate deep enough. It was known to us that very powerful forces within Japan resented the German arrogance and preferred to develop their own plans independently. But what was to become the Tripartite Pact soon afterward was already taking shape in Washington as well as in Japan.

I tried to line up the forces as they existed in 1936–37 and to separate the pro-Germans from the rest. At that time it was very difficult to find genuinely pro-German elements in the highest echelons of Japan's military and naval hierarchy. It was also a fact that on these levels there was a distinct opposition to co-operation with the Nazis and especially in circles close to the Imperial Palace. The Emperor himself was an enigma. I had met him in several separate audiences in his younger days and gained the impression that he was a man of average intelligence who regarded himself as a constitutional ruler somewhat in the British sense.

During those days of ferment the Emperor permitted himself to drift with the current rather than, as our diplomats averred, trying to swim against it. He watched events perhaps with open eyes but was unwilling to change their course. He acted neither as a brake on the militant jingoes nor as a stabilizing influence, as some of the observers preferred to regard him. In his inactivity he gave encouragement to our opponents, the chauvinistic group who were even then preparing for the so-called Greater East Asia War.

Aiding us were a few important personalities in both diplomatic and naval circles. They were not motivated by any pro-American feeling or genuine sentiment for our ideas or way of life. They were motivated by realism. One of these men was Admiral Kichisaburo Nomura, my old friend from the days when he was himself director of Japan's Naval Intelligence, and Admiral Yonai, the former Russian language officer who rose eventually to the position of Navy Minister. Both were definitely opposed to a pro-German orientation but had limited power to prevent it, although they did succeed in slowing it down. As far as we could ascertain, there was only one Japanese admiral to favor a German alliance, another Nomura (Naokuni), a submarine expert who was influenced by his admiration for German accomplishments in U-boat warfare. The Nazis worked on him, but he was still fighting a lone struggle inside the Japanese naval high command.

This then was the line-up. The militarists, misled by Oshima's glowing reports from Berlin and influenced by Eugen Ott's bribes in Tokyo, were drifting toward a Nazi alliance to aid the realization of Hitler's ambitious plot. The navalists were still sitting on the fence; and although they were turning to the south with glances gradually increasing in their expression of greed, they were still reluctant to risk bringing these desires to reality.

Back in Washington, the situation had quieted down. By means of the effective blows which we were able to deal, we had crippled the Japanese intelligence system in the United States. Yamaguchi had read in the newspapers of the indictments of his agents and could not fail to realize that his network was fully uncovered and that we knew as much about his activities as was wholesome for any intelligence organization to reveal. His dilemma was a considerable one. He had to decide whether to continue his work here or to give up the struggle. He decided for the latter course, and shortly after I left Washington, Yamaguchi also returned to Tokyo. He was far from being in disgrace. Shortly after his return he was raised to the rank of rear admiral, and joined the faction of Admiral Yamamoto and the group within the Japanese naval high command which was preparing for war.

In June 1936 I was ordered to sea duty in the cruiser *Richmond* with the knowledge that my work in Washington had been well done and the Japanese espionage ring was as good as destroyed. Upon receipt of my orders, which Captain Puleston delivered to me "with regret," he gave me this oral injunction: "You may be going to sea duty, but you must consider yourself always a part of Intelligence.... Continue your work wherever you are." I appreciated his expression of confidence; but while retaining my interest in intelligence, I necessarily devoted almost undivided attention to the exacting requirements of sea duty, especially when another fleet problem provided me with a singular opportunity to test Japanese potentialities from their point of view. In this new fleet problem, prepared for execution in 1937, my ship was to play the role of Orange, a designation now frankly referring to the Japanese. We were supposed to bring the war to American shores to determine whether a break-through by an enemy naval force was at all possible. While the 1933 fleet problem was of the greatest significance from our own historical point of view, this 1937 problem became of decisive influence in the shaping of Japan's own plans. There can be no doubt that its outcome and the lessons it provided in the sphere of grand naval strategy were instrumental in changing Japanese plans and even in reorienting their entire intelligence work from a haphazard collection of odds and ends to a determined preparation for war by whatever means intelligence provided.

A number of Japanese agents watched developments both on the west coast and in Hawaii. I would like to mention one in particular who was a German. His work was decisive, and his procedure typical of the methods at that time being employed by Axis agents. He was Klaus Mehnert, a young German intellectual fully embued with the idea of Teutonic grandeur and working in his own clandestine way for its realization. He was one of those Germans born without a country, born in the Prussian twilight of war and peace somewhere in the Baltic, and clinging with an almost morbid patriotism to his German allegiance when at last he was given a citizenship. He belonged to a group of German plotters who had their headquarters in Breslau and planned for a war against the Soviet Union. They called themselves the Osteuropa Gesellschaft or East Europe Society, and published a monthly journal in which they bared their imperialistic dreams as does a patient before a psychoanalyst. The implications of these dreams were clear to the political analyst. They represented groping efforts seeking the soft spot of Europe where best to strike the opening blow. They were from the first not convinced that Russia was the softest of all available spots, and when they finally arrived at their conviction that Russia would represent a tough nut to crack, they turned their attention in other directions. They joined General Haushofer's group of German geopoliticians, and Mehnert himself became a member of a small group of free-lancing geopolitical spies whom the Haushofer organization, with the aid received from Dr. Alfred Rosenberg's Foreign Political Bureau, sent everywhere in the world. In the United States there were several men active: one in Alaska; Philipp H. Lohman of Miami University, at Oxford, Ohio, in the Middle West; Fritz Bartz of the University of California at Berkeley on the west coast; and Mehnert at the University of Hawaii in Honolulu. They were left free to work because we were unprepared to combat the fifth column which betrays a nation through the treachery of spies, saboteurs, and traitors. We still felt that "it can't happen here."

Despite his dubious record Mehnert succeeded in obtaining a position in Honolulu which served as excellent camouflage. He was added to the faculty of the University of Hawaii at Honolulu as professor of anthropology. But he showed interest only in his own field—the huge Japanese population of the islands as a possible kernel of disturbance when the war came. In lengthy reports he advised his employers that the Japanese in Hawaii represented a definite threat to American security and predicted that in an emergency they would certainly join their native land and turn against the United States. Like so many other predictions and appraisals of Nazi political agents, this also turned out to be incorrect. I heard of these predictions, which were directly contrary to my own estimate and served to strengthen my opinions.

Mehnert soon wandered far afield from his subterfuge as a professor of anthropology and became interested in matters strictly naval. In this work he provided valuable information to the Japanese and was indirectly responsible for some of the details of the great strategic plan of the Japanese naval high command. His greatest work was his report based on our 1937 fleet problem, which he sent to Germany. There its publication reached the Japanese listening posts in Berlin.

Certain views of his were aired openly to explore the field for adherents at the university, but most of his work became evident in essays which he published in the magazine *Zeitschrift für Geopolitik,* of Haushofer, "former major general, conceiver of *Lebensraum,* trainer of spies for the Nazi foreign service, and chief braintruster to Hitler himself." Mehnert was a member of Haushofer's organization, Arbeitsgemeinschaft für Geopolitik, which served the political explorations around the world.

When the activities of these agents were made known to the heads of the universities concerned, the news met with varying reception, but usually incomprehension. However, in Hawaii the president of the university said he would investigate. As a result Mehnert departed for China on June 10, 1941, by the *Tatsuta Maru,* where he joined Fritz Wiedemann, formerly German consul-general in San Francisco and head of German espionage on the west coast. In Shanghai, Mehnert worked ostensibly for the *Shanghai News Review* magazine.

Hawaii had been directly under Wiedemann—well known as an adjutant of the Führer and wartime captain of the company in which Hitler was a corporal. It was while I was district intelligence officer at San Diego that I had a double agent plant a disconcerting idea with Wiedemann. I informed him that the United States wasn't concerned over Wiedemann's activities here because he was

going back to Germany soon anyhow. This was news to Wiedemann. He immediately enlisted one of his women workers to go
to Berlin to ask Hitler if there was anything wrong with his own
work. We don't know the answer given, but Wiedemann soon
left his San Francisco post. However, this not before suit was entered against him by a woman for $8,000 expenses for a trip she
had made to Germany for Wiedemann.

I need not go into details of this 1937 fleet problem except to say
that it revealed certain weak spots in our defenses and proved
the distinct possibility that a daring and skillfully executed Japanese maneuver could break through to our most vital defense installations. It was assumed that the weak spots would be corrected
by our high command. The conclusions which Mehnert reached,
and which he communicated to his employers, provided an ingenious pattern. He deduced from the published reports and discussions of the fleet problem that the United States had a life line
in the Pacific which it had to maintain if it wanted to survive as
a Pacific power. This life line extended from Dutch Harbor in
the north through Midway in the central Pacific down to Pago
Pago in the south, behind which the United States could be contained regardless of what happened in the rest of the Pacific Ocean
area. What we regarded as an essential *defense line* for our own
safety, our opponents viewed as the *prison fence* behind which to
lock us. The idea which this amateur strategist drew up with exceptional skill was simple enough:

He concluded that an opponent could paralyze the United
States if he succeeded in preventing us from breaking out of this
line, in which case he would have freedom of movement in the
area which lies beyond the line to the west. The Japanese could
paralyze us, Mehnert calculated, by destroying our fleet, our only
means of carrying the war west of Midway, and by occupying strategic spots just outside the crucial geographical line.

Here, then, were the essential clues supplied to Japanese strategists by our own fleet problem, which they did not fail to evaluate
for all it was worth. Looking back on the plans they made, we
cannot fail to see Mehnert's hand in the grand strategic plan of the
Japanese. But his report had also a different and immediate significance. It convinced the Japanese that we were vulnerable. It
convinced them that in a war against the United States they had
a chance for strategic success. And finally it convinced them that

there was a possibility of defeating us by merely locking us in behind our so-called defensive life line.

I do not know how Mehnert's report was received in Tokyo, but Admiral Yokoi, who was later Japan's naval attaché in Berlin, revealed in an exceptionally candid essay, written under the influence of the heady wine of temporary victory, that it was instrumental in bringing about the drawing up of the final offensive plan of the Japanese naval high command. Once the possibility of victory in a naval war against the United States appeared plausible to the plotters, they concentrated on perfecting the plan for it.

20

PRELUDE TO PEARL HARBOR

WE NOW HAD reached the historical turning point in our relations with Japan, although this fact was not immediately evident
to some of our diplomats who were observing the rapid development of events on the spot in Tokyo. From now on Japan's political and diplomatic moves were predetermined by military neces-
sities, all keyed to support the grandiose strategic plan which was
taking shape in the Army and Navy General Staffs. In reality, there
were two different plans in preparation, and they were not necessarily interconnected. One, which was drawn up in the War Ministry by the Army General Staff, still had China as its major objective. Another, somewhat less advanced than its military counterpart, which was being hatched in the Navy General Staff, envis-
ioned expansion toward the south. Secrecy was carefully maintained, not merely to conceal the two plans from unauthorized outsiders but also to conceal each plan from the staff preparing the
other. As I shall show on a later page, the Army was genuinely surprised when in September 1941 it was presented with the completed Navy plan prepared in minute detail and ready for implementation on a moment's notice. This secrecy was nothing unusual in Japan, where the Army clique was distinctly separated
from the Navy, one fighting the other, while in addition there
were smaller cliques forming within both branches of the armed
forces.

The Japanese political situation in the winter of 1936-37 was
fraught with tension and danger. The prelude to events was the
so-called Showa Restoration of February 26, 1936, when Army
extremists assassinated the Finance Minister, the Keeper of the
Privy Seal, and the Inspector-General of Military Education, re-
moving from their path at least a few spokesmen of the moderate
political forces. The rebellion of the extremists was put down, but
the Army had its victory; it gained definite influence on the political conduct of the country and succeeded in putting its own men

into key positions. The first climax of this development came on November 25, 1936, when the Army succeeded in forcing upon Japan the first alliance with Germany, the generally unpopular Anti-Comintern Pact.

The Army influence remained paramount even after the puppet premier Koki Hirota was overthrown by opponents of the pro-German orientation, scoring a temporary respite and a momentary victory destined to last for just one day. An attempt to appoint the moderate General Ugaki as premier failed because of the Army's violent opposition to one of its own generals. The manner in which Ugaki was prevented from accepting the premiership from the Emperor's hand was symptomatic of the Army's supreme influence. He was "privately advised" to reject the Emperor's invitation to form a cabinet, but proceeded with his plans and succeeded in assembling a form of coalition cabinet that appeared acceptable both to the Imperial Palace and the Zaibatsu (industrial and economic groups) backers of the elderly officer. It was late at night when Ugaki's cabinet list was completed, but not wanting to lose any time, he ordered his car and proceeded at once to the Imperial Palace to present his list to the Emperor. He was driving at midnight along the roadway which skirted the dark moat of the palace when his car was suddenly stopped by a man wearing the uniform of a general of the Military Police. The man was the commander in chief of the Military Police himself. Acting upon instructions from the highest Army clique, the general now warned Ugaki against accepting the Emperor's commission. The warning was explicit and unequivocal, bolstered by vivid recollections of the February incident. Though Ugaki had set out for the palace to present his cabinet list to form a government, his mind now was effectively changed. He continued to the palace merely to return his commission to Hirohito's hands.

General Ugaki was thoroughly disturbed by the incident. He swore that he would resign from the Army and never wear its uniform as long as he lived. Hirohito was now compelled by the Army to appoint the extremist General Hayashi, who intensified the aggressive policies of the Army clique but proved a dismal failure in settling the domestic difficulties with which any Japanese cabinet in the middle thirties was inevitably confronted. His failure brought Prince Konoye into the picture; and when the news of Konoye's appointment as premier reached me, I failed to share the optimism of most observers, who regarded him as a reasonable politician and viewed his appointment as a triumph of the moderates. I had known Konoye and regarded him as a practical politician who managed to put up a diplomatic front but was a willing tool of the militarists behind his smooth façade. It was during his tenure, on July 7, that the carefully prepared plan of the Army General Staff was put into action. On that day a skirmish at the Marco Polo Bridge served as the pretense for the Army to start its compaign against north China and to overrun vast territories —according to plan and schedule. From then on, Japan moved at accelerated pace toward global war. Soon Italy was brought into the orbit when on November 6, 1937, she joined the Anti-Comintern Pact; and then Japan recognized the Franco regime in Spain. A provisional government of puppet Chinese was set up in Peiping, and the Japanese began the long-term administration of northern China, preparing the territory for later moves toward the south.

Our answers to these moves were eloquent but impotent. On October 5, 1937, President Roosevelt made his historic Quarantine Speech in Chicago but failed to arouse the West to a more effective opposition against Japanese aggression. A few weeks later nineteen powers met in Brussels to settle Japan's ambiguous China affair but ended their negotiations in failure, since Japan ignored their efforts. All that resulted from the diplomatic attempts to stop Japanese aggression was a weak nonaggression pact concluded between the Soviet Union and China. More important, however, was Chiang Kai-shek's heroic decision to resist Japanese aggression under all circumstances. This commitment, carried out to the end in a skillful manner but often under the most difficult conditions, was a major factor in denying ultimate victory to the Japanese. In their historical studies the Japanese had forgotten the lessons of Napoleon at Moscow, which demonstrated that a country with unlimited land masses to which to retreat cannot be defeated.

It was obvious to observers that Japan was maneuvering for position, but there were a few empty spots in the picture which prevented us from making a comprehensive estimate of the situation. The Japanese Navy's attitude and plans were difficult to fathom. What were the Navy's own plans for immediate aggression? This one question had to be answered to give us the complete picture. In 1937 it was impossible to give the answer, but there were several straws in the wind which aided in our estimates and served to convince us that the Navy, too, had its plans and was getting ready to join the Army in carrying the war to still other areas.

One of these indications was the complete reorientation of Japanese intelligence activities. After a lull of almost two years (between 1936 and 1938) intelligence was again moved into the forefront of Japanese activities and became an important instrument of power.

But the intelligence setup with which our Japanese adversaries now confronted us was entirely different from the net we previously encountered. The roles were different, and they were assigned to different personalities. It was no longer confined to the Japanese Navy to conduct offensive intelligence against us; the plot was broadened to become total espionage, seeking military and naval as well as political data, so that the planners in Tokyo could draw up their final plans in the full knowledge of our intentions, strength and weaknesses, potentialities, morale, and political alignment. The Japanese required a different network for this enlarged organization—a network expanded far beyond the confines of Naval Intelligence. So they decided to base it on their consulates instead and appointed a co-ordinator working under a diplomatic guise within the sacrosanct confines of the Japanese Embassy on Massachusetts Avenue in Washington.

The man who was chosen for this responsible position seemed to have a minor rank and an insignificant job in the Embassy. He was a second secretary in the Embassy named Terasaki, the man who may be regarded as the one individual who developed into the leader of all Japanese espionage activities during this prelude to Pearl Harbor. I had known him quite well. He was a quiet, precise, intellectual type, uncommunicative and reserved, giving the impression of extreme modesty but with a facile mind impressing one with his considerable energy. He succeeded in concealing his espionage assignment with exceptional skill. In fact, we did not know for a long time that he was Japan's master spy in the Western Hemisphere. We were surprised to find him a lone wolf standing apart from the rest of the diplomatic crowd and mixing little in society when his diplomatic functions per se seemed strange and inconclusive. But we attributed these characteristics to his personal inclinations and did not suspect him of extraneous activities involving espionage.

Working under him was a vast network of spies, based on the various Japanese consulates situated at strategic points. Hawaii, of course, was one of the subsidiary headquarters, and it was in Honolulu that Japanese espionage was expanded to such an extent that it became an invading force, both in the number of spies employed and in the energy with which they worked. While I was still on the *Richmond* and had only infrequent opportunities to observe this development from close quarters, Terasaki was busily engaged in building up his network and system.

In the spring of 1938 I was again able to return to intelligence duties, since upon completion of my tour of sea duty I was detailed as district intelligence officer of the 11th Naval District with headquarters at San Diego, the very hub of the wheel of Japanese espionage. Just as I was leaving my ship the Japanese gave another indication of their active preparations for war. The Japanese National General Mobilization Bill was passed, technical and professional men were ordered to register with the military, and factory owners were ordered to plan for war production and store essential supplies. The bill meant just what its title implied. Japan was openly mobilizing for war.

Our naval intelligence activities are centralized in the Office of Naval Intelligence in Washington with its geographical desks and research facilities, and decentralized in the various naval districts where regional intelligence work is in charge of what generally is referred to as the DIO, or the district intelligence officer. The United States was very fortunate in having in the persons of its DIO's energetic and alert men who proved a match for their Japanese counterparts then flocking to the United States in ever increasing numbers. This was a period of great vulnerability, and security depended upon Naval Intelligence. San Diego was an exceptionally important outpost, embracing a large Japanese population and in a position to watch Japanese espionage activities offshore, centered in the fishing fleets in which scores of Japanese espionage agents sailed our seas. At this time over 50 per cent of the aircraft factories of the nation were located within my district.

Shortly before my arrival in San Diego, and while I was still on sea duty, an incident occurred which indicated to us the return of Japanese spies to action. Investigation revealed the presence of a paid American agent of the Japanese on board a United States cruiser. In order to avoid suspicion through unusual contacts, which are immediately noticed by men on a ship, I was asked to contact the commanding officer of the cruiser, and arrange the details for the investigative procedures necessary for the development of the case. When I revealed to him the presence of a Japanese operative on his ship, he was scandalized and exclaimed: "For heaven's sake, let's get rid of him at once!"

But this was not the proper technique for following up a case. We regarded the man as a minor agent, completely covered and therefore more or less harmless and even useful, since he might enable us to discover the man behind him and probably even the higher-ups in the Japanese espionage ring. I succeeded in enlisting this commanding officer's co-operation, and the man was permitted to continue his espionage activities under the strictest surveillance, never suspecting that his undercover work was fully known to us. He proved to be an exceptionally useful lead. He telephoned his contact, he wrote letters to him, and he frequented the race track where he knew the lure of gambling and the urge of feminine beauty would bring the Japanese. As in the Thompson-Miyazaki case, the Japanese agent who appeared at the races with a group of Japanese friends was a language officer of the Imperial Navy.

At the race track the little group of Japanese were distinctly annoyed at the undue familiarity of this American bluejacket in public. The Japanese Navy lieutenant obviously could feel the thousand eyes upon him as the persistent sailor, who had taken a seat just behind the group, insisted on trying to maintain a conversation with them.

We saw that nothing passed between the American sailor and the Japanese at this time. Shortly after this episode it became apparent that the Japanese definitely discontinued the use of this man as a contact. They were becoming too cautious to use contacts in the uniform of our Navy.

But this initial coverage had given us the necessary names and leads which we were to follow. The bluejacket later was sent to Hawaii where general court-martial charges were drawn up. In the compilation of our suspect list and the surveillance of the spies we worked according to a definite plan. It was not our intention to make arrests and thereby destroy the minor cogs in the ring who were by then fairly well known to us. We realized that we had to deal with a many-headed hydra which defied destruction, especially under the limitations imposed upon us by our domestic statutes. We were satisfied that as long as we knew the activities of as many enemy agents as possible we could exert an invisible control over them and reduce the efficiency of their work. And we would have them identified for the big day if it should come.

In this strategy we were encouraged by the experience gained in Britain just prior to the First World War. We recalled how Britain permitted the presence of twenty-nine key agents and a few hundreds of minor German spies prior to the war, only to round them all up at the outbreak of hostilities and thus destroy the spy ring when it was in a position to become most dangerous.

Accompanying the Kaiser to the funeral of King Edward VII in London was the chief of the German Military Intelligence, whose identity was known to MI-5. The sudden arrival of this officer alerted the British counter-intelligence, and it was decided to shadow this man throughout his stay in London. The officer was careless enough to contact one of his agents in London, a hairdresser named Ernst, and revealed through this call the identity of his other operatives. The British did not follow up this scoop with arrests. They permitted the German agents to continue their work under close surveillance, but on the day of the outbreak of war in August 1914, they hauled in the net so carefully laid in advance. This was an illuminating example of perfect technique from which we did not fail to profit. The objective of counter-intelligence is *not* to bask in the bright lights of spectacular headlines by premature arrests.

We continued our work unknown to the public and also to the enemy agents who were so closely watched. There was occasional veiled criticism in the press, undoubtedly inspired, but it did not alter our decisions. In the meantime, scores of public-spirited citizens came to my office with tips, most of which, of course, turned out to be useless, but it was our practice to follow up all leads no matter how fantastic they might seem at first sight. In this respect Naval Intelligence differed from purely investigative agencies, which are inclined to drop espionage leads when they do not produce immediate results. I recall distinctly two cases where Naval Intelligence scored definite triumphs by following up leads which had previously been considered unproductive by other agencies. In San Diego our counter-intelligence activities, which made us cognizant of the importance of what was to be the prelude to Pearl

Harbor, were broadened in scope to encompass all types of espionage and subversive activities of all nationalities. Every lead was followed, and, when expedient for security, prosecution was initiated and completed regardless of the direction in which the ax might fall.

One of these involved a Soviet representative in this country. He was Mihail Gorin, head of the Soviet Intourist Bureau in Los Angeles. Also involved was his pretty wife, Natasha. One morning in the winter of 1938 a pickup truck of a Hollywood cleaning establishment made a regular stop at the Gorin home. Mrs. Gorin gave the driver the clothes to be cleaned, and outside, at the truck, the driver went through his routine of examining the pockets of the clothes delivered to him. In one of the coats he found an envelope containing a fifty-dollar bill and several sheets of paper with notes on them. One note made references to the Communist inclinations of certain Japanese in San Diego and a fight which this had precipitated with another group of Japs. Other notes referred to Japanese espionage activities on the west coast.

The driver, impressed with the importance of the contents of the envelope, returned immediately to his shop and showed the papers to the manager. The manager directed him to proceed with all the articles to the Hollywood police station. There the driver found great interest. This station had no photostating machine, but exact copies were made by hand of all the contents of the envelopes.

Meanwhile, at his office Mr. Gorin had missed the envelope and phoned his wife. Excitedly she told her husband that the clothes had already been collected by the cleaners. Gorin hurried home, picked up his wife, and together they proceeded to the cleaning establishment in Hollywood, where the manager calmly assured them that "Mr. Gorin was certain to have his envelope returned safely if it had been in the clothes because all the employees had been carefully checked for honesty, and the driver should be coming in any minute now."

Gorin could not suppress his concern, and proceeded to pace the floor of the office while awaiting the driver's return. These actions convinced the manager that the envelope was really "hot," so he found an excuse to go out and telephone this conclusion to the Hollywood police station and asked that they tell the driver when returning to come in the back way and to act in a usual manner.

After the Hollywood police had made their copies, the driver returned to the shop with the original material as directed. Together with the manager and with all of Gorin's clothes in his arms, he proceeded to the front office where Gorin and his wife were rapidly reaching the hysterical stage. As the driver handed the clothes to Gorin he almost snatched them from him, so great was his anxiety to search that inside pocket of one of the coats. Much to his relief he found the envelope just as he had left it with all the papers intact and he and his wife departed smiling and confident.

The Hollywood police, noting the reference to Communists, sent the material to Captain William F. "Red" Hynes, head of the Intelligence Bureau of the Los Angeles Police Department. Hynes, after examining the material, decided that he would pass it to Major General R. H. Van Deman, U.S. Army (Retired), who lived in San Diego.

General Van Deman, the father of Army Intelligence, who had set up this activity in Washington under the greatest handicaps at the beginning of the World War, and later handled intelligence for General Pershing in Europe, continued his interest and activity on his own time even after his retirement. When I arrived in San Diego as the 11th Naval District intelligence officer, I found General Van Deman to be a reservoir of information, experience, and good counsel. It was natural that I should spend many hours in the little office of his home drinking in the words of wisdom not available anywhere else, even in the most extensive libraries. It was also natural that we should work together against those subversive forces which threatened to undermine our national security.

When the General received the material sent to him by Captain Hynes, he called me immediately and said:

"Zack, can you come up here right away? I have something which looks pretty hot."

"Yes, sir," I replied. "I will be there in ten minutes."

Upon arrival at his office, the General explained the circumstances and showed me the copies made by the Hollywood police. I recognized in them extracts from reports made up in my office less than two weeks before. This immediately suggested a leak in my San Pedro office. That was my next stop.

In the San Pedro office there was employed under civilian contract, as investigator, Hafis Salich, an energetic and capable man of Russian extraction who had been born in the Georgian region of southern Russia, where some of his relatives still resided. Salich had served many years of useful and efficient service with the Berkeley Police Department and knew some of the Japanese language. He had been hired long before my arrival and had come with the highest recommendations.

One day Salich informed the assistant intelligence officer at San Pedro that he had made the acquaintance of Mr. Gorin and asked if the contact should be followed up. Sensing the possibilities of "pressure" through the family connections when this report was made to me, I gave instructions that Salich was to be told not to meet with Gorin anywhere unless another member of our office was with him.

About this time Mrs. Salich came to the San Pedro office with a report of family difficulties and related that Salich had been engaged in much card playing and was keeping late hours. Also that he was continually short of money.

None of these conditions were likely to create a favorable impression in an intelligence organization, and thus it was natural that when General Van Deman showed me the report about the Gorin papers, a complete picture unfolded itself before me.

It was not difficult then to determine that Salich was meeting with Gorin alone, contrary to instructions, and that Salich had been receiving money from Gorin for papers which he had been seen typing in the San Pedro office. (The money, $1,700, was apparently lost in the card games, too.) When Salich was confronted with the evidence, he confessed and was placed in detention.

It was some time before the U.S. attorney could get permission to close in on Gorin, but that was finally allowed and the case presented no difficulties in obtaining a conviction of both men. Mrs. Gorin was acquitted. Later, while Gorin was out on $50,000 bail, he "disappeared" and made his way back to Russia by ship.

The responsibilities of a district intelligence officer stationed on the west coast were increasing every day as the influx of Japanese agents continued and as the resident agents became bolder as time passed. By now the network was organized on a vast scale with its own hierarchy, at the apex of which was the Washington headquarters reporting direct to Tokyo and receiving its instructions from there. On the next echelon, only slightly lower, were the service attachés and the various intelligence organizations maintained in a semiopen state in five American cities. These agencies were the Army and Navy "inspectorates" in New York, a cotton intelligence bureau in Houston, Texas, and various quasi-commercial organizations in Chicago, Seattle, and San Francisco. Below this group of highly placed operatives was the group of language students, several of whom were stationed at strategic points on the west coast. In a sense, these language students, all regular officers of the Japanese Imperial Navy, were the highest among field workers, establishing and exploiting contacts and providing the sorely needed professional supervision to haphazard collection of intelligence data by hastily trained, nonprofessional espionage personnel. On the same level were the Japanese consulates, exercising an immense influence on civilian Japanese scattered all along the west coast. Their power was derived from their control over these civilians, since they were always in a position to compel the return of a reluctant operative to his native Japan for appropriate action. Or they could use the persuasive methods of the "Tokyo Club," the narcotic and gambling ring which stretched the length of the west coast and had ample trigger men to meet the few necessary occasions. The Tokyo Club never failed to do the bidding of the Japanese officials as all of them were Japanese citizens, easily deportable if reported. This pressure on the club also produced funds to finance much of the espionage activity in this country. On the lowest echelon, representing quantity rather than quality, were the Japanese at large among whom the leaders of the intelligence network recruited their agents. While an overwhelming majority of the Japanese resisted the pressure, which at times became almost unbearable, especially for the alien Japanese resident, a minority succumbed to the pressure of threats and provided whatever information was available to them.

The quantitative approach to intelligence reduced the quality and effectiveness of Japanese intelligence in the United States. It was a case of knowing too much and therefore understanding too little. It was the time-honored conflict between knowledge and intelligence, and while the Japanese were eminent in the former, they revealed little of the latter.

Their task was made extremely easy by the fact that what a state usually regards as the secrets of its national security were all available openly in the United States. It may be useful to review the advantages and disadvantages to us of this fact in passing, since it is my conviction that the advantages outweigh the disadvantages. Foreign agents with whom I came in contact during my years in

Intelligence were unanimous in a peculiar complaint. They all averred that the United States was the most difficult objective of any espionage agent, for while we were usually wide open to espionage, we also confronted the operative with well-nigh impossible tasks.

A prominent German agent (Von Rintelen) once related to a friend of mine his impression that "on the surface, the United States had no secrets which an efficient and alert foreign operative could not procure. A trip to the United States Government Printing Office in Washington usually yielded data at a nominal price which agents elsewhere would have had immense difficulties in obtaining. Most of the Army's and Navy's manuals were offered for sale. The document rooms of the Senate and House were other sources of information. Very often we had to pay thousands of dollars for blueprints of new airplane designs in France or Britain, while we obtained all the necessary data for the price of a daily paper or a periodical in the United States. But in the final analysis, the United States was still safe from us for three reasons."

He proceeded to outline these reasons. "First," he said, "the United States is too vast, a continent by itself, with developments going on simultaneously at distances of thousands of miles, interrelated as they are and requiring simultaneous observation by operatives. But how can any foreign power station the great number of spies in the United States required to carry out this observation adequately? It would require hundreds of highly qualified agents scattered all over the immense country to check on all that is going on, and no intelligence service can afford to concentrate such a huge army of qualified agents in any one country.

"The second reason for ultimate failure is the improvised character of America's defense system. The system used in war is entirely different from the system maintained in peace. The nucleus forces which are maintained in peacetime have no similarity to or relation with the vast people's army and navy which the United States puts into the field or sends to sea when the emergency arises. In the truest sense of the word, the United States starts its wars from scratch, and all the data which foreign intelligence services are capable of accumulating in peacetime turn out to be useless, antiquated stuff in war, when espionage becomes difficult and virtually impossible. Moreover, America is a dynamic country where nothing is static, especially not in times of great crises like wars. A plan drawn up today is thrown out tomorrow, and a better or bigger plan is substituted for it. What is the use of obtaining the details of this one plan, when tomorrow it is no longer valid? The success of this improvisation, both mental and physical, baffles the foreign intelligence service. In Germany," this agent said, "we tried to find out the secret of this strange phenomenon, America's ability to turn from efficiency in peace to an entirely different kind of efficiency in war. We sent a man to the United States to study and analyze the mysterious transformation of the United States in material and moral matters from peace to war in 1917. But all he could find was the innate ability of the American to adapt himself to all conditions and to exercise the same efficiency in all situations. America is still a land of pioneers, and it is very difficult to keep track of its movements and developments.

"The third reason, believe it or not, is the abundance of material which America readily provides to the intelligence service. Thousands of sheets of paper pour in every day into intelligence organizations abroad, all revealing some seemingly secret information—but who can sift all these data and weed out the bad from the good? We usually discover that while we have too much information, we can make very little of it, since a co-ordination of the incoming material overtaxes the usually limited facilities of any intelligence agency.

"This third reason is inherent in the national characteristics of the American people. Without being chauvinistic, they are intensely patriotic; and while they are loquacious enough, they somehow know when and how to keep their mouths shut. While in France we had no difficulty in recruiting native operatives among dissident elements always opposed to the regime in power, in the United States even the lunatic fringe is reluctant to place its services at the disposal of an alien espionage organization. The foreign agent coming to the United States is at first overjoyed by the apparent willingness of the average American to talk about what to the foreigner seems dangerous subjects. Endless is the amount of gossip floating in Washington drawing rooms. People like to boast about their accomplishments, or play up the deeds of a relative or acquaintance working in some defense installation or on a secret national project. But when this incoming material is sifted and analyzed, it usually turns out just empty talk, exaggerated bravado, useless chitchat—nothing concrete for a serious-minded intelligence organization. On the contrary, it serves only to mislead and confuse the agent, who will soon find himself incapable of separating the valuable material from the useless, and succumbs to the temptation of playing up as factual information what is nothing but sophomoric gossip.

"Another reason is, of course, the efficiency of America's protective agencies, the Counter-Intelligence Corps of the Army, the Office of Naval Intelligence, the investigative agencies such as the Secret Service of the Treasury, the postal inspectors, the U.S. Customs Agency, and the Federal Bureau of Investigation, all aided by watchful patriotic citizens who usually prove intelligent observers and excellent sleuths themselves. How," the German complained, "can even the best foreign operative penetrate this phalanx with the means available to an agent usually dependent on his own wits as he operates in distant territories with but slight contact with his headquarters?"

To me, this catalogue of reasons for the failure of foreign intelligence services appeared largely an arbitrary one, showing that to a large extent we were safe from enemy agents only by default. The immense dimensions of our country and the improvised nature of our preparedness do, indeed, make the work of a foreign agent rather difficult. The watchfulness of our intelligence and investigative organizations helps to make it impossible. But we do talk too much for comfort, and our press frequently does reveal too much; and while we are protected to a certain degree by the quantitative mass of material we thus provide to a potential enemy, we still enable him to pick up enough of quality to form a proper estimate of our situation and even establish our intentions. We are by nature goodhearted and open-minded. These two characteristics of our people expose us to potential enemies and make the work of the protective agencies doubly difficult.

The task with which my own office was confronted in San Diego was an immense one, our district extending all along the coast line and considerably beyond it, far out into the sea. It is well remembered that Japan had two fleets. One was her combined fleet in distant waters, but the other was here at our doorstep, a huge Japanese fishing fleet off the west coast which was "fishy" indeed. This second fleet, serving the purposes of the first, spent most of its time off the coast of North and Central America, including Panama until it was told in no uncertain terms that its presence at that particular spot could no longer be tolerated.

These fishing vessels had a variety of tasks to perform. First of all they maintained contact with Japanese Intelligence by transmitting correspondence via Japanese merchantmen which these fishing boats contacted on the high seas. They transported agents, picking them up at sea and bringing them in disguised as fishermen. It can be assumed that there were many commissioned officers among these simple fishermen. Their numbers and our lack of identification requirements made any accurate check on them impossible. They charted our waters, both within and without the three-mile zone, and there was no reef, shoal, or any other obstacle to a submarine or a combatant fleet that remained unknown to these fishermen. From them the Hydrographic Office in Tokyo obtained all the necessary additional data which were not supplied in the regular contributions of our own Hydrographic Office.

The activities of this presumptuous fishing fleet off our west coast caused genuine concern to the Navy Department, and in April 1939 I was sent before the California State Legislature at Sacramento to present the official views of the department to the Fish and Game Commission of the Assembly.

When the time for my appearance approached, the corridors of the Legislature were filled with strangers of the sea. They were attracted to the halls of the Legislature by the subject under consideration, the proposal to prohibit aliens from operating fishing boats off the west coast. This affected many Portuguese and Italians, who, with the Japanese, represented major factors in the industry. They were alert enough to send their supporters into action prepared for all eventualities.

After indicating the dangers of the situation in plain language, particularly as it concerned the Japanese operating fishing boats, I was subjected to a series of questions. I was asked, among others, to state my political philosophy. I explained that this was something a naval officer is not supposed to have. The commission apparently decided to support this enforced attitude by voting seven to seven on this issue vital to our national security. It was considered by the opponents to be a national rather than a state issue.

It was in the spring of that year, while the clouds of war were gathering in Europe, that we applied to Congress for more money to cover this situation. In my contacts with Congress I have always found the Appropriations Committee willing to provide funds when necessity could be indicated in concrete form. On this particular occasion we were able to show the Congressmen some of the original documents obtained from a Japanese agent which indicated that this particular operative had completed ingenious arrangements to employ on a large scale certain fishing boats in case of hostilities. The committee was incensed and told us that we could have all we wanted: "How much is needed?" they asked. "Do you want a million dollars?"

But we assured them that $250,000 would be ample to meet the needs of our growing organization. Events in Europe intensified activities on the west coast as well, and we found ourselves compelled to mobilize our reserve officers by calling certain ones to active duty in order to aid in our silent war against the ever-increasing number of enemy agents, Japanese as well as Germans and Italians. There was by then a definite link between the three groups, and the extent of this co-operation became fully evident to me when on the eve of the Second World War the mail brought a note in the childish phrasing of a schoolboy of Japanese extraction, outlining in exasperating detail the seriousness of the situation in its one single phase of total espionage. Even from a distance of several years, the note has all the topical significance which it contained in 1939. It is today a historical document in itself, providing the blueprint of aggression as it was revealed to a frightened little boy whose Japanese ancestry did not prevent his being a good American. It was postmarked ———, Calif., February 23, 1939. The letter is most illuminating and interesting. It would be published in full here but for the fact that the clues contained therein might still reveal to some of the hostile elements the identity of this courageous boy, although the letter was anonymous. One pertinent extract was sufficient to impress us with the importance of the document. It read in part:

One . . . day is come to our . . . Japanese, . . . Italion . . . and . . . German . . . I cannot hear all but it is to do with war and Japanese men to breake water dams and power lines . . . Japan to make trouble in french islands so Italy can get Mediteranun forts and Germany to make big propaganda in South America and may be Japan to bomb Guam . . . as Japan now got plenty of soldiers in close by island with float boats to take men and guns quick after Japanese ships capture island. These men get drunk and talk about America terrible and what soon is coming in European and New York and all work together to make fleet spread out and air bomb before democrats get too good fixed this come soon now as we not ready for big war and they fool to wait but make war quick without telling first....

These complete preparations by alien groups, which we had suspected for some time, would seem to presage something serious in the event of hostilities between Japan and the United States. But our own plans were made to nullify the prospective moves of the saboteurs by simultaneous raids and quick roundup of all suspects, and by providing physical protection for vital installations. It was believed, however, that these emergency measures would not have to be taken before Japan's initial move. As explained elsewhere, it was fully expected that Japan would commence hostilities with an air attack on our fleet without warning or a declaration of war. Such an attack would set in motion our measures to counteract any sabotage before the enemy could begin operating. Uprisings and extensive sabotage require careful planning and leadership in their execution. The secrecy necessary to make an air attack successful eliminated entirely any advance notice to agents and removed any opportunity for them to take timely or successful action.

While this anonymous letter served the very valuable purpose of increasing alertness to the contingencies implied, it must be admitted that the writer was not discovered. The clues contained therein made it a case of pure investigation rather than counter-intelligence; therefore it was turned over to another agency for handling. If the writer should read these lines I would be highly gratified to learn of his identity to compliment him for his contribution to our national security.

21

YAMAMOTO IN THE PILOT SEAT

THE CLOSE co-operation between German, Italian, and Japanese operatives in the field of espionage was merely a blurred outline of the alliance on a far grander scale between the three aggressor nations which had fallen into the hands of unscrupulous military adventurers. "Powerful gangsters," President Roosevelt said, "have banded together to enslave the entire human race." The partners in this international banditry, reminiscent of the worst days of the Middle Ages when war was still the dominant issue and peace inconceivable to the rulers, were united in a shotgun wedding. In a sense, theirs was an unnatural union. The people of Italy, sophisticated and wise as they are with their backlog of civilized history, had nothing but contempt for the Germans; while the Germans derided the Italians as "unheroic, opportunistic, and decadent." The Japanese regarded the Germans with an attitude comprised of qualified admiration and unqualified suspicion, harboring old grudges and new grievances; while the Germans remembered the fact that it was their own Kaiser who had coined the phrase "the Yellow Peril."

Despite centuries-old national animosities and suspicions these three nations became united in their common aim to conquer the world and to share in the domination of vanquished humanity. The alliance had innumerable contrasts and contradictions far beyond the basic dislike of one so-called Axis nation for the other. The Nazis, for example, advocated the race principle of pure Aryanism but prepared to make war against other "Aryan" nations in co-operation with their "non-Aryan" Japanese partner. The Japanese coined the slogan "Asia for the Asiatics"—but were prepared to share the control of the continent, at least for the time being, with the German invader coming in from the west and planning to meet the Japanese avalanche somewhere on Indian soil.

In Europe the situation was pregnant with imminent war which the Munich conference postponed but failed to eliminate. Several significant incidents indicated to the intelligence experts that Germany was bent upon having her war at all costs, a cheap war if possible and a short one at that, but a war, nevertheless, to test the military machine now moving into high gear. Although their eyes were turned to the east, to Czechoslovakia and Poland, their spies were sent to the west, to France, Belgium, and England. We learned from official British admission, including a statement of Home Secretary Sir Samuel Hoare in the House of Commons, that by the spring of 1939 Germany was maintaining 3,000 spies in the United Kingdom and that several diplomatic agencies of the Third Reich were also active in espionage. One of the most daring espionage exploits occurred during this period. Britain was testing one of her new experimental fighter planes at the Farnsborough air station behind "hermetically" sealed doors. Only the designers and a few very high officials of the Air Ministry knew of the experimental flight, and all precautions were made to prevent a leakage, either to the public or to the innumerable German agents assigned to find out Britain's secrets in the air.

The test flight was started on schedule with two of the RAF's best test pilots in the cockpit of the hush-hush plane. They were to make a short flight over English territory at great altitude and return to Farnsborough with the data of the test. But the plane failed to return. When hours passed without word from the plane, counter-intelligence agencies were called in and the whole of Britain was combed for the missing aircraft. Squadrons of planes were sent out to survey the whole of Britain from the air, and posses were organized to search for wreckage of the plane, since it was supposed that it had crashed somewhere on British territory. But no trace could be found, and nothing was ever heard of the secret plane.

Possibly influenced by the overcharged atmosphere of these prewar days and possibly on the basis of reliable information, British Intelligence attributed the disappearance of the plane to an amazing incident. According to this theory—and I call it theory since I know of no definite substantiation—the Germans learned the secrets of the plane, the time scheduled for the test flight, and its exact course, which included a short detour to sea. They sent one of their largest U-boats to the very spot where the plane was to be farthest out at sea, and, when the aircraft appeared over the submarine in ambush, it was shot down, the pilots killed, the plane salvaged and taken to Germany for examination. This theory was apparently accepted by Lord Vansittart, who was then chief diplomatic adviser to His Majesty's Government and head of the Political Intelligence Division of the Foreign Office. This episode was similar to the complete disappearance of a secret experimental plane in its first flight from an aircraft plant outside Los Angeles, California. One of my agents, who knew aircraft and the incident, later reported to me that he had sighted a duplicate of this experimental plane in a Japanese factory.

Several other incidents, minor by comparison, also served to alert us to the growing danger of German espionage, which was becoming increasingly aggressive and bold. The car of a Royal Air Force officer was burgled and documents were stolen which outlined planned co-operation between the air force and ground troops. Agents were discovered in the Greenwich Arsenal and in several British defense plants, and a woman named Johanna Wolf was uncovered as the head of a spy network composed of hundreds of domestic servants employed by the families of Britain's key personalities, including the First Lord of the Admiralty. The German Embassy on the Mall was turned into a veritable fortress of espionage, with radio transmitters, teletypes, and batteries of coding machines installed by German workmen brought for this particular purpose from the Reich to London. Propagandists were dumped on England by the hundreds, and political espionage under the skillful Sophie, Baroness von Wangenheim, author of erudite articles on the British secret service, was flourishing in the drawing rooms clustering around Belgrave Square.

In Paris also German espionage agents were active. When Admiral Darlan signed an order alerting the French battle fleet during the days of Munich, the text of this order was obtained by German agents even before the French fleet received it. Another operative was uncovered who was providing the Germans with a complete list of French airfields and the exact strength of the air forces kept in readiness on them. Thousands of German spies worked in Poland and Czechoslovakia; and the fifth column received orders to go to battle stations in Norway, Denmark, and the Netherlands. The Western democracies were confronted with tens of thousands of German operatives, aided in their work by Italian and Japanese agents everywhere in the world.

In Tokyo events were rapidly implementing as well as supplementing Hitler's scheme of war. An office in the Navy Ministry was one of the centers of these activities. It was occupied by my old friend Admiral Yamamoto, who by then had moved up to the strategic position of vice-minister of the Navy and was the real power behind the Navy Minister's shaky throne. Yamamoto knew what he wanted but still was not certain how to get it. The dilemma with which he was confronted during his stay in Washington, the dilemma of war or peace, was now settled. He had decided for war and concentrated all his activities on preparations for it. But even now he had no definite plan and was still groping in strategic darkness despite the encouraging information received from operatives. Tamon Yamaguchi was at his side during these important formative years. After the collapse of his house of cards in the United States, Yamaguchi had returned to Japan. He was made a rear admiral and appointed chief of staff of the important Fifth Fleet, doing extensive work with carriers for his superior, Yamamoto. He continued the experiments which started in 1930 and was successful in completing them. By the end of 1939 he could report to Yamamoto that Japan for the first time in her history had a fleet in which air and sea power were perfectly integrated. He could report that Japan had at her disposal a considerable number of exceptionally highly qualified carrier pilots, that the rate of accident was reduced to an unavoidable minimum, and that Japan was ready with her carriers to deal whatever blow was considered necessary to cripple the United States fleet. On January 1, 1940, Rear Admiral Tamon Yamaguchi reached the climax of his career. He was appointed to the personal staff of Admiral Yamamoto in charge of translating the many theories of war against the United States into imminent action.

The decision to make war against the United States was the result of events in Europe as they were interpreted in Yamamoto's scheming mind. The year 1939 was far from satisfactory to these Japanese. While Germany was advancing relentlessly, occupying the whole of Czechoslovakia and enslaving Hungary, Bulgaria, and Rumania in a series of bloodless conquests, Japan was bogged down in China and threatened by various Russian moves in the wake of a 1938 frontier clash which ended quite differently from a similar clash in 1937, which had caused the Japanese to think that the Russians would not go to war. This time the clash ended with what Admiral Yamamoto considered the ignominious defeat of the

Japanese aggressors, who were spanked in the diplomatic field and harassed by innumerable domestic difficulties for which no remedy could be found. In the very midst of this situation the Russo-German alliance of August 23, 1939, hit the uninformed Tokyo plotters with the suddenness of an earthquake.

This strange alliance, concluded for a period of ten years but violated within two, caught the Japanese completely by surprise. It was the product of Hitler's morbid brain, and he refused to share his secret even with his closest Japanese collaborators, including the omnipresent General Oshima, whose infatuation for Hitler was not reciprocated by the Führer. Hitler, a movie fan—especially when it came to those pictures from which he hoped to learn the secrets of his potential enemies—was shown a motion picture sent to the German War Ministry by the Nazi military attaché at Moscow, General von Küchler. The picture showed Stalin reviewing a May Day parade, and when it was displayed on Hitler's private screen at Berchtesgaden, the Führer ordered that the sequences showing Stalin be repeated again and again, as if he were trying to fathom the character of the Russian leader through his features and gestures on the screen. Finally, he had the projector stopped at a close-up, looked intently at the picture of Stalin, then said: "I think I could trust this man." Acting upon his famous intuition, he ordered his Moscow embassy to contact the Kremlin and suggest closer co-operation with the Nazi Reich. It was a shot in the dark at extreme range; but to the astonishment of everyone concerned, perhaps even including Hitler, the offer was politely received in Moscow; and just a few weeks after Counselor Schnurre made the first inquiry, an alliance and nonaggression pact was signed by Molotov for the Soviet Union and Ribbentrop for Germany.

With the stroke of the pens of these two men the Anti-Comintern Pact of November 25, 1936, had become a scrap of paper. Tokyo was indignant and confused. Plaintive cables were sent to Berlin accusing the Embassy staff of negligence and failure—but Oshima and his colleagues were not at fault. The Germans had double-crossed them, too.

The signing of the Russo-German alliance, however, created an entirely new situation for Japan just as it did for Germany. For the Reich it secured the eastern frontier beyond what was to be conquered in Poland. For Japan it seemed to remove a persistent threat to her on the continent. With Russia thus tied to a friendly

Germany, a war between the Soviet Union and Japan was no longer considered as looming on the horizon. Russia thus eliminated as a potential opponent, Japan felt freer to turn her attention to the war against the United States and Great Britain, described as essential in the Tanaka Memorial but regarded as too risky as long as Japan had her commitments along the western borders of Manchuria and northern China.

The time had come for Admiral Isoroku Yamamoto to climb into the pilot's seat. He left the paper work in the Navy Ministry and assumed command of the First Fleet, his flag flying from the battleship *Nagato,* and incorporated the Second Fleet as well, combining the battleships, cruisers, and aircraft carriers of the two fleets into a mighty striking force for the first blow against the naval might of the United States.

Just as Yamamoto was departing for duty at sea the time had come for me also to change my work as district intelligence officer for command of a heavy cruiser. In San Diego we were in the very midst of an important and extensive piece of work which I had elected to do before my departure. It was the immense job of checking the address of every individual on our suspect list—some five thousand names. We were assisted in this tremendous task—at that time the only comprehensive checkup on suspects anywhere in the United States—by a popular and efficient Californian law enforcement officer, Sheriff Eugene W. Biscailuz of Los Angeles County, in whose territory the greatest number of suspects was concentrated.

A reserve officer in the United States Navy, Biscailuz was full of enthusiasm and had all the qualifications for doing an excellent job: "You give the orders, Captain," he said, "and I'll carry them out." This was the spirit I found everywhere along the coast, a contribution which greatly assisted my own work. We were ready to deputize a large number of trustworthy individuals to take care of any and all suspects at a time of actual emergency. The importance of the assistance I received from the Sheriff can well be understood when we remember that at this time over half of the aircraft factories of the nation were in my district. The Navy had a great responsibility and an immense job to perform, often in the face of opposition born of the complacency which still encumbered some of us. I recall the time I went to Major "Rube" Fleet, head of the Consolidated Aircraft Company, and advised him that the time had come when his organization should start the issuance of identification cards with photographs of its employees and should increase the number of guards. Fleet's reply, well meant though it undoubtedly was, was far from satisfactory. "Why," he said, "that would be too expensive."

I replied with firm finality: "But Rube, you are soon going to have it and like it. How about my talking to your personnel officer?"

"I guess it's O.K. Go ahead and do everything you think is necessary." The frugality of this business executive had been quickly overcome by the good judgment and inherent foresight which built this great American company.

When I sent to the Director of Naval Intelligence as my "swan song" the completed and checked suspect list, I recommended that every other district in the country be instructed to compile similar lists as quickly as possible. My recommendation was accepted, and the resulting lists provided the basis for the effective and simultaneous pickup of suspects when the news of December 7, 1941, was flashed to the nation.

Just as I was preparing to hand over my duties to the officer relieving me, an intelligence incident of major proportions was brought to my attention. A confidential informant reported to my office that a Japanese agent occupying a top position on our suspect list had inadvertently revealed a plot which appeared to have the greatest immediate significance. According to this agent, a suicidal attempt would be made by the Japanese to reduce our fleet by four battleships so as to establish a more equitable ratio with the Japanese fleet for "the Day." From the statement of the agent, the plot was planned as the act of individuals running amuck, for whom the Japanese government could apologize in seemingly good faith. But after the apologies the United States would be left with four less battleships.

The plot was explicitly outlined in a burst of emotional bravado by this indiscreet agent. Incensed at the sudden closing of the Mexican border at Tia Juana by the Immigration Department, he asserted that "the Japanese would soon open the border and keep it open." According to him, on the following day, October 17, 1940, a Japanese squadron of twelve suicide planes would suddenly appear at an American naval base where, according to information, four capital ships of the United States Navy were at anchor. The planes would come in sections of three each; four planes, one from each section, would make suicide attacks by diving down the stacks of individual ships, while the others were to drop their bombs and try to get away. This, incidentally, was the first indication that the Japanese were planning to use suicide planes, a plan fully carried out to our detriment in 1944–45, when the desperate Kamikaze Corps of Japanese aviation was brought into being.

The report electrified our office in San Diego. Fantastic though the plot seemed to us, it was our principle to take all information seriously so as not to be caught by surprise by any eventuality. The high reliability of our confidential informant, who was a skilled intelligence reserve officer with excellent contacts, and the outstanding position of the Japanese agent in the espionage organization of his country added significance to the report. We did not know how the Japanese planned to approach our ships—whether they were sending in a small converted carrier or planned to launch their planes from submarines so built as to accommodate one or two aircraft. But we were warned on October 16, 1940, that the attack was to take place the following day.

The atmosphere was conducive to such a suicidal attack. Germany had just completed the campaign in the west and was in the middle of the Battle of Britain. Southern England was being subjected to a cruel air offensive. The Axis was riding on the wave of unbroken victories; while Britain was living through what Mr. Churchill so eloquently called her finest hour. The co-operation between Germany and Japan was closest, while the nonaggression pact still in existence with the Soviet Union turned Axis eyes away from the Russian Far East. The United States, the "unofficial enemy," was suspected and hated as a nonbelligerent supporter of hard-pressed Britain; and it seemed quite plausible that Japan was assigned the role to deal with this mighty arsenal of democracy in a manner that was both effective and cheap to a reluctant aggressor.

There was no time to lose. First we ascertained whether there was anywhere on the west coast a concentration of four American battleships. Inquiry revealed that Admiral Richardson, Commander in Chief of the United States Fleet, had just arrived in San Pedro with three battleships and one heavy cruiser. Here then was the concentration of four capital ships which the Japanese had allegedly singled out for attack and destruction.

When at least part of the information was thus confirmed, I reported the matter to the commandant of the 11th Naval District, Admiral Charles Blakely, USN, who shared my apprehension and ordered me to get in immediate touch with Admiral Richardson on his flagship, the *Pennsylvania*. I jumped into a plane and flew to San Pedro, having advised Admiral Richardson that I would arrive with an important communication. This great American admiral was fully alerted and awaited my arrival on board. He listened to my report intently, contemplated the implications of the information, then asked: "Are there any Jap planes in the vicinity with which they could carry out the attack?"

"We are certain, sir," I said, "that there are no Japanese vessels within range from which such an attack could be staged. But I can give no assurance that there are no suicide planes hidden somewhere on Mexican soil. We have had several trustworthy reports of surreptitious activities of Japanese ships off that coast, and they could be involved in just such a plot."

"Well, I don't think we can ignore this report," he replied promptly.

"I agree with you, sir, we cannot ignore it."

No matter how remote and fantastic the plot appeared, Admiral Richardson was not the man to remain complacent in the face of a threat to his ships. "I will alert my antiaircraft batteries," the Admiral said, "and when you return to San Diego, advise Captain McCain, the commanding officer of the Air Station, to alert his aircraft as well."

Admiral Richardson was en route to San Francisco from Hawaii. On October 17, somewhat ahead of his schedule, he sailed, with his men at battle stations ready to meet and repel any Japanese threat. The day was one of anticlimax. We all waited for something to happen, but the day passed without incident.

It was impossible to ascertain whether the information was based on definite knowledge of Japanese intentions, or was merely the emotional outburst of a xenophobic Japanese agent who was constantly in contact with his naval and military officers visiting Mexico. It was possible, however, that Japanese Intelligence learned of the warning which had reached us and also of the alert at the San Diego Air Station and reconsidered the decision to "take care" of our four battleships.

There was, however, a lesson in this incident even though it evaporated in this uneventful manner. It was that the Japanese regarded our battleship fleet as an actual menace to their plans and thought that the elimination of at least four battleships was essential to create the nominal parity deemed necessary by them to prevent any interference by us in a Japanese movement toward the Philippines and Singapore. This strengthened my opinion that the Japanese were preoccupied with plans for an air attack against our fleet, wherever it was concentrated and in whatever strength.

When I again reviewed and analyzed this report, I arrived at the considered opinion that despite the inconclusive outcome of the episode there was more to the information than met the eye. I did not doubt that the agent had some information about Japanese intentions to bomb our battleships prior to a declaration of war. Furthermore, I did not doubt that he knew from conversations with informed Japanese naval officers that the Japanese would use their naval air arm for the preliminary attack to open hostilities. The pattern of the information, even though there had been no confirmation in practice, provided me with an additional insight into Japanese plans for the future; and I was, therefore, reluctant to dismiss the incident as merely a canard. From then on, I never ceased to be on the alert. I expected the Japanese to act, and to act in the manner which the agent's report indicated. From then on, I expected a Japanese attack on our fleet by aircraft momentarily, an apprehension shared only in the most perfunctory manner by those whose actual duty was the protection and safeguarding of these ships.

Fleet Problem 14 had set the pattern for the most effective means of attack against us. The incident of October 16, 1940, repeated the theme of four battleships which had to be sunk or disabled before the Japanese could move to the southward. This report had reached the commander in chief at the time, Admiral Richardson, and his successor, Admiral Kimmel. A detailed account also was immediately forwarded to the Chief of Naval Operations for the Director of Naval Intelligence.

22

THE SHOOTING WAR BEGINS

ON NOVEMBER 9, 1940, about three weeks after the "air attack which failed to materialize," I sailed by Matson liner for Hawaii to take command of the heavy cruiser *Salt Lake City*. Also en route to Hawaii and a passenger on my ship was the distinguished statesman Senator Owen Brewster of Maine. He was keenly interested in the situation in Hawaii and the potentialities of the months just ahead of us. In lengthy conversations with the Senator I outlined in some detail the situation as I saw it and stated my theories of impending events with a conviction fortified by my most recent experience and analysis. My apprehensions regarding the future were repeated to other people and definite points stressed as the position of the individual warranted, and all of them, except those who should have been most interested, remembered my apprehensions and forecasts as did the Senator himself. Six years later, when I was testifying before the Joint Congressional Committee investigating the Pearl Harbor disaster, he recalled our conversation. It was gratifying indeed to find that his memory was good while other memories seemed to falter under the strain of personal responsibilities and failures.

Remembering Captain Puleston's injunction, and acting upon my own inclinations that I was an intelligence officer first and foremost, upon arrival in Hawaii I went immediately to the Intelligence Office. I found it in a corner of the customhouse, tucked away in a two-room box, housing two officers, one yeoman, and a translator. This was the entire force on the eve of war.

But things were to change soon. I was told that Captain Kilpatrick, chief of staff of the scouting force, had just been designated by Admiral Richardson, the Commander in Chief of the U.S. fleet, to make a thorough investigation of all intelligence activities in Hawaii and that he wanted me to assist in these investigations.

There was little that could be accomplished with only limited facilities in the Intelligence Office in Honolulu. Appalled by the lack of counter-intelligence preparedness, I called the following morning, November 14, on Admiral Bloch, commandant of the 14th Naval District, to impress him with the necessity of improving his intelligence organization. I outlined to him our organizational structure on the west coast and suggested that a similar organization could be created in Hawaii. The fleet had been shifted to Hawaii, so it was his responsibility to provide facilities for its safety by increasing our intelligence preparedness. After listening intently he gave me carte blanche to have any personnel sent out I thought necessary. Acting under his authority, I wrote a number of letters the same day, and within a few weeks a comprehensive intelligence organization was functioning in Hawaii with concrete plans for further enlargement of personnel, training, and actual operations. Simultaneously I began to maintain contact with the woefully understaffed office of the fleet intelligence officer, Lieutenant Commander Edwin T. Layton, whom I had recommended for the assignment. He carried on his job despite the fact that he often "had his ears pinned back." Layton was under the jurisdiction of the Commander in Chief and beyond Admiral Bloch's authority. After obtaining a comprehensive over-all view of intelligence activities in Hawaii, I felt that I was well informed insofar as this particular phase of our preparedness was concerned. All these initial activities had to be performed at a feverish pace, since I knew I was to remain only two days. On November 15, after taking over command of the *Salt Lake City*, I was to sail for the Mare Island Navy Yard for needed repairs and an increase of antiaircraft armament.

I had learned of the prospective movements of my new command in a very roundabout way and in a manner which indicated that security aboard that ship was not what it should be. The incident through which I learned it was both amusing and serious. In those days of late 1940 we had already surrounded the movements of our ships with great secrecy, and it had been impossible for me to ascertain in San Diego before I left what her future schedule was to be. My family had been left behind in Coronado because I had decided that I did not want them in Hawaii if things were going to happen.

Several days after the Matson liner had departed from San Pedro, I was engaged in conversation with an elderly gentleman in the lounge and asked him what he was going to do in Hawaii. His reply interested me: "I have a son there who is a tailor and he wants to come back to our Long Beach branch because he has many orders for uniforms for two ships which are returning to the coast. So I am going to take charge out there while he is away."

"Is that so? What are the ships that are coming back?" I asked nonchalantly.

"One is the *Salt Lake City* and the other the *Pensacola*. They leave two days after we get in." He stopped short as he noticed the amazement I must have registered. Then he continued: "You seem surprised; are you interested in either of the ships?"

"Well," I replied, "I'm only going out to take command of the *Salt Lake City*. Where did you get this news and how authentic is it?"

"It must be true if my son is bringing me out here."

"Did he tell you not to let this be known?" I asked.

"No, it seems to be general knowledge."

"Thank you, sir," I said. "But I hope you're wrong."

Even before I arrived in Honolulu I had drawn up some comprehensive security measures which were to make the *Salt Lake City* the most security-minded ship in the fleet. Later when I found that stacks of cables were being filed in the Honolulu cable office with the ships' names as return addresses of the men, and that these cables were passing through innumerable Japanese hands, I was gratified to find that not a single *Salt Lake City* name was among them. But I reported the find to the Commander in Chief, and remedial measures were taken.

During the last phases of the three-month overhaul period at Mare Island the news reached me that my old acquaintance, Admiral Kichisaburo Nomura, whom I first met in Tokyo in 1920 when he was chief of Japan's Naval Intelligence, had been appointed ambassador to Washington. He was leaving for his post at once, and I expected him to pass through San Francisco, which he did. It seems that the Admiral knew of my presence in San Francisco, since upon arrival he inquired of Admiral A. J. Hepburn, USN, then commandant of the 12th Naval District, how he could get in touch with me. In the meantime I had talked with Admiral Richardson regarding Nomura's proposed visit and indicated that if there were no objections I should like to have a confidential talk with the new ambassador to ascertain if possible the object of his mission. Admiral Richardson asked me to send him a copy of the report which he knew I would make immediately.

When I arrived in Nomura's suite on the fourth floor of the Fairmont Hotel on February 7, 1941, the Admiral astonished his aides by ordering them out of the room. This was contrary to established Japanese custom, again proving to me that Nomura was ever ready to dispense with the formalism of his country's etiquette and act, as well as think, in our own Western ways. We talked for an hour and a half and covered a multitude of subjects, all bearing on the tense political and military situation. At several points I tested his desire to break off our talk, but he urged that we continue. Admiral Nomura was amazingly frank; and when I complimented him on his frankness, he indicated that I was one of the two persons in the United States to whom he could open his heart. The other he said, was Admiral William V. Pratt, USN (Retired), a former chief of Naval Operations and a brilliant naval officer. It was a gratifying answer to my own compliment—even though I realized that Nomura was by then a diplomat in fact as well as in name. I knew that there was one other, our Shimbashi teashop partner Mc-Claran, but he was retired and was unavailable.

In the course of the conversation Nomura made the following positive statements, which I am recounting here in order to show how one faction within the Japanese high command was thinking. Nomura stated:

1. His mission was to prevent a resort to force between Japan and the United States in settling present disagreements.

2. Japan had completely changed her views with regard to China, and early peace was now regarded as essential to both countries.

3. The signing of the Axis pact was done only after a sharp division of opinion in Japan and with only a slight balance of influence in its favor. The mistake was soon realized, but nothing could be done in the face of a *fait accompli*. It would have to die a natural death.

The Admiral apologized for the extremists in Japan; but when I recited to him the activities of these extremists, including those in French Indo-China and Siam, he made no comment and remained thoughtful for an appreciable interval. He seemed to be deeply fearful of the growing power concentrated in the hands of the extremists and knew of no way their power could be reduced at this late hour of tension.

When I left Nomura, I had arrived at a series of conclusions.

Above all, I felt that Japan regretted her partnership in the Axis and was greatly concerned over the prolongation of her China venture, Nomura being commissioned to do everything in his power to extricate Japan from her Chinese predicament by enlisting the good offices of the American government. He was also to try to prevent an embargo on oil and other essentials which the United States supplied to Japan, and was to request reconsideration on those items which were already under embargo.

He was quite frank in his expressions about a war between Japan and the United States. In 1921 he had made a statement to me. Now twenty years later he repeated it. "In such a conflict," he said in a statement which I now regard as historical, "Japan will be finished as an empire, and it will mean a great loss to the United States." He was deeply imbued with this thought, as he repeated: "A war against the United States will mean the finish of the Japanese Empire."

In my conversation with Admiral Nomura the war in China loomed largest. From the amount of time he spent in discussing the subject and the intensity with which he debated it, I deduced that the issue must have been foremost in all Japanese conversations on the highest levels, dominating the thoughts of Japanese military and political planners. But there seemed to be no end to Japan's adventure in China. Generalissimo Chiang Kai-shek was firmer than ever in resisting the siren songs of Japanese peace envoys, and we were backing him up with moral rather than material support, since, while we sent encouraging words to Chungking by the ton in diplomatic pouches, we were still shipping essential war materials to Japan, despite an extended embargo introduced late in 1940 in the wake of the signing of the Tripartite Pact.

If a confirmation of my gloomy views was still needed, this pact would have provided it. Nomura was astonishingly outspoken in his opposition to the pact, but so were other Japanese politicians in conversations with our diplomatic representatives in Tokyo. In May 1940, for example, the premier, Admiral Yonai, assured our counselor of the Embassy in Tokyo that Japan would never join a German-Italian pact as long as he was premier. But he was overthrown because of his stand, and this did not prevent Japan under the new Konoye cabinet from being a party to signing the Tripartite Pact just a few months later on September 27, 1940. I was particularly interested in Nomura's statement that the wheels of

Axis diplomacy were lavishly oiled with unvouchered German funds and many bribes were handed out to grease the palms of Japanese hands which were to sign the Axis pact. I refused to believe that the Emperor or Yonai could be bribed; but nevertheless, both had to chime in with others in hailing the pact as a great and noble act. The Emperor even invoked the hoary principle of the *Hakko Ichiu,* a blatant piece of Japanese falsification of history, claimed to be an injunction to Jimmu Tenno, the first descendant of the Sun Goddess in the sixth century before Christ, admonishing the Imperial House of Japan to "unite the eight corners of the world under one roof," interpreted to mean expansion for world domination.

It was impossible to learn the secret clauses of the Tripartite Pact, but there was little doubt that it abounded in unpublished preambles and protocols, the usual appendixes of wartime pacts concluded between belligerents and their seemingly neutral allies. When I tried to draw out Nomura on this particular subject, he protested both ignorance and innocence and assured me that there was nothing in the pact beyond what met the eye.

But co-operation between Germany and Japan was becoming close, not only in the political but also in the military sphere. From confidential information direct from our agents in Germany we learned that a huge Japanese military mission was being sent to Germany—but what astonished me was the fact that it was led by a flag officer of the Japanese Navy, another Nomura, Admiral Naokuni Nomura. This, then, was the game Japan was playing, symbolized even in the coincidental identity of names: one Nomura was sent to the United States to talk of peace, while another Nomura was sent to Germany to discuss war. Naokuni Nomura, our intelligence agents reported, made no secret of his sympathies. In fact, his actions in the Reich revealed that he had considered himself an active ally of the Germans in their war against Britain. He even participated in an operational cruise of a German submarine and was temporarily in command during the sinking of a British merchantman—without warning. In a sense, his trip was a shopping expedition, the Japanese trying to buy up as many German military inventions and secret weapons as possible. The Nazis, hoping to gain Japan as an active but neutral ally, obliged them by opening up all their arsenals and supplying everything the Japanese wanted. The shopping list of Naokuni Nomura was revealing enough in itself. It was no shopping list for peace. It was a harbinger of imminent war.

The German plans did not envisage Japan engaged in war against the United States. Hitler hoped to gain Japanese support for his war against the Soviet Union, a hope that was intensified a few months later when he discovered that Russian troops from the Far Eastern army were participating in the Battle of Rostov in November 1941.

His ambassador to Tokyo had been sending Hitler conflicting and contradictory reports, which were extremely vague about Japanese intentions, causing an entry in the official war diary referring to "the Japanese enigma." He hoped, however, that even a neutral Japan closely allied with Germany would remain a potential threat to the Far Eastern flank of the endless Russian front. In this hope, he had staged an elaborate hoax on October 7, 1941, proclaiming the Russian campaign virtually ended and the Red Army definitely broken. This hoax was intended to be at the expense of the Japanese, to lure them into the war against the Soviet Union by creating the impression that in view of the Russian collapse, a Far Eastern war would be an easy task for Japan.

But the Japanese, however, had different plans; and while they did everything in their power to keep the German-Japanese alliance at work, they did not share their secrets with the Nazis. When, on December 7, 1941, the Pearl Harbor attack became known at Hitler's headquarters, the following entry was made in the war diary: "The heavy veil which concealed Japanese intentions until today has now fallen. Japan attacked the United States and Great Britain." A special conference was called for the same afternoon at which Hitler gave vent to his disappointment in no uncertain terms. There can be no doubt that he was unaware of Japanese intentions to attack the United States; that he fully disapproved of the attack; and, thirdly, that he regarded the Japanese decision as greatly prejudicial to his own war plans.

A report of my conversation with Ambassador Nomura in February 1941 was prepared for Admiral Stark, Chief of Naval Operations. A copy was sent to Admiral Kimmel, who had by then replaced Admiral Richardson as commander in chief of the United States fleet. To Admiral Kimmel I wrote:

"It is my opinion that a new situation has developed which might or might not affect previous estimates."

There was no answer to this note, but Admiral Stark acknowledged my report by writing:

"I am more than grateful for your report of the conversations with the new Japanese Ambassador. It is intensely interesting and illuminating. I sent the original to the President and copies to ONI, Secretary Hull, and Secretary Knox. Many, many thanks."

Notwithstanding my conversation with Ambassador Nomura, other political observations had crystallized my opinion that Japan was moving toward war. It seemed that Nomura's visit could be the last constructive effort to forestall it. Ever since 1933, when I participated in Fleet Problem 14, already described, I had somehow visualized the course Japan would take on the eve of such an attack. I had no doubt that it would start, as Admiral Schofield anticipated in his own outline of the fleet problem, with a surprise air attack against our Pacific fleet wherever it was located at that particular time, to be followed by the destruction of shore facilities in Hawaii, also from the air. A fleet action in the conventional sense was out of the question because of the distances involved. On the basis of my studies of Japanese psychology, I expected that an unmistakable sign would be added to the usual indications of an impending aggressive move by Japan. The withdrawal of her merchant shipping from all sea lanes and marked increase in radio traffic are conventional and time-honored signs of the imminence of any war between sea powers. But in the case of Japan I anticipated the appearance of a Japanese submarine in the Hawaiian area.

It was with these thoughts and apprehensions that I sought an interview with Admiral Kimmel, the new commander in chief of the United States fleet, to lay before him my analysis and perhaps to place my knowledge of Japanese psychology at his disposal to aid him in forming an estimate of the situation. If I had any doubts in my mind that Japan had decided to join Germany in what then seemed a victorious march of unending conquest, they were now all dispelled. Despite Nomura's reassuring words and the protestations of other peace-minded or, rather, prudent Japanese of vision, I was almost convinced that a war between the United States and Japan had become inevitable.

I had known Admiral Kimmel but slightly in Washington when in 1935 I was in charge of the Far Eastern Section of ONI while he was director of ship movements in Operations. I remembered him as an approachable but serious and energetic type of man whose pinkish complexion and ruddy face suggested amiability. He was popular with many high-ranking naval officers, but contrary to widespread rumors, and as he testified before the Congressional Pearl Harbor Committee, he was not particularly close to President Roosevelt, whom he once served for an extremely short period as temporary aide while Mr. Roosevelt was assistant secretary of the Navy.

In Hawaii, Admiral Kimmel was known as a hard-working, conscientious Cincus, as the title of commander in chief was then abbreviated. In fact, observers said that he was working too hard trying to do everything himself. He was certainly entitled to better advice from certain members of his staff whose short memories and incorrect conclusions made possible a deduction that the chances of an air attack by the Japanese on Pearl Harbor were "none."

Kimmel's position in Hawaii was far from being an enviable one. The commandant of the Naval District was Admiral Claude C. Bloch, USN, himself a former commander in chief but now subordinated to a younger officer, a role no one is likely to cherish, wherever he may serve. It was common gossip in Hawaii that there was no love lost between the two top-ranking admirals, a situation which was by no means conducive to the harmony so necessary for accomplishment of security of the base and the preparedness of our fleet.

I had hoped that by carrying my concern to the Commander in Chief I should be able to round out the picture for him if only by providing him with the personal opinions and analyses of an officer who had spent the greater part of his years studying the Japanese. It seemed that Admiral Kimmel was eager to receive this information. After I stated to his chief of staff, Captain (now Vice Admiral) W. W. Smith, USN, that I should like to see the Commander in Chief, he notified the Admiral; and in a few minutes an interview was granted. On a March day in 1941 I was escorted by Smith into a map-studded office of the Commander in Chief to be cordially greeted by my highest superior in the fleet.

Our conversation opened with a detailed discussion of my report on the conversations with Admiral Nomura, a copy of which he had received. Then I related to Admiral Kimmel the details of the incident of October 16, 1940, when we were alerted by the report that a suicide squadron of Japanese planes would bomb four of our battleships the following day. Admiral Kimmel seemed to be intensely interested in the incident, which led us to a discussion of my conclusions. I told the Admiral of my conviction that if Japan decided on war with us she would open hostilities with an air attack on our fleet without a declaration of war, on a week end, and probably *on a Sunday morning,* by launching planes from carriers so that they could fly down wind from a spot as far away as possible in order to facilitate the escape of the ships of the attacking force. This spot, it was emphasized, was usually in the northern sector. He was specific in his questions, which I tried to answer in the same detail—and we even touched upon the lesser possibility of the Japanese lowering some seaplanes from merchantmen smuggled into the lea of one of the innumerable islands of the archipelago. This I said could easily be forestalled by declaring a five-hundred-mile section of ocean around the Hawaiian Islands an operating area requiring all merchant vessels coming into it to pass through specific points where inspection was possible. Ships found in other localities of the area would be liable to seizure.

Such an operating area was set up at a later date.

I told Admiral Kimmel that one of the earliest indications of hostile intent, the withdrawal of merchant shipping from the usual lanes, would be evident through the system established and set up by me in 1935 in Naval Intelligence. The other, markedly increased radio traffic, would be evident to his operators. I then concluded with the unmistakable sign and said: "When you have a report of an enemy submarine in the Hawaiian area, you can know that they are ready to strike."

Finally, Admiral Kimmel asked how I thought this air attack could be prevented. I told him, "Admiral, you will have to have patrols out at least five hundred miles daily."

He replied without hesitating, "Well, of course we have neither the personnel nor material to do that."

I pondered for a moment, then added: "Admiral, you'd better get them, because that is what's coming."

Our conversation lasted about ninety minutes, and I left the Admiral's office in the belief that it was a fruitful one.

About six months later I was approached by a civilian, Mr. Curtis B. Munson, who came to Hawaii late in October 1941 with exceptional credentials signed by Admiral Stark which caused him to be looked upon as a presidential agent. He said he had been told to see me because of my knowledge of the Japanese. He was interested in the probability of armed uprisings by Japanese on the west coast and in Hawaii in case of hostilities with Japan. He was therefore investigating the loyalties of Japanese residents of the islands. I outlined to him the reasons for my firm conviction that if Japan decided to go to war with us, hostilities would open with an air attack on the fleet at Pearl Harbor on a week end and probably on Sunday morning. Then I told him emphatically that he could eliminate any fear of uprisings or sabotage in either locality because of the utmost secrecy necessary to make a surprise air attack successful, and that that was the way the Japanese would commence hostilities. "Sabotage and uprisings require well co-ordinated leadership and advance notice which in this case would be impossible. Their main objective at this time is four battleships," I reiterated. I then said to him:

"You now have two Japanese envoys for Washington." (Kurusu was en route.) "When the third one arrives, you can look for things to break immediately one way or the other." I explained to him that there would have to be three Japanese envoys in Washington for a decision to be reached. My conclusion that at least three were necessary to decide anything or even to carry out a decision reached by others grew out of my analyses of the many inspection trips the Japanese used to make to this country during peacetime. We watched those visits very carefully, and discovered that on almost every visit they were interested in some important industrial activity or device. In each plant there was usually one item which brought a quick succession of three Japanese inspecting parties. After that, all interest was lost in this particular plant and in the item of curiosity. One Japanese cannot make up his mind. Two Japanese can hardly ever agree. They need an umpire in all their decisions, their innate trait of subordination influencing them to agree upon what the third person regards as the best course of action or the most reasonable decision. All this was reinforced by one of the proverbs which seem to guide all Japanese action: "Hear three times, believe."

World events were now moving with gunfire rapidity. Hitler was at war with the Soviet Union, their ten-year pact notwithstanding; and the Japanese Army for the first time was moving south into Indo-China. The Axis-satellite Vichy government, under pressure, approved the Japanese move and thus was providing a springboard for attack against Malaya and even the Philippines. Our answer to this was to freeze Japanese assets in the United States, an outstanding move unprecedented in its wisdom from the point of view of intelligence. No espionage network can exist without adequate funds, even though, contrary to common belief, intelligence is comparatively inexpensive. The funds at the disposal of Japanese espionage in the United States were concealed under a variety of titles and were kept by many commercial firms and other financial enterprises in letters of credit and similar negotiable papers. With one stroke of the Treasury's pen all access to these funds was barred, and Japan's local donors, like the gambling rings of the west coast, proved inadequate to finance sufficiently the work of Japanese espionage. This freezing of Japanese funds at the psychological moment was one of the contributory factors in rendering Japanese espionage ineffective during the war.

On September 16, 1941, I again wrote to Admiral Stark: "It is very gratifying that there is a possibility of resolving the Japanese situation, but we must not relax our vigilance until they have given concrete demonstrations of their sincerity."

The reasons for this were manifest in Japan's domestic obligations and international commitments. In the final analysis they were interconnected, and as one was caused by the other, the solution of the domestic problems also depended on the settlement of international issues.

But Japan moved on in other fields. In October the saber-rattling General Hideki Tojo, spokesman of the Kwantung military clique, took over the reigns from the pliable, fence-straddling Prince Konoye, providing still other evidence that Japan was rapidly moving toward war. On November 17 the second envoy of whom I spoke to Munson was received by the President.

The selection of Kurusu was one of those typical signs of Japanese arrogance in international relations when they feel that they have two jokers in their hand. Saburo Kurusu was another of my old acquaintances from Tokyo, husband of an American wife, and father of a boy whom I used to bounce on my knee when he was a little lad. But it was this same Kurusu who had been sent to Berlin to sign the Tripartite Pact with the Germans and Italians. A more flagrant violation of international etiquette and a more impertinent insult to the United States could hardly be imagined than to send a man to Washington to discuss peace who only a short while before had been the protagonist of an agreement spelling out war in capital letters.

I hoped that I would be asked by Admiral Kimmel to meet Kurusu on his arrival in Honolulu so that I might attempt to learn something of his mission, and I let it be known at headquarters that Kurusu had been a close personal acquaintance in Tokyo. But I was not called in from the minor activities in which my ship was engaged off Pearl Harbor. Kurusu's intentions therefore remained completely enshrouded.

The arrival of this second envoy increased my inner tension to the highest pitch, and it was under some emotional strain that I prepared myself for a cruise to Wake Island escorting the *Enterprise*, Admiral Halsey's carrier flagship, which was taking plane reinforcements to the Marines there.

On the eve of our sailing, November 27, I dined at the house of Lorrin Thurston, editor of the *Honolulu Advertiser* and head of radio station KGU. After dinner, with only Thurston's wife and himself present, we moved into the living room and there, for three hours, we discussed the situation. I revealed to them in detail what I had told Admiral Kimmel and Munson. Thurston was baffled and excited. Finally, as I concluded the careful analysis of past events and those soon to come, he suddenly exclaimed: "Here I am, a reserve officer in G-two, and I haven't even been advised what to send out over my radio in case of an attack!" I advised him to say: "We are having a sporadic air attack, everyone should keep calm and remain indoors. Do not go on the streets as it will interfere with the military going to their posts. There is nothing to worry about."

I did not share the confidence these words were meant to inspire when, on November 28, I sailed from Pearl Harbor with Admiral Halsey as part of Task Force Eight.

While at sea we monitored as usual all incoming news broadcasts of interest. In one of these on December 2 I picked up a most significant news item. According to the announcer, reading a press dispatch from Washington, the Japanese ambassador to Peru had just arrived in Washington. Here, then, I thought, were the three envoys from Tokyo. Nomura was the first to come; he was joined by Kurusu; and now the arrival of Tatsuji Sakamoto from Lima completed the circle. I was fully alerted, watching for the other sign of war: the appearance of a Japanese submarine in Hawaiian waters. It was on the morning of December 5 that a signal indicated the appearance of the expected submarine. We were advised by Pearl Harbor that an unidentified submarine had been reported in our own operating area south of the islands. I had not the slightest doubt that Japan was ready to strike. From six o'clock that evening, when short-wave radio reception from Tokyo became feasible, I sat at my radio until midnight trying to intercept any conversation which might be on the air. I hoped to pick up information which would justify a signal to Admiral Halsey for forwarding to Cincus at Pearl Harbor.

I did intercept a jumbled conversation, a fantastic group of sounds scrambled by a machine to prevent listeners from knowing what was being said. I was able to distinguish that the person on the receiving end was being given and was acknowledging orders. Ordinarily in Japanese conversation the one who is speaking does so in very short sentences at the end of which he says, *"Nei"*—meaning "Do you get me?" If understood, the listener says, *"Ha."* Thus a conversation sounds mostly like a series of *Nei's* and *Ha's*. If any part is not understood, the listener with a rising inflection, says, "Huh?" and the portion not understood is usually repeated.

On this evening, just two nights before Pearl Harbor, I could detect a distinct note of tenseness in the acknowledgments of the listener, and I knew that he was receiving orders. But I could not make out any part of the conversation because of the effective scrambling process. With only this circumstantial evidence available to me I felt stymied. I could almost hear Admiral Halsey's emphatic exclamations had I informed him in a signal: "I think things are about to break because I hear a Jap on the radio saying in very excited voice, 'Ha-Ha-Ha!' "

The sun rose on a very tense Saturday as we were returning to Pearl at the highest speed consistent with our diminished fuel supply. We drew within five hundred miles of Hawaii but could observe nothing of significance. I retired that night with an uneasy feeling, shared by many of my shipmates who knew of my concern and showed it. The tension grew by the hour, and the suspense kept me awake. I arose early that Sunday, December 7, 1941, well before the usual round of dawn activities. I had just returned to my cabin at exactly eight A.M. when my communication officer burst into my quarters with a look of consternation on his face. It was not necessary for me to hear him to know that something had happened. But he blared forth immediately, "Captain, a message just came saying, 'They're bombing Oahu . . . this is no drill. . . .' "

I rushed to my radio and switched it on to KGU, Lorrin Thurston's station, to get additional information. Shortly, as I listened intently to the words in the loud-speaker, my own draft message, suggested to Lorrin just about two weeks before, came back to me:

"We are having a sporadic air attack. Everyone should keep calm and remain indoors. Do not go on the streets as it will prevent the military from going to their posts. There is nothing to worry about."

These last words of my own making kept coming back to me, haunting my mind: "There is nothing to worry about. . . . There is nothing to worry about. . . . There is nothing to worry about," like the panting of the engines below my feet.

I wondered. But I knew that at last the shooting war had begun!

23

BEHIND THE TRAGEDY
OF PEARL HARBOR

THE IMPACT of the news was overwhelming. My shipmates regarded the news as a major catastrophe even before they had any information of the extent of the damage. Morale, generally uniformly high on our ships, was visibly sinking as additional information poured in on the radio. Experienced Navy men could read between the lines and realized that the Japanese had scored a major success. They were even inclined to exaggerate the Japanese victory in their minds and to regard it as a strategic triumph; whereas in reality it was a major tactical succcess.

It was my regular practice to check up personally on the morale of my crew even in peacetime. Whenever I noticed a slump or received an adverse report I stepped in to give morale a lift. I was proud of the fact that on my ships, from the *Dorsey* to the *Salt Lake City*, morale was always high, the crews efficient, and the atmosphere congenial.

The checkup on morale became an urgent necessity now that we were at war. Outwardly, as we sailed through the ocean that was no longer pacific, all wartime measures were functioning smoothly: the ship was blacked out, our radio was silent, our battle stations were manned. The calm water, the serenely wheeling sea gulls, the cloudless skies seemed to belie the grim fact that all the world was now at war. But the contrast was far from soothing. It was nerve-racking. To think that our base was now probably only a heap of rubble, that many of our best ships rested on the bottom of the bay, serving as steel coffins for some of our best friends, and that we were returning to a cemetery of American preparedness was by no means reassuring. As I watched these ideas permeating the minds of my shipmates I decided to intervene at the first opportunity and attempt by psychology to restore the morale on board.

My determination to speak to the crew was crystallized the morning of our entrance into Pearl after an all-night, fruitless search of the areas to the southward. As we approached the entrance, a signal came that a pilot would board us. Ordinarily we took no pilot going in to our buoy; this indicated that there were possible obstructions unknown to us. As we stopped near the entrance buoy, Mr. Sorenson, the oldest pilot at Pearl, came aboard. His face was the epitome of concealed grief. He was strangely silent where he was usually buoyant and voluble.

"Where's the fleet?" I asked Mr. Sorenson.

"Fleet?" he replied, looking at me with incredulous eyes. "There isn't any fleet; they're all sunk!" And then he expanded: "They are all gone! That fire you see is the *Arizona*. Others are upside down or almost out of sight. Right there across the entrance is the *Nevada*. The *Pennsylvania* was bombed in the dry dock, and the *Lurline* was sunk by a submarine."

"The *Lurline?*" I asked. "She was supposed to leave on the fifth, and I had hoped to get in to see some friends off on her."

"They got her, one day out." I stood for a moment appalled. All those innocent people gone at the hand of a treacherous Jap submarine. I felt myself stiffen appreciably, and I unconsciously uttered a deprecating allusion to the little brown "brothers."

"All right, Mr. Sorenson. That's all I want to hear. I'll talk later after I have put my ship alongside the oil tanker." It was very consoling when the pilot assured me that the tanker *Neosho* was undamaged, as were the navy yard storage and repair facilities.

The terrible scenes within Pearl Harbor have already been partially described. Someday the full picture will be painted. Once alongside the tanker, I had the word passed over the loud-speaker: "Let's get going on this oil and provisions. We're going out after those Japs as soon as we're full." This produced a burst of speed throughout the ship. After that I went below to my cabin to relax in an easy chair.

As I sat with eyes staring at the deck beams above I heard a light knock at the door. "Come in," I said pleasantly. It was the ship's medical officer, Commander James F. Hays.

"Isn't it terrible, Captain?" he began.

"What's terrible, Jimmie?" I asked.

"Why, all this terrible destruction. What on earth are we going to do?"

"Sit down, Jimmie," I said, pointing to another chair into which he slipped quietly as if not wanting to disturb the angry elements.

"The Japs have missed the boat, Jimmie," I began, "and they are going to be very disappointed when they find that we have not lost a single unit which we would want to use against them, and that they haven't touched our base, which is really the vital thing in this war for us. As you see, we have the fuel and supplies with which to pursue them. Jimmie, they are licked before they start."

Thus began a forty-five-minute dissertation on the mistakes of the Japs and on our own war potential of ten to one. Jimmie, at first a little doubtful, became more talkative and then began to smile. At the end of the forty-five minutes he arose from his chair, a broad grin on his face, and said exultantly:

"Why, Captain, I feel like a different person."

If that was the reaction of the ship's doctor, then my whole crew needed the same medicine, I thought. I went immediately to my desk and made copious notes on the conversation just completed and decided that as soon as possible I would give a talk to my crew along the same lines.

During the day I managed to get ashore to a telephone. I called the Intelligence Office. They had just completed the roundup of suspects. I asked one friend to cable my wife that I was safe. Then I called Lorrin Thurston.

"My God, Zack, I'm glad you're safe. Where are you? Come on over," he yelled excitedly.

"I'm sorry, Lorrin," I replied. "I won't be seeing you for quite a few days. There's work to be done."

"Well, you certainly hit it on the nose. When Stephanie saw that item about the third envoy arriving in Washington on December 2 we were both watching for things to happen. How's your ship?"

"She's all right, Lorrin, and you just watch her when she starts shooting."

"Good luck," Lorrin said. "Hope we'll see you soon."

When we were ordered back on a patrol to the northward after a very short sixteen hours in port, I went to sea with a crew whose spirit was far from satisfactory. The thoughts of my men were incoherent, as indeed the picture which presented itself to them at Pearl was incoherent, too, in its mass of twisted steel and chaotic rubble. If I could talk things over with the men, they would, I thought, find calm in my own calmness, and reassurance in my own confidence. I was one of the very few men on board who was not unduly alarmed over this sudden turn of history.

On Saturday, December 13, I decided the right moment had come. After the crew had been mustered on the quarter-deck, I left the bridge and walked aft with an air of complete confidence and even a slight smile. I felt that every eye was upon me as I stepped to the microphone on the quarter-deck.

"I have called you together for several reasons," I began. "First of all there are things which I feel you want to know, and there are several things which you ought to know. I appreciate exactly how you feel and have felt the past few days. We have had a tremendous shock. I have been through such a great calamity before and I know your feelings and reactions. I am, therefore, very deeply consoled by the fact that recovery is very quick, and I can see that you have recovered from it. I make reference to my experience in the big Japanese earthquake in Yokohama in 1923, where everything collapsed at that time. There was no opportunity to fight back, and there was very little in this case, but you will have your opportunity and satisfaction very soon."

Then I proceeded to read to them two dispatches which had come in from the Commander in Chief and the Chief of Naval Operations soon after December 7.

"Your actions have been splendid," Cincus signaled. "We took a blow yesterday. It will not be a short war. We will give many heavy blows to the Japanese. Carry on." The dispatch from CNO said: "While you have suffered from a treacherous attack, your Commander in Chief has informed me that your courage and stamina remain magnificent. You know you will have your revenge. Recruiting stations are jammed with men eager to join you."

Then I continued: "I am really sorry that the ship had to go into Pearl Harbor the other day and that you had to observe what had taken place there, because I think it has served to give you all an entirely wrong impression. It is a matter of fact that regardless of results of the raid on Pearl Harbor, the effect of what took place there is going to be greatly beneficial to us for many reasons. . . . We have lost one battleship and sustained some damage to others, but in this connection it is to be noted we have not lost a single unit which is now considered far more important. I refer to aircraft carriers, heavy cruisers, light forces, and submarines. The recent activities, the damaging of a few of our battleships, the sinking of the two British battleships at Singapore, and the sinking of the enemy battleship *Haruna* [so reported but actually not sunk] and another badly damaged in Philippine waters with the small forces available there, indicate that the large, more slowly moving battleships are going to be employed in the future in a different and limited manner.

"You will note that they did not get a single carrier or heavy cruiser and barely touched any of the light forces. They are going to be very much surprised and disappointed in this revelation. I know this to be a fact from certain information that I have.... I am not telling you these things to ease your mind, but I want to impress upon all of you that we have not lost anything. I hope that what I have told you will impress and convince you of this point and stop any concern. We have a particular job to do right now, and our part in this work is very important."

I went on to talk for a long time, explaining the necessity for the discomforts imposed upon the men by keeping all compartments closed below decks. I talked about safety measures, censorship, gas masks, and morale in general. I made it a particular point to warn them against rumors, illustrating every one of my arguments with appropriate little incidents.

I observed the men closely as I spoke, to note any reactions. There were many, and they were distinct. I first noticed the look of helplessness replaced by one of interest and anticipation. As the talk progressed, I saw men glance at each other as if seeking to bolster their own changed attitude. Soon I saw smiles of confidence being thrown back and forth; and finally, as I saw them nudge each other, or slap a neighbor, I realized that they were back to normal. At this stage I knew it was time to stop talking.

"I must compliment every one of you," I said in conclusion, "for the manner in which you have worked, the spirit which you have shown, and the stamina which is inherent in every one of you. I have noticed, and I have watched carefully, the manner in which everyone has 'snapped back' and particularly the manner in which you are eating." There was loud laughter. I had succeeded!

As soon as I had returned to my cabin, in came Dr. Hays, his face wreathed in smiles. I motioned him to be seated, and we lighted cigarettes.

"Captain," he started, "I've never in all my life seen such a change in a body of men as I witnessed today. Why, it was just unbelievable. I watched them all the time, and things progressed just as if they had been arranged."

"They were arranged, Jimmie," I replied. "You helped me do it in that talk we had in here the morning after Pearl Harbor."

Jimmie blushed a little, probably realizing for the first time that I had used him as a guinea pig, then he said:

"Well, it certainly was great, and I think every man that was in Pearl Harbor or has seen it since the raid needs just such a talk."

"That gives me another idea, Jimmie. I'll let you know if it works out."

Upon our return to port I went immediately to the public relations office of the Commander in Chief and saw Captain Waldo Drake, the officer in charge, and formerly one of my zone intelligence officers in the 11th Naval District. I told Waldo my experience with the crew and suggested the talk be furnished the other ships, without mention of me or my ship, as a guide in preparing something similar.

"That's wonderful," he said. "We'll make a press release of it, too."

The next day the Honolulu newspapers editorialized on my point of view and reprinted excerpts from my address.

This, then, was our part of the picture. I wondered at the time how the Japanese had received the news of Pearl Harbor and how satisfied they were with the results. These questions could not be answered then, but now we know all the answers in meticulous detail.

Pearl Harbor was of Yamamoto's making. The idea, which first took root in his fertile brain while he was still in Washington, became ever more crystallized as he climbed higher and higher on the ladder of the Japanese naval hierarchy. As the years passed, the war against the United States became a fixation with him, but only a very few men, his closest and most intimate collaborators, knew that all the Japanese war preparations which he inspired were really preparations for war against the United States.

Throughout 1941 the Japanese combined fleet participated in large-scale maneuvers while the fleet staff of Commander in Chief Yamamoto held so-called war games, both in the offices of the Naval General Staff in Tokyo, and on board ships anchored at Sukumo, Saeki, Kagoshima, and Kanoya, usually on board Yamamoto's own flagship, the *Nagato*. The opposing fleets were given meaningless designations during these exercises and war games so that only a very few initiated members of Yamamoto's staff knew that they were in reality preparations for the war against Britain and the United States.

Then a special meeting of all fleet staff officers was called at Tokyo for September 2, 1941. Attendance was compulsory, and members of the staff were advised that the war games would be of momentous importance on this occasion. So many officers were summoned to the games that the facilities of the Naval War College proved inadequate. So Yamamoto's staff adjourned to the Army War College, guarded by special detachments to prevent unauthorized persons from learning the purpose of the meeting.

When all members of Yamamoto's staff had assembled in the large auditorium, the Commander in Chief proceeded to share his closely guarded secret with all of them. He told them bluntly that this was to be last of the many war games. Once this war game was finished, the officers would have to prepare themselves for the supreme test of war. For the first time the opposing fleets were given definite designations. The attacking team, commanded by Admiral Yamamoto himself, was called the "N team," the letter standing for Nippon. An "A team," designating America, was commanded by Admiral Nobutake Kondo, while an "E team," the letter standing for England, was under the command of Admiral Chuichi Nagumo.

The operation plan was drawn up by a relatively junior officer, Commander Watanabe, chief of Yamamoto's plans and operations section, under the supervision of Admiral Ito, chief of staff, and Captain Kurojima, deputy chief of staff.

The great war game that, in Yamamoto's own words, was to decide the fate of the empire for centuries to come started on September 5, 1941, and continued, with short interruptions for meals and hurried rest, until September 13. On that last day the actual attack on Pearl Harbor was rehearsed and found feasible, although the game indicated that Japan would lose about one-third of the units participating in the Pearl Harbor raid. Unfortunately this proved a too pessimistic estimate, since the attacking vessels all escaped unscathed, even though numerous assault planes were shot down.

It was also on September 13, a day of infamy for Japan, that a fundamental disagreement between Admiral Ito and Captain Kurojima developed over the follow-up operations in the wake of an anticipated successful air raid. The question before the staff meeting was truly a Hamletian one: to land or not to land during the second phase of the raid. Captain Kurojima advocated an amphibious assault, and suggested that an emaciated American defense force would not be able to withstand the landing, even though the Japanese attempted it with only inadequate forces. Admiral Ito argued that Japan could not afford such a risky double operation, considering the initial risks involved in the air attack at such an immense distance from the home base. Logistics were a decisive factor.

There was long discussion with several flag officers participating. When the decision was made finally by Yamamoto, he decided against amphibious assault, thus embracing Ito's cautious attitude. This decision, despite its apparent manifestation of caution, revealed Yamamoto as the gambler he truly was. Although he realized that his forces were insufficient for a strategic assault and could, at best, score a major tactical victory, he hoped that he could bluff the United States into submission even with the weak hand he held. He counted upon the collapse of American morale. Japan lost the war on September 13, 1941, even before she embarked upon it, when a decision born of the realization of her own weakness prevented her from delivering what might have become a *coup de grâce* to our chief Pacific base.

Later, when the Battle of Midway supplied the final convincing evidence that Japan had overreached herself and miscalculated the relative resourcefulness of the two belligerents, Yamamoto realized his blunder as a sporting poker player usually does. It was then that he made a statement that reached us in a distorted form. He said:

"We would have to land on the west coast of America, fight our way east all across the continent, capture Washington and dictate the peace in the White House if we want to win this war. But all this is patently impossible." He must have been relieved, indeed, when the bullet from an American plane extricated him from the predicament into which his gambling nature had enticed him. But it must be said that he undoubtedly realized, with Nomura, that war with the United States was a great gamble at best.

From the war game Yamamoto returned to his flagship *Nagato* (incidentally the only Japanese capital ship to survive the war, though in a seriously damaged condition) and sailed for Kure for a meeting with Field Marshal Sugiyama, chief of the Army General

Staff. This meeting took place on September 15 and was as momentous in its consequences as was the war game itself. Yamamoto outlined his plan to Sugiyama and assured him that the initial major victory of the fleet would enable him to exploit an American defeat situation with the comparatively limited forces which the Army had available for ambitious conquests to the southward. It was only upon receiving this assurance, documented and supported by the record of the Tokyo war game, that Sugiyama agreed to commit the Army to Yamamoto's venture. Agreement thus reached, Yamamoto sailed for Saeki, where his plans and operations staff put the finishing touches on the actual war plan, while Sugiyama explained the plan to Tojo and obtained the Premier's support and political cooperation.

On November 1 the fleet received sealed orders to stand by, first for Y-Day and then to prepare for X-Day. Y-Day was the designation of the date on which the assault force built around six carriers was to sail from its assembly point in Hitokappu Bay in the Kuriles, while X-Day was the date on which the attack was to take place. On November 5, Y-Day was fixed as November 23, Japanese time, while five days later top-secret orders designated December 8, Japanese time, as X-Day. At the same time a code was designed, first to inform the fleet at sea of the concentration of American forces at Pearl Harbor, and then to order the attack. It was agreed upon that the signal "The fate of the Empire" incorporated in a seemingly innocuous broadcast would indicate that there were many warships assembled in Pearl Harbor. The code phrase "Cherry blossoms are in all their glory" was to indicate the presence of no warships. The all-important Navy code for "All forces attack" was "Climb Mount Niitaka." This should be distinguished from the diplomatic code which became the subject of considerable discussion and investigation. It has usually been referred to as the so-called Japanese "winds code" and the alleged "winds message." In the report by Admiral H. K. Hewitt, USN, formerly top secret, it was described as follows:

In the latter half of November, 1941, the Japanese Government by messages to Washington and elsewhere established two codes to be used for communication between Tokyo and elsewhere. The first has been referred to as the "winds code." In that code certain Japanese words were to be added in the middle and at the end of the daily Japanese language short-wave news broadcasts and could also be used in Morse code messages, which words would apparently be weather reports. Thus, the Japanese words "HIGASHI NO KAZE AME" which meant "East wind rain," would actually mean that Japan–United States relations were in danger. Words were also supplied for Japan-Russian relations and for Japan-British relations. The existence of this code was brought to the attention of the Navy Department late in November through the interception and decryption of Japanese messages establishing the code, and also through information to the same effect received from other sources such as the United States Naval Attaché at Batavia. It appeared that the use of the code words would indicate a breaking off of diplomatic relations or possibly war between the countries designated.

The Japanese also established, late in November, 1941, a code system which has been referred to as the "hidden word code.".... This code was intended to be used, when telegraphic communications might be severed, as a means of informing Japanese diplomats of the situation concerning the country in which they were located.

A preparatory "winds message" was sent on November 19, in Japanese diplomatic code, and gave the code words to be used in later fictitious broadcasts. The actual message read:

Regarding the broadcast of a special message in an emergency.

In case of emergency (danger of cutting off our diplomatic relations), and the cutting off of international communications, the following warning will be added in the middle of the daily Japanese language short wave news broadcast:

(1) In case of a Japan–U. S. relations in danger: HIGASHI NO KAZE AME (East wind rain).

(2) Japan–U. S. S. R. relations: KITA NO KAZE KUMORI (North wind cloudy).

(3) Japan–British relations: NISHI NO KAZE HARE (West wind clear).

This signal will be given in the middle and at the end as a weather forecast and each sentence will be repeated twice. When this is heard please destroy all code papers, etc. This is as yet to be a completely secret arrangement.

Forward as urgent intelligence.

This was a step taken by the Japanese Foreign Office to advise their *diplomatic* representatives throughout the world as to what was imminent. This preparatory message *was* sent and *was intercepted,* translated, and decoded by many stations of the Allies who were listening to the Japanese traffic.

The "execute" or the actual further transmission of one or more of these specified phrases at the end of subsequent weather broadcasts is the point that has been so much under debate. In the congressional hearings Captain Safford indicated that he had seen the "execute" message on December 3 or 4, 1941. Others with access to all messages said there was no "execute" message.

I was not in a position to see any of them before December 7. However, I have an opinion. I agree with Admiral Hewitt that "a Japanese message using the 'winds code' words relating to the United States, if received on 3 or 4 December, or at any other time prior to 7 December 1941, would have conveyed no information of importance which the Navy and War Departments did not already possess. Such a message would have indicated either a break in diplomatic relations or possibly war with the United States. That both the Navy Department and the War Department, and Admiral Kimmel as well, were already aware that a break in diplomatic relations or war with the United States was imminent, is clearly established by the November 27th 'war warning' to Admiral Kimmel, and by the repetition on November 28th by the Navy or the Army's warning dispatch to General Short."

At the same time, it seems incredible to me that the Japanese would have sent out the preliminary message and not have followed with the "execute" message, *unless* (1) the Japanese knew we were reading their codes and tried to practice deception by actually withholding the "execute" to make us feel that nothing was as yet imminent, or (2) the Foreign Office did not actually know that the Pearl Harbor blow was to be struck. But it was known to all of our forces that Japanese diplomatic representatives in Allied countries were burning their codes several days before December 7, a last positive indication that war is imminent. On December 3 Admiral Kimmel was handed a message by Layton, the fleet intelligence officer, which read:

HIGHLY RELIABLE INFORMATION HAS BEEN RECEIVED THAT CATEGORIC AND URGENT INSTRUCTIONS WERE SENT YESTERDAY TO JAPANESE DIPLOMATIC AND CONSULAR POSTS AT HONGKONG SINGAPORE BATAVIA MANILA WASHINGTON AND LONDON TO DESTROY MOST OF IMPORTANT CONFIDENTIAL AND SECRET DOCUMENTS.

Our own naval attaché in Tokyo burned his codes on December 5, the military attaché later, and the Embassy burned theirs only after they had received official word from Japanese authorities of the attack on Pearl Harbor. It is therefore apparent that both the Japanese Foreign Office and our Office of Naval Intelligence knew that things were about to break. These same facts were known to Admiral Kimmel and his staff at Pearl Harbor. It was not until the night of December 7 that a Japanese broadcast with "west wind clear" was intercepted at Pearl Harbor. By then, however, it was of no consequence, as Layton testified.

The latest word on the investigation of the winds message came from Tokyo in June, 1946. It was to the effect that the Foreign Office, with whom the "execute" message would have originated, did *not* send it before the Pearl Harbor attack but did send it immediately afterward. I feel that too much importance has been attached to the winds messages in all the investigations. These messages were not handled by the Japanese Navy, which was careful to safeguard the secret of its intentions to strike at Pearl Harbor.

It was on November 18, 1941, that the first Japanese unit under orders for this attack sailed from Hitokappu Bay. It was a "Surprise Attack Force" consisting of submarines, the slow speed of which necessitated earlier departure. Then on November 27, Japanese date, approximately four days after the date designated as Y-Day, the main Japanese battle force of six carriers, two battleships, two cruisers, and thirteen destroyers sailed under the smoke screen of absolute secrecy. Extreme care was taken to camouflage the mission of the fleet and the intentions of the Japanese high command.

The passage of the assault force was uneventful. It was never detected by non-Japanese ships, but it encountered a Japanese vessel, the *Tatsuta Maru*. In order to prevent even inadvertent disclosure of the encounter, the merchant ship was incorporated in the battle fleet and forced to make the trip to Pearl Harbor with Yamamoto's expeditionary force.

The rest is history. I have read many descriptions of the Pearl Harbor attack as Americans saw it, and some of them were truly gripping in their presentation of stark realities. It may be of interest to describe here the assault on Pearl Harbor as a Japanese naval officer saw it. The following is based on the diary of an anonymous Japanese commander who was in charge of two waves of airplanes in the attack.

"When we left Japan," he wrote, "nobody on board seemed to know that we were sailing into war. It was a cruise like so many earlier cruises. Still another fleet exercise, we thought. It was frightfully bad weather, but we usually had our exercises under just such atmospheric conditions. So did we sail for a few days, leaving the storm behind. We sailed in an easterly direction, that was all we knew. We have left the Bonin Islands far behind.

"There were many rumors floating on board, but nobody knew for certain what our destination was. Until at noon one day—I shall never forget the moment—a flag appeared on the mast of the flagship. We have seen that flag often in our lives, since it was one of the most cherished relics of the Japanese Navy. And now, flying from the mast of the flagship was the flag, the banner which Admiral Heihachiro Togo flew from his *Mikasa* in the Battle of Tsushima. It was the first sign that we were sailing into war. A peculiar feeling gripped us all, a feeling of elation but also of melancholy. We were Japanese men, and a Japanese sailor is not supposed to return alive from battle."

The Japanese commander then told in great detail the preparations and briefings on his carrier. The men were given a pep talk by Admiral Nagumo: "In a war against the United States," the Commander in Chief said, "Hawaii is the most important naval base of the enemy. It is America's Gibraltar. Whenever the enemy wants to send his ships to the Far East, they must stop and refuel in Hawaii. There exists no American vessel that could make the round trip, San Francisco to Manila, without refueling in Hawaii. And since America deploys her fleet at an advanced base we will find this fleet all assembled in the Harbor named after the Pearls."

"We did not underestimate the enemy," the commander's entry in the diary continues. "The main island of Oahu is one huge fortress. Allegedly 180 planes are assembled there. There are said to be aircraft factories in underground halls. Pearl Harbor has one of the largest dry docks in the world. And then Diamond Head. An old extinct volcano but when one is fortunate enough to observe it from close quarters, one sees nothing but fortresses, bunkers, casemates, anti-aircraft batteries. There are said to be 140,000 soldiers gathered there, housed in underground quarters, invincible, inaccessible." In typical Japanese poetry, which can mix the blood of battle with the beauty of a cherry tree, he called the place of the great encounter "the garden of War." Then he heard "the singing of the propellers, alert; then the order for the attack came.

"The weather is unexpectedly bad," he continued. "Although the ceiling is about 4,500 feet there are gloomy dark clouds everywhere the eye can see. The carrier is negotiating a minor storm with all the power it has until at 6:15 A.M. that last order to start at once is given. They fly on instruments, nerves tightened in the greatest suspense, high over the clouds, in almost complete darkness."

At 7:55 sharp he dives from the clouds into a fairyland underneath his wings.

"Below me," he related, "lies the whole United States Pacific Fleet in a formation I would not have dared to dream in my most optimistic dreams. I have seen all German ships assembled in Kiel Harbor. I have also seen the French battleships off Brest. And finally, I have frequently seen our own warships assembled for review before the Tenno. But I have never seen ships even in the deepest peace anchor at a distance less than 500 to 1,000 meters from each other. A war fleet must always be on the alert since surprise attacks can never be fully ruled out. But this picture down there? It is hard to comprehend. Have these Americans never heard of Port Arthur? Are they really unaffected by the events of the days just passed? Or are they so confident that they believe nothing could ever happen to them?"

His diary continues, describing in minute detail the whole attack and then a fourth wave in which he again participated. An American who may feel ashamed when reading the foregoing passage now can gain satisfaction from the Japanese description of the effectiveness of our defenses and the courage with which our battle-shocked men handled their antiaircraft guns. According to this Japanese commander, several more bombing waves were planned, but the withering fire of our ships' antiaircraft guns cut down the Japanese strength; and the attack was abandoned after the fifth wave dropped its bombs—by then aimlessly through the myriads of shells flying toward them, and doing little damage.

Thus ended the impressions of a Japanese observer on our "Day of Infamy."

In Japan, a thorough camouflage had prevented us from learning the imminence of the attack. The Japanese went so far in deceptive measures as to order all sailors attached to shore bases to take leave in Japanese towns to give the impression that the fleet was in port. Our own Intelligence had just one fragmentary hint of impending events. The fleet intelligence officer, watching radio traffic, noticed the "disappearance" of a few carriers—the same carriers which were soon to turn up off Pearl Harbor. No satisfactory explanation could then be given, by the intelligence officer as the available data were insufficient to deduce from it Japanese intentions. But their radio silence made him apprehensive, so much so that Admiral Kimmel was moved to remark: "What, you do not know where the carriers are? Do you mean to say that they could be rounding Diamond Head [the southeast corner of Oahu on which Pearl Harbor is situated], and you wouldn't know it?" Layton's reply was: "I hoped they would be sighted before now."

While the Japanese had comprehensive information of the movements of our ships, we had less than fragmentary information about the movements of their vessels. In a sense, the Pearl Harbor tragedy was a Waterloo of American evaluation, estimating, and planning. And that should now in retrospect be our greatest warning.

But there are already many signs visible that the lesson of Pearl Harbor is all but forgotten, although the memories of that infamous day are preserved in sentimental recollections. We must not view such things emotionally and sentimentally. We must make an inventory of our concrete mistakes and learn from them if we desire to avoid future Pearl Harbors.

24

THE LESSONS OF PEARL HARBOR

I. THE TEST OF INTELLIGENCE

It cannot be said that the complete unpreparedness in which the enemy caught our fleet on December 7 was shared to an equal extent by our Intelligence; but there were many naval organizational deficiencies which were reflected in our intelligence setup.

Before the Congressional Committee I indicated that the following organizational deficiencies were contributing factors to Pearl Harbor:

(1) That the planning officers were allowed to take over the intelligence function of evaluation. This resulted in individuals without a full knowledge of the Japanese or their psychology determining what the Japanese might do. This practice applied not only in Washington but also at Pearl Harbor, where the erroneous conclusion was reached by the planning officer that there was no chance of an air attack on Pearl Harbor.

(2) That the two purely technical organizations of the SIS, Signal Intelligence Service of the Army, and ONC, Office of Naval Communications, were allowed to take over the intelligence functions of decoding, translating, evaluating, and disseminating intercepted messages. I had fought for years to have these functions properly allocated to the Office of Naval Intelligence.

(3) That the selection of officers for Intelligence and the rapidity with which the directors of Intelligence were changed—seven directors between 1940 and 1945—made for inefficiency. The qualifications for Intelligence as set forth in my letter to the Chief of Naval Operations and reproduced in the Appendix are vital considerations to efficiency.

One of these deficiencies had practical application in the Fleet Intelligence Office, an agency charged with superhuman responsibilities but given extremely limited authority. In 1941 we had in this key post a fleet intelligence officer who was alert and imaginative, with a tremendous capacity for work—Lieutenant Commander Edwin T. Layton. When I arrived in Pearl Harbor and visited him in his office, I found the conditions under which he was compelled to work entirely unsatisfactory. He was assisted by only one officer, and the two were even then working day and night to cope with the manifold responsibilities of the job.

The fact that a lieutenant commander was in charge of this all-important intelligence office was characteristic of the attitude higher echelons had toward their intelligence arms. I do not mean to imply that for work a lieutenant commander is inferior in intelligence and imagination to a captain or a rear admiral. But it is an indisputable fact that he is inferior in rank and, hence, in influence. I had tried for years to bring about the designation of a captain as fleet intelligence officer, so that he might pound the desk of the planners if need be. But I had been unsuccessful; and until Layton was appointed, the job was only collateral duty. The higher echelons just could not visualize the important duties a fleet intelligence officer should perform.

This officer necessarily learns most about the enemy from immediate observation and, therefore, cannot avoid drawing his own conclusions. In the case of the Japanese he must make his own estimate of the situation influenced by his personal knowledge of the enemy and their psychology, which may not always agree with various estimates made on higher echelons. Even so, fleet intelligence officers are wont to present their opinions and outline probable enemy intentions based on their complete over-all view of the enemy's position; and this is an important consideration, since our fleet intelligence officers, in the nature of things, should know more about the enemy than anyone else. In fact, during the war our intelligence officers knew more about the enemy than the Japs themselves.

Eddie Layton, too, had his own ideas and drew his own conclusions, but he could not present them with the force necessary, since he was only a lieutenant commander. He himself felt that his ears were pinned back too often for comfort, and was reluctant to provoke the ire of superior officers who disliked intensely a junior officer interfering with their own ideas, especially when the junior was "only an intelligence officer." The old prejudices, subconscious rather than deliberate, traditional rather than natural, were extremely evident in Pearl Harbor, somewhat further complicated by the fact that the Commander in Chief failed to have a proper appreciation of the value of intelligence.

All this does not mean, however, that the Fleet Intelligence Office, though overworked and understaffed, was not working full time with the highest possible efficiency. There was another branch of Intelligence which was similarly efficient and was co-ordinated by Layton through personal friendship: Communication Intelligence, in charge of Lieutenant Commander J. J. Rochefort, USN, a highly trained specialist in two fields, being also a Japanese-language officer. These two intelligence activities followed closely the movements of the Japanese, but it was not the officers' "privilege" to deduce enemy intentions from the information they gathered. This function was usurped by the planners, whose main preoccupation should have been to take appropriate countermeasures to the Japanese moves culled from the incoming material, promptly submitted to higher echelons, and high-lighted by those who knew the Japanese.

I have now before me a fairly comprehensive record of the activities of our intelligence agencies at Pearl Harbor as they functioned between early November 1941 and the day of the attack. It may be useful to reconstruct from their reports the quality and quantity of their work and make a short summary of the information which they were able to place at the disposal of the Commander in Chief and his planners to enable them to make their estimate of the situation and their preparations.

Although radio traffic was found to be normal early in November, Communication Intelligence discovered several important signs of increased Japanese activities. Above all, Japan introduced an entirely new set of calls for her units afloat, while shore station calls and shore addressees remained unchanged. A series of high priority dispatches, sent from Tokyo to major fleet commanders, was also discovered.

On November 3 traffic volume was found slightly under normal, but this condition failed to mislead our Communication Intelligence. On that date Communication Intelligence Summary contained this significant information: "General messages continue to emanate from Tokyo communications. Such an amount is unprecedented, and the import is not understood. A mere call change does not account for activities of this nature. The impression is strong that these messages are periodic reports to the Major Commander of a certain nature."

Simultaneously an increase in dummy traffic (meaningless messages sent to keep volume of traffic at a certain level) was noted, also emanating from Tokyo radio. The Japanese commander in chief was found sending an urgent message to "all concerned," including major commanders, the combined fleet, the Naval Intelligence in Tokyo, the chief of the Naval General Staff, and the Bureau of Personnel. Then a significant note: "The Commander in Chief, Combined [Admiral Yamamoto], continues to be associated with the carriers and submarines."

This was the yield of just one day's radio monitoring work, and it must be admitted that it contained enough for contemplation. In retrospect, the information culled from intercepts was significant enough. Other information supplemented the findings of Communication Intelligence. On November 4, the Fleet Intelligence Officer reported: "The Fifth Fleet has its flag in a light cruiser at Maizuru, but nothing else is known about the force as yet. It is possibly the nucleus of a Japanese Sea Fleet." Subsequent events proved that it was.

By November 6 Communication Intelligence found traffic volume slightly above normal. Another deviation from long-established custom was also noted. Formerly Tokyo radio called the unit concerned when the dispatch was addressed to a member of that unit. Beginning this day all specific call-up was eliminated. All broadcast messages were now addressed to a single call without regard to the specific addressee of the message. This was properly evaluated as meaning another advance in communication security by the Japanese, and was another straw in the wind. On the same day Communication Intelligence was able to confirm a very heavy air concentration on Formosa. (A few weeks later Formosa was openly identified as the center of Japanese air activities against the Philippines.) Monitoring Admiral Yamamoto's traffic, Communication Intelligence made this significant discovery: "A large amount of Combined Fleet traffic is now appearing with secret (tactical) calls in use."

Traffic remained heavy the next day, but increasing security measures introduced daily by the Japanese made our analysts fight against overwhelming odds. "Greatest effort is being made," Communication Intelligence now reported, "to increase the number of identified calls to facilitate analysis of the traffic but Orange [the Japanese] changes in methods of handling fleet traffic render this more difficult than had been hoped."

On November 8 it was found that the Chichijima air station was included in much of the traffic between Empire offices and the mandates, and another important observation was made. "The area between Chichijima [Bonins], Naha [Okinawa], Takao [Formosa], Palau [Pelews], and Jaluit [Marshalls] appears to be particularly concerned with movement of air forces and auxiliaries," the summary stated, "while the formation of a force under Combined Air Commander in the Takao-Bako [Pescadores] area appears to be nearly completed as indicated by reports addressed to Commander in Chief, Combined, Naval Minister, Commanders of Carrier Divisions, Combined Air Force, First Fleet, and shore addresses generally associated with movements or organization changes."

The next day was a Sunday, but traffic was found to be heavy. The deployment of the two carrier divisions was found proceeding on schedule, and it was even discovered that the chief of staff of the French Indo-China force was in for a conference in Tokyo. A message sent for Yamamoto to the cruiser at Maizuru, flagship of the force which Intelligence previously had indicated as the possible nucleus of a high-seas fleet, seemed to reveal the presence of the Commander in Chief with this obscure force.

On November 10, traffic was dominated by Japanese Naval Intelligence addressing dispatches to all major commanders. Intelligence calls continued to occupy the air for several days afterward, even to the elimination of other messages. While increased activities made a definite establishment of ship movements difficult, it was definitely established that far greater than the usual movement occurred during these days. Obviously the deployment of the fleet was continuing without interruption, by now proceeding to their prearranged stations according to previous orders, which explains the accumulation of traffic between November 1 and 10, and the sudden reduction afterward.

On November 15, when Communication Intelligence discovered "an apparent movement of Fourth Fleet units in prospect or underway," the Office of Naval Intelligence revealed that it was fully alert to the general political situation. Its fortnightly summary of the current national situation began with these ominous lines: "The approaching crisis in the United States–Japanese relations overshadowed all other developments in the Far East during the period. Saburo Kurusu, former Japanese Ambassador to Berlin, is flying to Washington with compromise Japanese proposals. No one apparently expects his mission to succeed, the envoy himself reportedly expressing extreme pessimism." Again, the evaluation of ONI proved more realistic than the evaluations of certain higher echelons to whom this important intelligence function was then wrongly assigned.

On November 16 Communication Intelligence discovered that Japanese Destroyer Squadron One was assigned to operate with the carrier divisions and battleship division; while the Fifth Fleet, dubbed by intelligence officers "the mythical fleet," remained obscure. Yamamoto's circuit was becoming increasingly busy, especially in contact with the commander of the Second Fleet. Evaluating this information, Communication Intelligence made the following deduction, to be revealed as correct when later all information became known: "Commander in Chief, Second Fleet will be in command of a large Task Force comprising the Third Fleet, Combined Air Force, some Carrier Divisions, and Battleship Division Three." This force, just three weeks later, provided the assault force for the attack against Pearl Harbor.

On November 20-21 Communication Intelligence definitely established the progressing concentration of Japanese fleet units, and also found increasing activity by the Tokyo Personnel Bureau. "The traffic load on the Tokyo-Takao circuit," the summary reported, "was very heavy on the 21st, so heavy that the circuit was in duplex operation most of the mid-watch." Traffic volume remained above normal on the twenty-second—the date which we now know as Y-Day. An intercepted message indicated that "Combined Fleet tactical exercises are now completed." Tokyo Intelligence was also found on the air with a long message to its addressees. On that same day the Fleet Intelligence Officer at Pearl Harbor received a significant message, the reliability rating of which could not be established. "Dutch authorities in the Netherlands East Indies have received information," the report stated, "that a Japanese Expeditionary Force which is strong enough to constitute a threat against the Netherlands East Indies or Portuguese Timor has arrived in the vicinity of Palau. If this force moves past the line through Davao-Waigea-Equator, the Governor General of the NEI will regard it as an act of hostility and will consider war to have begun."

While high-priority traffic now almost monopolized the air at the Japanese end, with "increased activity among Third Fleet addressees with a high percentage of what appears to be movement reports," our Chief of Naval Operations sent a dispatch to Cincus: "The chances of any favorable result coming out of the present negotiations with Japan are very doubtful. It is his opinion that this, coupled with the statements of the Japanese Government, and the movements of their military and naval forces, indicates that they may make a surprise aggressive movement in any direction, including an attack on the Philippines or Guam."

It was about this time that the Japanese task forces left their assembly points and, accordingly, traffic returned to an ambiguous normal. Only Tokyo Intelligence remained on the air, transmitting additional information to addressees who received it all without the necessity of acknowledgments. To mislead our monitors by keeping traffic up to normal at a time when no further orders were transmitted to the fleets sailing under their own prearranged or sealed orders, Japanese radio stations began to *retransmit all messages,* a fact noted and mentioned by Communication Intelligence as having considerable significance. On the other hand, Japanese Intelligence increased its radio activity from day to day. On November 29, for example, a large share of the day's traffic was made up of messages of an intelligence nature. Tokyo Intelligence alone sent eleven messages during the day to major commanders both ashore and afloat, while the radio intelligence activity at Tokyo sent four exceptionally long messages to major commanders. So heavy was the traffic that the Yokosuka transmitter had to be enlisted for the transmission of these messages.

Agent reports, received in Pearl Harbor, also indicated increased activity, not merely afloat but on land as well. Thus, for example, on November 27 a reliable agent stated that Imperial Headquarters had assumed control over certain increased air activities; while a British Intelligence source stated categorically that "Japan will commence military operations on December 1 against the KRA Isthmus and Thailand," proceeding from Formosa, where Communication Intelligence had previously detected the concentration of these forces.

On November 28 a report from another British source informed the Fleet Intelligence Officer of the Japanese procedure to be carried out on Japanese news broadcasts in the event that diplomatic relations were on the verge of severance, repeating the words *"Higashi-Higashi"* five times to indicate break in Japanese-American relations. On December 1 our attaché in Bangkok sent word that an "absolutely reliable agent" had reported conferences taking place in Bangkok preparatory to the commencement of hostilities, and a further report followed, that another agent had reported on November 30 that the Japanese ambassador to Thailand had obtained permission to burn his papers and codes.

By then it was inevitable that we should discover something imminent. On December 1 all Japanese call letters were changed again, inducing Communication Intelligence to point out: *"The fact that service calls lasted only one month indicates an additional progressive step in preparing for active operations on a large scale."*

The remainder of the evaluation is of equal interest: "A study of traffic prior to 0000, December 1 [when all calls were changed again] indicates that an effort was made to deliver all dispatches using old calls so that promptly with the change of calls there would be a minimum of undelivered dispatches and consequent confusion and compromise. Either that or *the large number of old messages may have been used to pad the total volume and make it appear as if nothing unusual was pending."*

It was obvious from this proper deduction that our Intelligence was not deceived by the Japanese trick.

By December 2 our Communication Intelligence had succeeded in definitely establishing that the Japanese high-seas fleet was on the move. Of course, radio intelligence is largely based on circumstantial evidence and deductions, and it is pitted against and compared with information obtained from other sources. The whole intelligence which we are after is rarely told on the air, and the decoding of certain messages takes time. Even so, the deductions which can be made on the basis of experience and practice usually provide a lead for other agencies on higher echelons to make their own estimates of the situation.

Just five days before Pearl Harbor our Communication Intelligence informed all those concerned that certain radio intercepts as well as the absence of normal radio traffic, indicating *radio silence* of the Japanese fleets, was a sign of impending events. The fleets which until recently had been worked and serviced by the

Takao (Formosa) radio were no longer receiving their signals from this station. In several instances it was found that instead of signaling direct to the fleets, as was the previous custom, Takao radio now forwarded traffic to Tokyo for transmittal to these fleets.

From this and from other indices, Communication Intelligence made the following deductions, included in their daily summary on December 2:

1. The First Fleet was relatively quiet. It appears that there may have been a split in the Combined Fleet Staff and there may be two supreme commanders with their staffs. (This could indicate operations in two widely separated areas.)

2. The Second Fleet was obscure. "This is partly due to lack of new identifications but contributes somewhat to the belief that a large part of the Second Fleet is underway in company."

3. In so far as the carriers were concerned, there continued an almost "complete blank of information." Not one carrier call had been recovered since the change of calls, leading Communication Intelligence to regard this as a sign that carrier traffic was at a low ebb.

4. The Combined Air Force was reported to have "undoubtedly left the Takao area." And then, the most important over-all deduction:

5. "Summing up all reports and indications, it is believed that the large fleet made up of Second, Third, and First Fleet units has left Empire waters." Closer identification was impossible by these means, since Communication Intelligence was dependent on radio traffic and no such traffic originated from the phantom fleet, while the traffic beamed to it was heavily camouflaged, the Japanese trying hard to practice radio deception.

Next day, December 3, it was reported again: "No information on submarines or carriers." And the reiteration of previous deductions: "It is the impression that both Second and Third Fleets are underway." On the fourth the Commander of the Second and Third Fleets, described in the summary as a "previously very talkative commander," was found to be ominously quiet. The Second and Third Fleets were completely absent from the air and, accordingly, also from the summary. Suddenly, on December 5, traffic volume became very heavy. All circuits were overloaded with Tokyo broadcasts going over full twenty-four hours. The air was filled with high-precedence messages, and pressure must have been so great that, occasionally, there was no time for coding. A Captain Okawa, for example, addressed a signal to a certain Fujihara, described as chief of the Political Affairs Bureau, in *plain language,* saying: "In reference to the Far Eastern crisis, what you said is considered important at this end, but proceed with what you are doing; specific orders will be issued soon."

There was just one fragmentary message from the two phantom fleets at sea, but it was, especially when viewed in retrospect, significant. It was addressed to the commander of the Fourteenth Army aboard the *Ryujo Maru.* A number of transports were in communication with the Third Fleet without, of course, receiving answers.

On Saturday afternoon, December 6, the office of the communication intelligence officer had drawn up what was to become its last peacetime summary. By then all Japanese radio stations were going full blast, radio volume was extremely heavy, and Tokyo was represented with three distinct and separate broadcasts. Other messages emanated from Saipan, Ominato, and Takao. Naval Intelligence again dominated the air with prefixes of high priority. And then the stereotyped entry: "Still no traffic from the Second and Third Fleet Commanders."

The pattern which one can receive from this detailed analysis in the knowledge of all subsequent events and information obtained since the end of the war is an interesting one and may be described briefly. An expeditionary force was formed of units of the First, Second, and Third Fleets, divided in two, one moving on the Philippines with transports attached, the other moving against Pearl Harbor. The carriers were in this latter force. The submarines were identified as being definitely in the Marshalls, obviously left there to go north to interfere were we to pursue the retiring Japanese fleet on its way back from Pearl Harbor.

The Japanese plan was simple enough. It was this simplicity and the daring which was inherent in its simplicity that made its execution appear impossible to some people who did not know the Japanese. Even so, Intelligence succeeded in alerting the Commander in Chief, and at noon on December 5, 1941, he received from his war plans officer, then Captain (now Vice Admiral) C. H. Mc-Morris, USN, a short memorandum significantly entitled, "Recommended Steps to be taken in case of American-Japanese War within the next forty-eight hours." The imminence of war was evident in every one of Captain McMorris' memoranda. On December 1 he had submitted another in which he assumed war "within the next twenty-four hours."

The plan was a good one if viewed with the eyes of the conventional seaman who is dependent upon traditional textbook learning in drawing up his plots. It was a good plan but was oriented to the wrong direction. It was doomed to failure, and was never to be executed in practice because our planners could not conceive what the Japanese could do: throw Western conventions overboard and apply what they had learned from history, their own history at Port Arthur—surprise attack without a prior declaration of war.

I was properly asked by the Congressional Pearl Harbor Committee why I thought the Japanese would start the war with an air attack on our fleet. I told them there were four sound reasons:

(1) The Japanese could not be expected to make the grave strategical blunder of a movement to the southward leaving our fleet intact on their flank. This, in spite of the fact that the Japanese then had at their disposal in the Pacific 180 ships to our 102, because they well knew that by the time we could assemble an expeditionary force on the west coast, the rest of our fleet would come around to the west coast. Therefore, it was obligatory that they attempt to sink or cripple seriously at least four of our battleships in order to bring us down to a nominal parity with them.

(2) The Japanese are great students and could be expected to know all the fundamental principles of war and the lessons of history. They had seen the effectiveness of surprise at Port Arthur and could be counted upon to realize the possibilities of a successful surprise air attack on our fleet at Pearl Harbor.

(3) The Japanese knew to the most minute detail the situation in Hawaii, the scheduled movements of our forces, and everything necessary to make such an attack successful if we were not alert to it. The large number of agents at their disposal and the complete information obtained by them was an open invitation.

(4) The Japanese had discussed in books, in considerable detail, the chances for success of an air attack on Pearl Harbor. In one of these books collected by our naval representatives in Japan was a most pertinent paragraph. A translation was handed to the

Pacific Fleet war plans officer in October 1941. In fact it was translated in the Fleet Intelligence Office. It read:

The American Commander-in-Chief has been occupied by various
secret plans but the three points which he is the most concerned are:
(1) Will a Japanese fast *striking force* made up of cruisers and aircraft carriers come on a scouting or striking mission?
(2) Will Japanese submarines hover near the Islands to attack or
harass the Fleet?
(3) Will a Japanese Expeditionary force be sent overseas?
The first of these is the most fearsome. Suppose Japan were to form
a fast striking force composed of such speedy battleships (whose speed
America cannot match) as the *Haruna, Kongo* and *Kirishima,* the aircraft carriers *Akagi* and *Ryujo,* and the *Nachi* class of heavy cruisers?
This would be a fast-stepping force that would be truly matchless and
invincible! Were they opposed to even the large guns of American
battleships, they could utilize their superior speeds, thus leaving their
slow adversaries behind. If opposed to a cruiser force they could close in
and with telling blows crush the opposition. Truly, this would be a
peerless force; able to close to battle, or open out, if out gunned! If
this Fast Striking Force should meet misfortune, losing one or two fast
battleships or aircraft carriers, they would surely be a severe blow to
Japan and we would have to grit our teeth, smothering our rage until
the day of a decisive Main Engagement to obtain our revenge!
Maybe such a bold venture would be too great a risk, who can say?
On the other hand, warfare is a risk and he who hesitates, or fears the
risks of bold venture, cannot wage war! Moreover, an attack off Hawaii
would be the first battle of the Pacific War and if in the very first engagement one can wrest the courage away from the enemy by one's own
daring, it would put him in a funk or give him the jitters. . . .*

I think it is proper to emphasize that my analysis has been prepared some years after the events to which it refers. The indices
which appear so convincing today might have been overlooked
then—although I still maintain that they were crystal clear and
should have induced a greater preparedness rather than an infer-
ential relaxation of caution. While the South China Sea, the Philippines, and even Guam figured prominently in the summaries
and intelligence reports, there was no reference to Pearl Harbor,
since the fact that Japan was to start the war with an all-out attack
on our fleet at Pearl was their greatest and best-kept secret.
Even so, the imminence of war was recognized by all concerned.

* Excerpt from *When Japan Fights* by Naosaku Hirata.

Regardless of whether or not it was to include the Philippines, Guam, territory bordering on the South China Sea, or areas farther to the south, all far distant from Pearl Harbor, this Hawaiian outpost was our main Pacific naval base and as such was automatically involved in any and all naval activities of a hostile nature. Therefore I could never sympathize with the argument that the lack of an alert at Pearl Harbor was due to the fact that hostilities were expected to be started elsewhere. Moreover, in 1941 it was not so much the base as the fleet anchored there which was the center of Japanese interest. While the base is immobile, the fleet is mobile. It has, in fact, no fixed geographical location; and if the war does not come to the fleet, it is the fleet's mission to go to the war. This was the focal idea which motivated all Japanese plans when they went after our fleet. It was my conception of Japanese plans based on the four reasons, given previously, which convinced me that Japan would commence hostilities with an air attack on our fleet. The total absence of consideration of this possibility in our planning was a partial cause of our failure. War reaches a climax at its very outset, the Battle of the Marne being a splendid example. That battle revealed that while a major power, with its initial moves, can hardly expect to win the war against another major power or coalition of powers, it can very well lose the war then and there if appropriate and energetic countermeasures are taken by the opponents. This was the position in which we had the Japanese at the time of their bold venture against Pearl Harbor. If we had been alert and able to deliver an effective attack on their carriers, the whole trend of the Pacific war could have been drastically changed.

In summary, then, of the activities of Intelligence just prior to the Pearl Harbor attack, it becomes obvious from the foregoing selections from our own intelligence reports that our high command was given repeated indications of the concentration of large Japanese forces and of the movement of a powerful Japanese force coincident with the most determined Japanese attempts to cloak their movements and messages in secrecy. And furthermore, I have never heard the following question asked of those concerned with preparations at Pearl Harbor: "In arriving at your estimates, did you consult in detail the opinion of those who were best qualified to state what the Japanese might do in the premises?"

II. THE TEST OF LEADERSHIP

The reader of the foregoing analysis may properly ask the same question posed by the Congressional Joint Committee on the investigation of the Pearl Harbor attack: "Why, with some of the finest intelligence available in our history, with the almost certain knowledge that war was at hand, with plans that contemplated the precise type of attack that was executed by Japan on the morning of December 7—why was it possible for a Pearl Harbor to occur?"

We should not be concerned any longer over the effectiveness and seriousness of the warning given to Admiral Kimmel and General Short in highly classified dispatches passing from Washington to Hawaii. It has been established definitely that ample information and warning *was* provided, both from Washington and by the proper observers on the spot, to enable Admiral Kimmel to prepare his command for the emergency. But what about the additional vital information in Washington not sent to them? one may ask. By their own admission, oriented as they were only to war in the Far East, it is inconceivable that Admiral Kimmel and his staff would have reacted any differently to the additional information available in Washington.

Anyone who read the daily papers in Honolulu would have known that war was imminent by merely scanning the headlines. The following items were displayed prominently by the *Honolulu Advertiser:* November 13, 1941. "TOKYO RADIO ASSERTS WAR IS ALREADY ON—ANY MILITARY MOVES ONLY LOGICAL RESULT OF ENCIRCLEMENT POLICY, JAPANESE STAFF SAYS."

November 14: "JAPANESE CONFIDENT OF NAVAL VICTORY."

On December 3, an editorial in the *Advertiser* said bluntly: "There is nothing further to be gained by stalling in Washington. ... The immediate future of U.S.-Japan relations is gloomy.... Unless there is immediate and complete reversal of Tokyo policy —the die is cast. Japan and America will travel down the bloody road to war."

On December 5, an almost last warning: "PACIFIC ZERO HOUR NEAR. JAPAN ANSWERS U.S. TODAY."

The Joint Committee, recounting some of these headlines, commented that "it would seem difficult to imagine how anyone— upon reading the newspapers alone—could have failed to appreciate the increasing tenseness of the international situation and the unmistakable signs of war."

This prominent idea was similarly expressed by former Secretary of War Stimson when, referring to the commander on the spot, he said: "If he did not know that the relations between Japan and the United States were strained and might be broken at any time, he must have been almost the only man in Hawaii who did not know it, for the radio and the newspapers were blazoning out these facts daily, and he had a chief of staff and an intelligence officer to tell him so. And if he did not know that the Japanese were likely to strike without warning, he could not have read his history of Japan or known the lessons taught in the Army schools in respect to such matters."

Admiral Kimmel did read the newspapers. In his own testimony he made a point of the fact that after the warnings of November 27 he was dependent on the newspapers for information concerning the state of negotiations, and while he added that he did not act on newspaper information, he obtained a major portion of his "diplomatic information from the newspapers."

Who, then, was at fault, and where must we seek the responsibilities for the failure to be alert? The specific failures of the Hawaiian commands as set forth by the Joint Committee indicates comprehensively what those commands failed to do and thereby constituted lack of alertness. The report states:

8. Specifically, the Hawaiian commands failed—

(a) To discharge their responsibilities in the light of the warnings received from Washington, other information possessed by them, and the principle of command by mutual cooperation.

(b) To integrate and coordinate their facilities for defense and particularly in light of the warnings and intelligence available to them during the period November 27 to December 7, 1941.

(c) To effect liaison on a basis designed to acquaint each of them with the operations of the other, which was necessary to their joint security, and to exchange fully all significant intelligence.

(d) To maintain a more effective reconnaissance within the limits of their equipment.

(e) To effect a state of readiness throughout the Army and Navy establishments designed to meet all possible attacks.

(f) To employ the facilities, material, and personnel at their command, which were adequate at least to have greatly minimized the effects of the attack, in repelling the Japanese raiders.

(g) To appreciate the significance of intelligence and other information available to them.

9. The errors made by the Hawaiian commands were errors of judgment and not derelictions of duty.

These failures, at least on the part of Admiral Kimmel and his staff, are best summed up in the words of Admiral King when he said:

"The basic trouble was that the Navy failed to appreciate what the Japanese could, and did, do."

Here, then, is the concrete reason why we were not alert at Pearl Harbor on December 7. It was for the specific purpose of eliminating this "basic trouble" that I called upon Admiral Kimmel and related to him and his chief of staff, Captain (now Vice Admiral) W. W. Smith, in March 1941 the details of just such possible moves by the Japanese in case of hostilities which they undertook exactly as predicted.

Admiral Kimmel did expect war—but by a rationalization for which it is difficult to find an explanation, he excluded himself and his command from participation in that war. Of course his mind was predisposed by the statement of his planning officer, Captain McMorris, made at a joint conference with General Short, that there was little chance of an air attack on Hawaii. And his chief of staff did not inquire as to the reasons for the Army alert that week.

Sufficient facts are now known for the historian to pass judgment even today. All of the documents are available. We know that Pearl Harbor was a test of leadership. And we know that when this test came, the leadership was found wanting.

It was said of Admiral Jellicoe after the Battle of Jutland that he was the only man in history who could have lost the war for Britain in one afternoon, by exposing his fleet to the torpedoes of the German high seas fleet. It may now be said of Admiral Kimmel that fate had given him the opportunity to save the United States in one morning, by repelling the treacherous attack and turning Japan's victory into Japan's defeat.

In Admiral King's opinion, the following courses were open to Admiral Kimmel:

"(1) He could have used patrol craft which were available to him to conduct long range reconnaissance in the more dangerous sectors. . . .

"(2) He could have rotated the 'in port' periods of his vessels in a less routine manner ...

"(3) If he had appreciated the gravity of the danger even a few hours before the Japanese attack, it is logical to suppose that naval planes would have been in the air during the early morning period, that ships' batteries would have been fully manned and that damage control organizations would have been fully operational."

In the light of the Japanese statement that three remaining waves of their attack were called off because of the heavy resistance put up by the ships after they were firing and because the attacks became increasingly ineffective, it is interesting to speculate on the results had the ships been initially alerted.

All these factors of a tragic past are significant only in their importance for the future. The Joint Committee was abundantly conscious of this fact when it concluded its report with a series of recommendations ranging from such truisms as need for unity of command to elimination of personal jealousies.

Of particular importance for our future security is the recommendation that "effective steps be taken to ensure that statutory or other restrictions do not operate to the benefit of an enemy or other forces inimical to the Nation's security and to the handicap of our own intelligence agencies."

Most important is early and effective action upon the realization that "operational and intelligence work requires centralization of authority and clear-cut allocation of responsibility."

The Joint Committee further recommended that "the coordination and proper evaluation of intelligence in times of stress must be insured by continuity of service and centralization of responsibility in competent officials." The committee voiced the opinion that the security of the nation can be insured only through continuity of service and centralization of responsibility in those charged with handling intelligence, adding that "the assignment of an officer having an aptitude for such work over an extended period of time should not impede his progress nor affect his promotion."

In my own testimony before the Joint Committee I dealt extensively with these basic problems, and I am gratified to find some of my own analyses and recommendations are now so fully incorporated in the committe's report.

Surveying the tragedy of Pearl Harbor in the lessons which it teaches, the Joint Committee introduced its report with words which bear repetition:

> The Pyrrhic victory of having executed the [Pearl Harbor] attack with surprise, cunning, and deceit belongs to the war lords of Japan whose dreams of conquest were buried in the ashes of Hiroshima and Nagasaki. History will properly place the responsibility for Pearl Harbor upon the military clique dominating the people of Japan at the time. Indeed, this responsibility Premier Tojo himself has already assumed.
>
> We come today, over 4 years after the event, not to detract from this responsibility but to record for posterity the facts of the disaster. In another sense we seek to find lessons to avoid pitfalls in the future, to evolve constructive suggestions for the protection of our national security, and to determine whether there were failures in our own military and naval establishments which in any measure may have contributed to the extent and intensity of the disaster.

This is the proper spirit in which the tragedy of Pearl Harbor must be viewed and the only approach which may enable us to escape a similar disaster in the future. If we succeed in learning the lessons of history's cruel teachings, we may yet say that the agony of Pearl Harbor was not in vain and that we succeeded in gaining strength from our own shortcomings.

25

AN INTERMEZZO AT SEA

FROM THE first days of the war there grew in my mind the question of how we could best defeat the Japanese at the least cost to us. I was of the opinion that it would be a long war, with the European commitments, the need for repairing and replacing our damaged ships, overcoming the distances, deploying our forces for the kill.

I felt certain that they could not withstand our war potential of ten to one against them. But I did not doubt that we would have to show the Japanese how to surrender.

At the outset of the Pacific war I felt that we should begin immediate retaliatory action, hitting the Japanese wherever we could with whatever means we had at our disposal. It was essential, I thought, to carry the war into Japanese-controlled waters at once, to prevent the enemy from consolidating his gains with complacency or from strengthening his forces without interference. Little did I think when I presented my tactical suggestions to a new member of Cincus' staff, at his request, that I was to participate in our first attempt at a comeback in the first raids against the Gilbert Islands at Wotje, then Wake, Marcus, and the *Hornet*'s trip to "Shangri-La" for the first raid against Tokyo. (I heard "Radio Rose" the night before that famous raid say: "It was reported today that a foreign plane was seen over Japan. I just want to say emphatically that it is impossible for a foreign plane to come over Japan." The next night she could not continue her broadcast. Neither could her assistant, as both were too choked up with tears and fears.)

So we were on the offensive from the first day of the war, a historical fact all Americans should proudly remember whenever they lament over the spilt blood of Pearl Harber. Outnumbered, outgunned, and outsmarted as we were in those early days, we surpassed the Japanese where they thought they were far superior: in fighting spirit. The officers and men of the ill-equipped destroyers, the lone-wolf submarines, and the few cruisers and carriers which returned the ball to Japanese waters in suicidal thrusts and daring forays—all are the unsung heroes of those dark days of the war. It gives me immense satisfaction and fills me with justified pride that the *Salt Lake City*, affectionately referred to by Bob Casey as the *Swayback Maru* or "the One-Ship Fleet," was part of this nuclear force which preceded the final release of nuclear energy by almost five years.

In those early days of the war I did not have time to analyze from the viewpoint of history. I was living it. I had never cherished the idea of war. I had hoped that I would never be compelled to participate in another one after the first world war to end all future war. But now that we were again deeply involved, I was at sea in command of a heavy cruiser which, in our estimate, was to play an important part in the fighting, at least for the time being. I devoted all my thoughts and energy to combat. I tried to visualize and determine exactly what I would do when suddenly confronted at close quarters by a superior Japanese cruiser force or by a battle cruiser, both of which conditions developed for our ships during the war. It is not for me or for this narrative to tell the many details of war as they manifested themselves to us at sea. They have been told in excellent detail by such outstanding writers as Fletcher Pratt, Gilbert Cant, and especially Captain Walter Karig and his various able collaborators in their unsurpassable *Battle Reports*. The exploits of my own ship, the *Salt Lake City*, were described with inspired pen by the great war correspondent Bob Casey of the *Chicago Daily News* in his *Torpedo Junction*.

There is, however, one rather abstract or theoretical fact providing a proud remembrance for all of us. Our fleet, perfectly balanced prior to 7:55 A.M. on December 7, was thrown off balance a few minutes later. It was with this unbalanced fleet that we had to embark upon war. We had only cruisers, a few carriers, destroyers, and submarines left, most of them in a peacetime condition, with inadequate antiaircraft batteries vastly inferior to those of our later ships which poured from the shipyards.

But there was a spirit which inspired this rudimentary fleet to offensive action. It was a spirit of the ruthless offensive, exemplified by the order of the new Commander in Chief of the United States Fleet, Admiral E. J. King, USN. His order to the fleet was short: "Do the best you can with what you have on hand." We did even better than best. We remained on the offensive throughout those dark days in our naval history and continued to harass the Jap until we were strong enough to hit him in force. Only the submarines remained of what was once our Asiatic fleet. But these submarines, left to themselves without a proper fleet organization and denied the vital co-operation of General MacArthur's aircraft in the Philippines, went after the Japanese on the day hostilities started and conducted a highly efficient attack of their own.

We suffered a grievous loss in the Battle of the Java Sea, but so did the Japanese. But our fighting spirit was demonstrated when our four destroyers engaged a whole Japanese force of cruisers, destroyers, and transports at night and inflicted extensive damage on them by torpedo fire. The badly battered United States was neither down nor out. It was in the war doing its best with the little then on hand. Our own initial activities afloat were led by an indomitable spirit: the spirit of Admiral William F. Halsey.

After the battles of the Coral Sea, Midway, and Guadalcanal it was Japan's turn to be thrown off balance. While we continued on the offensive, the Japanese withdrew from action and remained on the defensive for eighteen months, until they were forced to join action when we arrived off Saipan. There remained just one major action in which the Japanese were willing to participate and in which they again suffered a disastrous defeat, the second battle of the Eastern Philippine Sea which included the epic battle for Leyte Gulf in which Admiral Jesse B. Oldendorf shone so brilliantly. The fine record of the Japanese Navy very early in the war is beclouded by its caution and ineptitude shown subsequently almost throughout the war. It is this aspect of the Pacific war which proved the soundness of the American Navy's often revolutionary strategic principles and its absolute tactical superiority over its opponent. These should dominate all considerations of our Navy's role in winning the victory.

It was the *Salt Lake City*'s privilege to fight in the vanguard of this earliest offensive action. On February 1, 1942, the people of the United States, carrying the burden of the war with lowered morale, were electrified by headlines announcing this first major offensive action against the Japanese. It was the raid against the Gilberts and the Marshalls, planned and executed by Admiral Halsey in the manner which foreshadowed his emergence as our foremost fleet commander.

The *Salt Lake City* was given the atoll of Wotje as a target; and we moved in, rather ill prepared, since our charts were inadequate and our intelligence incomplete for such a daring expedition. I considered it essential to benefit from our close approach to the island also in a purely intelligence sense, and was greatly supported in this decision by a guest on board, Lieutenant C. H. Coggins (MC), USN, who may be remembered from earlier chapters as the spy-catching doctor. Ever since our first chance meeting over the Thompson case, we had been close friends and indefatigable coworkers in intelligence; and it was this friendship and his keen observation which induced me to ask the Commander in Chief's permission to take him on the raid. Until we had sailed, he thought it was to be only a normal cruise. Others on board were Bob Casey and Bob Landry (*Life* magazine).

Intelligence methods in combat were then embryonic, and no preparations had been made to gather topographical data from air reconnaissance on combat missions. We were at a distinct disadvantage, too, with the type of planes at our disposal. Even so, we made plans to conduct what to my knowledge was the first air intelligence operation in the Pacific war. Two planes were spotting for our ship-borne artillery, and two were standing by, but we were thinking of information for future activities. Our planes utilized private cameras, formerly locked up on board, to photograph the whole island as they were guiding the fall of our shots on important targets.

We could not help recalling the previous extensive efforts to gain information of this area through visits of our ships and the opposition of our own State Department to these "controversial" issues. In fact I prepared a note to be dropped by our aviators on Wotje addressed to the Gaimu-Sho (Foreign Office), Tokyo, and marked: "Please deliver to Mr. Eugene Dooman, American Embassy." It read: "Have arrived and inspected the Gilbert Islands in spite of opposition—Zacharias." In the confusion of our preparations it was not given to my aviator, so Mr. Dooman continued to remain in ignorance.

The intelligence data which my aviators collected in their spare time seemed to justify the effort and open up entirely new vistas for air intelligence. From the photographs they acquired on their mission we prepared a detailed map of the island which was the basis of information used with great effectiveness during later attacks.

Coggins was put in charge of the work and was delighted to be permitted again to act as an intelligence officer ad interim. He interrogated every officer who had flown over Wotje during this operation, including carrier pilots. Soon the carrier photographic officer came over to watch the technique. I told him to quote me to Admiral Halsey as saying: "We should have a camera in every plane."

Thus I was enabled to put to the test ideas I had long been advocating to the department. I had initiated the first large-scale photographic activities by calling a conference in Washington of all interested bureaus in June 1940, at which Merian Cooper, a famous aviator, explorer, moving-picture executive, and a boyhood neighbor and friend, had presented views on the photographic needs of the Navy. The efficacy of our later air photographic work needs no comment.

Our little task force under the command of Admiral William F. Halsey, USN, flying his flag on the carrier *Enterprise,* consisted of the flagship, the heavy cruisers *Northampton, Chester,* and *Salt Lake City,* and screening destroyers. Although our mission was limited in scope, it entailed considerable risk since we went in virtually blindfolded, having no information on Japanese installations, and our Combat Intelligence was still too young to advise us of the exact whereabouts of the enemy. We went in not knowing what might confront us, in the air, on the surface, or under the surface.

Even in this operation Halsey acted in his typically courageous manner only after he had convinced himself that there was no disproportionate material risk involved in his action. His move was unorthodox to the orthodox naval man. But it was also the unorthodox handling of their fleets which made Nelson and Cunningham of the British Navy the great leaders, one in the past and the other in the recent war.

It was a great thrill to serve under Admiral Halsey. He was then not yet nationally known, although in the Navy we knew that he was one of our natural tacticians, destined to become *the* naval leader of the Pacific war. He is a born commander who knows instinctively what to do in all situations. His daring is the result of absolute reliance on instinct and judgment, which has served him well in many tight situations and aided him in the death struggle off the Solomons when the Japanese kept coming down "the Slot." It was Halsey's brilliant handling of his fleet which caused the impassive Marines, in the words of their commander, General Vandegrift, "to doff their battered steel helmets to the Navy." The public does not have quite the right picture of Halsey, just as they had no accurate picture of Dewey or Sims or even Farragut, Jones, or Lawrence. But while in the case of some of our naval leaders of history the retouching hands of time glossed over certain shortcomings, in Halsey's case popular idolation glorified a "shortcoming" which in fact is nonexistent. The public calls him "Bull" Halsey and attributes to him the irrational, unreasonable, swashbuckling acts of his namesake. It is a fact that Halsey was willing to take considerable risks, especially when they involved him, too; but his actions were carefully weighed and minutely planned. What makes these actions appear so improvised in their daring is the facile mind which finds the proper answer instinctively rather than through somewhat slower intellectual processes; and his own confidence in the soundness of his decisions makes him act on them many times as soon as the apparent solution has materialized.

The caution and calculating prudence which are equally inherent in him and emerge whenever the occasion requires were evident a few months later when under the leaded sky of a wet April we escorted the *Hornet* to launch Doolittle, then a lieutenant colonel, on his epic flight to Tokyo. Although the story of this operation has been told often, its practical significance has never been made clear in the telling.

The sky over Japan was as unknown to us as had been the waters around Wotje. Clever Japanese propaganda had emphasized the tale that air conditions over the islands did not permit operations of aircraft and thereby tried to create the impression that Japan was protected from an air offensive against Japan proper by "divine winds" and "divine air pockets." In a sense, therefore, the Doolittle operation was an intelligence mission on the largest practical scale. It was his job to determine air conditions over Japan and answer many questions before an air offensive could be planned on the scale which General Hap Arnold even then had in his mind. From this point of view the Doolittle mission was far more than the morale lifter which it was called. When several years later the first B-29's appeared over Tokyo, they were utilizing the experience and lessons gained under trying circumstances by Doolittle and his fliers.

On our voyage to escort the *Hornet* to its destination "Shangri-La" the first active co-operation between the Navy and the Air

Force bore fruit. It began long before, when the Navy detailed capable young officers as instructors for the Doolittle fliers, teaching them the tricks of take-off from a carrier. While co-operation was complete, an incident toward the end of the joint voyage seemed to leave an unwarranted scar on General Doolittle's memory in so far as the Navy is concerned. It may be remembered that, despite comprehensive precautions to ensure absolute security. Admiral Halsey's force steamed into Japanese waters with its precious load of B-25's and was sighted by a fishing-trawler patrol of the enemy. The encounter demanded quick action. No one could know how much the trawler's crew had seen or whether its radio had reported the sighting to Tokyo. At that time we were operating on a shoestring, and these carriers and cruisers were vital to future offensive operations. We could not possibly risk them, since such risks could have entailed tragic consequences. As subsequent events proved, had we lost any more ships after the tragic encounters in the Macassar Straits, we should not have been able to start and sustain our offensive in the Guadalcanal area—a vital point in our campaign.

It was in this atmosphere of careful calculation that the decision had to be made when the Japanese trawler was sighted: The planes must be launched at once. Here then was what Doolittle probably regarded as the monkey wrench in his minutely prepared plans. We were still a considerable distance from the spot where he had hoped to take off. As a result, while his main mission was successfully executed, the increased length of the flight created insurmountable difficulties for many of his planes in trying to reach a landing point. But the decision of Admiral Halsey could not have been otherwise and it was in such crises that his true greatness became apparent. It was his combination of daring and caution which stood at the cradle of all his victories.

The war was by then, even in its earliest stages, moving toward an unexpected climax. A strange encounter in the Coral Sea revealed to us a new side to Japanese strategy. It revealed that, despite their tremendous initial successes, they were not quite sure of themselves. The Coral Sea battle was fought between two fleets which never saw each other, although Vice Admiral F. J. Fletcher watched on the screen of our radar the Japanese planes being recovered by the carrier. Japanese carriers were deployed beyond the horizon, while our own *Lexington* also remained out of Japanese sight. The battle was fought out by the planes launched from the respective carriers. It was conclusive only because it stopped the Japanese by their own caution rather than by the effectiveness of our counter-measures. To me this was a significant indication and confirmed my belief that, far from being the daredevils their propaganda represented them to be, the Japanese Navy under conditions of near equality moved with caution and uncertainty.

At the same time our continued offensive convinced them that the basic strategic plan on which their grand strategy was based was not working. We were *not* locked in behind the Dutch Harbor–Midway–Pago Pago line; the life line to Australia was *not* cut; in fact, we still commanded the sea on the routes to our advanced bases then in the process of preparation under General MacArthur on Australian, New Caledonian, and New Zealand soil. Admiral Ito's caution, which prevented landings on Hawaii in the wake of the Pearl Harbor attack, had presaged a trend which had proved to be costly; and the war which Japan hoped to win in a blitzkrieg fashion with the first bold stroke developed into a war of attrition, which the Japs dreaded.

It was then that Tokyo decided on another bold venture to remedy the situation by sealing the imaginary line and keeping us east of it. Grandiose plans were drawn up for simultaneous landings on Midway and at Dutch Harbor and then Hawaii, and the transports which failed to sail for Pearl Harbor in December 1941 were now pressed into service against Midway and the Aleutians. America was facing another threat properly recognized by Admiral Nimitz as one equally as dangerous as Pearl Harbor.

It was just such a situation that I had visualized; and the awareness of its possibility had caused me to draw up for the attention of Admiral Nimitz my memorandum of March 17, 1942, which was later made a part of the record of the Congressional Pearl Harbor Committee.

In this memorandum I indicated that I felt the local situation as it then existed in Hawaii was an open invitation for the Japanese to return—this time *in force* and prepared to take the Hawaiian Islands. There were various rumors prevalent which I recognized as typical fifth-column technique; and this, I said, "not only softens up our own people but it is throwing the second generation Japanese into the laps of enemy agents many of whom are still *not* in custody." At that time only 369 Japanese had been picked up. These were the ones considered most dangerous or on whom the records showed something definite, but it was estimated that there were at least 1,000 active agents in the islands. Typical of those still at large was a former waiter at the Royal Hawaiian Hotel whom I saw there for the first time in 1941 when he served me dinner. I was in civilian clothes. During the course of the evening when I tried out my Japanese conversation on him, my host asked the waiter: "Jim, does he speak good Japanese?" Jim replied "Oh, yes, he speak excellent Japanese. He now captain, soon be admiral."

Early in March 1942 when I checked up on Jim at the hotel, the assistant manager informed me that Jim had left suddenly after the attack and had never come back. Our investigators then found him working at the City Café.

This and other conditions increased my concern. There had not been made a house-to-house search for Japanese agents or for weapons in the hands of enemy aliens; only 8 per cent of the radio transmitting sets in houses of Japanese aliens had been collected, although an admonition against use of sending sets had been sent out; no search had been made of isolated areas or ravines for enemy fliers who might have landed; and enemy aliens still had freedom of movement on the edges of Pearl Harbor.

After conferring with several intelligence officers who shared my concern, I decided to report the facts and opinions to my highest superior on the spot, Admiral Nimitz, by speaking to his chief of staff, then Rear Admiral Milo H. Draemel, USN. I told him: "My conversation with you is impelled from a sense of duty because of what I consider a serious situation existing in Hawaii. Once before in such a situation, I gave concrete opinions and advice which apparently could not break through preconceived ideas." This referred to my meeting with Admiral Kimmel and his chief of staff, Captain W. W. Smith, in March 1941, in which I pointed out that the Japanese in the event of hostilities with us would begin them with an air attack on our fleet, on a week end and probably Sunday morning.

After my talk with Admiral Draemel he suggested that I draw up a memorandum for the Commander in Chief so that he could read it and then talk to me regarding it. In this memorandum I documented for the first time the fact of my conversation with Admiral Kimmel and Captain Smith nine months before Pearl Harbor in which I had presented to them my estimate of the situation. Extracts from this previous conversation were included in the memo for Admiral Nimitz for the sole purpose of making him feel that I knew what I was talking about before Pearl Harbor and that I was just as well informed now.

In less than three months just such a situation eventuated and resulted in the Battle of Midway. But for our intelligence work, and the superb performance and sacrifices of our own aircraft torpedo squadrons, who dedicated themselves to history as the *first* suicide airmen, we would have been confronted with a catastrophe even greater than Pearl Harbor.

I ascertained that Admiral Nimitz had passed my memo around to his staff and that all but two of them felt that I was correct in every detail. The dissenting two had commented: "Selfish interest involved." I took that to mean that certain ones, holdovers from Admiral Kimmel's staff, felt that I was their nemesis unless discredited.

I never ascertained exactly what Admiral Nimitz felt about the memo. He spoke momentarily about it the afternoon before I sailed for "Shangri-La," but his remarks had no bearing on his opinion of its merit. But on the morning of June 6, just after the Battle of Midway, when I had flown into Pearl Harbor, I encountered Admiral Nimitz approaching his headquarters. He crossed the street to intercept me and gave a hearty handshake, his face wreathed in smiles, and I felt that he wanted to say: "Now I know what you meant." He had realized that the Midway action could become a decisive battle of the war, either in the enemy's favor or our own, and he had realized it as soon as his Intelligence reported to him the Japanese plans and intentions. It is beyond the scope of my narrative to analyze the naval leadership in preparing for and executing the Battle of Midway. But it is proper for me to emphasize the decisive contribution which Intelligence made to victory.

Just as the Pearl Harbor disaster was partly due to failure to consider intelligence data in its proper perspective, the great victory at Midway was the triumph of properly recognized intelligence. Even today all that I am ready to disclose is that certain intelligence officers deserve as much credit for the victorious conclusion of the battle as the officers who planned and executed the action, largely on the basis of brilliant intelligence work.

The battle itself not only again revealed to me a series of clues in the field of Japanese psychology, but also manifested the spiritual superiority of our own forces. When long after the battle I read

Japanese diaries of men who died on other battlefields after having been compressed like sardines on Japanese transports, ready for the landings on Midway and Hawaii, I fully realized the cycloid traits in the Japanese character. The diaries revealed men who were fully heartened and gloriously ready for still another victory. They disregarded the discomforts of their transport, the hardships of their voyage, the possibility of imminent death in battle. All this was overshadowed by the imminence of triumph. But as these same men viewed from the distance the deadly clash between their own fliers and ours, as they saw their carriers wrapped in flame and then going down forever, their so-called and much-vaunted "spiritual superiority" turned into distinct psychological inferiority. The entries in the diaries changed rapidly from confidence to hope and from hope to despair.

It was evident to me that the Japanese were susceptible to psychological influences, no matter how complete and apparently successful their moral training and indoctrination.

In fact, even their combatant ships at Midway did not fight to the last. On one of their carriers was an old acquaintance of mine, my perennial shadow and opponent, Admiral Tamon Yamaguchi, suffering the brunt of our attack. This was a climax he did not expect and for which he came completely unprepared. As our heroic aircraft torpedo squadrons conducted one suicidal attack after another in which our best men perished, Yamaguchi gave up the battle even before all his means of resistance were exhausted. He decided for himself that further resistance was impossible, so he prepared to die by the hand of inevitable fate. He called the crew to listen to a farewell address even while the battle was still in progress. He took the men away from their battle stations, just to "banzai" with him and await the end in inaction. It was an anti-climactic end to his career, his ultimate failure when the war for which he had so arduously prepared himself and which he had helped to plot became stark reality. To me, the Battle of Midway represented the end of an era which I may call the Yamaguchi era. It was in a sense symbolical. It heralded the end of Japan.

The failure of the Japanese in this battle ushered in a new phase of the war, a phase which was marked by our own deployments and maneuvering for position. The quiet which settled on the waters around Midway was shattered in other regions—around the Solomons when on August 7, 1942, our first expeditionary force of Marines invaded the islands. I was no longer at sea, but watched events from a battle station removed from the actual scenes of combat.

I was ordered to report to Washington, to the Chief of Naval Operations, and arrived in late June for duty in OP-16. This code stood for the Office of Naval Intelligence, and I was to assume the position of deputy director of Naval Intelligence, with all the responsibilities which the job entailed in wartime. As I prepared myself for the new job, the highest thus far in my career as an intelligence officer, I reviewed the years which were behind me, the years of war between the wars.

I had fought them on many visible and invisible battlefields. They had provided me with thrills and frustrations, with opportunities and disappointments, and had yielded a glorious adventure which was forever implanted in my mind and heart. It had been an uphill fight I had waged, but every minute of it had been worth while if only because it had been a fight. The years had not been wasted. They had been devoted to hard work yielding results in the many improvements and better recognition of intelligence, as was manifested to me when I returned to the third floor of the Navy Building to the desk that was to be my bridge for one year.

The war also had taught me many lessons, and I was determined to apply them in practice now that I was given the opportunity. I had one major aim upon assuming my new job: to add brain to the brawn which was then abundantly building in our shipyards and armament factories. Confined to an intellectual field of battle, I was determined to find ways and means by which we could gain victory sooner and more cheaply. In this sphere I recognized the primary task of wartime Intelligence and its great challenge to justify its importance, and indeed, its existence.

BOOK THREE

THE WAR OF WITS

26

WASHINGTON AT WAR

IF EVER A nation started a war from scratch, the United States was that nation in 1941. There is a saying from which we seem to derive a peculiar satisfaction—that only totalitarian countries are ever prepared for war. As usual with generalizations, this one has come to be accepted without critical qualification. But once it becomes a truism with us, it contributes even further to our notorious unpreparedness.

Wars are usually waged against the status quo, against existing conditions in one nation which another nation, after having felt its muscles and judged them sufficiently strong, decides to change. In 1937 the Germans made this design public. During the party congress in Nuremberg, Rudolf Hess, echoing Hitler, proclaimed that "the Old Order had outlived its usefulness and must be replaced by the New Order." He was thus presaging the inevitable clash with us, since he regarded the United States and Great Britain as representatives of the "Old Order," while Nazism and Fascism were "torch-bearers of the New World."

This statement carried the declaration of war against us—but we failed to recognize the menace in its challenge. So we continued to live our life of the status quo, failing to prepare to defend our heritage with the same energy and selflessness with which the Germans and the Japanese organized to destroy us.

It is true, and proper, that the democracies never think in terms of a war of aggression. Our traditions, moral heritage, and written constitution prevent us from waging a war in the German and Japanese manner without declaration or warning, pouncing upon an unsuspecting opponent lulled into complacency by means of diplomacy. But the events of the past should teach us a valuable lesson. This lesson can be stated in the simplest terms: While we should continue to refrain from aggressive war for aggrandizement, we must not fail to be prepared to wage a defensive war.

In the war just ended we succeeded, perhaps for the last time, in saving the status quo of our American way of life. We can continue our system of government, the pursuit of private competitive enterprise, and live the life we have developed for ourselves—rides in the country, going to church on Sundays, playing golf in the afternoon, listening to jive music blaring forth from overworked juke boxes— provided we recognize these privileges as symbols of freedom and do not take them for granted. It is no Fourth-of-July oratory to say that what we have is worth holding. We can keep it only if we are willing to defend it. The pioneers of America were deeply religious and prayed by disposition, but they also fought, and fought well when it was necessary.

America has immense hidden strength—not merely in its natural resources, but chiefly in its people, who normally turn these resources into great industries, skyscrapers, roads, schools, and hospitals. In the past whenever the need has arisen America has been capable of changing her latent resources into ships and guns and planes as well. However, its accomplishment was dependent upon one other vital element: time; time to act before the enemy could destroy our powers of resistance. But now, in the words of President Truman, "Never again can we count upon the luxury of time to prepare our defense." This applies to all of our armed forces and particularly the Navy, which must intercept the enemy far from our shores. And it applies to our intelligence agency because now *knowledge is truly power*.

We were in the very midst of preparations for the top-secret mission to "Shangri-La" when a letter diverted my thoughts to the Office of Naval Intelligence. Captain Puleston's admonition was still alive both in my heart and mind, and I regarded myself first and foremost as an intelligence officer. But the pressure of war did not allow of as much attention to the problems of wartime intelligence as I desired. Communications were slow, and weeks passed without contacts with the hinterland. I imagined, however, that Intelligence was active, fighting the war by its own means now that it had become a fateful reality. A letter, dated February 3, 1942, brought me the first authoritative news. It was from an old and dear friend, the late Colonel John W. Thomason, Jr., U.S. Marine Corps, who was as great a writer and artist as he was a brilliant strategist, tactician, and able soldier. In a few lines written in his characteristically forceful manner Colonel Thomason gave me the summary so eagerly awaited since the outbreak of hostilities:

"I am still in ONI," he wrote, "with very poor prospects of getting out. I have the American Republics Section: South America hangs around my neck like the ancient sailor's albatross. I made a three months' tour by air of the whole damned place last fall, returning just before December 1. Now, God help me, I'm an expert. But it's a long war, the way our Kriegsherren are going at it, and I'm sure there will be trouble enough to go around."

He was all for immediate offensive action, this fighting Marine, and against what he called a "step-by-step war." But he was resigned to the bureaucracy of war as he wrote:

"Oh well. I just work here. I'm an old mercenary. I don't have to blush for what these Yankees do or don't do."

And finally turning to shoptalk closest to both of us, he doled out a bit of information on ONI:

"I would say, my dear Zack, that our department resembles more than anything the outside fringe of a cyclonic or whirling storm. Everything being tossed about. King is superimposed on Stark, having absorbed most of the latter's functions: simply another planet of the first magnitude added to our galaxy: both shine, perplexing to the navigator.

"Wilkinson has ONI, the third chief in a year and a half. Bill Heard has the Foreign Branch; Waller, Domestic. Your old desk is in the entirely capable hands of McCollum. We are swollen enormously: never was there such a haven for the ignorant and well connected. As a matter of fact, ONI isn't bad, so far as collecting information goes. But what good is information if it isn't used? Here the museum idea seems to prevail."

Thus in a few lines did Colonel Thomason put his finger on the age-old trouble of Intelligence. His letter saddened me, since it awakened memories and kindled a nostalgia. It made me yearn to go back to Intelligence, where I felt there was vital work to do. Counteracting this desire was my present duty, one of the best possible assignments a captain in the Navy could ask for in time of war—command of a heavy cruiser in the active theater of operations. I felt that I was letting my crew down by even thinking of something else. We had "grown up" together in these past seventeen months. I was part of the team.

In the spring of 1942 the two posts of Chief of Naval Operations and Commander in Chief, United States Fleet, were combined by President Roosevelt for the duration; and Admiral King was named to the united command.

My relations with Admiral King had always been gratifying, since he seemed to have a constructive understanding of intelligence and valued the work I had been privileged to do in former years. He was once quoted as saying: "If I ever become Chief of Naval Operations, Zacharias is going to be my director of Naval Intelligence."

Not long after Admiral King's assumption of his new post I was ordered to proceed to Washington upon arrival of my relief, and to report to the Chief of Naval Operations. Admiral King was instrumental in bringing me back to Washington at this time. But these indications were to be only partly fulfilled; and for the first time I was to experience what is called "department politics."

It was several months before my relief was able to catch up with my ship but finally, in June 1942, after the Coral Sea battle, I found myself hurrying to Washington, my twelve days' delay for leave at home being canceled because of "services urgently required."

I arrived on the eve of still another turnover within ONI: Admiral Wilkinson, a seafaring man at heart, was preparing to return to the fleet, and Captain Kingman, the assistant director, was also about to be transferred to sea duty. Awaiting these changes and what seemed to be the probable and logical advancement to the top, I was given temporary charge of the Foreign Branch, relinquished by Captain Heard, who, too, went to sea.

A few weeks later the new "slate" was announced. On this slate a Captain Harold Train, USN, an officer who had been passed over in the regular selection process for rear admiral and who had never had one day's experience in intelligence work (he had attended several international conferences) was named director of Naval Intelligence. I was given the post of assistant director, shouldering under Train, who was advanced to the rank of rear admiral, the great work of reorganization.

A few weeks in ONI convinced me that we had to start from scratch and do a complete job of overhauling if we were to make ONI an efficient wartime intelligence organization; and I was often reminded of Thomason's prophetic words that the museum idea still prevailed. My assignment as assistant director was, therefore, the greater disappointment, since I knew that the traditional system of the chain-of-command would slow down the realization of my prepared plans, but I hoped that I would receive complete support from Admiral Train, who was a newcomer to Intelligence and not familiar with any of its peculiar problems and their solutions. But the months ahead of me proved extremely difficult. I was compelled to wage an uphill fight; even so I was able to carry out at least a part of my program, fighting, as I went, against obstruction and inertia.

Washington was a beehive in the spring of 1942. The impact of Pearl Harbor was still visible in the confusion and occasional chaos, in the duplication of effort, although the bureaucratic machine of the American war effort was gradually emerging from the shock. But not Intelligence.

The word itself seemed to have an undue fascination to many untutored minds, who perceived in it either a romantic escapade of war, or simply an escapade. There were many applicants for intelligence work. So great was their number, and so little their real qualifications, we were confronted with the difficult task of saying "no" to myriads of newcomers armed with powerful letters of recommendation. Simultaneously I began the weeding-out process, particularly the deadwood in key positions. All of this met with great approval in lower echelons and was evident in a sudden spurt of morale within the organization throughout the United States. Many came in to express their gratitude. I knew that it would not fail to have its reverberations on upper levels, but I closed my ears to these unpleasant noises.

Intelligence was then a fashionable activity in Washington. Intelligence groups and organizations were mushrooming everywhere in the capital, each new agency regarding it as its first duty to establish its own intelligence outfit instead of drawing on available organizations with their backlog of experience. While this situation existed, we found that very little truly valuable information was produced which higher echelons could accept as absolutely reliable and useful for orientation and action. The principle of "too much too soon" was thus applied to wartime intelligence, quantity dominating where quality was absolutely essential.

These deficiencies of the situation were most keenly felt by the military organization which was created as our successful answer to the problem of unified command, the Joint and the Combined Chiefs of Staff. Organizing the over-all direction of a global war was indeed the first challenge President Roosevelt had to face, and the problem he had to solve in a satisfactory manner if we were to prosecute the war with the businesslike efficiency which it fully required. His answer proved to be a stroke of genius providing the smoothest organization in all history for the conduct of a coalition war.

Acting upon the advice of his military commanders, and particularly Admiral William D. Leahy, USN, his own chief of staff, the President created two top-ranking command organizations, one American, the other Anglo-American. The American organization was the Joint Chiefs of Staff, composed of the President's Chief of Staff, the Army Chief of Staff, the Commanding General of the Army Air Forces, and the Chief of Naval Operations. The international organization was called the Combined Chiefs of Staff, and consisted of the American Joint Chiefs and their British equivalents. In these two organizations was created a command machinery which was unique in its composition, unprecedented in the smoothness with which it functioned, and unparalleled in its subsequent accomplishments. If one sole organization can be singled out at all and be given credit for the greatest single contribution to victory, it is the Joint and Combined Chiefs of Staff, an international brain trust of war.

The Chiefs of Staff were meeting every day in a setting that would have done credit to a Hollywood director. The white marble Public Health Building on Constitution Avenue was provided as headquarters and turned into a top-secret building with barbed wire and armed guards thrown around it. Machine guns were concealed under the bushes, an ingenious electric warning system was installed to announce uninvited visitors who might have wanted to venture beyond limits, and at night powerful searchlights illuminated the grounds to enable the guards to detect intruders. Inside the meeting hall of the chiefs, intricate maps were hanging from the walls, a motion-picture screen was kept in readiness to show military operations in slow-motion details, and direct communications were provided to enable the chiefs to follow the war as if they were in the thick of it. They had their own communication officers, their own staffs—but they were lacking their own intelligence organization.

The lack of an intelligence agency directly attached to them and providing information to them on the highest echelon was most keenly felt, and caused Admiral King to summon me to his office one day to discuss this problem. The idea which emerged from this conference was that of a joint intelligence organization, to be formed by pooling the intelligence resources of the Army and Navy, and to incorporate under the Joint Chiefs of Staff all intelligence agencies of the government in order to provide necessary intelligence data for the President and the Joint Chiefs. Admiral King approved the idea of drawing up a specific plan.

Memories came back to mind of old Tokyo days when Captain Watson had produced what we came to call our M-Plan. The man who gave his name to this plan, Sidney F. Mashbir, was now in Washington, where he had come to reside when he resigned from the Army in 1923 and after the Japanese earthquake had destroyed his organization in Japan. He had enrolled in the Military Intelligence Reserve G-2 and become a lieutenant colonel. Subsequently, he engaged in some secret work for the Navy in Japan, trying to implement his M-Plan for us. He had been advised by us to keep away from our military and naval attachés to avoid arousing suspicions of the Japanese authorities. He was to exploit as far as possible his former Japanese business associates and the Pan-Pacific Union, of which he was a member. All of this aroused the suspicions of the military attaché, who suggested Mashbir be investigated when he next came through Hawaii. This was done, and influenced by the military attaché suspicions, Hawaii played safe and turned in a prejudicial report. A copy of this report reached me in San Diego and I recognized it as being based upon completely erroneous assumptions. Meanwhile this report had had an unfavorable effect in G-2; and advantage was taken of Mashbir's failure to fill in a form reporting a change of address, or something comparable, to disenroll him. Although a secret report was later made by me to the head of that organization explaining Mashbir's activities for the Navy, nothing was done to clear it up. The whole thing is an illuminating story in itself, and, as I explained to the Roberts Committee, this was one of the reasons why we did not have more information on Japan before December 7, 1941.

However, with the outbreak of hostilities Mashbir was sought immediately by the Signal Corps because of his wide technical skill. He was later "borrowed" by G-2 to send to Australia, an action which caused the raising of several eyebrows. But there, his executive ability and quick accomplishments brought him promotion to full colonel by General MacArthur after only one month of reorganizing an important activity, the Allied Translator and Interpreter Section, Southwest Pacific Area, of which he was given full charge. Since then he has been in the forefront of General MacArthur's intelligence activities and will be remembered in the motion picture of the preliminary surrender negotiations at Manila as the man who thumbed the Jap general along as he attempted to shake hands.

Knowing Sid's background and interest, it was natural for me to turn to him for advice and aid, inviting him to join me in drawing up the plan for a joint intelligence organization. The next four months were ascetic indeed. I spent full days in the Office of Naval Intelligence reorganizing and working on immediate problems, while my evenings were spent with Sid Mashbir in the most complete seclusion drawing up "the plan" for Admiral King. When it was completed, it seemed to contain most of the answers to existing questions, and to provide an organization that would fill the gap so urgently felt by the Joint Chiefs. The new organization created on paper was called the Joint Intelligence Board, and established for the first time in our history a highest-level intelligence organization fully capable of aiding the war effort with top-quality intelligence.

When the plan was presented to Admiral King, he devoted considerable time to its study and considered every aspect of the solution which our draft seemed to suggest. I watched him as he read the draft and could detect even in his impassive face signs of approval as he turned from page to page. When he finished reading our document, he lifted a pencil to change but one single word in the whole draft. He changed the name of the proposed agency from "Joint Intelligence Board" to "Joint Intelligence Agency." He then put the draft in a drawer and said: "I'll see what can be done about it." He was later quoted as saying: "If I live, this will go through." This was tantamount to his approval.

However, that was as far as the plan progressed. After being fully prepared, presented, and approved in at least one of the highest echelons, it was suddenly pigeonholed because of unknown influences, filed—and forgotten. Some day all the obstructive tactics which resulted in actual interference with the Army and Navy intelligence services in time of war, I hope, will become known. At the time I was powerless to combat these influences because of lack of support in my own office. Military Intelligence, under General Sherman Miles, encountered them, too; but he was fortunate in having the sympathetic understanding and backing of Secretary of War Stimson. Our splendid censorship organization remained unhampered because of the determination and power of its director, Byron Price. I am sure that in future reorganizations which must take place, the Congress will include this situation in one of its investigations, because it is one which has a bearing on the whole future of our country. Even at the time of this writing when the new Central Intelligence Authority, an agency the importance of which is recognized by all concerned, is taking its first stumbling steps, I feel that same invisible hand reaching out in its predatory efforts and lust for power.

Here, then, in 1942 was I confronted with the second war which we were waging: the never ending battle of Washington, in which memoranda clashed with memoranda, and draft proposals were the usual casualties.

27

DEPUTY DIRECTOR OF
NAVAL INTELLIGENCE

As soon as I arrived in Washington, I had opportunity enough to confirm Thomason's remark that "ONI isn't bad, so far as collecting information goes." The Office of Naval Intelligence was now a big and still-growing organization where able men by far outnumbered "the ignorant and well connected." Here again I saw the hidden strength of America come to life. Men who only a few months before had been peaceful private citizens, newspaper publishers, lawyers, insurance salesmen, bankers, writers, radio commentators were now rapidly becoming ingenious and even brilliant intelligence officers. But the situation was discouraging on the whole. Only perfunctory use was made of the Office of Naval Intelligence; the old prejudices carried over into the war; and we had to fight for recognition, virtually sell our material to the staffs, no matter how valuable it might have been.

The problems of wartime Intelligence are vastly different from its peacetime tasks. Above all, everything is speeded up, since there is no time left for leisurely research and analysis. Those in the battle areas need their information at once, and the flow of intelligence to them must be maintained. The accent now shifts from strategic to tactical intelligence, from general information of a probable enemy's designs to actual enemy movements, at least insofar as volume is concerned. Operational intelligence is added to the responsibilities of Intelligence as a whole, material for the commanders in combat zones, information of immediate value for action.

While the volume of work increases, the task is somewhat facilitated by an easier access to the enemy's secrets. It is a truism that wars cannot be conducted behind closed doors. Planes fly over the enemy's territory, returning with minute pictures of his installations, terrain, deployment proceedings, and all those secrets which, in peacetime, intelligence officers have difficulty obtaining. Weapons and instruments, and sometimes ships, are left behind on abandoned battlefields ready for analysis and study revealing the most closely guarded ordnance secrets of the enemy. Documents are captured, diaries are found, all providing data to which there is but limited access in peacetime.

The question with which Intelligence is thus confronted is one of embarrassing riches: quantity seems to predominate, and quality is submerged in the mass of information which thus becomes more available every day that the war progresses. The duty of the good intelligence officer is to make a qualitative selection from the mass of data that comes to his desk. Another challenge is in the field of security and counter-intelligence. The enemy desires to learn as much about us as we are learning about him. It is now the foremost duty of Intelligence to prevent the enemy from gaining a similar access to our secrets. At all times our efficient censorship organization, co-operating fully and functioning perfectly under the very able leadership of Byron Price, kept us informed of enemy agents. It was Price who first discovered and reported to us the use by the enemy of microfilm in which a whole story is told in a single dot disguised as a period in a letter or hidden under an unused flap of the envelope. When magnified a thousand times, the little dot discloses that it is more deadly than a 16-inch projectile. It was the gratifying co-operation of his organization which made possible the identification of certain agents in Central America. And when a small group of these individuals were arrested there occurred simultaneously the sudden disappearance of the German submarines operating off the Atlantic and Gulf coasts. An outline of this activity was included in my testimony at hearings of the Senate Judiciary Committee on December 14, 1942. I said:

"Through information coming to us we were able to identify certain individuals who we believed were engaged in the refueling of submarines in that area. I must say that the number coming to our attention in the very beginning was limited, but through a search of the communications passing among them we were able to identify approximately six times as many so engaged. . . .

"The Army and the Navy intelligence organizations almost simultaneously got knowledge of the activities of these individuals which knowledge was also presented to us by communications from censorship. It was all rather simultaneous and it is difficult for me to say just who discovered the information first, but it was equally as important. . . .

"Because of the seriousness of the situation it became obvious that action had to be taken, which resulted in the incarceration of certain individuals. With that incarceration the communications to all of them suddenly subsided and with the subsiding of the communications submarine activity off the coast suddenly disappeared. . . ."

I regarded it as my first task to accelerate the transformation of Intelligence into a valuable tool for our commanders in the field. But there seemed to be no co-ordination. Because everybody was bent upon doing his own intelligence work, duplication abounded in virtually every government agency. The Navy for the time being had its ONI, but the Office of Communications was also doing its own independent intelligence work and passing it directly to the Commander in Chief. The Army had G-2, with the Secretary of War just about to set up still another intelligence agency under his own jurisdiction and independent of G-2. There were intelligence organizations at the headquarters of theater commanders which maintained an independent attitude, unmindful of the needs of Washington. The Office of Strategic Services was trying its wings. The Treasury Department, Commerce Department, State Department, Office of Censorship, and several other agencies were busily engaged in intelligence work; and the first thing the newly established Office of War Information did was to establish its own intelligence service.

I assumed that the Office of Naval Intelligence with its experience would be a directing agency to help co-ordinate other efforts, but I was sorely disappointed to find that much of the intelligence work in other agencies was conducted by inexperienced personnel who appeared reluctant to gain from experience or benefit from the advice of ONI.

Training of personnel was our primary problem, since we had only an inadequate intelligence school chiefly concerned with the preparation of officers for investigation duties, known as "gumshoe activities" among those in a belittling mood. Complaints heard in the field offices decided me to make training my number one project. Radical changes had to be made, and I took it upon myself to make them immediately.

The old school was abolished and two new schools were created:

one in Frederick, Maryland, called the Basic Intelligence School, to introduce newcomers to the elementary principles and techniques of intelligence; and another, the Advanced Intelligence School in New York, to train intelligence officers on an operational level. This second school grew out of the realization that Naval Intelligence in war has somewhat different tasks from those of Army Intelligence. The elements of ground combat and the problems which it raises are largely nonexistent in naval warfare, so that what the Army calls its combat intelligence has but limited application in the Navy. What we needed was operational intelligence, an activity between strategy and tactics providing in intelligence everything a commander might need to take his ships into combat or to conduct amphibious warfare. The immense mobility of fleets and the wide expanse of our watery battlefield necessitated a broadening of intelligence work, too; and we felt that our operational intelligence would take all these factors into consideration. We planned to train hundreds of operational intelligence officers by driving them through a hard curriculum compressed into a comparatively short time. We actually trained a thousand—and as I now look back upon this project, and the demands which soon poured in upon us, I feel that we were not disappointed in our expectations. My faith in Lieutenant (now Commander) John Mathis, USNR, who headed this school, was well founded. His legal mind, pleasant personality, and keen investigative abilities gave me confidence. Ably assisted by an outstanding faculty of men high in the educational field, such as Lieutenant Richard W. Hatch, Lieutenant Garrett Mattingly, and others, the success of this undertaking was assured.

In the meantime an agency was being nurtured within ONI which proved of the greatest significance and was, in my opinion, one of the two agencies which made the greatest contributions to American intelligence during the war. Even though the U-boat war was still going against us, we sank an occasional German submarine off our coast and brought in prisoners for interrogation. It had been foreseen that prisoner interrogation would be an important function of Naval Intelligence, and preparations had been made far in advance, even before we were actively in the war. A prominent New York lawyer, Ralph G. Albrecht, who had long and intimate knowledge of German intelligence work since he had represented American firms in their claims against the German government in the long-drawn-out suit for damages resulting from German sabotage in World War I, was the first to organize a prisoner interrogation branch within ONI; later the activity was broadened and set up as a semi-independent branch within Naval Intelligence under Commander John J. Riheldaffer, USN (Retired), who returned to active duty.

The work of this agency is beyond praise. The results which its activities yielded may indicate the efficiency of this organization. To mention but one, it was this agency which discovered a potentially dangerous German secret weapon long before the Germans were ready to use it. This weapon was the acoustic torpedo, a device which was to be attracted to our merchant ships by the very noises which the ships emitted, infallible in finding its mark. Commander Riheldaffer's organization succeeded in obtaining a complete blueprint of this weapon approximately six months before the Germans applied it in combat, and thus enabled our Navy to develop a simple countermeasure. When the first acoustic torpedo was fired by a German submarine, we were ready to counteract it; and the carefully guarded new weapon on which Germany was pinning great hopes turned out to be a dud.

This was just one of the many accomplishments of Commander Riheldaffer's organization, which, I regret to say, did not receive the recognition it fully deserved.

Another important innovation in Intelligence was suggested to us by the problems with which we were confronted in the wake of our North African landings. The intelligence organizations afloat and in the field failed to recognize the future planning value of intelligence picked up in their operations, and after culling the immediately usable tactical intelligence data from the material to which they obtained access in combat, they discarded the rest. The planning activities of the Washington Departments were entirely forgotten. The Office of Naval Intelligence felt very keenly this practice of the combat forces which deprived the Navy Department of its most valuable source of material for future planning. We decided to do our own collecting on the spot with officers and men specially trained for the job. The first graduates of the New York school were just joining us, and we decided to form them into teams under a newly created organization operated in co-operation with the Army, and called JICA, the Joint Intelligence Collection Agency. Working with my assistant, Captain Edward A.

Hayes, USNR, one of our brilliant reserve officers, we prepared a comprehensive plan, which, as it contemplated joint action with the Army, we took to G-2 and showed to the director of Military Intelligence, the late Major General George Strong.

The plan met with a gratifying reception in the War Department: "This is just exactly what we've been talking about," General Strong said after a short study of it. He then volunteered to present the proposal to General Marshall immediately with a view to obtaining his approval. Apparently, when the Army Chief of Staff saw the plan, he realized at once its scope and importance and approved it. General Strong indicated to us that he had no trained personnel immediately available, but I told him that we would set up the organization in Africa and he could add his personnel as they were trained and became available.

We then got in touch with General Donovan, the head of the Office of Strategic Services. He had many operatives throughout the world and particularly in the European theater. Their activities of espionage and sabotage had a direct relationship to Military and Naval Intelligence. They provided us with information of the enemy on which to base operational plans; they often gave us leads which were beneficial in following the efforts of enemy operatives and nullifying them before they could interfere with our military procedures; and we co-operated in preparing for activities such as the "McGregor" project prior to the invasion of Italy. After explaining the purposes of the JICA we offered him the facilities provided by this organization and invited him to participate as far as possible. He accepted heartily, and his agents in the field were delighted with this system which provided them with instant contact with their headquarters. Our "salesmen" had obtained the promise of one seat per day for our couriers on planes going to or coming from the forward areas. This assured us of almost twenty-four-hour service with the front lines.

Here then was the first specific effort toward large-scale Army-Navy co-operation in the field of intelligence. It provided the highest strategic intelligence setup the United States had ever had. The system was later expanded to East Africa (Cairo), Europe (Italy), and Asia (New Delhi); and we placed a JICA team in every city of importance as soon as captured.

With the arrival of our previously trained and well-briefed intelligence teams in the African theater of operations under the able leadership of Captain Earl Major, USNR, there began immediately an endless flow of documents to JICA headquarters on the fourth floor of the Navy Department. It was gratifying indeed to see the coatless representatives of the several agencies gathered around the large table poring over the fabulous wealth of documents as they were passed from one to the other for each to signify immediately his own department's interest in the material. This informal selection eliminated the useless copying and distribution which ordinary methods of interdepartmental handling entailed. I dare say that the higher echelons never knew the reasons for the sudden speed with which pertinent information began to come into them from the forward areas.

As soon as the system was on a definite footing, my first thought was to increase its usefulness by making its facilities known in the Navy Department. Among the first I saw were the logistic planners, then under Rear Admiral Oscar Badger, who had the responsibility for maintenance of port facilities after landings were made. I said to him:

"Oscar, is there any information you need from Africa?" He regarded me for a moment as if he thought I were teasing him about a recent outburst of his subordinates with regard to the lack of information on which to base constructive planning. Then I added: "Tell us what you want, and Intelligence will serve it up to you." That broke the ice, and he exclaimed: "Do you know that I have one hundred and eighty million dollars' worth of material waiting to go to Oran and I don't know whether they have a single damned crane with which to take it from the ships?"

"That's what I'm here for," I said. "Let me know what you need, and we'll get it."

In short order he had detailed all his difficulties and desires.

"Would two weeks be too long to wait for this?" I asked.

"Where in hell are you going to get this within two weeks?" he asked disbelievingly.

"You'll get it," I answered as I gathered up my papers and left his office.

The following morning a courier was winging his way toward Oran, with a detailed urgent job for the Oran team.

In this same port not long before, our first intelligence team had run into an immovable stone wall in the commanding officer: he was in command there, and every individual would do as he was told; he didn't want any intelligence men snooping around there! So the team found themselves shunted to the Communication Office to help with decoding work. With the aid of Army direct wires we received immediately this discomforting news in Washington. It was sent right back, but to Admiral H. K. Hewitt, Commander North African Naval Forces, who fortunately was an officer with a fine appreciation of the scope and importance of intelligence. After confirming the facts, Admiral Hewitt moved, and so did the unsympathetic commanding officer at Oran—back to the United States.

Within two weeks of the time I had left Admiral Badger's office I was back again. This time I laid upon his desk a neatly bound folder with a dignified label: "The facilities of the Port of ORAN."

As he thumbed through the pages, he uttered unprintable expressions of amazement, and it was not surprising that a few days later the Director of Intelligence sat reading in amazement a highly commendatory letter on the efficiency of ONI. It was signed O. C. Badger.

I often visited the JICA room as the atmosphere there was so refreshing compared to the "humidity" of other offices in confused Washington. One of the big moments occurred upon the arrival of the secret report of accomplishments of the intelligence team which landed with the first wave in Sicily with glowing results to be related in another chapter.

This "baby" of mine had certainly come of age!

28

OP-16-W

ON A SNOWY December day in 1942 a yeoman of the United States Navy went to a store on F Street in Washington to buy a recording of Wagner's *Flying Dutchman* overture. There were only five people in the whole country, and the yeoman was not one of them, who knew that this purchase was part of a military operation. The record was needed by a secret branch of the Navy Department carrying the code name OP-16-W to begin an all-out psychological warfare campaign against the German Navy. A few bars from the overture, chosen for their popularity with German music lovers and the symbolism of the opera which they so forcefully introduce, were to serve as the theme of regular broadcasts.

At this time many innovations were being tried out by the various planners in the Navy Department. Considerable latitude was afforded for trying out new methods and devices, and ingenuity was widely encouraged in an atmosphere which was formerly clothed in conservatism. Some of these innovations were on a gigantic strategic scale, as, for example, the organization of the service forces, and on tactical levels many new secret weapons were developed with our British ally to combat and defeat the German submarine.

Most of these innovations, no matter how revolutionary, moved along traditional naval lines and fitted into the customary pattern of naval thinking. But here in OP-16-W was something entirely different which could not be fitted into any category of naval warfare. The idea had its origin in a basement room of the British Admiralty where a lieutenant commander of the Royal Navy developed the notion that Germans, especially members of the German Navy, were vulnerable to psychological attack. He felt that their morale was susceptible to undermining by certain adverse psychological factors, such as the basic inferiority of their arms, the protracted idleness of their ships, and the prolonged isolation in U-boats, pictured as steel coffins, on operational cruises.

The British lieutenant commander, a reserve officer with a journalistic background, presented his plan to Commander Fleming, himself a reserve officer but in 1942 serving as confidential aide to Admiral Godfrey, Britain's director of Naval Intelligence—one of the two great intelligence chiefs the Royal Navy has been fortunate to have in times of war. Approval was immediately forthcoming, and a branch called NID 17-Zed was created to conduct psychological warfare against the German Navy by all means known for this type of campaign—by radio, leaflets, and subversive means through the spreading of rumors by agents. Also on the radio the Germans were advised to avoid submarine duty by contracting certain diseases.

Shortly after its inception 17-Zed scored its first major triumph and justified its existence even to the perennial skeptics who stand at the empty cradle always hoping that the child will be stillborn. A recruiting campaign was being conducted by the German Admiralty to obtain additional men for Admiral Doenitz' U-boat arm, which then was on the eve of considerable expansion. The building program of 1941 envisaging scores of submarines coming off the ways was just about to become a reality, and thousands of young Germans were needed to man these splendid new boats. Doenitz preferred volunteers since he regarded high morale, usually engendered by volunteering, as essential to the success of his branch.

NID 17-Zed went into action with a series of radio broadcasts and cleverly designed leaflets, both given wide distribution in those German towns where Doenitz hoped to have the greatest success in his recruiting campaign. The material put out by 17-Zed emphasized the hardships of life on a U-boat, the hazards of the U-boat war, the short life expectation of a U-boat man, and many other factors which made service in Doenitz' fleet anything but a romantic experience. When the effectiveness of the campaign was tested through various means of validation, such as censorship, prisoner interrogation, and captured documents, it was found that the recruiting campaign was far from being the success Doenitz expected it to be. It is impossible to ascertain in psychological warfare how far results can be attributed directly to the campaign itself, since a variety of factors contribute to the effectiveness of a psychological offensive, some of which are merely exploited by this intellectual warfare rather than supplied by it. There was no doubt, however, that 17-Zed achieved its goal. Doenitz did not get the number of volunteers he hoped for.

The activities of 17-Zed were called to the attention of our naval attaché in London, and Admiral Harold C. Stark, the commander in chief of our naval forces in that area. Several specialist officers serving under them became convinced of the effectiveness of this new arm and suggested to the Navy Department in Washington that an American counterpart to 17-Zed be established for co-operation with the British outfit. But nothing was done.

At about the same time one of our intelligence officers, Lieutenant Commander Ralph G. Albrecht, USNR, was in London discussing improved methods of prisoner interrogation. He was a highly qualified German expert, a prominent international lawyer who specialized in sabotage and espionage cases against Germans from World War I, whose German was flawless. During his stay in London he was pressed into service by 17-Zed to make two broadcasts to the German Navy to call attention to the comradeship which existed between the U. S. and Royal Navies and to point out the eventual contribution our Navy was to make to the joint war effort.

Upon his return Commander Albrecht reported his experience to me and suggested that we, too, embark upon a psychological campaign along lines suggested by the British. He was energetically supported in his recommendation by Commander Riheldaffer, who pointed out that his section's work of prisoner interrogation yielded masses of so-called incidental intelligence which could be effectively used for the psychological offensive.

It required no argument to convince me, as it was my opinion that total war had a powerful implement in the psychological weapon. Even as I listened to the first description of the Japanese attack against Pearl Harbor, I realized that a highly emotional nation like the Japanese would require psychological as well as physical attack to force her to her knees. But still, in 1942, I felt that the time for a psychological war against Japan was not yet ripe, even though the British successes in this field revealed that it was potentially effective against the Germans. I therefore approved the plan for the establishment of a psychological warfare branch within Naval Intelligence in August 1942, and looked around for the man to head it up. I did not have to look far since the best man available for this unusual job was then working for Intelligence on other important assignments, such as contact with and control of certain Japanese residents in Hawaii. He was our old friend the doctor, now Lieutenant Commander Cecil H. Coggins of the Navy's Medical Corps.

My enthusiasm for the new branch was not generally shared, I was told: "We are fighting this war with ships not with words," and again: "What good can come from a series of broadcasts? Nobody will listen to them!" Another immediate superior said: "Why do we need a doctor in Intelligence?" My patience was sorely strained. But I closed my ears and went ahead.

The four of us—Riheldaffer, Albrecht, Coggins, and myself—continued the work in the face of considerable opposition and antipathy. We encountered other natural difficulties, not the least of which was the recruiting of top-notch personnel for the job. Coggins was now working directly under me. He planned his branch as a secret one; and we were determined to keep it on an extremely limited scale with a staff of just three or four people, in contrast to the rambling and overpopulated organizations maintained for psychological warfare by the other agencies, including the Army. But while Coggins limited quantity, he put no ceiling on quality, a condition which complicated for him the job of finding the right persons for the work. However, in his extensive reading on intelligence, espionage, and counter-intelligence matters, he had been impressed with two books which suggested to him the personnel for his branch. One was *Total Espionage* by Curt Riess, and the other was *German Psychological Warfare* by Ladislas Farago. After conferring with me and obtaining my approval, Coggins got in touch with the authors and arranged a meeting. He interrogated these men for two days; and when he had satisfied himself that he had found the nucleus for his branch, he returned to Washington to talk things over with me, and finally the Special Warfare Branch was established and Riess and Farago were employed as the first two members of its staff.

The establishment of what we called the Special Warfare Branch (we feared that by calling it Psychological Warfare Branch we should engender even greater hostility by opponents of everything psychological) was greeted with extreme enthusiasm by the Office of War Information, which then found co-operation with the armed forces a very difficult task. Elmer Davis, director of OWI, became our champion, and whenever attempts were made to abolish our branch, he pleaded with our highest echelons and borrowed time for us so that we could continue our activities.

We worked in the closest and most harmonious co-operation with OWI, which was the sole vehicle for the dissemination of our material. The broadcast recordings were prepared for OWI in a studio of the Interior Department then under the able direction of Shannon Allen, and manned with capable technicians. The broadcasts were put on the air by OWI seven times a day, three days a week from all outlets OWI then had in the United States, North Africa, and Great Britain. In addition we prepared for them a program called Prisoner-of-War Mail, an arrangement by which German and Italian prisoners kept in this country could send greetings to their relatives and friends in their homelands. This was the first such attempt made in the United States, and it yielded splendid propaganda results. We also worked with OWI in drawing up propaganda directives insofar as naval warfare was concerned, and this close co-operation proved that a military and a civilian agency could work together smoothly on what was undoubtedly an important military operation.

This arrangement also gave us an opportunity to watch the machinery of the Office of War Information, and we became convinced that in certain phases at least it was an efficient and effective agency far removed from the ballyhoo propaganda agencies of previous wars. Later, too, when our campaign against Japan started, it was Mr. Davis' office and the tireless personal handling by his able overseas director, Edward Barrett, which made the execution of the plan possible over obstacles and against odds the description of which must be left to another chapter.

Great care was taken to conceal the existence of our Special Warfare Branch and the fact that the United States Navy was engaged in psychological warfare. I conducted preliminary negotiations with the staff at my home and then gave instructions to regard the new branch as secret. As a result only a handful of people knew of its existence. Even so, outside efforts were made to bring about its abolishment, and I had to fight hard for its continuance. The branch continued to operate with little change until May 1, 1946, while similar agencies were subjected to experimental major operations. The promising child maintained by the Army finally suffocated from overcrowding and died early in the game.

Our plan for psychological warfare was simple enough: We were to prepare our own broadcasts, creating an officer spokesman of the U. S. Navy to address members of the German Navy; prepare leaflets for distribution from England; and prepare guidance notes on naval matters for other American and British agencies engaged in psychological warfare. Operations began on December 7, 1942, just one year after the attack on Pearl Harbor, and Commander Albrecht was designated to act as our German spokesman. This was a very fortunate choice. Albrecht became undoubtedly the most effective instrument the United States had on the strategic level of wartime propaganda throughout the Atlantic war. In the course of operations Albrecht made 309 broadcasts to the German Navy, and their effectiveness was attested by the Germans in a document our forces captured at German naval headquarters at Cherbourg. The document proclaimed that his broadcasts "had a crushing effect on the morale of German naval personnel."

Because of his civilian background as a prominent international lawyer we had given him the cover name of "Commander Robert Lee Norden, USN," or, in German, "Fregattenkapitän Robert Lee Norden der Amerikanischen Kriegsmarine."

The idea behind the so-called Norden broadcasts was a revolutionary one never before attempted in psychological warfare. We decided to utilize information in even highly classified intelligence data for his broadcasts, to give the impression of absolute omniscience; and very often "Norden" sounded as if he knew more about the German Navy than the Germans themselves, which was often the fact. The files of OP-16-W were bulging with a novel kind of intelligence. We collected data on all friction within the German Navy, picked up innumerable items of gossip, little or major scandals. And by utilizing our intelligence machinery for the gathering of this type of incidental intelligence, we ascertained in exact detail incidents in the family life of Admiral Doenitz, the sweethearts of German naval officers in France, the deficiencies of new boats, down to such minor (but from our point of view significant) details as Admiral von Friedeburg's refusal to permit one of his officers to marry a young lady of simple circumstances—but unblemished virtue.

The first broadcast went on the air on January 8, 1943--describing in detail activities of a German naval officer who continued his own Gestapo methods, for which he was notorious, even in an American prison camp. The revelation of intelligence data was regarded with misgivings in higher echelons, but we were fortunate to have as Cominch security officer Captain T. T. Patterson, USN, whose understanding of our work made the initial attempts quite easy from this point of view. He gave us almost unlimited freedom of action, and with such ammunition we could not fail to score a success even at the earliest stages of our campaign. We had destroyed the "museum" idea which formerly surrounded our files. But quite often I had to confront higher echelons to prove mathematically that we were saving American lives by our work. "We can quit," I said to Admiral R. S. Edwards, "but you are betting American lives against the possible effects of hoarding information. Intelligence is no good unless you use it." I usually won out with an admonition to "Be careful," a warning superfluous to the trained intelligence officer.

The U-boat war was at its height when "Norden" went on the air. Two days after his debut the Germans succeeded for the first time in wiping out half of an oil convoy going to our forces in North Africa. Despite bad weather in the Atlantic, German U-boats were scoring impressive victories, and the unrestricted submarine warfare was to be intensified during February in what Nazi propaganda confidently called the irresistible Doenitz offensive.

It was German propaganda technique to play up the U-boat victories by announcing cumulative data on sinkings, ringing a bell for each Allied ship which was sent to Davey Jones's locker, and issuing so-called special bulletins (*Sondermeldungen*) for particularly impressive sinking claims. But there was confidence in our office since we knew that the potentially very effective counterweapons which we had assisted in furthering were in production; and Admiral King was able to announce that the U-boat war would be under control within six months. Nevertheless, German propaganda exploiting the successes of their U-boats was an important element of morale promotion in Germany. They now used it to counteract effectively the adverse influence of the Stalingrad debacle. Our task, then, became one of preventing the Germans from using the U-boat's successes to gloss over their defeats in North Africa and in Stalingrad. Accordingly, a special operational plan was designed to throw them on the defensive in their U-boat propaganda as well. We decided to question German claims and to expose them as exaggerated by proving that U-boat commanders falsified their reports of success to Admiral Doenitz and were notorious for mendacity in their claims.

The whole month of February was devoted to this powerful offensive. "Commander Norden" harped on the untruthfulness of German U-boat commanders in every one of his broadcasts. We released to the press, both in the United States and neutral countries, a list of the ten German U-boat commanders who were best known for their mendacity, and cited facts and figures to show that ships which they claimed as sunk were still afloat, carrying vital war goods to the battle fronts.

Toward the end of February our campaign had drawn its first blood. The Germans started to answer us first by indirection, publishing the methods by which U-boat commanders ascertain their successes, and then by answering "Commander Norden" directly. It was evident the Germans were on the psychological defensive and that faith in their claims was definitely undermined. Even so, their sinkings represented serious inroads into our shipping, and we intensified our propaganda to prevent the Germans from ever claiming the sinking in a month of one million tons of Allied shipping, a figure which German propaganda represented as essential for victory in the U-boat campaign and which the German U-boats were actually accomplishing in the month of February, 1943.

The success of our campaign was to be revealed definitely after March 1, when the Germans were to issue their monthly sinking claim. The results were more than satisfying. Obviously intimidated by our campaign, for the first time in the war the Germans claimed less than they actually succeeded in sinking and the figure remained more than 100,000 tons under the one-million mark.

At about the same time another incident revealed to us that the Norden talks were effective right from the beginning. German U-boat commanders were usually given a high Nazi decoration called the Knight's Insignia of the Iron Cross for sinking our ships. We discovered, however, through intelligence that only one petty officer in the whole German Navy had ever been awarded this decoration apparently reserved for commissioned officers. With the facts lined up, we started another campaign criticizing Admiral Doenitz for his discrimination in the failure to award the Knight's Insignia to men of the lower deck as well, who were, Norden argued, sharing all the hazards of operational cruises without being permitted to share the rewards.

We did not have to wait long to draw blood. After the third broadcast the German Navy announced that two petty officers had been awarded the Knight's Insignia, the announcement saying: "The Führer, upon the recommendation of Admiral Doenitz, Commander in Chief of the German Navy, awarded the Knight's Insignia to...."

A few hours after this award became known in 16-W, "Commander Norden" was on the air, congratulating the two men who received the awards. Then he said: "There was, however, a slight error in the citation. It was not upon the recommendation of Admiral Doenitz but it was upon the recommendation of the United States Navy that these awards were made to these petty officers."

By spring "Commander Norden" was well known within the German Navy, and we learned that his German listeners referred to him by the nickname "Bob." On one occasion when a young German naval officer was captured after his boat had been sunk, he volunteered a suggestion to change the time of the Norden broadcast, since Norden's schedule coincided with the change of the watch on U-boats and deprived many of his German fans of the opportunity to listen. Final confirmation of his effectiveness came when a U-boat commanded by Lieutenant Heinz Eberhard Müller was sunk. Both the sinking and the German submarine's resistance represent a saga of the sea, the German commander fighting to the last and abandoning ship only after he had been seriously wounded and could no longer organize resistance. An American destroyer fished survivors from the sea, and Lieutenant Müller was taken to a hospital to be patched up. Hardly was he able to talk again when he turned to a pharmacist's mate who was attending him and asked: "Would it be possible for me to talk to Commander Norden?"

This request created considerable confusion since no trace of "Commander Norden" could be found in the Navy Register or in the Navy Department's telephone directory. In fact, our operation was conducted in such secrecy insofar as our end was concerned that nobody outside of 16-W and 16-Z knew of "Norden's" existence and occupation. However, Müller repeated his request to an interrogating officer from 16-Z who called at his bedside, and he was given immediate assurance that Norden would visit him at once.

For this visit Albrecht had to have another half stripe put on his sleeve since he was a full commander only on the air, while in reality he was a lieutenant commander in our Naval Reserve. As an added precaution, we entered the name of Commander Robert L. Norden, USN, in the Navy Department's mail-room directory, and when later "Norden" began to receive fan mail from his enemy audience via Switzerland, the mail room knew how to route those letters. For all practical purposes "Norden" was not a phantom broadcaster but a living person brought to life by Albrecht's complete self-identification with the character he was supposed to create and his outstanding performance under the assumed name.

His interview with Müller yielded the final confirmation that the so-called Norden broadcasts were hitting their target and that with them we had a definite instrument with which we could influence German naval thinking and even tactical action. But the opportunity which this form of offensive provided as part of a co-ordinated campaign was not appreciated in higher echelons, and was completely neglected by the Cominch antisubmarine group, the one agency which was created for the purpose of combating the German submarine. It was known as the "Tenth Fleet," a phantom organization under the personal command of Admiral King. Although increasing confirmation of Norden's effectiveness removed tendencies to belittle the psychological warfare effort, the complete absence of training in this field is responsible for the general lack of knowledge of the scope and importance of such work. This precluded full support which should have been forthcoming with necessary data for participation in the activities. A major campaign planned by Norden involving the surrender of German U-boats was completely disapproved, as being an unnecessary post-V-E-Day activity. This created the impression that certain officers regarded victories scored by psychological warfare as unworthy of naval tradition. Later the British used successfully the very tactics that had been proposed.

While we continued in Washington our psychological warfare efforts under the handicaps of lack of appreciation and sometimes hostility, the British went ahead full speed with their operations and gained the support of highest echelons, including the commander in chief of the Mediterranean fleet, then Sir Andrew Browne Cunningham, RN. It was, indeed, in the Mediterranean theater that British psychological warfare was used with the greatest effectiveness and scored its major victory. This was largely due to careful planning and the wide latitude which it was given by Admiral Cunningham.

There, it was the Italian fleet which was attacked by psychological means. It was an easy target since the Italian Navy was known to be fundamentally opposed to war against the Western Allies in co-operation with Germany. This opposition was partly based upon the knowledge of the fleet's own weakness and the tremendous defeats it had suffered early in the war. At least part of these defeats were brought about by brilliant intelligence work, which enabled the Royal Navy to sink more than twenty Italian submarines between June and November, 1940, by exploiting certain information which the British Division of Naval Intelligence procured in Rome on the eve of Italy's entry into the war. The torpedo-air attack against the naval base of Taranto was another blow from which the Italian Navy found recovery difficult; and Germans, notorious for their lack of tact in coalition warfare, failed to make Italo-German naval co-operation a working proposition.

Although we tried never to underestimate an enemy, a sense of proportion was maintained in adjudging the Italian Navy as a major opponent, and there was a little quip making the rounds in both of our navies which somewhat characterized the attitudes and sentiments. It said that while milk shakes were favored in the American Navy and the Royal Navy preferred rum, the Italian Navy stuck to Port. Nevertheless, the nuisance value of the Italian Navy, supported as it was with extreme effectiveness by a few German air squadrons stationed in the Mediterranean theater and the U-boats the Nazis managed to smuggle through the Straits of Gibraltar, was very high. The British Mediterranean fleet, under orders to keep the Mediterranean open to Allied traffic at all costs, suffered heavy casualties in its heroic campaign and was hit by Italian suicide raiders even in such ports as Alexandria, Gibraltar, and Oran, revealing to the world that Italians, too, could fight hard and with self-abnegation if they put their hearts into the struggle.

Toward the end of 1942 and early in 1943 the Germans began secret conversations with their Italian allies to activate the Italian fleet to support some of the ambitious projects Hitler designed for the Mediterranean theater. Among these projects was an operation called by the code name "Hercules," aiming at the capture of Malta, and another operation going under the code name "Anton," concealing the planned capture of Gibraltar. Both operations were designed to counteract our successes in North Africa and to lend more effective support to Rommel's hard-pressed Africa Corps.

Our intelligence agents reported both plans to us and also sent in information about a trip Admiral Doenitz was making to Rome to discuss personally with the Italian admiral Riccardi closer co-operation between the German and Italian Navies. A strategic evaluation of the situation suggested to us that, with our deployment still in its earliest stages, an intensified naval warfare in the Mediterranean was contrary to our interests, since it was bound to slow down our advance toward Sicily and then Italy proper. Admiral Cunningham decided to enlist psychological warfare in preventing such co-operation, and inspired a conference between the psychological warfare departments of the British and American Navies to draw up an operational plan best calculated to frustrate Italo-German co-operation.

The question which the psychological warfare experts asked Admiral Cunningham was a simple one: "What do you want?" they asked. "Do you want the Italian fleet to come out for battle in which your forces may have a chance to annihilate it as a major striking force? Or do you prefer to keep the Italian fleet inactive for the duration?" With supreme confidence in their own weapon, these mental warriors assured Admiral Cunningham that they would be able to accomplish either one of these strategic aims by psychological means alone.

Admiral Cunningham's decision was motivated by his own needs. He was confident that he could annihilate the Italians in battle, but he was himself operating on a shoestring and preferred not to risk a single one of his major vessels in unnecessary combat with the Italians, who would, he calculated, be effectively supported by German air units. So he gave instructions to the psychological warfare group to do everything in their power to keep the Italians in port.

An ingenious plan was thereupon designed and put into operation, calculated to drive a deep wedge between the Germans and the Italian Navy and prevent their co-operation on a major scale. There was revealed to the Italians information gathered through our intelligence agencies which convinced them that the Germans regarded the Italian Navy as cannon fodder and were prepared to sacrifice it if they could save Rommel's Africa Corps by so doing. It was learned through secret sources, including agents planted even within Italy's own naval intelligence organization, that Italian merchantmen were to be pressed into service to evacuate Rommel's German troops while the Italian forces would be left to their fate. As soon as this top German secret was learned, it was put on the air and told in convincing detail to our eager Italian listeners. The results were gratifying indeed! Psychological warfare proved to be an effective aid in maintaining the Italian Navy in an inactive status throughout our advances toward Italy. This was frankly admitted by several pro-Allied Italian naval officers of high rank such as Admiral Bergamini, now the commander in chief of the Italian Navy. And it was kept from interfering with our operations even when we started our eastward move and captured Italy's own Gibraltar in the western Mediterranean, Pantelleria, and then landed on Sicily.

Our combined intelligence activities yielded immense results in the Sicily operations. Aside from the success of our psychological warfare in keeping the Italian Navy away from these crucial areas of operation, another intelligence team which we created in JICA scored a major triumph on the day of our landings on Sicily. Extracting information from a reluctant Italian pilot as to the exact location of Italy's naval headquarters in Sicily, these specially trained intelligence officers from New York City raided the building, blew the safes open with hand grenades, and captured documents and other invaluable information which made our subsequent naval operations in the area a comparatively safe enterprise. Maps showing Italian mine fields and important data on seaports, and even organizational data on the Japanese Navy were among the prizes.

As the Italian campaign reached the mainland, psychological warfare was intensified with the aim of causing the surrender of the Italian fleet intact. Plans for this operation were drawn up in London in co-operation with the Foreign Office's own political warfare executive, which was kept posted on the political situation in Italy. Early in June the psychological warfare personnel were told that Mussolini's collapse was imminent and that behind the collapse loomed the total defeat of Italy. By then we were in direct contact with certain dissident elements in the highest echelons of the Italian Navy and prepared through them the surrender of the fleet. Validation of the psychological efforts by contacts with the Italian Navy revealed to us that the fleet was amenable to surrender, and early in July a proclamation was drafted to be issued at the most favorable moment, calling upon the Italian fleet to come over to us.

This psychological moment came in the late summer when parallel negotiations with Marshal Badoglio, then head of the Italian government, and commanders of the Italian Navy indicated an early collapse of Italian resistance. These negotiations had to be conducted in utmost secrecy; while a few key men on the Italian ships knew of impending events, the rank and file were not aware of the plans we had prepared for them and had to be advised of their fruition through means which made a reception of our climactic proclamation possible: by sending through radio channels permanently monitored by the Italian Navy including their own secret wave lengths, ascertained by radio intelligence, together with the distress channel.

By late August the Italian fleet's mood had been rendered sufficiently conducive to surrender, and when Badoglio decided to cease resistance, we could call upon the Italian ships to come over to us. No greater proof of psychological warfare's effectiveness in modern war can be provided than the eventual success of this major campaign which was conducted without letup from February 1943 to September 1944. The Italian fleet was the only service of Italy's armed forces which actually carried out the surrender stipulations in the exact manner prescribed by us, according to plan and schedule, and as designed when we first set out to bring about this end by means of psychological warfare.

Major credit for the Italian psychological campaign belongs to the British. Throughout this period the psychological warfare efforts of our 16-W followed the major trend of the war and concentrated on campaigns against the Germans. But gradually the campaign against Japan came to occupy our attention, and plans were made to enlarge our staff by including experts on Japan in addition to our German specialists. But just when the stage was being set for our psychological campaign against the Japanese enemy at the proper moment, I was ordered to sea in command of the battleship *New Mexico*. All of my subordinates were amazed that I should be sent back to sea just when I was at the top of my successes and was planning new ones. And so was I. Even now, I do not know what caused that action or whether it was justified. It will have to be credited to the fact that I was moving too rapidly, and was becoming too strong for the good of more ambitious individuals and agencies. That happens in Washington.

Regardless of this new splendid command, I was leaving Naval Intelligence with a heavy heart. In spite of exhausting and discouraging uphill fights which prevented me from carrying out my program in full, I could look back on the accomplishments of my one year in Naval Intelligence with justifiable pride. Our two schools were graduating excellent intelligence officers who were received with open arms by the fleets. Our Operational Intelligence, carefully nurtured under Commander Charles F. Baldwin, USNR, was bringing concrete results, and our teams were landing with the first waves. The Joint Intelligence Collection Agency was functioning with top efficiency, as were, indeed, the many branches of the Office of Naval Intelligence, with officers and men displaying an energy and devotion born of the highest possible morale. It was a far cry from the conditions which I had found in Naval Intelligence when I arrived in Washington in July 1942. This was no reflection on my predecessors. Our success was due to the application of years of experience which until then had not been applied.

And last but not least, I left behind a psychological warfare branch which was ready to go into action against Japan on a moment's notice. My subordinates felt that these were personal accomplishments. I didn't care what others felt.

Those in 16-W were most depressed. They all knew the hard fight I had put up, and they feared that the forces which had always worked for the abolition of 16-W would now have their own way unobstructed by my efforts to protect the Psychological Warfare Branch from outside influences. But I knew that their big day would come; success had made their fears groundless. Later, necessary personnel were added to round out the efficient crew for the work ahead. The day of this comprehensive campaign, far more intensive and better co-ordinated even than the Italian venture, was still more than a year away. But much physical fighting had to be done before we could start firing effectively our penetrating verbal bullets. And it was again my good fortune to share in this physical fight in command of the battleship *New Mexico*—much to the confusion of *all* my enemies.

29

DETOUR TO SEA

I LEFT Washington on September 5, 1943, to take command of the *New Mexico,* one of the three battleships of the *Mississippi-Idaho* class, three ships not present in Pearl Harbor on December 7, 1941. This was my first battleship command, and those who know the Navy can well appreciate that it is an entirely different experience from command of smaller ships. The intimacy which characterizes the relationship between the commanding officer and his shipmates on destroyers, and to a certain extent even on cruisers, is completely lacking on a huge battleship with more than 1,700 men in the crew. It is virtually impossible to know all of them, and direct personal contact can be maintained with only a few on the ship. This made it impossible to exercise command by direct personal relations, which I had found so successful in the past. Even so, I decided to do what I could to weaken the barriers which usually exist between the commanding officer of a battleship and the men and officers under him.

One of my methods used previously had been to address the crew from time to time, explaining to them the over-all trends of war, thereby trying to create in them a feeling of actual participation in the great events of which they were a gallant and important part. It was also my custom to pass through the crew quarters as often as possible when the noon meal was being served, to show interest in their food and comforts. I made it a point to be critical of the quality, temperature, and manner in which it was served. Preoccupied as I was with the psychological problems of war, I fully realized that morale was one of the most important factors; especially on a battleship, I have always felt that food and the soda fountain were the basis of contentment, and contentment the basis of morale.

At the time I took command of the *New Mexico* we were in the stage of the war which Admiral King termed "the defensive-offensive phase," meaning the departure from purely defensive measures and a gradual going over to the all-out offensive.

The change-over from defensive to offensive was a deliberate sequence in our strategy. Admiral Nimitz had become confident that he had enough in ships and men to venture into Japan's own sphere of domination. And his planning for the break-through to the Japanese island fortresses was materially aided and influenced by another triumph of Intelligence. In August 1942 two submarines carried a small raiding force of Marines to Makin Island for a commando attack against that Japanese outpost under the leadership of Colonel Evans Carlson and Lieutenant Colonel James Roosevelt, both of the Marine Corps. It was planned as a small-scale operation, to harass the Japanese garrison and conduct reconnaissance as far as possible. This operation, in which only a few hundred men participated on both sides, and which on the surface appeared to be rather inconclusive, nevertheless yielded the "ammunition" which radically changed our plans for the Pacific war. The men returned to Pearl Harbor with many captured documents which the Japanese abandoned on Makin as they fled into the wooded areas from the headquarters, which was situated near the shore and overrun by Carlson's raiders in the initial assault.

This was the first major haul insofar as enemy documents were concerned, and our intelligence officers, long and meticulously trained for this occasion, concentrated upon the material. It soon became evident that although the Makin outpost was a minor one it was supplied with all major documents—a grave intelligence blunder. In the mass of material were found plans, charts, and battle orders, including one top-secret map which revealed the exact air defenses of all Japanese Pacific islands, the strength of the air forces stationed on them, their radius, methods of alert, types of planes used—and above all, operational plans for any future emergency. It was assumed that the capture of these documents would bring about changes in the plans, but the Japanese were by then so committed that they could not make radical changes; improvising also is contrary to their national character. Most of the plans were left unchanged despite the knowledge that their secrets had fallen into our hands. In fact, it was during the Iwo Jima campaign in 1945 that we found the first deviations from Japanese defense principles.

By November 11, 1943, the *New Mexico* was on her way, with Makin and Tarawa as the first stops in a campaign which was to continue throughout 1944, moving ever closer to Japan proper in the most gigantic island-hopping project the world has ever seen. The Japanese radio was still putting out fantastic claims that they were still "winning the war" in the Solomons. But false victory in one remote, by-passed area was the only elixir Japanese propaganda could dole out to forces in active operational areas which could not know the over-all situation and regarded their own plight as local and insignificant in the whole picture.

Far more significant was a statement made by Premier Tojo on the eve of our deployment for the break-through. I felt that a note of desperation and despair had crept into his words as he said: "If we lose this war, we will lose our birthright." Here was a different Tojo speaking. For the first time in his wartime career he was holding out the possibility of defeat. Until then there had been nothing "iffy" about the Japanese war pronouncements. And the possibility of losing their "birthright" was never even considered. It seemed that Japanese propaganda, like Japanese strategy, was changing over to the defensive.

The story of Tarawa and Makin has been forever immortalized, and I am glad that I had the honor to command a major combatant unit throughout that campaign and its close successor, the conquest of the Marshall Islands. But that is another story.

On February 4 Kwajalein was declared secured; and the day after, I landed and inspected the effectiveness of our bombardment, examined huge piles of captured documents, and talked to the Nisei (Japanese-Americans) who had the difficult task of sorting and translating them for immediate and future use.

The next five months were decisive in the Pacific war, with the devastating raid on Truk and soon thereafter the assault on Saipan and Guam. With the reduction of Saipan the last barriers to our advance to the inner seas of the Jap Empire had fallen; but over and beyond the purely military consequences, and of even deeper significance, were the political implications of the campaign. The true situation of Japan was laid bare in the diary of General Saito, commander in chief of all forces stationed on Saipan, which our intelligence found in his final headquarters.

This document was of the greatest significance. It revealed an extensive controversy between field commanders and the Imperial General Staff on the one hand, and between this military command and the Emperor on the other. According to Saito's record, he was deceived when reinforcements definitely promised failed to reach him, and the fleet, under Admiral Toyoda, the commander in chief, failed to come to his aid.

Saito waited and hoped. But he was doomed to disappointment, since the promises had no foundation in fact. In an outburst of sincere indignation he turned against the "Tokyo clique" and even against the Emperor when he said: "How senseless it is to die for the Emperor when those who are responsible for my plight, and indeed, for the plight of Japan, continue to live their careless lives in Tokyo."

In a last attempt to acquaint the Emperor with the truth, he sent a message by radio in code to Tokyo advising the Emperor of the true state of affairs and also of the hopelessness of his situation. It may be assumed that the Emperor never received this sensational dispatch; but we were fortunate enough to capture it intact, with a copy finding its way to OP-16-W, where its significance was immediately recognized.

A psychological campaign plan was designed by 16-W based on Saito's records and diary, envisaging documentary disclosures and bringing the Japanese general's accusation into the open. It was expected that such a disclosure would precipitate a political crisis in Japan and affect accordingly their will to resistance. Unfortunately, the plan was vetoed by the security officer, who failed to recognize the significance of the document and preferred the "museum idea" to the psychological scoop which undoubtedly the disclosure would have scored.

By the end of July 1944 the tide had definitely turned against Japan, and the war was entering a new and final phase. We had succeeded in piercing the armor of Japanese resistance. The war had been "lost" by the Japanese in the furious actions between October and the following July. It was to be "won" by us in the few months to follow.

As on July 30 we headed east for Bremerton Navy Yard to replace the guns worn by intensive use, I felt that my detour to sea was drawing to its close. The time had come to bring to bear new weapons both physical and spiritual.

30

PRELUDE TO SURRENDER

LATE IN December 1943, while listening to reports of Radio Tokyo, I picked up a proclamation issued by the Emperor of Japan which I believed to be of the utmost significance. I did not overestimate the Emperor's powers, but neither did I underestimate the role he was playing as the "universal stabilizer" between the various factions of Japan's political life. After many years of close contact with Japanese politics it was not difficult for me to recognize his place in Japan. While some individuals in certain circles were trying to make their calculations without the Emperor, I decided to base my plans on Hirohito as the one person able to tip the balance decisively at the psychological moment.

On that eventful day in December 1943 the Emperor made the following statement: "The situation is the most critical in the long history of the Empire."

Similar remarks had been made before from lower echelons, chiefly to spur the people to greater sacrifice and to dispel the mood of superficial complacency which until then had characterized the Japanese war effort. From competent observers who had returned to the United States on the first trip of the exchange ship *Gripsholm*, and from other intelligence sources, we had put together a fairly accurate picture of the trend inside Japan. The blitzkrieg atmosphere attending the early victorious stages of the war now belonged to the past. The moment of glory in Japanese history had faded. It was being replaced by an incoherent feeling of uncertainty, not only among the people but also among the political and military leaders, who now realized that they had embarked upon an enterprise which was overtaxing their material and moral resources.

Japanese history had been my guide throughout these complex months, and I found that a similar situation had existed during the Russo-Japanese War of 1904-5. At that time we had had several highly qualified military observers with both the Russian and the

Japanese forces. Their objective professional appraisals had enabled us to sift facts of that war from the mass of propaganda which typified subsequent reports. Captain Peyton C. March, later to become chief of staff of the United States Army, was one of the observers; and it was one of his reports which now served as my guide in evaluating the Japanese situation. His report Number 6 of January 3, 1905, described the so-called Battle of the Sha River in which the Japanese suffered their first setback. "The effect of this battle," he wrote, "was clearly shown upon all the Japanese generals with whom I came in contact. They seemed to realize for the first time, or at least showed openly for the first time, that they realized the magnitude of the conflict upon which they had entered."

It was under the impact of such an unexpected turn of events that the Japanese requested President Theodore Roosevelt to act on their behalf in seeking peace—a fact which, as has already been narrated, had been admitted to me on a quasi-social occasion in the Washington apartment of one of Japan's alert diplomats.

It was inductively certain that the Japanese would again turn to some intermediary once they realized that the tide had turned against them. And the Emperor's statement was an indication that at least some of the leaders of Japan had been awakened to this realization and regarded the war as irretrievably lost. Not only was it obvious that the Emperor was proclaiming the thoughts of his advisers, but it was also obvious to those who knew the technique of Tokyo palace politics that the Emperor was endorsing the views of others.

In a sense Hirohito was the weather vane throughout the war. When in the wake of the disastrous Battle of Midway he agreed to issue an imperial rescript dignifying it as a glorious victory, I knew that he was under the complete influence of advisers who felt it vitally necessary to picture that debacle as a passing event to be compensated for by other victories. Until the end of June 1942 the Emperor was still very much on the side of hope and confidence; but by December 1943, when he made his gloomy pronouncement regarding the critical situation, the war and he had taken an entirely different turn.

On the basis of my experience in Japan, my subsequent studies, and the scant Japanese intelligence material available to me while at sea, it was not too difficult a task to identify the influential group which had persuaded the Emperor to make this last significant statement. The Japanese themselves, and certain observers in the United States, looked upon the late Prince Konoye as the man kept in the background for use when conversations were to be started. However, I discarded Konoye altogether as an acceptable or even a possible candidate for a peace negotiator chiefly because he had been an integral part of the indecisive Japanese political leadership which had permitted the militarists to carry Japan into the war. Other men appeared to me to be plausible candidates for membership in a peace group: Admiral Nomura; Admiral Yonai, then holding the position of minister of the Navy; Admiral Okada, though behind the scenes; and Admiral Suzuki, a former grand chamberlain to the Emperor. This imperial circle, composed of elder statesmen and practical politicians, was not opposed to gaining victory; but they could also be counted upon to salvage whatever they could from defeat. If my deductions were correct, they provided a basic group against which to attempt a campaign of psychological warfare when the time was ripe.

Of added significance was the realization that at the time it was made, the Emperor's somber declaration seemed premature. Despite setbacks and the damages wrought by our war of attrition the Japanese fleet was intact in many of its essentials. A spirited and efficient aircraft-building program was yielding results, and Japanese planes continued to appear in the skies in ever-increasing numbers despite the enormous attrition caused by our radar fire control, contact influence fuses, and other innovations, not to mention our own aircraft.

As 1944 dawned, nowhere in the whole Japanese armor did there appear a single decisive break—in fact, their psychological preparedness seemed greater than ever. If surrender in defeat is accepted as an indication of lowering morale, there was no sign of that. Surrenders were just as scarce as earlier in the war: the realization of defeat had not altered the attitude of the individual on the combat front.

Until this stage our psychological warfare against Japan had been conducted on a small scale by the Office of War Information, which was broadcasting from a very great distance. In the Pacific theater of operations psychological warfare was virtually unknown. No preparations had been made to attack the Jap's Achilles tendon, as revealed by history—his moral stamina. Haphazard and inadequate efforts were being made in the southwest Pacific under General MacArthur, who was making up as best he could for the lack of early organized effort by drawing on his own knowledge of Japanese psychology and his ability to adapt his campaign accordingly. A psychological campaign in a distinctly tactical sphere was also being conducted by Admiral Mountbatten in the India-Burma theater, but it did not radiate beyond the immediate combat zone; and while it yielded good results in Burma itself, where the number of surrenders was gradually increasing, it had no influence whatsoever beyond that theater, and even there it had limited effects.

The greatest need for psychological warfare was in the Navy's own theater, the Pacific Ocean areas, where we were now going over to the offensive, close to the Japanese homeland.. But there its importance was not recognized, and nothing was being done. A few free-lance psychological warriors in very low echelons who tried to change the situation by introducing methods which had proved effective in the European theater found themselves faced with lack of understanding and were hamstrung.

The Office of War Information experienced great difficulty when it tried to join the offensive against Japan. According to the presidential directive which established the OWI, the theater commander had complete control of everything in his zone; and psychological warfare could be conducted, if at all, only with the approval and under the supervision of the local commander in chief. For reasons which I still cannot understand but which must be similar in background to those which caused Pearl Harbor, Admiral Nimitz was persistently advised against the use of psychological warfare against the Japanese. This advice was based upon a shallow conception which took as a fact an imaginary situation actually created by Japanese propaganda itself: the delusion that the Japanese would never surrender and that any attempt to interfere with their mental processes would be doomed to failure. This concept was never tested, it was just accepted. And for two years of war the Japanese benefited from it.

But working under very difficult conditions and at times confronted with open hostility by higher echelons, a small group of young Marine officers decided to take things into their own hands and make an attempt at psychological warfare during the Saipan operation. They prepared crude instruments: a hand-operated printing press and a homemade loud-speaker system mounted on a "requisitioned" jeep—and thus the first tactical psychological warfare team in the Pacific Ocean area was born. Makeshift efforts of individuals as early as Guadalcanal cannot be considered as an effective attempt.

The Saipan operation provided considerable opportunity for psychological warfare in more ways than one. Leaflets were used for deception purposes, a great number of them being dropped over areas where we did *not* intend to land, giving the impression of imminent operations in that area and luring the enemy away from places where the actual amphibious assault was to take place. During operations, too, leaflets were used with great effectiveness, especially against the civilian population. The Japanese used these civilians as a shield to protect their military forces as they were retreating, and some were even forced into guerrilla fighting against us. When the island was declared secured, we had the first large haul of prisoners, the majority civilians; and the first proof was obtained that the Japanese were not as impregnable to psychological attack as their propaganda so often tried to represent. From that time this type of psychological warfare had more support, but it never came into systematic usage throughout the Pacific war.

While I considered tactical psychological warfare of the utmost importance in lessening resistance and hastening the cessation of hostilities in isolated areas, I was preoccupied with planning a psychological campaign on the strategic level—not against individual military or naval units in the combat zone but against the leaders in Tokyo, who, from their comparatively safe position behind the curtain, moved their forces like so many marionettes.

The loss of Saipan produced in Tokyo the commotion we expected. The capture of the island and the loss of over five hundred planes in one sea action—the Battle of the Philippine Sea—brought home to members of the Tojo government the hopelessness of their stand. The cabinet resigned in the wake of this spectacular defeat right on their own doorsteps. The disappearance of General Hideki Tojo from the political scene of Japan was a major political event, the significance of which did not escape us. His successor, General Koiso, was another member of the so-called Kwantung group which had dominated Japan's political machine ever since the outbreak of the war—but still, Tojo was relegated to a place of nominal importance by appointment to the Privy Council. It was inevitable that his influence and prestige would suffer in the crisis. I felt confident that the Koiso cabinet was a caretaker government destined to yield to still another cabinet if, and when, the situation deteriorated further. The important question in my mind was: Who would follow Koiso? A return of Tojo would have meant resistance to the bitter end, and such a return was by no means impossible. But if Koiso should be followed by a politician close to the Emperor and fitting into my category of surrender-conscious "peacemakers," it would definitely give us an opportunity to bring about Japan's collapse by means of psychological warfare.

The return to the mainland of the *New Mexico* for re-gunning was shortly followed by my transfer to the 11th Naval District as chief of staff. My new post enabled me to review my own analysis on the basis of more adequate information not accessible in the midst of operations to the captain of a battleship.

Events then followed with a rapidity which made Tojo's return appear exceedingly remote and Premier Koiso's position highly precarious. The beginning of his downfall came late in October 1944 with the Battle for Leyte Gulf, in the course of which the Japanese combined fleet was annihilated as an effective striking force. As the picture unfolded, with Japanese ships going down, one after another, in the narrow straits of the Philippines, with General MacArthur consolidating his foothold on Leyte, and Admiral Halsey dealing finishing blows, I realized that the important moment in the war had arrived. The time had come to begin a psychological campaign on the highest strategic level. Japan was confused and was vulnerable to a stroke by psychological warfare alone.

I weighed the possible methods by which this could be initiated. As I paced the floor of my office, my assistants regarded me questioningly and wondered what momentous problem was confronting the district. I was thousands of miles away. It was obvious to me that I would have to overcome many preconceptions if I were to gain a trial for my abstract weapon. But I could also visualize at least a hundred thousand of our dead piled up on the shores of the Japanese main islands. I felt I must do something; and on December 16, 1944, I took the first step. I wrote a letter to Captain Waldo Drake, USNR, a former zone intelligence officer and more recently chief of public relations under Admiral Nimitz on loan to the OWI as a tactful intermediary between Pearl Harbor headquarters and that agency. My letter read:

Dear Waldo:

I was surprised to hear of your new job but know that you are glad to be back on the Continent again and it should provide you with much latitude and many things of interest.

I know you feel as I do about leaving the scenes of activity at a time when you are really stepping up, but I find that the new job here as Chief of Staff of the District enables me to incorporate the "front line" ideas into those of the back area. Of course, if it must be shore duty, you know how much I enjoy returning to my old surroundings where everything was able to go forward with interest, enthusiasm, and devoid of obstructions.

You know that I am watching the Far East with great interest and at times with some concern. However, things seem to be going along nicely, and, with a new serious setback to the Japs, I expect a change of government in which more liberal influences will come into being. That makes it all the more necessary that your office should at this time be hitting at and talking directly to the High Command in Tokyo instead of concentrating on the fringes in the field. Knowing the vulnerability of those individuals who now control the Army and Navy from Tokyo and their peculiar sensitiveness to straight talk from an official spokesman, I am greatly surprised that your office has not instituted such a procedure. This activity requires particular technique, far different from the approach to the leaders of other nations, but I am convinced of its efficacy in breaking them down and resulting eventually in a great saving of lives and shortening of the war.

As you know, it is no satisfaction to visualize certain contingencies and then watch them eventuate as a surprise to many people who are unfamiliar with the peculiar conditions and psychology inherent in the Japanese. You know of several of those which have developed as visualized. Therefore, it is hoped that something can be done in this matter. It can be done only by those who know how. I have seen many projects fumbled because of lack of necessary knowledge connected therewith. Therefore, I am a strong believer in the axiom that the planner must be responsible for and have a part in the execution of his ideas. It may be that you will see Admiral Nomura the next Premier, and if so that will be the signal for us to work rapidly in your field.

Less than two weeks later I received Captain Drake's reply, and it was promising in many details:

Am most grateful for your kind and interesting letter of the 16th inst. I feel exactly as do you about leaving the center of effort when so much is happening, but feel most fortunate in being able to work for Elmer Davis.

I took the liberty of letting him read your letter, in which he found so much of interest that he asked permission to show it to George Taylor, Chief of the Pacific Division of the Overseas Branch. Taylor is likewise in agreement and impressed with your remarks and, at Taylor's suggestion, Elmer Davis has instructed me to urge you to further develop your ideas in another letter.

By then the physical facilities for a psychological campaign were already available on the west coast, in Hawaii, and on Saipan. Elmer Davis found it necessary to travel himself to Pearl Harbor and then on to Saipan to gain Admiral Nimitz's support for intensified psychological warfare activities in the Pacific Ocean areas. A skeleton staff of OWI psychological-warfare personnel was working under Admiral Nimitz—but the only accomplishments so far were negligible and confined to the tactical level. My plan envisaged an all-out strategic effort. So on February 1. 1945, at a time when my ideas were fully crystallized and my operational plan almost ready for immediate action, I wrote:

I was quite pleased with the reaction to my last letter as indicated in your recent one to me and I would have liked nothing better than to be able to get to work on some concrete plans for you. You must know how snowed under I am, digging into this new job, particularly with the Pacific activities stepping up as they are.

At the same time, you know how difficult it is to convey to others in a few words, ideas of the nature that I touched upon. Particularly is it true with effective approaches to Japanese psychology when these approaches must be made on the basis of the individual characteristics of the individuals to whom I referred. Undoubtedly, many people probably feel that they can, and are, covering these approaches properly. That may be true in the ordinary sense. However, I doubt that any of them have ever talked to Japanese Naval and Military men or had an opportunity to observe their actions and reactions under varying conditions.

It would sound as if I were trying to make a job for myself but this is not the case. My sole desire is to emphasize that for the Japanese there are certain definite approaches which must be made if they are to be effective. I mentioned that we should have an official spokesman speaking directly to the high command. By this, I mean selecting individuals in the Japanese Army and Navy to whom to address the broadcasts personally. Such broadcasts must be made by a high official of our Naval or Military Service whom they know and also whom they respect, as regards ability and service reputation. You may be sure that their files cover these points.

The effectiveness of such approaches can be realized only after witnessing their reactions and recorded actions, during repeated conversations with them over a long period of time. What I got out of Admiral Nomura on his way to Washington was possible only through such approaches. Those who are now in command in Japan are no more astute than he was. Such broadcasts must have the theme repeated for several days consecutively and then again after a short interval. If possible, the official spokesman giving them should do so in Japanese, and, to let them be certain of the identity of the person who is addressing them, he should repeat it to them in English. This would serve not only to identify the individual but would also impress them with the fact that we are so intent upon getting the message to them that "we repeat it in English in order that it should lose nothing in translation, and our poor ability in the Japanese language." This is the round-about method to which they are accustomed but which past experience has shown is the most effective one.

I know that the above sounds like a technical manufacturer setting up his own specifications but I can assure you this is the only positive approach. Unfortunately, when you seek to fulfill those specifications, you can find very few people who can meet them. That is due to the lack of association which resulted after the Japanese earthquake in 1923 and the Immigration Bill effective 1 July 1924. [The Japanese felt rebuffed and had withdrawn socially into their shells.]

However, no single person can do this job. But it requires only a small organization for Japan, such as that which we had just begun to set up when I left Washington in September 1943. This contemplated organization was desirably small, probably five people at the point of origin, maybe less. How many do you have on it now?

Recalling that my previous letter suggested the advent of a liberal cabinet very soon, and with Nomura at the head, would indicate a forthcoming proposal of peace, I still feel that we cannot help with this trend too soon in order to give this very small group ammunition on which to approach other officials to stop fighting. After all, that is what we want the Japs to do and it will not be necessary to indicate any weakening of peace terms. All we have to offer them is something on which to hang their hat, both the high officials and the soldiers in the field who will feel disgrace for a short period after defeat is realized.

I hope that you heard last Sunday's broadcast by Dorothy Thompson. What she mentioned is somewhat along the lines that I propose, but the inherent peculiarities of the Japanese will require very specific treatment, particularly in our approaches to the Military and Naval people. I am certain that it can be done, and should be done, and I am also certain that the speed and effectiveness with which it is delivered will spell the difference in thousands of lives.

Once again, I would like to emphasize that the work along the fringes will have no bearing whatever on this effort. What we want to accomplish is disintegration at the top, and the lower echelons will fall automatically.

You know that I am always glad to help wherever I can, particularly in the Japanese field. So, please give Mr. Davis my regards and say that I wish that I could be of more concrete service. He has done a splendid job and I would like to see him do what many people think is impossible.

The stage was being set for my work, not in this correspondence, which was merely the backdrop to the drama, but on Iwo Jima, where we again found the offensive difficult despite the series of setbacks suffered by the enemy in other localities. What had been evident to me now became evident to others and emphasized the truth of my statement that "the work along the fringes will have no bearing whatever on this effort. What we want to accomplish is disintegration at the top, and the lower echelons will fall automatically."

The Secretary of the Navy, the Honorable James Forrestal, was a witness to the difficult battle of Iwo Jima. He saw men die for the possession of a steppingstone the conquest of which brought us nearer to Japan, but not to conclusive victory over Japan. He was greatly concerned over the undiminishing fury of Japanese resistance to our tactical assaults. When he reached San Diego, on his way back to Washington, he was seeking an answer to the basic question which persisted in his mind: How can we stop this bloodshed and conclude the war with victory by exploiting *all* means available in our arsenal? He was frankly worried and could visualize the tremendous cost in lives which would be entailed by a forced landing on the main islands of Japan.

During his brief stay in San Diego I was introduced to the Secretary, and in the short conversation which ensued I felt that he was aware of my plan for hitting at the Japanese high command. Traveling with him was a friend and classmate, Rear Admiral L. E. Denfeld, and I knew that I had come into their discussions on the return trip from Iwo Jima. It was obvious from what the Secretary said to me that he had something definite in mind, but the first definite inkling was to come through our own grapevine. My assistant chief of staff, Captain Maurice C. Sparling, USNR (whose keen mind is now occupied as superintendent of banks in California, canalizing trends of a different nature), strode into my office with a knowing look on his face.

"What's this about you leaving us for duty in Washington?" he whispered. My surprise as well as my interest was undisguised, and I asked:

"Where did you get that idea? There is nothing to it as far as I know."

He edged closer and confided: "Well, you'd better get your bags packed, because the Admiral's chauffeur just gave me the tip. Yesterday, as they were driving the Secretary about, you were thoroughly discussed; and the Secretary wants you to help with something in Washington."

Throughout that day it happened that many things had to be referred to the Admiral, but never once did he volunteer the information I awaited so anxiously. Even Joe, Sergeant Joe Husong, the Admiral's orderly and the "sees all, knows all" of the district, had nothing to add.

I knew it was possible that in Washington the Secretary had been told by Elmer Davis in greater detail of the project which had developed in correspondence. It must have been apparent by then that there was no time to lose. Japanese broadcasts and information given to us by various neutrals indicated imminent changes in the Tokyo political setup and a tendency in at least some Jap circles to look for a way out rather than insist on resistance to the end. It was in this atmosphere of a thickening plot in Tokyo, the repercussions of which became visible in Washington as well, that a signal was received from the Navy Department:

"The Secretary would like to have Captain Zacharias in Washington for about ten days temporary duty if it is agreeable to you— Please issue him the necessary orders."

31

OPERATION PLAN 1-45

IN THE placid surroundings of San Diego, far removed from the sophisticated atmosphere of Washington, but also from intelligence data available to our war agencies in the national capital, I imagined that the authorities shared my optimistic views about the possibilities of a Japanese surrender. I felt encouraged in this belief by the letters I had received from the Office of War Information and the promptness with which Mr. Forrestal had acted upon my orders for temporary duty in Washington. When, however, I arrived in Washington, I found a rather gloomy atmosphere prevailing in both the War and Navy Departments, in the Joint Chiefs of Staff, and in our diplomatic agencies. The situation was quite remarkable as all those "in the know" realized our strength and Japan's weakness; but they were almost without exception victims of skillful Japanese propaganda and were awed by Japan's so-called spiritual strength.

There were two top agencies holding the key to the problem and retaining for themselves all decisions in connection with my plan. One was the White House, where President Roosevelt still retained personal control over the conduct of war, especially insofar as its diplomatic aspects were concerned; while the other was the Joint Chiefs of Staff, the only American agency which had a complete over-all view of the situation and could make decisions in the complete knowledge of all facts. The bridge leading from one agency to the other was Admiral William D. Leahy, USN (Retired), who was the President's personal chief of staff, and in this capacity was also the senior member and chairman of the Joint Chiefs. In neither place was there any inclination to take Japan's imminent or even potential surrender seriously.

When I arrived in Washington, President Roosevelt was in Yalta, attending what was to become his last conference with Generalissimo Stalin and Prime Minister Churchill. He took to Yalta voluminous intelligence material and evaluations thereof, and it seems that all these conclusions indicated a long and hard war. This atmosphere was an aftermath of the difficult Iwo Jima campaign, which increased the peculiar inferiority complex of our military leaders. Knowledge that a similarly difficult campaign was ahead of us on Okinawa influenced their judgment of the military situation and caused them to see the picture in a far more unpleasant light than the real conditions of relative strength could have warranted.

Imbued with this feeling, President Roosevelt went to Yalta with one major purpose in his mind: to obtain Russian participation in the war against Japan in order to bring the struggle to a more rapid conclusion even at the price we should have to pay for Soviet intervention. Even then the atom bomb was not considered a weapon which would permit absolute confidence in it as a decisive factor in terminating the war, and Russian participation seemed to him essential.

A very peculiar situation existed in the State Department, where Mr. Grew, our former ambassador to Tokyo, was serving as acting secretary of state. He was surrounded by men who knew Japan and the Japanese well enough, but they were influenced in their attitude toward the war in the Pacific by frequent accusations from certain impatient and intolerant left-wing elements of favoring the Zaibatsu of Japan, the financial and industrial powers who, wittingly or unwittingly because of frequent assassinations, notoriously supported all the aspirations of the military. It is possible for me to state categorically that these accusations lacked foundation. Mr. Grew and his advisers had in the past regarded the Zaibatsu as the most trustworthy element insofar as Western orientation and pro-American policy were concerned, but now they regarded Japan as an enemy entity and made no differentiation between the various factions. They were patriotically and wholeheartedly bent on defeating Japan totally so as to deprive her even of the possibility of rising again as a military power. But, probably as the result of intimidation by their loquacious and vociferous accusers, they failed to detect within Japan those forces which were potentially and actually ready to talk peace instead of continuing war. In all my negotiations in Washington I found Mr. Grew and his advisers most determined, first, to continue the war to Japan's total defeat, and, second, to avoid any deals with the Emperor. This, indeed, was in stark contrast to the impression I gained of the State Department's policies and attitudes by reading certain New York newspapers and journals.

The intransigence of the State Department and its apparent inability to recognize the cracks in Japan's diplomatic armor *ipso facto* disqualified it to act as an important instrument in our dealings with Japan, and thus a situation arose in which our top diplomatic agency was practically left out of all activities connected with our gradually mounting political warfare.

However, the greatest surprise I was to encounter in Washington was that the Office of War Information, too, viewed the situation in a rather gloomy perspective and accepted as the main motif of its propaganda directives the line that Japan was still very strong and capable of prolonging the war for several more years. It was due undoubtedly to directives and instructions received from other and higher quarters that this line was taken, but it rendered our propaganda largely ineffective, for it supported Japan's own propaganda contention that she was still strong enough to present insurmountable obstacles to our victory.

There was only one agency in Washington which I found in full agreement with my estimate and ready to formulate plans for intensified political warfare against Japan in view of her obviously deteriorating military situation. This agency was OP-16-W. Before I left Washington I had made certain that 16-W would conduct comprehensive research to lay the necessary groundwork in anticipation of the time when my ideas could be translated into action.

Dr. Farago, in charge of research and planning, had conducted a huge project to determine the best means by which we could attack with psychological weapons the seemingly invulnerable enemy. Every Japanese conflict of the past had been carefully scrutinized in order to establish whether there were historical precedents for surrender, and, secondly, to study the circumstances of surrender. In addition, Farago had collected material revealing cracks in Japanese morale and tendencies furthering surrender. Immense quantities of historical data had been accumulated; and the conclusion was reached by 16-W that the Japanese, despite their protestations to the contrary, were definitely susceptible to psychological attack. The research material now placed before me revealed that far from refraining from surrenders in the past, in most instances when Japanese fought among themselves the campaigns ended with the surrender of the defeated side, and not, as

Japanese propaganda claimed, with the mass suicide of the vanquished. This was confirmation of my own opinions, resulting from
my years of study of Japanese character.

More important, however, were recent intelligence reports disclosing a definite Japanese trend which could be exploited to move
the Japanese toward surrender, or at least a termination of hostilities prior to our invasion of Japan proper. Among these was a very
significant report given in the utmost secrecy to one of our intelligence officers in a neutral capital. It outlined in great detail the
course Japan intended to take and stated that General Koiso would
soon resign and permit the appointment as prime minister of Admiral Suzuki, an old confidant of the Emperor and leader of what
I even then had come to call the "peace party." Moreover, the document indicated that the Emperor himself was leading a group of
influential personalities desirous of obtaining peace terms under
the most favorable circumstances. And finally, the document informed us that when such a formula could be worked out and our
unconditional surrender terms modified to permit the continuation
of the Emperor on the throne, Admiral Suzuki would resign in
favor of an imperial prince who would effect Japanese surrender
and guarantee the execution and observance of the surrender terms.
The report—as early as December 1944—even named this imperial
prince as Prince Higashi Kuni. It is not known to me whether any
agency outside of 16-W gave to this most significant report the attention it deserved or whether it was ever brought to the attention
of the White House or the Joint Chiefs. It is possible that distribution was restricted because it arrived in an atmosphere in which
Japan's collapse was entirely ruled out as a possibility. I am convinced that had this document, later to be proven correct in every
detail, been brought to the attention of President Roosevelt and
his military advisers, the war might have been viewed in a different
light, both Iwo Jima and Okinawa might have been avoided, and
different decisions could have been reached at Yalta.

Mr. Forrestal permitted me to report to him personally on my
observations and then allowed me to prepare for him a strategic
estimate of the situation and an operation plan for the psychological campaign which I thought should follow.

This document, entitled "A Strategic Plan to Effect the Occupation of Japan," together with Operation Plan 1-45 for the implementation of the psychological phase, I delivered to the Secretary

of the Navy on March 19, 1945, just two weeks before our landings on Okinawa. Because of its significance in historical perspective, I reproduce the plan here in its entirety, if only to indicate the situation as it existed in March 1945, and the conclusions reached on the basis of our analysis.

SECRET

A STRATEGIC PLAN TO EFFECT THE OCCUPATION OF JAPAN

Any invasion of Japan is assumed to be based on three major premises:

(a) That we seek no material gain whatever in Japan.

(b) That occupation is for the purpose of effecting the peace and taking the necessary steps to ensure its permanence.

(c) That it is desirable to effect the occupation of Japan with the least possible loss of life consistent with the early termination of the war.

Premises (a) and (b) are generally accepted and require no comment. Premise (c) prompts the consideration of plans which might make it possible to effect the occupation of Japan with the minimum use of armed force. This would be possible only if the will of the Japanese High Command could be broken prior to the normal time when full-scale invasion is indicated. This would require the four following lines of action:

1. The continuation of our advance through adjacent islands, particularly the Ryukyus, and selected coastal areas of China, in order to continue our pressure against all communications between Japan and the continent.

2. Increased pressure against the "life-line" of Japan by concentrated bombing of Japanese western and southwestern port terminals in order to prevent shuttle traffic with the continent.

3. The avoidance of all deliberate attacks upon the Imperial Palace, the Ise Shrine, and the Imperial Family.

4. Intensive psychological warfare designed (a) to discredit individuals in the Japanese High Command, thus reducing its effectiveness through indecision and internal conflict; and (b) to discredit the High Command in the eyes of the Japanese People.

Course 1. The necessity for this line of action has undoubtedly been covered in previous estimates of the situation. It is sufficient to say that it will be necessary in the carrying out of any plan, and is supplementary to (2), (3), and (4) as herein proposed.

Course 2. The Bombing of Western and Southwestern Port Terminals. The western and southwestern port facilities of Japan are stressed because they are within easy reach of important shipping points on the continent, which are presently out of convenient bombing range. The bombing of these terminals in Japan would have not only the effect of actually destroying facilities but would produce psychological demoralization as a result of the severance of sustenance. This plan, like Course 1, is assumed to have been fully covered in current estimates of the situation, but it is mentioned in order to point out its potentially important contribution to the final yielding of Japan without a full-scale armed invasion.

Course 3. *Safeguarding the Imperial Palace, the Ise Shrine, and the Imperial Family.* The problem of bombing or safeguarding the Imperial Palace, the Ise Shrine, and the Imperial Family is one which requires most careful consideration. The Emperor is considered by the Japanese as a divinity descended from an unbroken Imperial Line over 2600 years old. Regardless of the facts which contradict this belief, to the great majority of the Japanese it is eternal truth itself, the catalyst which has made possible the efficient cohesive factor in Japanese military morale and discipline.

If an Emperor should die or even if his immediate family should be entirely wiped out, precedent is such that there will always be some individual, no matter how distantly blood-related, who will succeed as Emperor, and who will be the Imperial puppet available for use by the High Command for their own purposes. Thus the Japanese concept of the "One Imperial Line" which is "Unbroken for Ages Eternal" is, particularly in time of war, extremely difficult to destroy. However, the tremendous effect upon the Japanese of an enemy destroying the Emperor and his immediate family by force would be used by their High Command to produce a determination on the part of every man, woman and child to fight such an enemy to the last and thus gain a "glorious death." Against such fanatical resistance, the cost to us of a full-scale armed invasion in lives would be prohibitive.

The advantage of bombing the Palace, the Ise Shrine (the so-called "Grand Shrine" of the Sun Goddess, believed to be the divine ancestress of the "Imperial Line") and destroying the Emperor could, at best, result only in the destruction of minor military targets consisting of anti-aircraft batteries. It is believed that there would be some mass harakiri, even in high circles, but that would further strengthen the determination of the Japanese people as a whole to resist to the end.

It is therefore proposed that the policy of avoiding these targets be continued.

(Note.—The present discussion does not take account of the disposition of the Emperor after the cessation of hostilities, since that problem will be dealt with separately in connection with the consideration of post-war problems.)

Course 4. Intensive Psychological Warfare against the Japanese High Command. Careful observation of the Japanese under varying conditions and activities, such as conferences, military inspections, and crises, has led to the inevitable conclusion that no Japanese, regardless of rank or position, is so constituted that as an individual he is willing or able to assume responsibility for important decisions without the benefit of lengthy and repeated discussions sufficient to convince him that he does not carry the responsibility alone. This continued demonstration of a feeling of individual inferiority—appearances to the contrary notwithstanding—is the Japanese weakness which must be exploited to the fullest.

For the High Command also shares this weakness. If suitable seeds are planted in the highest echelons and nourished by continual demonstration through facts easily substantiated by those within close range, it would be possible to produce doubt, debate, difference of opinion, and open disagreement of the most deleterious variety.

This possibility is supported by such evidence as the results of the extremely suppressive measures adopted by the Japanese government in the attempt to control "dangerous thoughts" and to deal with "thought problems." The efforts at control produced much quicker dissemination of these forces than would otherwise have occurred. Similarly, the susceptibility of the Japanese to the rapid spread of disruptive rumors by means of the intensive "grapevine" in ordinary domestic life is a matter of extensive personal observation.

Furthermore, when we consider that the Axis pact was signed, according to Admiral Nomura, "by the narrowest margin, and then only after extensive bribery and the distribution of large sums of money in Tokyo," and when we recall that bribery and blackmail have attained the highest degree of success in Japan, it is obvious that there were and still are groups in Japan who were opposed to the alliance with Germany. These factions must not be looked upon as "liberal" in our sense of the word, but rather as other nationalistic groups who preferred to promote the welfare of Japan by other means. These groups, now eliminated from active control and reduced in power by enforced resignations, are nevertheless still intact. And as the embarrassment of defeat gradually comes to engulf the High Command, these latent factions will be ever on the alert to regain their former position. It is believed that this situation is capable of effective exploitation.

The possibility of breaking through the censorship and control of the high command and thereby bringing about the disintegration at the top increases as the trend of events continues unfavorable for Japan and our forces approach the homeland. The method for bringing about this disintegration is one requiring the most precise technique of psychological warfare and is possible only through direct approaches to individuals in the high command whose individual characteristics are well known. The approach must be made by one who is known to them personally and who is respected by them. The language must be direct and forceful, but with the appeal that has been found to be effective by reason of its very difference from the usual approaches and verbiage.

The effectiveness of such an approach can be appreciated only by one who has personally witnessed the reactions of certain individuals within the Japanese High Command during repeated, intimate conversations with them over a long period of time, and who has carefully studied the record of their activities. When Admiral Nomura was enroute to Washington on a certain occasion, such an approach was effective in obtaining important information from him. Those who are now in command in Japan are no more astute than was he. The accurate prediction of past Japanese actions has been the result of such approaches. The activities of the next few months offer the greatest possibilities for effective psychological warfare with its attendant process of disintegration and submission.

To be sure, some will doubt the effectiveness of such a proposal, but only because they have a limited knowledge of Japanese military psychology, or because they have sought in the past only limited results through entirely different approaches. It must be emphasized that the ordinary methods customarily followed in diplomatic channels are based upon a common school of thought in which the Japanese have become masters themselves. It is true that such activities also have psychological implications, but they connote only a "peaceful" approach.

As such, the goal is to enforce one's own will upon the adversary by peaceful means. In the event of failure, the consequences to the particular individuals involved are rarely serious. The "maneuvers" are not the result of correlated actions in force or even of taking a firm position. The elements of both personal interest and combat are lacking. Often there is no alternative but eventual disagreement.

It must be emphasized that such a characteristic diplomatic approach is entirely foreign to those whose military backgrounds enable them to envisage the saving of a hundred thousand lives, an achievement which might be possible if the will of the Japanese High Command can be broken.

We now face an enemy who knows that he is defeated. In spite of the fatalistic tendencies of the Japanese—involving individual disregard for life and appreciation of the glory of dying for their Emperor—they are nevertheless realistic people as regards the lessons of history and hopes for the future.

Our terms are still unconditional surrender, and urging their withdrawal from the war will involve no conciliatory measures whatever.

In view of the manner in which the Japanese nation was forced into the war, the present state of their naval forces, and the effectiveness of our air attacks, we may be sure that with the collapse of Germany, the present Japanese High Command will be provided with a suitable pretext for withdrawal from the war. Every move made by us should be designed to facilitate this decision.

It is believed that by following the four courses outlined above the desired results may be achieved. If we would avoid the necessity of an invasion of the Japanese homeland, involving very heavy losses to ourselves, such a program should be initiated at once. There is nothing whatever to be lost in the attempt, and the results may be of inestimable value to us.

The four courses suggested in this plan were intimately interwoven, and the success of one depended on the other. I have reason to believe that this was the only strategic plan drawn up by any American military authority to combine material and psychological warfare on the strategic level, by giving equal status to physical and psychological assault, and by trying to exploit the psychological impact of physical means of offensive, and vice versa. In a sense it represented a pattern for modern warfare in which physical and psychological means of attack are closely interwoven and in which the effectiveness of one can be heightened by the proper application of the other. While it is gratifying that toward the closing stages of the war this type of strategic planning received both attention and support, it is equally regrettable that no similar plans existed earlier in the war and that there was complete disregard of all the possible effects psychological attacks might have had on the enemy if applied in a strategic sense.

The only plan remotely resembling our strategic project was drawn up under General Eisenhower's supervision at SHAEF in Europe, but there psychological means of assault were so far subordinated to military means that the effectiveness of the psychological campaign was completely dependent upon the success of our military offensive, without yielding results by itself or paving the way for success of military arms.

Secretary Forrestal received my plans with thorough understanding and became a top-level advocate of the courses suggested therein. Without his help the strategic plan would have been relegated to limbo along with the innumerable memoranda which were then being produced in Washington by the hundreds. His position was a difficult one, and it is a high tribute to his intellectual integrity and personal courage that he decided to give us his support despite some apparent skepticism regarding the plans. He was himself subjected to many influences, and some of his advisers were providing him with data which did not seem to bear out my own estimates and conclusions. Moreover, his experience at Iwo Jima had convinced him of the immense tactical and psychological striking power still left in the Japanese on the fringes. When, in opposition to many opinions, he decided to lend us the support we so badly needed, he did it because he felt that the situation was sufficiently serious to warrant an attempt and because he was by disposition in favor of the unorthodox. Virtually the only support we had, besides that of the Secretary, was from the Office of War Information, where Mr. Davis and Edward W. Barrett pursued the project with unending vigor.

President Roosevelt returned from Yalta and made his report to Congress on March 1, and outlined the meaning of our unconditional surrender formula insofar as it concerned the Germans. He also indicated that certain secret military arrangements had been made with the Russians but asked permission of Congress to leave these arrangements in the category of secrets, since they involved military operations and their disclosure would have aided the enemy. We of 16-W assumed, however, that they involved Russian participation in the Pacific war; and we were frankly opposed to the arrangement, because in our considered opinion Japan was on the eve of surrender, and we needed no additional or outside last-minute aid to bring about the capitulation of the Japanese.

It was in this general atmosphere and in the midst of the Okinawa campaign that I settled down with two members of 16-W, Ladislas Farago and Stefan T. Possony, in a secluded office in a former garage building on the fringes of Washington to draw up the details for Operation Plan 1-45. I was closeted in that office for one whole week. But at the end of it, on March 19, 1945, I was able to deliver by hand to the Secretary of the Navy our plan, and expressed the earnest hope of obtaining the necessary approval for it on the highest level, meaning the White House. The operation plan was patterned after similar plans drawn up for standard naval operations. It stated the "mission" or the goal of our policy together with our propaganda objectives. It provided all the available information as well as assumptions based on experience and study. It was followed by a "decision" and the courses designed to implement the decision, and concluded with an outline of "logistics," to show that no additional personnel or material were needed for the execution of the plan.

I am reprinting here the entire operation plan, as it provides considerable illuminating material even in retrospect:

SECRET

OPERATION PLAN 1-45

1. *MISSION:* (Policy Goal)

To make unnecessary an opposed landing in the Japanese main islands, by weakening the will of the High Command, by effecting cessation of hostilities, and by bringing about unconditional surrender with the least possible loss of life to us consistent with early termination of the war.

This to be accomplished by providing valid and powerful arguments for those in high places who are actually or potentially desirous of an early peace, and by canalizing their views which are divergent only as to means;

(Propaganda objectives)

   (a) To convince highly placed leaders of the hopelessness of further resistance,

   (b) To convince the High Command that there is an alternative to complete annihilation and enslavement,

   (c) To explain the meaning of "unconditional surrender,"

   (d) To create dissension, confusion and opposition among those enemy leaders who remain adamant in their opposition to this plan.

in order to impose our will upon the enemy.

INFORMATION:

   (a) The Japanese main islands are now isolated except to the continent and are faced with threats from all directions.

   (b) Our present and future positions outside of the Japanese main islands will afford means of exerting all coercive pressure necessary.

   (c) Certain members of the Japanese High Command realize that the war is irretrievably lost; the others of the High Command recognize the seriousness of the present situation which is bound to deteriorate in the future.

(d) The plans for victory of the Japanese High Command are contingent upon continued unity of thought between the Army and Navy and upon an all-sacrificing prosecution of the war.

(e) Great conflict of opinion exists within the High Command as to the past, present and future conduct of the war.

(f) Field commanders in highest echelon are blaming the High Command for inept leadership in the war.

(g) Great difference of opinion and dissension exists among commanders in the field and at sea.

(h) For the first time since the Russo-Japanese war, the Premier has been instructed to participate in the deliberations of the High Command, thus establishing an immediate link between the political and military leadership of the empire, carefully separated since 1868.

(i) For the first time in 24 years, criticism of the government and the High Command is openly voiced.

(j) The Axis pact of September 27, 1940, was signed by Japan by the narrowest margin and only after extensive bribery in Tokyo and distribution of large sums of money.

(k) There are a great many highly placed individuals in Japan who realized that war with the United States meant "the finish of the Japanese empire and a great loss to the United States."

(l) It is known that foreign broadcasts are monitored in Japan and transcripts have a comparatively wide distribution.

ASSUMPTIONS:

(a) That Japanese strategy anticipated fatigue of the United States in the prosecution of a prolonged war and consequent withdrawal therefrom.

(b) That unless the will of the High Command is broken their continued leadership will stimulate every man, woman and child to sustained resistance with its attendant cost in lives and money.

(c) It is known that groups already exist whose position in favor of a cessation of hostilities would receive the required stimulus and support for concerted action in the direction desired by this plan.

(d) That cessation of organized resistance in Germany or a request for peace by Germany would give the Japanese High Command the pretext for withdrawal from the war, particularly if such a "face-saving" course is encouraged.

(e) The execution of this operation plan will offer the encouragement and suggest the means to those in the highest echelons to exert their effective influence and cause the cessation of hostilities before Japan is totally destroyed.

(f) The increasing dependence on law-enforcement agencies for the execution of the total mobilization plan and the general reaction to recent air raids indicates the deterioration of Japanese morale on the home front with its resultant effect on the High Comn.and.

(g) The enemy statements regarding means with which to repel landings on the main islands and new secret weapons indicate a realization of inherent weakness.

2. *DECISION:*

The United States will conduct an intensive psychological campaign against the Japanese High Command through an official spokesman of high rank in order to accelerate and effect the unconditional surrender of Japan without the necessity of an opposed landing in the Japanese main islands.

3. *COURSES OF ACTION:* (Implementation)

The official spokesman will:

(a) Lay the groundwork for the implementation to follow by addressing personally individual naval, military, political and economic leaders in a factual, direct, intimate and suggestive type of speech which experience has shown always commands their attention. He will carefully discuss their accomplishments or failures in order to enhance the prestige of desirable individuals and discredit those who hold the reins of remaining power and are in favor of continuing the war.

(b) Exploit the cliques and groups, formed and forming in the High Command, who feel that the war is irretrievably lost or disagree with present strategy.

(c) Explain in the most detailed and concrete terms the hopelessness of the situation for Japan and the futility of continued resistance.

(d) Exploit all Japanese admissions of their own weakness and the confessed impossibility of remedy.

(e) Exploit the loss of Japanese seapower and its relation to an island empire. Couple with this their inferiority on land and in the air.

(f) Emphasize by detailed casualty lists of ships and personnel the progressive reduction of Japan's war-making capacity.

(g) Emphasize the tremendous power that will be added to that great force already being exerted against the Japanese homeland, upon the collapse of Germany.

(h) Exploit the desertion of their ally Italy and the return of France as a powerful war factor with its direct bearing on and interest in Japanese controlled areas.

(i) Exploit Japanese inability to evaluate the Russian position in the war, particularly the startling events immediately preceding Japan's entry into the war.

(j) Exploit existing and potential friction between Japan and Germany on all levels.

(k) Exploit Japanese fear of invasion evident from bombastic predictions of action to be taken for defense of the main islands. (These duplicate the utterances of German military and naval leaders prior to the Normandy landings.)

(l) Explain that unconditional surrender does not mean other than complete cessation of hostilities and yielding of arms as outlined by President Roosevelt to the Congress of the U. S., in order to clear out the destructive forces now entrenched. He will cite examples of Germany and other occupied territories, including Japanese territories already occupied, to prove that no violence has been or will be practiced against any individuals unless found guilty by a legally constructed War Crime Commission, and emphasize with authority what we will *not* do, but avoid any specific commitments as to what we *will* do, in order to combat present Japanese atrocity predictions.

(m) Exploit the existence of alternatives for the Japanese as contrasted with the hopelessness of Nazi leadership in Germany.

4. *LOGISTICS:*

No additional machinery or personnel will be required for the execution of this plan.

5. This plan will be effective immediately upon promulgation.

This plan will not prejudice any existing policy regarding peace terms or the conduct of the war.

All psychological operations will be co-ordinated both as to times and trends in order to avoid reduction of effectiveness of this main operation.

The official spokesman will broadcast three times a week for a period not exceeding fifteen minutes each. The broadcast will be repeated at least twice. The Japanese text will always be followed by the same speech in English in order to obtain maximum clarity and effectiveness, and to enhance the authenticity of the talks.

Secretary Forrestal approved the plan immediately, and it was shortly approved by Fleet Admiral King as well. I can recall vividly the occasion when I gave Elmer Davis and his staff, assembled in his office, the news of Admiral King's approval. He threw up his hands in disbelief and exclaimed, "What?" As I nodded confirmation he slowly lowered them and with a broad smile said, "Praised be the Lord." The problem now was for OWI to secure War Department approval prior to submission to the Joint Chiefs and then to have it endorsed by the President. All these steps were necessary before we could go into action.

The War Department had no objections to the plan, and we were assured that the Joint Chiefs looked upon it with benevolent eyes—but definite approval was not immediately forthcoming. In the meantime we had arrived at the decision that it would be necessary to start our campaign with a psychological bombshell if tedious months of build-up for the spokesman were to be avoided. This was possible only by a declaration of the President of the United States explaining in detail the meaning of unconditional surrender as suggested in section 1 (c) of our operation plan.

Accordingly we drew up a "Declaration by the President of the United States," a short statement to be approved by President Roosevelt and to be read in his name on what was to become my first broadcast. The draft was given to Elmer Davis, who in turn presented it to President Roosevelt, then spending a few weeks at Hyde Park to recuperate.

But meanwhile, as we were thus preparing our own bombshell, the Japanese provided one of their own which merely served to fortify us in our conviction that the propitious moment had arrived. On April 8 the cabinet of General Koiso fell and was replaced, as predicted by our confidential agent in his December 1944 report, by a cabinet headed by Admiral Suzuki. It was evident that Japan was now ripe for a termination of the war and that we were reaching the eleventh hour insofar as our psychological warfare campaign was concerned. In the midst of these Japanese events, President Roosevelt arrived in Washington to spend one day at his desk in the White House before continuing his journey to Warm Springs, Georgia.

While we were thus awaiting the approval of the presidential declaration, we gained another advocate for the whole psychological warfare plan. Senator Elbert Thomas of Utah, who had lived for many years in Japan, reached independently the same conclusions and in a letter to Admiral Leahy urged the immediate beginning of such a psychological warfare campaign. By then Admiral

Leahy was fully aware of our plan and forwarded Senator Thomas's letter to me for handling. I had a long conference with the Senator during which we reached complete agreement, and I was able to report back the Senator's sentiments and suggestions to the President's Chief of Staff. But just then the tragic news of President Roosevelt's untimely death struck us; and with his relinquishing of the helm of state, we felt that our whole plan was doomed to collapse.

In the tragic days which followed the President's death nothing could be done to bring the plan to President Truman's attention, but I spent my time in perfecting the opening broadcast to be put on the air the moment the President approved and released the statement.

It was nerve-racking indeed to watch men dying on Okinawa and realize the bloodshed which could be avoided through a psychological campaign. OWI felt that we should go ahead without the presidential proclamation, but I was insistent that the success of the whole project would be jeopardized unless we could have an opening gun to give it authority.

National attention had been focused on events in Germany, where our forces under General Eisenhower's supreme command were cutting Germany's armed forces into ribbons. The end was coming in days rather than in weeks. Peace negotiations were being attempted by several parties, including Heinrich Himmler, who in this last tragic hour had turned against Hitler and was appearing as a leader of a peace party within the Reich. Then the news came reporting Hitler's last resistance in the Chancellery bunker in the Wilhelmstrasse, the approach of the Allied forces to Berlin, the collapse of the German armies, and several battlefield surrenders.

Our own project was completely submerged in this tremendous rhapsody of European events; and we felt relegated to a secondary place as Germany's surrender occupied all attention. As I visualized again those hundreds of thousands of casualties which would have to be sacrificed needlessly on the shores of Japan, I decided to move into action myself.

Ed Barrett had been called to New York on urgent business. His assistant knew nothing about the status of the statement, and I scouted the whole of OWI to find the best contact with the White House. I learned that Samuel R. Davenport was a close friend of Matthew J. Connelly, one of the President's secretaries, so I phoned

Davenport and asked him to come around to Barrett's office as there was an urgent matter for consideration. I had never met Davenport, but learned upon his arrival that we had had a close mutual friend in the late Jack Cody, a former American businessman in Japan. I told Davenport that it was Jack who had taught me much of the technique for getting things done and added: "That is why I am asking your help."

As he knew something about Japan himself, it was not too difficult to explain to Davenport the urgency of getting out the unconditional surrender statement and the results which would ensue from each day's delay in beginning the broadcasts. After hearing my story he agreed to see Connelly immediately, and within two hours I received a telephone call from Davenport informing me that the statement was now on the President's desk awaiting his approval. He also assured me that it would not be allowed to be buried by other papers. I considered this a good day's work and went home.

On May 8 the German surrender was already an accomplished fact, prematurely announced and known to millions throughout the world. We waited, however, for the official proclamation by President Truman, scheduled to occur at nine A.M. Eastern War Time, from his office in the White House.

At ten minutes before nine o'clock Washington was in the midst of a heavy downpour of rain. I settled comfortably before the radio at home. The radio announcer was running through the preliminary descriptions preceding the President's address when the telephone rang violently. I jumped up and answered it and was greeted by the excited voice of Ed Barrett:

"Hurry up, Zack. Get down here . . . we're in trouble."

"What sort of trouble, Ed?" I asked fearfully, quickly trying to recall the things that I had done and those I had left undone.

"We're not in trouble. I mean we're late," he added.

"Late for what?" I asked, feeling much relieved.

"The President is releasing the unconditional surrender statement now. We must get it out.".

"All right, Ed. I'm all set to listen to him now. I will call you back as soon as he has finished the address. I want to check what he says."

Throughout the impressive address the President made no mention whatever of Japan. My confidence was again restored—I had feared that release of the statement before it could be sent to Japan in my first broadcast would destroy completely the calculated effect of my whole project. I called Barrett again and said:

"The President didn't say anything about the statement."

"I know he didn't. But he has already handed it to the press as a press release—just before the address. Hurry up. Get on your horse."

"All right, Ed. Get a leased wire to San Francisco for eleven o'clock. I will have the broadcast records finished by that time, ready for transmission. I'm on my way."

Great guns! We are late, I thought. It's already on the press wires. I quickly called my office and had them arrange for the use of the Interior Department studio immediately. I hurried to the studio. On the way I picked up two assistants, Lieutenant John Paul Reed, USNR, and First Lieutenant Dennis McEvoy, USMCR, together with my scripts.

The studio was alive with excitement. Shannon Allen greeted us cordially and assuringly. "Everything is ready for you," he said, as he led us into the large studio. It was like the curtain call of the first opera of the season. Finally, the technician inside the glass enclosure raised his hand and then leveled his finger directly at us. We were on the air—in Japanese.

McEvoy made the opening announcement, and then I followed with fifteen minutes of Japanese text—the longest fifteen minutes of my life. The record was played back, the three of us checking every word with the script. It was better than I had hoped for.

San Francisco was on the wire and ready to receive it. Soon the machines were grinding out the words to the west coast while we went ahead with the English text. This was somewhat less of a strain, and the tension was lessened. San Francisco reported that their reception had been perfect and that Japanese monitors were now picking up the broadcast in Tokyo. The opening gun for "Surrender" had been fired. My own words, in both Japanese and English, carried the President's proclamation:

"Nazi Germany has been defeated.

"The Japanese people have felt the weight of our land, air and naval attacks. So long as their leaders and the armed forces continue the war the striking power and intensity of our blows will steadily increase and will bring utter destruction to Japan's industrial production, to its shipping, and to everything that supports its military activity.

"The longer the war lasts, the greater will be the suffering and hardships which the people of Japan will undergo—all in vain. Our blows will not cease until the Japanese military and naval forces lay down their arms in *unconditional surrender*.

"Just what does the unconditional surrender of the armed forces mean for the Japanese people?

"It means the end of the war.

"It means the termination of the influence of the military leaders who have brought Japan to the present brink of disaster.

"It means provision for the return of soldiers and sailors to their families, their farms, their jobs.

"It means not prolonging the present agony and suffering of the Japanese in the vain hope of victory.

"Unconditional surrender does not mean the extermination or enslavement of the Japanese people." *

* See pages 399-401 of Appendix for full text of the opening broadcast.

32

MESSAGE FROM TOKYO

IN AN environment so different from the bridge of a ship and far removed from the shooting war I nevertheless felt that I was still in the thick of battle; and the campaign proceeded according to plan and schedule with the precision of a military operation.

When my scripts were prepared, they were submitted to OWI, the State Department, and our own security officers. As soon as they were approved by all these agencies, I made the recordings in an Interior Department "confidential studio," normally used for the recording of secret proclamations prepared in advance for future use. The records were then sent by airplane or leased wire to San Francisco. From there they were beamed to Japan by short wave. Honolulu intercepted them and again beamed them to Japan by short wave. This wave we knew would be picked up by the official monitoring stations in Japan. From Saipan our station sent out the intercepted broadcasts on the medium wave used by Radio Tokyo so that the five million Japanese listeners who had private sets could also listen surreptitiously.

Important passages were lifted from my talks and printed on leaflets for wide distribution over Japan by the bombers of General LeMay and General Kenney. Also in the Southwest Pacific area, General MacArthur's increased and efficiently functioning psychological warfare staff, sparked by the energy of my old friend Colonel Mashbir and Brigadier General Bonner Fellers, made the most of the contents of my talks.

But the real battles were fought over the scripts in Washington. Seated with me at a table was Lieutenant Commander John Paul Reed, USNR, who acted as my own personal executive officer—and I could not imagine a better man for the job. He was a scholar in his own right, a sociologist of great reputation, author of *Kokutai*, the basic reference book on what is called "the national structure of Japan," that mixture of secular and sacred elements of propaganda and faith which insisted on the divinity of the emperor and made his supernatural person the focal point of Japan's modern state philosophy. Reed had spent several years in Japan, was fluent in the language, and knew the people well. With a background of Intelligence during the war, he knew the details of our target and was a sound adviser, especially when our discussions around the table in the terrible humidity of that early summer grew overheated. His contribution was of inestimable value.

Next to him sat another Japan expert and experienced newspaperman, Dennis Griffin McEvoy, then serving as a first lieutenant in the Marine Corps Reserve. Despite his youth Dennis was an important member of the team, full of ideas and suggestions, with an excellent easy style adapted to Japanese psychology. He, too, had mastered the difficult language and had an intimate acquaintance with many Japanese personalities. In addition he acted as my liaison officer with other sections of the Navy in collecting additional information we needed.

The third member of the team was Francis Royal Eastlake, one of the greatest linguists I know. He was born in Japan of a prominent American father and a Japanese mother, whose family was numbered among the highest nobility left over from the Shogunate. But he had spent the greater part of his life in the United States. Languages were his hobby, and he spoke fluently thirteen of them, with Japanese occupying the place of honor in his own personal Tower of Babel. In addition to mastering those languages he was an accomplished poet in six of them and turned out Japanese, German, French, and even Persian poems with the same ease with which he wrote English verse. He was my adviser on linguistic problems, and also contributed many vital suggestions from the psychological point of view.

Next in the circle was a member of my staff whose identity I cannot reveal even today. He was a man of Japanese origin, a great liberal who had decided to abandon his native land for the liberties which the United States offered. His presence in the circle greatly increased our effectiveness, since he advised us on all matters from military history to the use of proverbs. He also criticized my much-practiced delivery and was instrumental in providing my talks with the convincing fluency in style which was later praised by so many Japanese listeners.

On the other side of the table sat Stefan T. Possony, an expert in psychological warfare and a military scientist who had come into the Navy from the Institute for Advanced Study, at Princeton, New Jersey. He is an author of note in the field of military and naval strategy. For several years he had been in charge of the German activities of 16-W, where he turned out more than 250 Norden broadcasts.

At the lower right-hand corner of the table set the stormy petrel of the group, Ladislas Farago, in charge of research and planning, the idea man of the team and the one who provided us with the research material we needed to make these talks both authentic and plausible. Every time Farago disappeared into the Library of Congress he turned up later with important additional data. But more important was his contribution as planner, designing each broadcast to carry our major theme but at the same time making them appear new and often sensational to the listener. He carried over much of his Hungarian temperament into our discussions and frequently was an autocrat around the conference table. Quite often when objections were raised to his suggestions because of peculiar Japanese psychological aspects, he would get up and resign on the spot. We eventually decided that this was a trick of his to test the validity of the arguments rather than to have his proposals accepted.

This, then, was the unbeatable team which I had the privilege of heading in our concentrated efforts to show the Japanese high command why, how, and when to surrender unconditionally. As I now look back upon my "shipmates" in this unique undertaking, I am grateful that we were successful in assembling this ingenious and highly efficient team. Anything less would not have sufficed. They all worked with unselfish devotion, and their passion for anonymity made them keep in the background even when the broadcasts became international news and the undertaking was in the headlines. There was not a single security violation throughout this difficult mission, and at no time was there more than a word or a phrase that we were requested to delete from the finished scripts. The contribution of the team to our common cause was immense, and I am glad to pay this tribute to them both collectively and individually. As a result of their work, at least a million of our young men who would have been casualties had we invaded Japan now are living normal lives.

At this point I must also call attention to the other tireless workers in the office for their patience in typing and retyping the smooth scripts (cut to pieces at repeated conferences) and for their endless efforts to put the unintelligible Japanese sounds on paper. Our gratitude goes to Mrs. Cecelia Hansen, Miss Elizabeth Willis, and Miss Anne M. Brown. And finally for all the leg work which had to be done between the OWI, the Navy Department, and the sixth floor of the old garage building on 5th Street, gratitude must be expressed to Commander W. Howell Cullinan, USNR, head of OP-16-W, who is now back at his broadcasting post in Boston, and his assistant, Lieutenant Jacques Futrelle, USNR, now filling again the columns of the *Washington Star*.

The magnitude of the task can be appreciated when it is remembered that each script had to be constructed on four fundamental principles:

(a) It must support existing policy and directives.

(b) It must not disclose matters which might endanger security of plans or operations.

(c) It must have content both timely and psychologically effective.

(d) It must avoid offending our public, particularly certain sections of the press and certain commentators.

This last precaution was important because of the fact that for reasons already indicated the broadcasts were repeated in English text after they were made in Japanese. This made them susceptible to interception by any of our radio fans.

It is difficult to visualize the amount of minute work which had to go into the preparation of these talks. I shall describe here in detail the preparation of a single broadcast, one which proved to be particularly effective and which is reprinted as number seven in the Appendix. It was built around a short news item broadcast from Tokyo which indicated that Rear Admiral Yokoyama was relinquishing his post as senior aide to the Navy Minister. He may be remembered as the Japanese officer who had journeyed to Newport, Rhode Island, to obtain my opinion and advice on the political situation in October 1933. We could therefore represent him as an expert on the United States and one of those sound Japanese who realized that the war was lost. We could picture him as a scapegoat, a man who had outlived his usefulness. By attributing to him certain advice unpleasant to the ears of intransigent Japanese leaders we could suggest to our listeners that those who knew all the details and realized the consequences of a ten-to-one disparity in war potentials were being relegated to subordinate tasks because their advice made them *personae non gratae* among those who insisted on the continuation of the war.

To make the broadcast plausible we needed many details of the character and especially the professional career of Yokoyama as well as so-called incidental intelligence to render my talk more intimate and personal. The use of intelligence material in my talks was calculated from the very beginning. It was important to give the impression of omniscience on my part, to show that I was in possession of detailed information and that nothing was concealed from me. In the case of Yokoyama we traced his movements in the United States and even found that he used to spend Christmas in a Baltimore boardinghouse. We mentioned the date of his visit there, and many more intimate details, which served merely to increase the intimacy and authenticity of the talk.

In another broadcast we used an intercepted telegram. Our intelligence succeeded in obtaining a copy of a message which a prominent Japanese newspaper correspondent in Europe had sent to Foreign Minister Togo shortly after the journalist managed to escape from the German holocaust. The publicist reported to the Foreign Minister in great detail on Germany's collapse, pointed out in blunt language the mistakes Hitler and the Germans had made, and warned against duplicating the blunders in Japan as well. It was a person-to-person message, and I am not certain that it ever reached Foreign Minister Togo. But we used the text in full, mentioning the name of the sender, making a careful Japanese observer say all that was really my own theme: that further resistance was both criminal and fatal and that *"Time is running out for Japan."*

Many secret intelligence reports were used as the basis of the broadcasts in an unprecedented exploitation of this classified material for the purposes of propagating the truth as an effective weapon of warfare. There is little use for this important data if it is filed and forgotten. In our scheme of things we made this dead material work for us and even used such top-secret information, suppressed in Japan, as the arrest in Tokyo of the son of General Eugen Ott, German ambassador to Japan, as an espionage suspect. By the use of items susceptible of verification we were able to illustrate Germany's machinations against Japan in our own attempt to drive a wedge between those in the enemy camp.

From information transmitted by agents abroad, and more, direct from Tokyo, that reached us through the monitoring of all Japanese transmissions, we knew soon after my second broadcast that we had accomplished our aim of making the Japanese take cognizance of my talks. On May 20 we were informed through the same sources that the talks had been discussed in a cabinet meeting at Tokyo but no definite decision was reached regarding them. The use of an "official spokesman" by the United States government was an unorthodox procedure, and our Japanese listeners did not know just how official my status really was. As they waited, they also followed my talks with extreme care and eventually formulated their policy regarding them. But it was nineteen full days before they made their first direct answer to my broadcasts.

However, the day following the first talk on V-E Day, May 8, there were several indications of its reception and the reaction to it. A Tokyo news flash stated: "Prince Takamatsu has been designated as a proxy for the Emperor to visit the shrine of the imperial ancestors at Ise."

Those who were aware of the Japanese inner situation immediately recognized the significance of Takamatsu's appointment. Prince Takamatsu is the Emperor's younger brother. He had been conspicuous by his long absence from the news. This was virtually his first emergence from obscurity since 1931, when I had traveled with him as aide during his two months' tour of the United States. This sudden reference to him in the Japanese news just a day after I had referred to him in my first broadcast was the ambiguous Japanese way of informing me that my message was duly received and understood. The same technique was used on a more ambitious scale when Rear Admiral Yokoyama, whom I had used fully in my seventh broadcast, was named to represent the Japanese Navy during preliminary armistice negotiations in Manila.

In other radio flashes from south China and Manchuria, over the Japanese-controlled Singapore and Hsinking radios, came inspired feelers, making oblique reference to my talks, seeking clarification or trying to discredit me. The discrediting technique we dismissed as the obvious third-degree tactics first used and abused by the German propaganda machine. But the feelers we took seriously. We knew that these secondary radios on the propaganda fringe would be used before Radio Tokyo joined in the battle of the airways.

In my fourth broadcast, there was a discussion of certain leaders who had brought Japan to the brink of disaster. I named names. Some of them have already taken the way out in typical Japanese fashion. Others are now sitting in war criminal trials. Still others have already paid the penalty for their crimes. As the carefully worded text of this script was completed, I turned to my staff and said: "This will draw blood." It did, both literally and figuratively. While thus creating dissension within the war party, by citing facts well known to them and their critics at home, the psychological attack was so designed as to strengthen the hands of the peace party.

In this broadcast number four, I said: "Now, for the first time, the Japanese people have the opportunity to evaluate fully for themselves the quality of the political leadership which maneuvered their country into their ill-fated alliance with Germany. The men who advised the highest authority [we decided to make no direct reference to the Emperor until a later date] to link the fate of Japan with that of Germany, who schemed to plunge Japan into a hopeless war against the most powerful nations on earth—these men now stand revealed as lacking in judgment and in statesmanship.

"Let me recall to your minds the names of these men: Field Marshals Hata, Sugiyama, and Terauchi; General Hirosi Oshima, recently found hiding in southern Germany by the United States Army [a side remark to show that not all Japanese commit harakiri in a defeat situation]; General Tojo, Koiso, and others. Among these are some who worked secretly for German interests in Japan, and caused Japan to cast her lot with that of Nazi Germany which now has surrendered unconditionally."

I was convinced that there would be a direct answer to this talk. The provocations of my broadcasts were going very far. The Japanese did not know what to make of my talks and were feverishly seeking clarification. What was it I could offer? What were the concrete purposes of my talks? What was I driving at? And then again, how could they exploit my talks to serve their own aims?

Then on the nineteenth day of my campaign, the first direct reply from Tokyo was monitored by the FBIS. I might add that everything went according to schedule. The answer came when and as expected. I was confident that the mentioning of certain specific names would provoke Japanese replies, for they would regard the mentioning of these names as "pillorying" of the Army high command.

Dr. Isamu Inouye was delegated by the Japanese government to seek the answers to these questions and "to discuss" with me on the air, in unorthodox fashion, the question of Japan's unconditional surrender. Inouye was chosen as official spokesman on the Japanese end because he claimed to know me personally from the days when he edited a Japanese newspaper in Los Angeles. He was introduced as the overseas head of the Domei News Agency, the official government organ. Later he was appointed vice-chief of information in the Japanese Home Ministry, obviously in accordance with Japan's technique of increasing the status of her spokesmen.

When we received the full text of Inouye's cagily worded reply in my office, we analyzed it carefully to determine his real objective. It requires considerable experience to filter the true meaning from the typically Japanese indirect approach. After studying the English translation sent in from the FCC monitoring station on the west coast by teletype, it was decided that we should have to examine the original text of Inouye's address. When both the original and the English translations were scrutinized, we concluded that Inouye's broadcast was designed to achieve one or both of two objectives: to have the psychological warfare campaign discontinued or discredited; more probably, chiefly to obtain clarification of the unconditional surrender formula and, indeed, to bring about its amendment.

In line with the Japanese custom of the "indirect approach," the message of Inouye abounded in oblique statements. "Japan would be ready to discuss peace terms," he said, "provided there were certain changes in the unconditional surrender formula." Although the changes which the Japanese had in mind were not specified, Inouye said in conclusion: "We should like mutually to join hands in constructing an international machinery which strives toward world peace and the good of humanity." This line we interpreted as *the* message of the whole broadcast, coming, as it did, at the end of a long talk, after much verbal shadowboxing.

Inouye's reply to my fourth broadcast indicated the most direct acceptance to date of over-all American peace policy and demonstrated a basic Japanese inclination either to adhere to or benefit from it. What made this answer particularly significant were the thirteen concluding words. Inouye expected an answer since he stated: "I should like to know what Zacharias thinks of these words from Japan."

The Japanese text of the Inouye broadcast revealed a significant and interesting side light which was lost in the English translation. In the last paragraph he addressed me as Zacharias-*Kun*. Previous references were to Zacharias-*Taisa* (captain), and ordinarily, when referring to "Mr.," the word *San* is used. The word *Kun* is one used by Japanese only between close friends or intimates. Therefore its injection here was a significant gesture and appeal which carried the fullest of hidden meanings. Literally translated the implication was "my good friend" Zacharias.

Dr. Inouye's message not only indicated a frame of mind; it also proved to us that my broadsides were hitting the target. Other Japanese broadcasters followed Inouye's example and by quoting literally from my talks provided additional evidence that they were monitored and recorded in Japan.

The original operation plan had anticipated this development. We know that every important American broadcast was printed in a daily monitoring digest which the Japanese Board of Information placed at the disposal of about five hundred carefully selected Japanese political, industrial, and military leaders, and trusted publicists. It was to this audience that our talks were primarily directed. It was a qualitative rather than a quantitative selection. Although their number seemed infinitesimal among the more than seventy million Japanese, it was this group of five hundred who held the power of decision. If they wanted to continue the war, compel us to invade Japan and fight it out on Japanese soil, they had the power to do so. If they wanted to discontinue resistance, to embark on peace talks, or to surrender unconditionally, they also had the power to carry out their decision. Although we hoped that the broadcasts were also reaching the Japanese people, we considered them helpless because of the ineffectiveness of Japanese public opinion.

Copies of the monitoring report were supplied to the Imperial Palace. This was the manner by which we hoped, from the very outset, to reach the Emperor's own circle. The answers we received proved that our expectation was justified.

The catastrophic events for Japan which had been coming thick and fast since October reached their climax in March: the Koiso government finally fell. We knew this was the critical moment. The return of Tojo would mean a fight to the finish. On the other hand the appointment of a top admiral would mean that the Army diehards had lost control. For it was evident to the Japanese Navy that after the loss of the fleet in the Philippine battles the war could not be won, and the only hope for the Empire was a negotiated peace.

Our fondest hopes were realized by the designation of Admiral Suzuki as premier on April 6, 1945. For I felt that his appointment created the best possible political situation in Japan for us. I knew that he understood the United States and would be under no illusions as to our determination and capacity to fight the war through to a successful conclusion by invading the Japanese homeland. Because of his close association with the Emperor, I believed that he would be the master mind of the peace party. But younger men like Admiral Yonai would have to implement any actual program.

We recognized the Navy's role in the peace movement and did everything to drive deeper the wedge between the two branches of the armed forces. It would have been easy to harp on the ineffective showing of the Japanese Navy. But this would have been a faulty technique, and this theme was therefore barred from our talks. The Japanese Navy was, in the propaganda sense, fighting on our side. Any derision would necessarily have weakened its hand while automatically strengthening the hand of the war party, spearheaded by a clique within the Army, and led by ex-Premier Hideki Tojo himself from his nominal retirement.

In the cabinet Suzuki seemed to have only one opponent: General Anami, a colorless military bureaucrat whom the Tojo clique designated to represent the Army. He proved a fatal choice and was largely responsible for the bad showing of the warmongers. He was too weak to match wits with the shrewd Navy group or to muster strength against the palace clique. Tojo himself had made a fatal mistake by not preventing the Suzuki government from coming into power. By the time Tojo and his clique went into action to block the peace movement by eliminating the Suzuki group, and even the Emperor if necessary, the peace party was too well entrenched and controlled so many key positions in the country and overseas that the plot was doomed to failure. Tojo did not anticipate that Suzuki would be able to make the radical changes in the domestic administration, such as local governors, police chiefs, public prosecutors, etc., which served to strengthen the latter's position unexpectedly and thereby weaken Tojo. We knew that his clique within the Army was plotting a *coup d'état,* but we also recognized that conditions within Japan no longer favored such a coup. Even within the War Ministry various cliques were intriguing against each other. Field Marshal Count Terauchi, whose influence was second only to Tojo's, was too sick and too far away in Malaya to exert his influence. General Okamura, who commanded the armies in China, seemed to side with the peace party.

When Suzuki accepted the premier's office, he had hoped to retain at least part of Japan's wartime gains. The Philippines were lost, which made Japan's southern conquest virtually untenable. But he hoped to get out of the war and retain possession of Manchuria and Korea. He was encouraged in this hope by reports from his ambassador in Moscow who fully *mis*understood Russian intentions and assured the Premier that the Soviet Union would stay out of the war altogether.

The house of cards which Suzuki was laboriously building collapsed on the day when Okinawa was secured by our forces.

We had waited for this day and were ready to strike still another blow in the form of a special broadcast, in which I declared:

"The Battle of Okinawa reveals that your thorough preparation over a long period, the best efforts of your picked troops, and shortened supply lines to Kyushu and Honshu could not affect the outcome of this decisive battle. At Okinawa the United States forces have again reached their chosen objective. In many ways the Okinawa campaign resembles the Solomons campaign. Guadalcanal was essential. It represented the furthermost point of Japanese advance. It had to be held at all costs if Japan were to continue her *offensive*. Okinawa had to be held at all costs if Japan were to be successful in her *defense*. In Guadalcanal the Japanese Navy was subjected to attrition from which it never recovered. In Okinawa it was the Japanese air force which was sacrificed in vain. So future historians will say that while in Guadalcanal Japan *lost* the war, in Okinawa the United States *won* it.

"Can any thinking Japanese sincerely believe that the pattern and outcome of future operations will be different? At the end of this battle we have won territory of paramount strategic importance; our naval, air, and land forces have pushed open the very door of Japan. These, then, are the true lessons of Okinawa. They must be made as clear to you as they are to the rest of the world. Will you follow the example of the defeated German leaders and allow deceptive arguments and wishful thinking to destroy your country, now that it is evident that the war is irretrievably lost for Japan? Will true Japanese patriots allow this to come to pass?"

And Secretary Forrestal placed at my disposal a significant warning which I read to my Japanese listeners:

"I can find no American who feels that in this war, forced upon us by reckless and ill-advised Japanese leaders, the task will be too great or the cost too high to ensure final victory and a future free from further threats. Our careful planning has taken into consideration the possibility that the Japanese will fight with tenacity and fury as our *full* power is brought to bear against their homeland. We have seen evidence of that fury at Iwo Jima and Okinawa, and it has been overcome. In the same manner, we shall reduce the Japanese military power wherever necessary. We shall, in short, secure the unalterable objective which I know to be the will of this country, namely, the unconditional surrender of Japan and the liquidation of Japanese militarism."

The Suzuki cabinet was badly shaken. It could no longer conceal from the people at large that the invasion of the Japanese main islands was the next Allied move. It had to act and act quickly if it were to save at least a fraction of its own plans. Japan was ripe to ask for peace—and more than that, to beg for it if need be. The campaign was entering the home stretch. Every move we made in this situation was of the highest diplomatic significance, as, indeed, my talks now became part of a grandiose diplomatic warfare that was progressing in several countries with such divergent protagonists as the Kremlin and the Vatican.

33

DECISIVE BROADCAST

It was on June 9, 1945, at 8:25 A.M., that I made my fifth broadcast, in which I incorporated the message sent from Switzerland by the prominent Japanese newspaperman Jiro Taguchi to Foreign Minister Togo in Tokyo. A copy of this dispatch had been obtained through the superb efforts and espionage technique of the Swiss branch of the Office of Strategic Services and was a splendid example of their co-operation when they sent it to me as of possible value for inclusion in my campaign. We immediately recognized the great significance of this message but also the paradox of the situation. The addressee was the same Togo who on December 6, 1941, as foreign minister of the Tokyo government, had confronted Ambassador Grew in the latter's abortive attempt to get President Roosevelt's message through to the Emperor at midnight on December 6, while riding high on the waves of impertinence and confidence.

We could not escape the thought that the wheel of history had indeed made a full turn, and the involvement of one of the protagonists of the Pearl Harbor treachery added a piquant touch to the diplomatic spectacle. Mr. Taguchi was another protagonist. He had represented a jingoistic Japanese newspaper in Germany for several years and had prided himself on being in the confidence of the Nazis' inner circle. But now it was his turn to be humiliated, to offer humble advice to the broken foreign minister, counseling him to sue for peace if he wanted to avoid Germany's fate.

Taguchi went far beyond giving advice. He took upon himself the responsibility of trying to conduct peace negotiations in Bern, Switzerland, by approaching our minister there, Mr. Leland Harrison. He employed the good offices of several neutral intermediaries to lend added weight to his overtures. But it was by no means an official approach. Taguchi was acting as a free-lance peacemaker, and consequently his suggestions could not be taken seriously. However, his activities were seconded by the efforts of other Japanese in Bern, including representatives of great financial concerns, who added their endorsements to the pleas of Taguchi, hoping thereby to elicit an answer for transmittal to Tokyo.

By then peace feelers were coming in to Washington in amazingly large numbers. The most persistent of these came via the Vatican, although it must be emphasized that the Vatican acted only as a mere transmitting agency and made no recommendations of its own.

It was reported that the Emperor himself was seeking mediation by the Pope through the Archbishop of Tokyo, who happened to be the brother of a former foreign minister, the late Yosuke Matsuoka. This provided still another ironical touch, since Matsuoka had once been the strongest advocate of German-Japanese co-operation and had become the stooge of Hitler and Ribbentrop. Indeed, it was Matsuoka who had taken a leading position among the warmongers during 1941 and upon his return from a trip to Berlin had urged immediate hostile action, having guaranteed to Hitler that Japan would enter the war by seizing Singapore, which act, however, was not supposed to involve the United States. While one member of the Matsuoka family was thus instrumental in unleashing the war, another member was now making strenuous efforts to stop it short of the invasion of Japan proper. The Vatican was informed openly that the Archbishop of Tokyo was acting upon the Emperor's behest and that his role was merely that of an intermediary. But occasionally he added his own to the purported pleas of the Emperor, and some of them were remarkable for the urgency with which they implored the Pope "to do something."

These approaches began to reach the Vatican in April and continued throughout May, blowing hot and cold, playing a primitive form of psychological warfare by today protesting Japan's determination and strength, and tomorrow admitting complete exhaustion and failure. It was easy to recognize the crudeness of the diplomatic show being staged in Tokyo; and while we regarded these pleas as a possible indication of Japan's anxiety to conclude peace at the earliest moment, it was impossible to evaluate the requests because of the ambiguous nature of the campaign.

Without making a direct move, we registered these overtures as possible straws in the wind and adapted our campaign to them. In my opinion the most significant and probably the most enlightened approach was that of Taguchi. The urgency of his advice was well calculated to impress Togo and his circle in Tokyo. He placed special emphasis on a fatal German miscalculation. The Germans had deluded themselves with the thought that the Allies did not have sufficient fighting spirit to carry the war to total victory. As I revealed this passage of the Taguchi radiogram to my listening audience in Tokyo, I commented: "Do not these words have a familiar ring? Have you not heard leaders among you say that the United States does not have the spiritual strength to wage war to its predestined end? Mr. Taguchi described this fatal miscalculation of the Germans as the result of basing strategy upon imaginary ideas which have no foundation in reality. Has not the strategy of Japan been built upon a similar, nay, an identical basis?"

Mr. Taguchi informed Foreign Minister Togo that in 1943 after the Battle of Stalingrad, Germany's leaders realized the war was irretrievably lost. We had information which revealed that the Germans had become defeatist even before Stalingrad. As early as the fall of 1941 after the collapse of the German blitzkrieg against Russia, British Intelligence captured in a U-boat a highly significant document containing a speech made by the German Admiral Warzecha to a gathering of top-ranking German naval officers in which he insisted that all calculations had gone astray and that Germany was no longer in a position to win the war. Another report disclosed that the German General Staff was of the same opinion and that similar views were expressed by General von Wietersheim at a gathering of top-ranking Army officers. A joint memorandum was then prepared for Hitler suggesting and even urging him to work for a negotiated peace. They suggested that by relinquishing some of his loot he would be able to keep the most desirable parts of it.

Hitler in characteristic manner rejected the proposal and purged his generals. A few weeks later, early in December 1941, he assumed personal command of Germany's armed forces and began what in the history of warfare will be remembered forever as his campaigns of intuition. He did succeed in rallying both the people and the armed forces for a prolongation of the war, and did make a significant contribution to war technology by giving orders to concentrate on novel weapons against which there would be no defense. His basic calculation was sound. With the V-weapons, the new U-boats and their instruments enabling them to remain submerged for indefinite periods, and with possible success in atomic research, he could have been in a position to decide the war in Germany's favor. But by the time he had made this important military discovery, Germany had exhausted .her strength and the resultant fatigue prevented her from accelerating her scientific research. When the new weapons finally made their appearance, it was a case of too little and too late.

Taguchi reiterated this analysis as he pointed out that the same spirit which had induced Hitler to prolong the war after the collapse of the first Russian campaign had again prevailed after Stalingrad. "Instead of meeting the changed situation with political wisdom," he wrote to Togo, "instead of considering the future interests of the nation, they took, and intensified, oppressive measures."

By then Japan was following Germany's example. She was intensifying police measures to keep the people in line and to bolster their fading enthusiasm for what came to be labeled the "Hundred-Year War." Special sessions of district attorneys were held in Tokyo by the Minister of Justice, Mr. Matsuzaka; and the Procurator General, Nakano, was placed in charge of "morale promotion," which by then had become morale enforcement. My purpose in citing Taguchi's dispatch was far more than just to provide an intelligence scoop to enliven my broadcasts. I was quite explicit in drawing conclusions for my Japanese listeners, who are habitually slow in arriving at decisions unless assisted in their thinking. "The outstanding lesson which clear-sighted men like Mr. Taguchi learned from Germany's defeat was this," I said: "The continuation of a hopeless war not only failed to help Germany but compromised the entire future of that country. Mr. Taguchi said that the cost was immense. German cities were destroyed; the middle class disappeared; securities were turned into wastepaper; and in the very words of Jiro Taguchi: 'Everybody lost everything. The German nation lost its sovereignty.' "

This was a powerful argument, since reliable information now indicated that all Japan hoped to salvage from the war was her sovereignty. This word has a peculiar significance for the Japanese. It has a theocratic undertone in addition to its legalistic meaning. Sovereignty is closely linked to the sovereign in a combination of sacred-secular interpretation reminiscent of the feudal interpretation of the term, when the sovereign was God, the last representative of an unbroken line of divine rulers descended from the Sun

Goddess, an irrational dogma elevated to the rank of anachronistic political philosophy.

Admiral Suzuki, the new premier, was particularly concerned over this question of peculiar Japanese sovereignty. He was very close to the Emperor, having been grand chamberlain for many years. The imperial house and the classical interpretation of the imperial institution were deeply imbedded in his mind and heart. What he called the "national structure" of Japan meant the divinity and political prerogatives of the Emperor. This was his guiding principle, and now he was concentrating his efforts toward saving Japan by saving her national structure, i.e., the continuity of the ruling house said to be "unbroken for ages."

On the other hand, he was more than willing to heed the Emperor's desire to bring about peace—but his loyalty to the Emperor made him refrain from doing anything about it until he could ascertain what the Allies had in mind regarding the future fate of the imperial house. In his plight he decided upon what in retrospect appears to have been a desperate move. In June he instructed Mr. Sato, the Japanese ambassador to the Kremlin, to make representations to Marshal Stalin and ask him to intervene with the Western Allies on Japan's behalf in order to obtain a further clarification of the unconditional surrender formula, and, if possible, peace terms. What he really wanted was an assurance that Japan's sovereignty would be respected even if she had to pay for the privilege with her empire.

The fact that such a peace plea had been forwarded to Stalin, and Japan's plight bared to the Soviet leaders, did not receive here the attention it seemed to warrant. The Soviet Union by Suzuki's move was given a clear indication of Japan's inner plight and her willingness to surrender. Thus when on August 8, 1945, the Russians joined in the war against Japan, they acted upon intelligence provided by the Japanese themselves that they were at the end of their rope. Russia joined in the war in the knowledge that Japan had admitted defeat.

It is left to the judgment of history to explain why it was necessary for the Soviet to take its course of action and why the Allies, assuming they knew of Japan's approaches to the Soviet, refused to exploit the opening provided by Japan herself. If the detailed interpretations of the unconditional surrender formula had been forthcoming in June rather than the end of July, the war would have ended without Soviet participation and before the dropping of the atomic bombs on Hiroshima and Nagasaki. Although the historical perspective is insufficient as yet to provide a complete picture as it existed in June 1945, it is an undeniable fact that the diplomatic situation provided an opportunity for peace many weeks before mid-August, at which time it was generally thought that Japan had bowed to the supernatural force of the atom bomb.

I had always been under the impression that Russia would not enter the war unless there was something specific to gain thereby. I felt very strongly about this, and so reported whenever my advice was sought. I also felt that there would be endless complications, particularly in Manchuria, if Russia should enter, and therefore advised the Secretary of the Navy that she should not be allowed to do so if it could possibly be avoided.

The Soviet Union had a tremendous stake in Manchuria; but while the war against Germany was still going on, she had no means to protect that stake. Her Far Eastern forces had largely been shifted to European battlefields and were in the spring of 1945 engaged in fighting the decisive battles in Germany. This became quite obvious during the subsequent Manchurian campaign, for which forces had to be redeployed from Europe and for which commanding generals had to be named with European rather than Far Eastern experience. Marshal Vassilievsky and Marshal Malinovsky, the two top-ranking commanders shifted to the Far East, may be cited as examples to prove this point. Russian generals known to have been stationed in the Far East, such as General Gregory Stern, were conspicuous by their absence during the short Manchurian campaign of the Red Army.

It is questionable, therefore, whether the Russians were eager to join in the Pacific war as it stood in the spring of 1945. On the other hand, it is fair to assume that a considerable portion of official and public opinion in the United States favored Russian participation, editorials in American newspapers even turning the old "second front" argument against the Russians. When President Roosevelt went to Yalta he was determined to obtain Russian participation in the Pacific war, since he was of the opinion that a Soviet entry into the Far Eastern war would hasten Japan's collapse. He must have been under the influence of military advisers who habitually overestimated, first, Japan's power of resistance early in 1945, and second, the strength of the so-called Kwantung

Army stationed in Manchuria. This army has frequently been described as "the cream of the Japanese Army" even by such military observers as Colonel Evans Carlson and General Joseph Stilwell. It turned out to be far inferior to the Japanese forces met on other battlefields, chiefly because much of it had been withdrawn to fight in the Philippines and elsewhere against us.

It is now known from secret documents since published that Stalin asked a stiff price for his participation in the Pacific war and that we were willing to pay that price. In assessing the historical events of February 1945, we must blame ourselves as much as we are now inclined to blame others for the difficulties we are now experiencing in liquidating the Far Eastern war.

There always existed considerable confusion in Washington and, indeed, throughout the country regarding the diplomatic concept of the term unconditional surrender, and it became obvious that a further clarification of the unconditional surrender formula was necessary, not merely for the Japanese but for the people of the United States as well.

We presumed that the policy of the United States was formulated in five documents: one was the Atlantic Charter which distinctly stated that it applied to victor and vanquished alike; another was the 1944 New Year's declaration of Generalissimo Chiang Kai-shek. The third was the series of declarations issued after the Casablanca, Teheran, and Yalta conferences. The fourth was President Truman's proclamation of May 8, 1945, concerning unconditional surrender; the fifth was Justice Jackson's declaration on war criminals. With these documents in mind and their application clearly outlined, I felt that contrary to general belief we did have a concrete policy, and from then on my campaign was based on making this policy known to the Japanese.

By the end of June the plight of the Japanese had become desperate, and as Admiral Suzuki received no answer to his plea from Russia, he called an extraordinary session of the Diet in which he discussed in remarkably frank terms the entire war situation.

We recognized the significance of this move and gathered around the ticker bringing to our office the momentous speech. It was evident from the very outset that while Suzuki was talking of war, he was thinking of peace. Now, it was no longer a material consideration such as the retention of Manchuria or Korea which prevented him from saying in so many words that he would accept our terms.

The only doubt which still forestalled a decision was the future status of the Emperor. "I have served His Imperial Majesty over a period of many years," Suzuki said, "and I am deeply impressed with this honor. As bold as it may seem, I firmly believe there is no one in the entire world who is more deeply concerned with world peace and the welfare of mankind than His Imperial Majesty the Emperor. The brutal and inhuman acts of both America and England are aimed to make it impossible for us to follow our national policy as proclaimed by the Emperor Meiji. I hear that the enemy is boasting of his demand of unconditional surrender by Japan. Unconditional surrender will only mean that our national structure and our people will be destroyed. Against such boastful talk there is only one measure we must take—that is to fight to the last."

With our knowledge of the background of this extraordinary session and of Suzuki's speech, I made an important broadcast to the Japanese on July 7 inviting them to ask openly for peace. "Japan must make the next move," I said in clearly accentuated words. "Japan must make her choice without delay, for reasons which Admiral Suzuki knows. I have told you before that the time is running out for Japan. You must move and move quickly. Tomorrow it may be too late."

We analyzed the speech again for future action, and as subsequently proven by events and confirmed by Suzuki himself, our analysis was accurate. Our problem now was the method by which we could reassure Suzuki on this score, and indicate that there was no decision to destroy what he ambiguously described as the national structure of Japan.

This time our answer was not confined to another broadcast. Instead, there was selected a method as devious as those chosen by the Japanese themselves. We decided to answer Premier Suzuki in an anonymous letter written to a reputable American newspaper and to bring this letter to his attention in the quickest manner possible. The *Washington Post* was selected as the vehicle with full coöperation of its editors. The letter contained all the answers to Suzuki's query. Some of its passages may be worth quoting:

Insofar as Japan is concerned, the clamor for an "explanation" of the unconditional surrender formula is difficult to understand, since it has been both specified and clarified in various official documents.

Our policy of unconditional surrender can, therefore, be stated in simple terms:

(1) Unconditional surrender is the manner in which the war is terminated. It means exactly what General Grant had in mind when he stated his terms to General Lee, namely, the acceptance of terms without qualifying counter-arguments.

(2) The conditions which will obtain after surrender have been explicitly stated in the Atlantic Charter, the Cairo Declaration, Generalissimo Chiang Kai-shek's declaration of New Year's Day, 1944, President Truman's declaration of May 8, 1945, and Justice Jackson's statement on war criminals. These documents contain the conditions of which Japan can avail herself by surrendering unconditionally and thereby fulfilling the prerequisite of peace, namely, the cessation of hostilities.

(3) The Atlantic Charter and the Cairo Declaration clearly state that we seek no territorial aggrandizement. The Atlantic Charter, moreover, assures certain definite benefits to victors and vanquished alike.

(4) American military law, based upon historical precedents as well as a decision of the United States Supreme Court, clearly specify that conquest or occupation does not affect the sovereignty of a defeated nation, even though that nation may be under complete military control. . . .

If the Japanese desire to clarify whether or not unconditional surrender goes beyond the conditions contained in the five documents cited above, they have at their disposal the regular diplomatic channels, the secrecy of which precludes any public admission of weakness. They are aware that we know that Japan has lost the war. Such an inquiry could not possibly be misinterpreted, or display any weakness beyond that which now actually exists in Japan. It is presumed that this was the meaning and purpose of Mr. Grew's statement and in this sense it deserves the fullest endorsement of the American people.

If, as Admiral Suzuki revealed in the Diet, their chief concern is over Japan's future national structure (Kokutai), including the Emperor's status after surrender, the way to find out is to ask. Contrary to a widespread belief, such a question can be answered quickly and satisfactorily to all those who are concerned over the future peace of the Orient and the world.

The letter attracted considerable attention in the United States, and the *Washington Post* was bombarded by callers who wanted to learn the identity of its anonymous author. My telephone also rang. Washington correspondents, accurately gauging the technique, tried to make me confess authorship. Typical of the many efforts to determine the source of the letter was a syndicated article by Duke Shoop, Washington correspondent of the *Kansas City Star,* who wrote:

A provocative open letter inviting the Japanese to open negotiations on unconditional surrender is being widely discussed here since it is believed that Captain E. M. Zacharias, the "official American spokesman" of American radio broadcasts to the Japs, is the author.... This provocative letter is like something out of a mystery thriller, but it is not at all out of the question that some such method might be taken to convey further to the Japanese what we mean by unconditional surrender. Through neutral countries they have almost immediate access to comments in American newspapers. Whether this was the purpose or not, the letter is a significant contribution to the psychological phase of the war which has its purpose advising the Japanese of what unconditional surrender does and does not mean.

The letter was reprinted in many American dailies from coast to coast. We felt certain that it would be picked up in Washington by the listening posts of the Japanese government.

Simultaneously another broadside was prepared along more conventional lines. I was now called upon to prepare a radio script on the highest diplomatic level. I fully recognized my tremendous responsibility and devoted special attention to this one talk. We worked on the script day and night for almost a week, drafting and redrafting it, listening to suggestions, submitting it for approval, weighing every single word with the greatest of care. When at last I went to the broadcasting studio, I had its fourteenth draft in my pocket.

For this broadcast we selected a little room specially built for highly classified recording to guarantee security. As unobtrusively as possible, guards were posted around the studio to see that no unauthorized person could obtain advance information of what I was to say. But this secrecy was maintained for only a short period. When my recordings were put on the air a few days later, the text of the broadcast was released to the American press by the OWI, using this publicity as another means of reinforcing and emphasizing the message.

I was introduced as "an official spokesman of the United States government," in line with the stipulation of the operation plan. But the Japanese had indicated doubt as to my true authority. Was

I "official spokesman" in fact, as well as in name? Did my statements carry higher endorsement? Or was I merely a cog in the wheel of the American propaganda mill? With the release to the press we hoped to dispel their doubts, and the reception which the American newspapers accorded to this talk surpassed our most optimistic expectations. The news of this broadcast broke on July 21, and the evening papers were the first to feature it. "U.S. Warns Japan to Quit Now, Escape Virtual Destruction," headlined the *Washington Post,* and next morning the *New York Times* gave it front-page display and reprinted the whole broadcast. Other prominent papers similarly featured it.

The broadcast reiterated the themes of my letter to the *Post.* The message it carried was incorporated in four sentences: "The leaders of Japan have been entrusted with the salvation and not the *destruction* of Japan. As I have said before, the Japanese leaders face two alternatives. One is the virtual destruction of Japan followed by a dictated peace. The other is unconditional surrender with its attendant benefits as laid down by the Atlantic Charter." The urgency of the situation was formulated in words which were adapted to Japanese psychology when I said: "Your opportunity to think over these facts is rapidly passing.... If the Japanese leaders still prefer to delay and hope for miracles, they should remember that the cemetery of history is crowded with the graves of nations—nations which were doomed to extinction because they made their decision too late."

In the midst of the domestic clamor which was manifested in editorials printed in virtually every American daily, the Japanese kept a significant silence. As I waited for their answer, I visualized the conclaves going on in Tokyo, in which possible strategy and tactics were being discussed in an endeavor to find the most propitious answer. As it was, we did not have to wait long. The Japanese answer was delivered at 12:15 A.M. (EWT) on July 24, by another Inouye, Dr. Kiyoshi Inouye this time, who was introduced as Japan's outstanding authority on international relations. I remembered him quite well as a former professor at the University of Southern California, at Tokyo University, and as delegate to various international conferences.

The message entrusted to Dr. Kiyoshi Inouye was of momentous importance. In effect, he was to indicate Japan's willingness to *surrender unconditionally,* if and when Japan was assured that the

Atlantic Charter would apply to her. He stated: "Should America show any sincerity of putting into practice what she preaches, as for instance in the Atlantic Charter excepting its punitive clause, the Japanese nation, in fact the Japanese military, would automatically, if not willingly follow in the stopping of the conflict. Then and then only will sabers cease to rattle both in the East and the West."

This was not the final word of the campaign. But it was the next to last. In retrospect, the Inouye broadcast of July 24 must be accepted as evidence of the Japanese decision to terminate the war then and there; to terminate it on the basis of the terms outlined in my series of previous broadcasts culminating in my twelfth talk. The Japanese answer was delivered on the eve of the Potsdam Declaration in which the meaning of unconditional surrender was clearly outlined and spelled out. It was delivered *thirteen days* before the first atomic bomb was dropped on Hiroshima, and more than two weeks before the Soviet's entry into the war. Japan was ready for surrender. To reap our harvest we had only to shake her like a tree full of ripe apples.

Subsequent investigations on the spot after Japan's surrender revealed that the Emperor was fully aware of our psychological warfare activities and had access to the monitoring service. He felt that we understood clearly the situation inside Japan and that at the end of June 1945 the time had come to seek peace.

Several Japanese in high positions who were in constant touch with the Emperor were thoroughly interrogated. One official of the Foreign Office said: "The Zacharias broadcasts were influential especially in government circles," and added: "The outstanding feature of the Zacharias broadcasts was the difference between unconditional surrender and dictated peace. The Japanese knew how Germany was being administered under such a peace. Zacharias promised that if Japan accepted unconditional surrender they would have the benefit of the Atlantic Charter. The people began to look with favor on such terms, claiming that it was not what the militarists had said. It seemed to the people that Zacharias' explanation of unconditional surrender offered a way out."

Mr. Toshio Shiratori read the copies of my broadcasts at the Foreign Office. At first he was somewhat skeptical, then became a thorough believer. A copy of each broadcast was taken to the Emperor by Mr. Matsuda. He stated that the information in these talks influenced those in the Emperor's circle as well as the Emperor himself.

Another official of the Foreign Office stated: "The broadcasts of Captain Zacharias were the object of unusual attention." He felt that these talks were influential because (a) they claimed to represent the official views of the United States government; and (b) they reiterated the pledge of President Truman that the Japanese would not be enslaved.

The highest and latest official word on this subject was received in a letter from Mr. Dennis McEvoy. It was dated August 29, 1946, and was sent just after McEvoy's return from Tokyo, where he had gone after V-J Day to set up *The Reader's Digest* in Japanese.

It will be recalled that Mr. McEvoy, as a first lieutenant of Marines, was a member of the unbeatable team in the psychological warfare against the Japanese high command. His letter reads:

Just before leaving Tokyo I had dinner with Prince and Princess Takamatsu, whom you knew and mentioned in your first broadcast. The Prince told me on this occasion that "the Captain Zacharias broadcasts provided the ammunition needed by the 'peace party' to win out against those elements in the Japanese government who wished to continue the war to the bitter end"—and after looking over personally the fortifications the Japanese had prepared for us, I am convinced it would have been a very bitter end indeed. The Prince's statement was in exact accord with the estimate of the situation which you made before you began to talk to the Japanese on the radio. Other pre-war contacts of mine in Japan, both in and out of the government, who were in a position to observe the crucial political situation which terminated in Japan's surrender, confirmed Takamatsu's assertions. I believe that this is rather convincing evidence of the tremendous value of your work in helping bring the war to an early close, thereby saving countless lives.

There was unanimity among Japanese newspapermen that our propaganda not only shortened the war but made the bloodless occupation of Japan possible. This was the goal set forth in the "decision" of my Operation Plan 1-45.

34

BEHIND THE POTSDAM DECLARATION

Although my "operations" were conducted behind a screen of semisecrecy, sufficient facts "leaked out" regarding the contents of my broadcasts and the over-all purpose of my campaign to inspire a prolonged discussion revolving around the unconditional surrender formula.

Some of these discussions paralleled my own efforts. Probably the most important, and certainly the most influential, was a spirited editorial campaign conducted by the *Washington Post*. The chief editorial writer of this most important daily, Herbert Elliston, was reaching conclusions startlingly similar to my own, and in a series of brilliant editorials, written with the force of conviction, he urged the United States government to go to the limit in its clarification of the surrender formula.

The *Washington Post*'s campaign reflected the customary courage of that paper to advocate seemingly unpopular but sound ideas and educate its readers to their acceptance and support. There were other similar efforts in the nation, but they were not pursued with the intellectual force and material vigor of the *Post*'s campaign. They were, moreover, discredited by the isolationist background of the men who appeared to be behind some of the proposals, revealing them as appeasement attempts rather than means of political warfare. At the other extreme were the editorial pages of other newspapers which steadfastly denied that the collapse of Japanese resistance was at all a military possibility short of actual invasion, and castigated those who dared to attempt the methods of political warfare. Such editorials were written from a narrow point of view by persons who must have been overimpressed by the Japanese propaganda which had been conducted ever since the Meiji Restoration in 1868 and which boasted of the so-called psychological or spiritual strength of Japan so much played up by her military leaders—but not really taken seriously by these planners, who calculated in concrete facts and figures and not in abstract jingoistic terms.

On June 6 Raymond Gram Swing joined the discussion with an important fifteen-minute talk in which he said: "Captain Zacharias, former captain of the battleship *New Mexico,* who knows Japanese and Japan very well, is doing some broadcasts which reach Japan on the medium waves which ordinary sets can pick up. He is trying to explain to the Japanese people that they need not fear unconditional surrender. And he is doing it so effectively that the Japanese radio is having difficulties to answer him. His effectiveness would be many times greater if he did not have to use the words 'unconditional surrender,' in discussing peace. I should oppose reducing in any way the severity of the terms Japan must meet. But I also oppose putting up what may be an artificial barrier to the earliest possible ending of the war on those terms."

The problems of "unconditional surrender" were among the primarily psychological questions of the war with which my staff in OP-16-W had long been preoccupied. Several investigations into the origin and practicability of the formula were conducted in 1944 and 1945, and the experts of 16-W came to the following conclusions:

1. The proclamation of the term was based on a historical misapprehension.

2. In view of the explicit provisions of the Hague Convention, which clearly distinguishes between the responsibilities of combatants and noncombatants in warfare, the term could refer only to the manner in which hostilities are terminated and not to the future fate of whole nations.

3. It was a contradiction in itself, since the term "surrender" alone by itself represented a prima-facie condition.

4. The enemy exploited the term in its own propaganda and compelled our psychological warfare to assume a defensive tone, explaining and clarifying what we actually meant by the formula, thereby answering enemy accusations.

Similarly it was felt by high Allied military authorities that our political insistence on a so-called unconditional surrender tended to increase the difficulties of our complex military task. General Eisenhower's opinion of the subject was revealed on August 12, 1943, when Captain Harry C. Butcher, USNR, his naval aide, wrote in the diary he kept for the Supreme Commander: "What had appeared to be a quick collapse of Italy has disappeared into uncertainty, with the definite knowledge that the Italians are solidifying their opposition to us and are really fighting. Around headquarters, we are inclined to attribute this to the hard-boiled attitude of the Prime Minister [Churchill] and the President, who publicly insisted upon 'unconditional surrender' as soon as Mussolini was out. No surrender ever was made without some conditions."

On April 14, 1944, the famous diary revealed the General's views in even more explicit terms. "There have been discussions with Edward Stettinius, Jr. as to the meaning of 'unconditional surrender' as applied to Germany," Captain Butcher recorded. "Any military person knows that there are conditions to every surrender. There is a feeling that, at Casablanca, the President and the Prime Minister, more likely the former, seized on Grant's famous terms without realizing the full implications to the enemy. Goebbels has made great capital with it to strengthen the morale of the German Army and people. Our psychological experts believe we would be wiser if we created a mood of acceptance of surrender in the German Army which would make possible a collapse of resistance similar to that which took place in Tunisia. . . . To accomplish the proper mood, there would need to be a new American-Anglo-Russian statement to define 'unconditional surrender.' . . . After the three governments had agreed and announced such definitions, our staff feels that the Supreme Commander should make a declaration after the landings to the German commander in the west, reciting in soldierly language the principal points of surrender terms. General Ike strongly advocates this view and asked Ed Stettinius to transmit it to the President, which he did by cable."

President Roosevelt's reluctance to consider any change in the original formula was well known to the staff of OP-16-W, which, in fact, was one of the psychological-warfare agencies referred to in Captain Butcher's entry as preparing expert opinions on the subject. The Joint Chiefs in Washington shared General Eisenhower's long-standing apprehension, and, as early as February 1944, commissioned the Navy Department's Special Warfare Branch to prepare a memorandum on the subject, including possible recommendations. The question which the experts of 16-W were supposed to answer were, first, whether the unconditional surrender formula was conducive to increasing or stiffening resistance of the enemy; and, second, how we could alter the formula without losing face or doing damage to our political prestige.

The memorandum prepared by 16-W for the Joint Chiefs pointed out that the Declaration of Casablanca, in which the formula was first stated, was an outstanding psychological scoop inasmuch as it revealed both our determination and confidence to carry the war to a victorious conclusion at a time when the military situation did not seem to warrant such optimism and confidence. That it was effective was later confirmed by the top-secret Official German War Diary, kept for the German high command on a day-by-day basis. An entry shortly after the Casablanca Declaration paid high tribute to Allied propaganda, which, in the opinion of the German diarist, was alone responsible for sustaining the morale of the Allied peoples and their friends in occupied lands.

"This propaganda," the German diarist added, "is an extremely bold one, since the over-all military situation of the Allies does not permit recourse to such sweeping statements, indicating a belief in victory, and, indeed, giving the general impression that the Allies have already won the war."

When first proclaimed, the formula served notice on the Germans that we would never yield to shallow peace feelers unless they were made unconditionally on the basis of the 1935 status quo, i.e., prior to Hitler's reoccupation of the Rhineland. Moreover, it indicated that we would make no "promises," like President Wilson's Fourteen Points, the observance or nonobservance of which was made the subject of violent German postwar propaganda and claims.

But what in early 1943 was an excellent propaganda argument now tended to work against our best interests. Above all, as so often claimed and restated even by Captain Butcher, it had no genuine foundation in historical precedent.

President Roosevelt, a keen student of history, but acting probably on the basis of a misapprehension, borrowed the term from General Ulysses S. Grant. Our investigations revealed that in 1865 the formula was given an entirely different meaning from that of 1944. In the Civil War, General Grant was given power to accept the Confederacy's surrender "unconditionally"—which then meant that General Grant did not have to obtain the approval of President Lincoln or his cabinet for his acceptance. Other Northern generals were given a similar power only "conditionally"—which meant that they had to obtain the approval of President Lincoln *and* General Grant prior to making surrender arrangements. Thus it was evident that unconditional surrender was an administrative term, referring to the manner in which surrender could be accepted and not to the manner in which it was to be demanded or offered. In fact, it referred to the Union rather than the Confederacy, or, in the light of 1944, to the Allies and not to the Axis, inasmuch as it referred to powers of commanders in the field for the acceptance of surrender on terms approved by higher political authorities.

Detailed research, including the study of original Civil War documents in the National Archives, also revealed that much of the so-called historical evidence cited in support of the formula was of doubtful authenticity and that the importance attributed to the unconditional surrender incident between Grant and Lee was a legend. This was explicitly and convincingly stated in the 16-W memorandum prepared for the Joint Chiefs.

They were advised, however, to sustain the formula for the sake of prestige, but to confine it to the military sphere, explaining that it referred to the armed forces of the enemy and not to the nations as a whole. It was emphasized that a declaration of the Allies should clarify that unconditional surrender is the manner in which hostilities are terminated and does not refer to conditions to prevail after the war which have to be made on the basis of explicit peace terms, and not under the blanket dictation implied in unconditional surrender. No action was taken on the recommendation, and the formula continued to haunt our psychological efforts.

By early 1945 the situation had undergone considerable change. The Russians, in fact, failed to adhere to the unconditional surrender formula and maintained a coterie of captured German general officers, who broadcast appeals to the German armed forces to surrender *conditionally* to the Soviets. Then on March 1, 1945, President Roosevelt in his address to Congress after his return from Yalta went to considerable lengths himself to clarify the formula insofar as it concerned Germany. The proclamation issued on May 8 by President Truman served the same purpose insofar as the Japanese were concerned. But, apparently, both specifications failed in their purpose, chiefly because they were still vague and did not go far enough. Unconditional surrender remained a dreaded and mysterious term, at least in the imagination of the enemy population, and served to reinforce his propaganda effort.

It was finally decided, therefore, in highest Washington circles to define the conditions of unconditional surrender. In this decision was reflected the very contradiction of the original term, and also the fact that by the spring of 1945 the original formula had outlived its usefulness. The War and State Departments now both expressed the opinion that the formula required immediate clarification and specification, thus concurring in the opinion long voiced and advocated by the Navy Department.

The clamor of certain extremist elements in the United States against this change in policy was fully unjustified. There was never a desire to "sell out" to the Japanese in eliminating an unworkable formula. There was no desire "to make peace with the Zaibatsu"— as certain left-wing critics persistently maintained. In fact, there was a very great determination, not only in the White House but also in the War, Navy, and State Departments, to deal as severely and harshly with the enemy as the Rules of War permitted, to have no dealings with reactionary elements in the enemy camps, and to apply unconditional surrender in fact—without, however, harping on prejudicial words.

President Roosevelt died at the moment when he himself had just become an advocate of the changed formula and assumed leadership of the forces which proceeded to specify, clarify, and explain the meaning of unconditional surrender. But President Truman accepted his decision and was determined to carry out the policy of his predecessor.

In the meantime press items indicated that preparations were being made for the President to meet with Stalin and Churchill at Potsdam for a momentous conference to decide the fate of fallen Germany as well as the future of Japan. There were rumors that on the basis of previous agreements it was expected that the Russians would join in the Pacfic war either before or coincident with the Potsdam conference. One newspaper indicated that a document was drafted calling on the Japanese to surrender unconditionally— but specifying the terms of surrender in eight generous and explicit conditions. Marshal Stalin's name was included in the original draft of what later became the Potsdam Declaration to Japan, but as President Truman left for Potsdam on board the *Augusta* prior to the Soviet's entry into the Pacific war, and there were no signs that the Russians would join the war during the conference, the declaration was slightly redrafted to omit Stalin's name from among those of the signatories. Mr. Churchill's name was replaced by that of Mr. Attlee, who became prime minister in the wake of the July elections in Britain.

Just as President Truman sailed across the Atlantic with one missile calculated to increase the effectiveness of our psychological campaign, an American cruiser was crossing the Pacific with an entirely different type of missile which some thought would decide the war in the purely military sphere—the atom bomb.

It was without knowledge of the atomic bomb that on July 21 I went on the air with the most important broadcast in my series of talks. This broadcast was clearly understood in Japan, although it gave rise to many misunderstandings in the United States.*

President Truman and Secretary of State Byrnes were both in Potsdam when the news of my broadcast was flashed to the world. For a moment it seemed to them that it represented a premature disclosure of the Potsdam Declaration, the issuance of which, unknown to me, was scheduled for July 26. While the AP correspondent Mr. Vaccaro reported from Potsdam that the President and Mr. Byrnes tacitly approved my broadcast, several attempts were made by uninformed or misinformed individuals to be critical of me. This condition invariably results when information is sought on highly important matters from members of departments not in touch with the situation. These were surely ill-advised moves in the face of the effectiveness of my talks in Japan itself. At a moment when my efforts were yielding definite results, certain biased American publicists and uninformed commentators took it upon themselves to question my authority and thereby undermine my usefulness in the campaign itself. My position, however, was clarified by Arthur Krock, Washington editor of the *New York Times*, who in an article entitled "Objects of Our Propaganda to Japan" stated:

Uneasiness has been expressed in this country over a passage in the President's flag raising speech in Berlin (in which he stated that we have no territorial aspirations in the Pacific) and the broadcast to Japan by Captain Zacharias, USN, that was made the next day. . . . Captain Zacharias, though reiterating the requirement of unconditional surrender, told the Japanese people they can make "peace with honor" at this juncture and that the benefits of the Atlantic Charter will go with it; and this has aroused fears it will persuade the Japanese

* See Appendix, page 421 f., for complete text of the twelfth broadcast.

we are weakening and that they can get even better terms if they hold out.

Officials here have an explanation of both statements, which they think should correct any impression that we plan to give up the islands, or that there is confusion or loose thinking in our propaganda policy. ... Captain Zacharias was working on a twofold problem this Government faces in the Pacific war, and the line he took in his broadcast is the high official attempt to deal with it directly. He sought (a) to persuade the Japanese people that their military leaders lie when they predict pillage, enslavement, dismemberment of the home islands, rapine and the overthrow of their sacred institutions as the inevitable consequences of unconditional surrender, the hope being that, if the Japanese masses can be brought to realize this, the war will be shortened and many American lives will be spared. He sought (b) to show the American people the effort that is being made to save those lives.

This particular broadcast was published for reason (b) [Mr. Krock continued, then added later in his column]: He is an officer of the Navy, but his work is with the Office of War Information, to which he is accredited and which has responsibility for what he has been beaming to Japan and, in this instance, to the American people as well.

For the sake of the record it can be stated that this broadcast went through the usual channels for approval as previously indicated and that I made the broadcast with the fullest support of the Office of War Information, although it was prepared on my own initiative.

On July 26, about four o'clock in the afternoon, I was sitting in the office of Secretary Grew in the State Department when Mr. MacLeish, in shirt sleeves, rushed in with a copy of a momentous document just released by the Office of War Information—the Potsdam Declaration.

35

VICTORY

I WORKED throughout the night preparing for my broadcast number thirteen, which was to reinforce the Potsdam Declaration. The opening paragraphs of this talk are of special significance in the historical perspective:

"Today," I said, "I am addressing *both* the leaders and the people of Japan at a time when Japan as a nation is confronted with her crisis of death—or life. Japan must make a choice, upon the wisdom of which her whole future will depend. In the light of the alternatives presented in the Joint Proclamation, this choice should not be difficult. One alternative is prompt and utter destruction. If the Japanese people are forced by their self-willed militaristic leaders to choose an alternative of ruin, *centuries of sweat and toil will be brought to naught in a cataclysmic end of a tragic war*. The other alternative is the end of war. One simple decision will allow tranquillity again to return to the city and the countryside. The homeland of Japan will be saved to continue a sovereign existence under a peacefully inclined and responsible government."

By then my mission was almost completed. On August 4, when still unknown to me the atomic bomb was already being loaded on its carrier, I made a last appeal: "If the Japanese leaders have any loyalty and wisdom left, there is but one choice left to them. They must recognize their present situation, and take suitable steps to correct the tragic mistakes of the recent past. They must plan for their inevitable defeat and for Japan's future with whatever loyalty, intelligence, and courage they can still command."

On August 6 the first atomic bomb was dropped on Hiroshima. On August 8 the Russians joined us in the war against Japan, cutting through Manchuria with astonishing speed against little or no resistance. But by then Japan was virtually no longer in the war. She had been frantically trying to extricate herself from it.

The final move came on August 10—a note from the Japanese

government which was released by the Department of State early next morning. Simultaneously a Japanese broadcast announced the "break" from Radio Tokyo in what then were still oblique but to me easily understandable terms—explicitly referring to me by name and to the broadcast in which I had confronted them with their crucial alternatives. There was no doubt in my mind that Japan was rapidly collapsing in the manner predicted in my plan and in the form outlined in my series of talks. But still in Washington important voices could be heard that Japan, even after the note signifying readiness to accept the terms of the Potsdam Declaration, was playing for time. And when Mr. Byrnes answered the Swiss note, by emphasizing that "from the moment of surrender the authority of the Emperor and the Japanese Government to rule the state shall be subject to the Supreme Commander of the Allied powers who will take such steps as he deems proper to effectuate the surrender terms," it was widely felt that Japan would, after all, prefer to continue the war to the bitter end.

It is still vivid in my mind how anxiously everyone awaited the Japanese answer to Mr. Byrnes's note of August 11. In the Navy Department the pessimists seemed to prevail, and even the head of the Cominch Intelligence division volunteered the opinion that at the last moment Japan would back out and leave us holding the bag. In an opinion carefully prepared on the basis of my acquaintance with Japanese psychology I assured the Secretary of the Navy that the Japanese surrender would be forthcoming and, furthermore, emphasized that it should arrive before the sixteenth. I voiced the same belief in OWI, where skepticism largely prevailed. The invariable reply was, "I hope you're right."

There *was* a last-minute effort within Japan to prevent surrender with a *coup d'état*. As soon as the Japanese note arrived in Washington, I urged caution and circumspection. I felt I knew how the Japanese would react. It was evident to me that a gigantic drama was being played on the stage of Japanese politics, which in such a crisis would simulate the intrigue found only in the best Japanese drama. The fact that the surrender offer had not been announced on the home broadcasts of Radio Tokyo suggested further caution. The palace circles, which were in fact responsible for the surrender offer, were playing a dangerous and delicate game, which would require that they prepare the ground and establish themselves firmly before they took the people of Japan into their confidence.

I advised that during this period Japan be left unharassed in order to prevent interference with the Emperor's efforts. There was no immediate need for a propaganda exploitation of the diplomatic note. My apprehension of this period was fully confirmed some months later, when an OWI mission in Japan investigated the circumstances of the surrender. Frank Schuler of the OWI, an indefatigable worker all through my campaign, was a member of this mission. He discovered that the delay in acceptance of surrender was caused by a leaflet prepared in the field which informed the Japanese people prematurely of the surrender offer but after it was released in Washington.

The Japanese people who first learned of this fact from those leaflets were stunned. Moreover, there was no way for them to know that the Emperor was fully behind the offer. In their confused thinking they resorted to actions which made negotiations difficult for the imperial circle. But the leaflet did even greater damage. It incited certain Army officers of the palace guard to revolt against the Emperor and attempt large-scale assassinations to remove from the scene those who were in favor of the surrender. In the confusion created by this one leaflet there were hours when it seemed that the Emperor and his advisers would not be able to carry out their own surrender offer. On August 12, the general in command of the *gendarmerie* assigned to guard the Emperor's palace had informed his officers that Japan was going to surrender. He told them that he had just been advised of that fact by the Minister of War, General Anami. By this time the younger officers were highly incensed, and they tried to take matters into their own hands. One captain in the Army Air Corps seized a plane, took off from the airfield later used by General MacArthur on his arrival, and dropped leaflets over Tokyo urging the people to resist the surrender decision; two lieutenants went to the houses of members of the Emperor's household department and tried to assassinate important persons, including Marquis Kido and also the Premier, Admiral Suzuki.

Later dispatches stated that the Minister of War, General Anami, was a participant in the plot, and that is given as the reason for his suicide shortly after the surrender. Of the dissident group, five young officers were arrested and the plane pilot, Captain Minami, who had dropped the leaflets, crashed his plane as a final demonstration and died.

In Washington after Mr. Byrnes sent his reply to the Japanese note there was nothing to do but wait and hope. Few if any realized at the time how easily the favorable situation could have been upset with drastic and tragic results. It required very great political skill to straighten out this situation—but then on the fifteenth, the world's long vigil as well as the Pacific war was over.

The stunning effect of the atomic bombs on world-wide popular imagination caused an instant belief that the Japanese surrender was solely the result of atomic bombing. And that erroneous belief still persists very widely.

The surrender of the Japanese was brought about by three factors, of which the atomic bomb was only one, and, I am convinced, the least important.

It was the first factor, the military and naval success of United States arms in the Pacific, which brought Japan to her knees physically. This was made possible by the superb teamwork of our sea, land, and air forces. Our victory was physically assured when Japanese forces had been defeated in the Marianas, at Iwo Jima, and on Okinawa, and the Japanaese homeland left stripped of her vital naval protection by the United States Navy's progressive destruction of Japanese air and ship strength from the beginning of our Pacific offensive to our Philippines naval victories. But the Japanese spirit was not yet ready to accept the idea of surrender.

It was the second factor, our psychological offensive, specifically the Japanese broadcasts, which brought the Japanese emotionally and spiritually to their knees—and definitely hastened the implementation of the physical victory we had already won.

The Japanese note delivered August 10 makes this perfectly plain in its statement that "several weeks ago the Japanese Government asked the Soviet Government . . . to render good offices in restoring peace . . ."—that is, several weeks *before* the first atomic bomb was dropped.

The Japanese war, then, had been lost for Japan on the sea and islands of the Pacific, and that loss had been accepted by the Japanese as a fact inseparable from surrender—before the first atomic bomb was dropped. And the culmination had been brought about by our physical victories perfectly complemented by our psychological victory.

Japan would have accepted our surrender terms even without the prodding which the two atomic bombs provided. I am convinced that the dropping of those two bombs did not decide the outcome of historical events in the Pacific. I felt at the time that we should have given Japan a little more time in order to move in answer to the Potsdam Declaration, since the Japanese habitually require time to arrive at decisions. The Potsdam Declaration confirmed the application of the Atlantic Charter to Japan. This provision, as indicated by Dr. Inouye in his reply to me on July 24, was the one on which Japan was really ready to surrender unconditionally.

The atomic bomb, as did the bombing of Pearl Harbor and the bombing of London, could have strengthened instead of destroying morale. One Japanese said: "These bombs might well have decided every Japanese to fight to the last man, woman, and child."

Aside from its stunning and horrifying impact on human imagination and its production of a spectacular war climax, the atomic bomb's effect on the Japanese war was only to hasten, by a very short time, the Japanese expression of a decision already made.

On the night of August 15, 1945, when the air waves were full of the news of Japan's final acceptance of our terms, I was sitting at my radio, listening to the events as they developed with gunfire rapidity. Washington was rejoicing, and so was the whole nation. The radio brought to me exuberant demonstrations from distant cities, and the light evening breeze of the Washington summer carried snatches of the wild merrymaking which had the nation's capital in its grip.

My wife, who sat beside me, noted the apparent impassivity with which I absorbed the world-shaking news.

"You don't seem to be elated," she remarked.

"I am elated," I answered, "but I am also realizing that our real work is just beginning."

Under the impetus of this feeling I began on the following day the work on a comprehensive plan for the effective psychological reorientation of the Japanese mind in order to ensure the peace of the future.

It was gratifying, in the days following the Japanese surrender, to receive the praise of the press and such personal tributes as that offered by Admiral King, who said: "I want to congratulate you on your good work in making the Japanese see the light and bringing surrender." The citation accompanying one of the Legions of Merit which was awarded to me for work during the war more explicitly repeated these same words:

For exceptionally meritorious conduct in the performance of outstanding services to the Government of the United States as spokesman for the United States Government Psychological Warfare Program, from May 8 to August 4, 1945. Undertaking his assignment during a critical period of the war, Captain Zacharias achieved distinctive success in executing this phase of the Psychological Warfare Program against the Japanese Empire. He contributed materially to the reduction of Japanese morale. Administering his responsibilities with care and broad vision, he rendered invaluable service in the initiation, coordination and execution of plans for the basis of the Psychological Warfare Program. His devotion to the completion of a mission vital to the success of the Armed Forces of our country reflects great credit upon Captain Zacharias and the United States Naval Service.

But there persisted in my mind the thought that we had reached, not only the end of the war, but the beginning of something far more important—world-wide determination to secure lasting peace. What was past was only prologue. And I knew that what lay ahead was the great task of turning all the strength and skills we had developed in time of war and for the purposes of war to the purposes of peace.

My conviction is even stronger today.

Epilogue

VISTAS OF THE FUTURE

AMONG OUR great skills in war were those with which I have dealt in this book—the two intellectual forces of intelligence and psychological action. As we face the future, with man's universal hopes focused on peace, we shall be willfully blinding ourselves if we shut our eyes to the fact that these twin skills, so instrumental in effecting victory in war, can be equally instrumental in assuring peace.

A highly effective intelligence organization is an inescapable necessity as a preventive of war. Intelligence anticipates conflict. Only intelligence makes possible a workable, fruitful diplomacy to prevent conflict—the vital function of diplomacy. We must now integrate and build and sharpen our intelligence organization as an implement of peace.

The force of ideas, proven by the success of our psychological warfare in the Mediterranean against the Italians, in the Atlantic against the Germans, and in the Pacific against the Japanese, is now undeniable. And psychological action, like intelligence, and springing from intelligence, far from being solely a weapon of warfare, is a natural means of implementing peace. It is the surest, in fact the only, means of orienting the peoples of conquered nations to the acceptance and understanding of the principles of human existence and government for which we fought.

There is a tendency in the United States today to discount and disband intelligence and psychological action organizations—a national feeling pervading even government and naval and military circles that the usefulness and necessity of such organizations terminates with the termination of hostilities. If that feeling becomes, as it threatens to do at this time, national policy, it may well be fatal.

Shortly after V-J Day, an editorial in the *Washington Post,* entitled "Job in Japan," summed up the accomplishments of the past and the task of the future. It urged that the experience gained through my activities between V-E and V-J Days "should now be turned to account in the task of re-educating the Japanese and uprooting their cult of militarism."

The very idea which the last sentence of the *Post*'s gratifying editorial thus expressed was foremost in my own mind as well. The question before me on the morning after V-J Day was a complex one, but I realized that I had to answer it conclusively and comprehensively, if only to guarantee my own peace of mind.

In the course of my activities as a spokesman of the United States government I have always regarded myself as a "propagandist." The word as I understood it was completely devoid of all sinister meaning. It stood for a constructive activity. The facts I used in my talks could not be denied, questioned, or otherwise challenged. The arguments I voiced were admittedly sound. The theme was: A prolongation of Japanese resistance would merely deepen Japan's doom. Actually, I harbored no ill feeling toward my enemy listeners. I felt with them in their plight and hoped to help them to emerge from it.

In this sense, Admiral King hit the nail on the head with his congratulatory remark. We did succeed "in making the Japs see the light."

But the very sincerity of my efforts now placed an obligation on us as a nation and on me as the government's spokesman. Both in my talks and in the Potsdam Declaration we held out hopes and made definite promises. Personally I was keenly aware of the necessity of keeping these promises if we were to sustain our prestige after victory and also if we were to prevent the Japanese from feeling betrayed and disappointed, two factors conducive to generating discontent and resistance.

But while I thus weighed the moral implications of our activities, I did not fail to view the new situation created by Japan's surrender realistically, in its implication for the future. Were the Japanese really defeated? Were they stripped of all power to prevent them from rising again and confronting us with another problem ten or twenty years hence? Was the peace of the future secured by our victory in August 1945?

Once in 1939 a native authority listed seven elements which gave strength to Japan as an imperialistic power. Now, the morning after V-J Day, two of them, the military power of Japan and her Greater East Asia propaganda, no longer existed. But five elements of the original list continued to lend inherent power to the Japanese even in defeat. They were, and still are today, Japan's demographic strength, the homogeneity of the race, the family system, the imperial throne, and the so-called "Japanese spirit" or national morale. This last named is reinforced by Shintoism (in its non-political variety) ; Zen-Buddhism, which is left untouched although potentially more dangerous than state Shinto; the Confucian O-Yomoi; and the plebian Shiingaku, teaching the veneration of the virtues inherent in the foregoing elements of national strength.

Far from being "spiritually" defeated, Japan's moral situation resembles that of Judea at the time of the Romans when Titus succeeded in reducing the fortress of Jerusalem. Under the influence of these lines of thought, I sat down on the day of surrender, and while the world celebrated the climax of a gigantic war effort as enacted on board the USS *Missouri,* I drew up for the Secretary of the Navy an estimate of the situation and a plan for Japan after surrender.

The plan is still valid today. The peace is going to be won only by reorienting the minds of the Japanese people. The strongest present motivation of the Japanese for any action is their desire for recovery from defeat. They will do anything to make such a recovery. Contrary to their claims and propaganda, the primary cause of their defeat was their abandonment of their traditional ethical code of decency, justice, righteousness, and fair play, and their adoption of a course of aggression, terrorism, and brutality, as well as the might-over-right policy. The war they started by treachery and carried on brutally was far from what they claimed—a holy war. It ended in their defeat since the cause was unjust.

These are the ideas which the reorientation of the Japanese must emphasize. Recovery may again make Japan strong, but the Japanese with a changed mental outlook will no longer represent a menace to the peace of the world.

Japanese history has shown that the best of the tradition and the ethical code to which the Japanese people subscribe are not inconsistent with our own democratic ideas and ideals, although they are expressed in different words. I hoped that these similarities would be pointed out and our democratic ideas inculcated in the people, not as an imposition of something new, but as a further cultivation of the best of their own culture.

Without the good will and co-operation of the defeated adversary, peace, or rather lasting peace, will never be assured. Without their good will, their passive resistance will bring the failure of the peace and the failure will necessitate the continued use of a large armed force within Japan for a protracted period with atttendant disorders and loss of life. What needs to be done was outlined in my memorandum to the Secretary. Our mission is:

1. To promote Japanese adherence to the terms of the Potsdam Declaration.

2. To promote Japanese attitudes and sentiments conducive to the selection and maintenance of a peacefully inclined and responsible government in accordance with the freely expressed will of the Japanese people, by effecting a reorientation of the Japanese mind and by facilitating the penetration of democratic ideas and ideals.

I then suggested the establishment of a Reorientation Unit, specially organized to plan for and co-ordinate the activities of *all* Allied reorientation groups. I proposed that the head of this unit be an American with the designation of High Commissioner. I further suggested that he should function with the rank of ambassador under direct appointment by the President of the United States, and be responsible only to the President.

Then I outlined the functions of this Reorientation Unit, and by recounting those functions here today, for the record, I intend to show how much still remains to be done:

(1) daily supervised commentary on situation and events to clarify the picture for the Japanese;

(2) provision of facilities for the proper reception of such commentaries and announcements (radio receiving sets, public address system, publication distribution, motion picture theaters, etc.);

(3) the guidance of existing public information services;

(4) preparation of the first objective history of Japan; *

(5) preparation and provisions for a free discussion of the Emperor's constitutional position as an organ of state along lines suggested by Professor Minobe (possibly formation of a Japanese Constitutional Society, a scientific group under Allied supervision to stimulate such discussions); †

(6) the organization and promotion of sincerely pro-democratic and pro-American elements within Japan, especially professional, educa-

* On August 20, 1945, the Domei News Agency announced that the Education Ministry sponsors a National History Compilation Board for the obvious purpose of preparing still another official and biased Japanese history. This must be counteracted by sponsoring an objective nonofficial history and giving the finished product wide distribution.

† This was anticipated by the Emperor in his rescript announcing defeat.

tional and other intellectual groups (including student associations, an English teachers' association, utilization of international radio amateurs, members of international correspondence clubs, etc.);

(7) educational preparation for an understanding of democratic principles and processes by a dissemination of information about democratic functions in the United States and Great Britain;

(8) provisions of all kinds of diversions, including popular food, entertainment, vocational retraining, positive group activities, active political participation on a mass basis and on a municipal level, and formation of trade unions, in order to convince the Japanese of the sincerity of our intentions and demonstrate the advantages accruing to them, as well as to prepare them for political action on higher levels;

(9) education in civil liberties and preparation for the ultimate revision of the repressive police system;

(10) socio-psychological preparation for industrial, agricultural, and other economic reforms and reorganizations;

(11) the creation of a proper psychological atmosphere for the handling of war criminals;

(12) education of the Japanese people to the realities and obligations of defeat to prevent recrimination and revenge;

(13) proper preparations for an eventual free press;

(14) discouragement of disturbing and undesirable anarchistic and extremist political movements;

(15) propaganda against militarism and aggression;

(16) complete renovation of the co-operative system;

(17) exploitation and explanation of existing democratic ideas and tendencies in Japanese history and culture, insofar as they are in harmony with our own interpretation and ideas of democracy;

(18) possible co-ordination of Western (Christian) and Japanese ethical principles or alleviation of conflicts arising from differences;

(19) preparation for Japan's eventual admission to the family of nations on an equal social and economic footing, with the complete exclusion of Japanese ideas of militarism, navalism, and expansionism;

(20) elimination of present conception of Japan's racial inferiority and discredit the co-prosperity-sphere propaganda.

Our program of psychological warfare was in a sense an introduction to that reorientation campaign which, I am convinced, can do a far better job along these lines than thousands of soldiers and all our fleet deployed around the islands of the Japanese homeland. In this important sense, our propaganda effort was far from being wasted. On the contrary, it has an immense long-range value, the fruits of which will still be evident ten or twenty years hence.

It is fortunate and gratifying that much of the work suggested in my "Plan for Japan" is being accomplished by General MacArthur. But "no army of occupation can completely transform a society by force," Geoffrey Gorer wrote.

What our occupational authorities are doing today is an attempt to enforce a simulacrum of institutions outlined in a policy program drafted in haste two weeks *after* the surrender of Japan. The effectiveness of this program is guaranteed, not by its inherent practicability, but by the occupying forces and by the absolute impotence of defeated Japan; but because of the very nature of these guarantees, the success of the program can only be temporary. It is distinctly a short-range program, even though we may not now recognize its limitations. The present submissiveness of the Japanese, including the Emperor, must not be accepted as a proof to the contrary. The Japanese are rather slow in reacting to great political provocations. This is revealed by their history. It was only nine years after the event that the Satsuma rebelled against the Meiji Restoration, and ten years after his enforced abdication that Daigo II tried to regain his lost throne by force. When projected against the screen of their history, the present submissiveness and compliance fail even to indicate the definite success of our occupational policy.

What is needed even at this stage of the occupation and rehabilitation is a *specific long-range program* the successful accomplishment of which is not dependent upon the maintenance of an army of occupation in Japan. If no such program is provided at the outset, we will have to prolong the occupation of Japan indefinitely, if only to enforce our policy by armed supervision.

Our problem now as well as our immediate task is to foster a co-operative Japan. The latter can be produced only by the recognition and promotion of those aspects of the Japanese character and traditional institutions sustained by this character which are conducive to co-operation and democracy.

The sooner we can establish a civilian government in Japan which could provide the guarantees which we now perceive only through the maintenance of armed forces in the country, the better for everybody concerned. I feel that Great Britain's recent relations with Egypt show us a method by which this transfer can best be accomplished. In Egypt there exists a dual form of government, one the so-called sovereign government of the country with British advisers aiding the cabinet members, and the other invisible government of the British ambassador, who has a specialist for every need of the government.

We, too, could well establish the system of Allied advisers attached to Japanese government posts, first to supervise the peaceful conduct of its administration, and second to provide guidance along lines desired by us. Parallel with the Japanese government we should establish a high commission of civilian status within Japan, with a high commissioner and his cabinet of commissioners, duplicating the needs of the Japanese government in individual subcommissions. Under this system, the commissioner for security and order should be a military man, the only member of the military left in the administrative system. He should have adequate armed force at his disposal; but with the administrative machinery functioning smoothly, this force could be kept at a minimum.

The question of Japan's international control could also be solved rather easily if and when this system is adopted. While I advocate that the high commissioner be an American, I also suggest that individual commissioners be delegated by the countries which now share with us the military supervision of Japan.

And when in due course the system of commissioners is abolished, we must maintain the system of advisers within the Japanese government. Such a system would be beneficial for all concerned, and I have reason to believe that Japan would welcome such a move.

While the vistas of the future are honeycombed with many uncertainties, I feel that the solution suggested above would enable us to liquidate the Pacific war with as great a success as could be expected under the circumstances.

Of course, the future of Japan is not the only problem which today confronts us, demanding a conclusive solution in the interest of a lasting peace. The role of Japan in the Pacific was duplicated by Germany in Europe. Similarily, a return of Japanese militarism presents problems identical in many ways with those of a return of German militarism. The European picture with Germany as its focal point is necessarily complicated by other conflicting influences, none of which are impossible of solution.

The future security of the world depends on an objective approach to the basic problems and on a most propitious employment of means which in the past proved successful in the elimination of controversial aspects. I have a firm belief in the inherent ability of human nature to face and solve the issues once they are clearly and intelligently presented.

Psychology plays an outstanding role in these problems. It enables us to perceive and understand the characteristics of others with whom we have to deal and then provides the vehicle for mutual understanding so vital to the accomplishment of mankind's basic aim: permanent peace and security.

It is because of these circumstances that I do not regard my mission as terminated.

Appendix

FOURTEEN BROADCASTS TO JAPAN

Number One

Release 8 May 1945

ANNOUNCER: You are about to hear the first of a series of special broadcasts which we have announced previously. Near the end of this broadcast the official spokesman will read to you a declaration by the President of the United States dealing with matters vitally concerned with the destiny of Japan.

And now the official spokesman, Captain Zacharias, United States Navy.

CAPTAIN ZACHARIAS: This is Captain Zacharias of the United States Navy speaking from Washington, D. C.

I am beginning today a series of talks addressed to responsible and thinking Japanese. I propose to convey a message to you which is of the utmost importance to the whole future of Japan and to those who have the welfare of Japan at heart. And I am speaking to you at a time which your own generals and admirals have described as the most critical moment in the long history of your native land.

I have been recalled from the fighting command in the Pacific theater, to come to Washington at this crucial time, first because the collapse of Germany, which the world has now witnessed, spells Japan's inevitable military defeat. Let me emphasize that I am speaking only of Japan's military defeat. I am sufficiently acquainted with your military situation and I am intimately familiar with our own military potentialities to be able to evaluate the military chances of Japan in a scientific and objective way. There is not the slightest doubt that Japan will be defeated definitely and decisively.

Secondly, I was chosen as spokesman to interpret for you the true meaning of events now shaping up, because in twenty years of peace, in Japan as well as here in the city of Washington, I have always acted as a friend of the Japanese people and have done everything in my power to prevent the catastrophe which has already begun to envelop your homeland.

Those among you who know me personally, and there are many in the highest places, will confirm this fact.

Admiral Yonai will recall our many conversations after his return from Russia as a language officer.

Admiral Nomura Kichisaburo will remember my frank discussions, both

399

in Japan when Admiral Nagano often attended, and on his way to Washington to his last official assignment.

Mr. Kurusu will know my regret in the loss of his son whom as a young boy I often patted on the head.

Generals Matsumoto, Washizu, Teramoto, and Hirota will remember my frequent advice.

Likewise Mr. Debuchi, Mr. Wakatsugi, Mr. Horinouchi, and the staff of late Ambassador Saito.

Your Premier Admiral Baron Suzuki may remember our meetings when he was chief of the Naval General Staff. My impression of him was fully confirmed by his recent sympathetic statement regarding our loss in the death of Franklin Delano Roosevelt.

And finally, their Imperial Highnesses Prince and Princess Takamatsu will recall when, as their aide-de-camp, I accompanied them during their tour of two months in the U. S. in 1931.

In the present war, as a naval officer, I have fought against your armed forces. As long as you continue the war it is unavoidable that we remain on opposite sides. In spite of this I am inclined to believe that those of you who have known me personally will trust me. I cannot expect that all of you will have confidence in me or will *want* to believe me. But even those will have an opportunity to examine my facts. They will then not be able to deny that events have borne me out. My arguments, I am confident, will speak for themselves. My devotion to my military duties of today does not prevent me from thinking of the problems of tomorrow.

Let us look at the situation in which you find yourselves today. Your empire in the Pacific has crumbled, the lands which your forces seized in the early days of war have all been either recaptured or cut off from the homeland, and Japan itself is today under direct attack. Your navy has suffered losses which no navy can suffer and yet endure as an effective fighting force. Your land armies have suffered losses in the hundreds of thousands in dead, wounded and missing. And additional hundreds of thousands are waiting helplessly in the cut-off areas for a fate over which neither they, nor you, have any measure of control.

The men who have brought this misfortune upon Japan are repeatedly asking the question: "What will happen to Japan?" They know that everybody in Japan is also asking this question. What answer have they given you?

They tell you that the situation is the most serious in Japan's long history. They say the only choice left the Japanese people is victory or extermination.

I am in a position to guarantee with authority that the desperate phrase "victory or extermination" is a deliberate misrepresentation of fact. You know that Japan's situation is the most serious in all her long history. And I can state categorically that Japan has no chance left for victory. But at the same time I deny most emphatically that your only alternative to victory is extermination.

Now listen carefully, for I am going to read the official message which I have to convey to you.

"STATEMENT BY THE PRESIDENT OF THE UNITED STATES

"Nazi Germany has been defeated.

"The Japanese people have felt the weight of our land, air, and naval attacks. So long as their leaders and the armed forces continue the war, the striking power and intensity of our blows will steadily increase and will bring utter destruction to Japan's industrial production, to its shipping, and to everything that supports its military activity.

"The longer the war lasts, the greater will be the suffering and hardships which the people of Japan will undergo—all in vain. Our blows will not cease until the Japanese military and naval forces lay down their arms in *unconditional surrender*.

(I am still reading from the statement of the President of the United States regarding Japan. The President continues:)

"Just what does the unconditional surrender of the armed forces mean for the Japanese people?

"It means the end of the war.

"It means the termination of the influence of the military leaders who have brought Japan to the present brink of disaster.

"It means provision for the return of soldiers and sailors to their families, their farms, their jobs.

"It means not prolonging the present agony and suffering of the Japanese in the vain hope of victory.

"UNCONDITIONAL SURRENDER DOES NOT MEAN THE EXTERMINATION OR ENSLAVEMENT OF THE JAPANESE PEOPLE."

(That concludes the text of the statement of the President of the United States regarding Japan.)

You can understand from this forthright statement that your true alternatives are as follows:

Either cessation of hostilities with unconditional surrender, and this is the only way left for the preservation of your families, your homes, your economy, and your country.

Or a futile prolongation of resistance which will inevitably result in the needless desolation of your country and destruction surpassing in scale even that in Germany.

Let me assure you again and again that my country is determined to fight this war to its predestined end and I cannot find any who think that our victory will be too hard and too costly to win.

Therefore familiarize yourselves with this thought:

Your future lies in your own hands. You can choose between a wasteful, unclean death for many of your forces, or a peace with honor.

ANNOUNCER: You have just heard the first of a special series of broadcasts by a spokesman of the United States Government, Captain Zacharias.

Please note that in all these broadcasts, the English text is the official version. The Japanese is an unofficial translation.

Number Two

Release 12 May 1945

When I addressed you the last time, I was able to read to you a solemn declaration which the President of the United States has promulgated regarding all the people of Japan. The President's declaration is a document of the highest importance to the whole future of Japan, and also to the future of every Japanese family and individual. Hence, should not any important decision made by you be viewed in the light of this proclamation? It is *imperative* that you ponder the President's declaration and understand its full meaning: In order that you may better familiarize yourselves with its content, I shall now repeat the text of the President's message. . . . [See previous broadcast.]

As you follow the President's words carefully, you will note that his declaration is composed of two distinct parts. First, the President desires to remind you of the fundamental realities of your present military situation. Secondly, the President outlines a program for the future; the only one in fact by which you will be able to restore to Japan the hope for a gainful future. In my next talk I shall comment in detail on this important second point, namely the solution offered to you for what your own leaders have described as the most momentous crisis in the entire history of Japan. Today, I shall devote myself to comments on the first part of the declaration.

(Now) what are the fundamental realities of your present military situation? First, as you know, Japan has already lost the war. Second, the United States is determined to continue the war until no vestige of resistance remains. There is, however, an acceptable course of action for you, and it is your only hope. By discontinuing resistance, you yourselves can save Japan. Compare this alternative with the prospects of continued fighting in a war in which the issue has already been decided against you.

I realize that there are some among you who, however sincere, still shut their eyes to these realities. It is difficult for a Japanese to admit the tragic fact that his own country has lost a war. The acknowledgment of such a fact necessarily encounters many spiritual obstacles. But thinking Japanese are capable of facing facts. This I know from long and intimate personal experience. That is why I am talking to you today.

You will recall expressions of angry protest in the 86th session of the Imperial Diet voiced by such men as Tanaka Mitsugu, who asked, "How can one be sure of Japanese victory after the loss of Iwo Jima?" Tanaka Isōji questioned the efficiency of the High Command. This confirms the suspicions that many facts have been hidden even from those who are in high positions. It is now abundantly clear to thinking Japanese that those who made the estimates three years ago and promised you quick victory over the United States are now trying to conceal the facts in order to hide their own utter failure, the result of which can only be inevitable defeat. The shadows of this defeat are definitely evident in the communiques of your own High Command.

Have you examined these communiques to discover what they really reveal? Do they announce offensives initiated by the Japanese? No! The communiques of your own High Command speak only of attacks which we Americans launched against your forces—these forces which in every case proved inadequate to prevent our victory on Kwajalein, Saipan, Pelelieu, Iwo, and the Ryukyus.

Despite individual heroism, when and where were your forces able, even once during these past three years, to repel any of our attacks and thwart our offensives? Have your forces been able to hold the Marshalls, the Marianas, and the Philippines? Indeed, in what areas did your Navy retain command of the sea? Were the fleets of the United States hampered when they cruised at will off your coast and struck at your very heart—Tokyo, Nagoya, and the Inland Sea?

Regardless of the intensity of the resistance of your forces, the battles invariably ended with the complete victory of our arms. Remember, a lost battle remains forever a lost battle.

And still, in the face of continuing reverses, Vice Admiral Kondo counsels you to have patience. But what has happened while you have been exercising patience? We attacked Hollandia with 200 ships, Saipan with 600 ships, Iwo Jima with 800 ships, Luzon with 1000 ships, and Okinawa with *1400* ships. Thus within the last year we increased the strength of our attack against you seven times. In the same year we landed in Europe and defeated Germany.

Meanwhile, Admiral Kondo and others continued to advise you to exercise patience. Will your patience alone sustain you until, and especially *on* the day when the combined might of thousands of our ships, tens of thousands of our planes, and millions of our men will be poised for attack, awaiting the command "FORWARD"?

Number Three

Release 19 May 1945

In my two previous broadcasts, I read to you a solemn declaration which the President of the United States has promulgated regarding all the people of Japan. In my last broadcast I interpreted for you the first part of the declaration which dealt with Japan's hopeless military situation. Surely it is not necessary for me to review this situation in detail, for all around you it is everywhere in evidence. Daily the full strength of our armed forces moves closer to your homeland. Soon this strength will be augmented by the tremendous forces freed for action in the Pacific by the collapse of your ally, Germany.

Let me read again the full text of the President's declaration....

Today I shall examine the second part of the President's declaration which sets forth in unmistakable language the only course open to Japan to ensure its future as a nation. The course is unconditional surrender, and I can reiterate authoritatively that unconditional surrender is a military term, meaning the cessation of resistance and the yielding of arms. It does not entail enslavement. It does not entail the extermination of the Japanese people.

Now let me ask you this question. How have the words "enslavement" and "extermination" come to be associated with unconditional surrender in the minds of the Japanese people? Only through the desperate utterances of a group of your leaders.

To mention only one, your former Premier, General Koiso, injected the untruth that America plans the extermination of the Japanese people. This was an ignoble device to compel your people to continue a hopeless war. The bankruptcy of Koiso's leadership was recognized in the overthrow of his cabinet.

The desperation of such leaders is understandable. Did they not tell you, after the fall of Nanking, that the China Incident would soon be terminated? Did they not din into your ears the slogan "Sign the axis Alliance!" and plot behind the scenes to plunge your nation into the German war of aggression—a war whose European finale was written with the lives of countless Germans in the smoldering ashes of their principal cities? Did not such leaders as Tojo, Koiso, Shimada, and Yamashita promise you victory in this war? Have they not made countless other unfulfilled promises and commitments?

And now these same desperate leaders, realizing, as all of you do, that hope of victory has vanished forever, say that unconditional surrender means extermination or enslavement.

Their basic war slogan in the past was *victory*. But now it is victory OR EXTERMINATION. Why did they add this second concept? It was born of their present despair. Thereby they have unwittingly confessed to the whole world that Japan is on the road to inevitable defeat.

As you now know, certain leaders of the *Gumbatsu* have been planning the present-day war for many years. Japan has actually been at war since 1931. In making their war plans, these leaders have made two fatal errors. First, they assumed that Japan's ally, Germany, would win her war in Europe, and second, they thought that fighting spirit was a Japanese monopoly. But now Germany has collapsed. And the American fighting spirit is now admitted even by these same Japanese war leaders. Thus, in desperation, they commit *yet another fatal error* when they say Japan's only alternative is *extermination*.

But Japan has other leaders today who know better. They know the slogan "Victory or Extermination" was coined to serve the selfish interests of a few Japanese leaders. They know that in no sense does it serve the interests of Japan.

Let me cite a few more facts—facts which have been admitted in the Imperial Diet by your own former ministers of war and navy. Tens of thousands of Japanese soldiers and civilians live under American rule in Saipan, Tinian, and Okinawa. They are well-fed and contented. They are already rebuilding their homes in the cities of Garapan and Charan-kanoa. The wheels of the sugar mills turn again. The rice paddies are cultivated again.

I regret that men like General Koiso cannot see these people. I was on Saipan. I have talked with these people personally and I know.

Think it over. After all, you can check on these facts for yourself.

Why, then, do you responsible leaders of Japan permit your reckless colleagues systematically to deceive the nation by talks of "Extermination"? Today tens of thousands of Japanese benefit by our policies. When a hundred million cease resistance, why should we change our standards of treatment?

The American tradition of ending wars was reflected in the words of President Lincoln, and you heard them repeated by President Truman:

"With malice toward none ... let us strive ... to do all which may achieve ... a just and lasting peace."

Number Four

Release 26 May 1945

It is difficult at this time to appraise the full impact which the collapse of Germany will have upon Japan. I have no doubt that it will become evident, in all its implications, as the war is intensified against Japan. But the collapse of Germany has rendered Japan one service. Now, for the first time, the Japanese people have the opportunity to evaluate fully for themselves the quality of the political leadership which maneuvered their country into their ill-fated alliance with Germany. The men who advised the highest authority to link the fate of Japan with that of Germany, who schemed to plunge Japan into a hopeless war against the most powerful nations on earth—these men now stand revealed as lacking in judgment and in statesmanship.

Let me recall to your minds the names of some of these men: Field Marshals Hata, Sugiyama, and Terauchi: General Hiroshi Oshima, recently found hiding in southern Germany by the United States Army; Koki Hirota and Toshio Shiratori; Generals Tojo, Koiso, and others. Among these are some who worked secretly for German interests in Japan, and caused Japan to cast her lot with that of Nazi Germany which now has surrendered unconditionally. In Berlin, General Oshima collaborated to bring about the signing of the Tripartite Pact, and made commitments on behalf of the Japanese nation, and, more particularly, although an army general, he made commitments on behalf of the Imperial Japanese Navy.

I realize that this is a serious indictment against a Japanese army officer. But remember, I promised to give you the facts.

As you know, there was a German invasion of Japan. Can it be called by any other name? This German invasion of Japan began with the signing of the pact of 1936. At this time, German military men, propagandists, and so-called professors began to arrive in large numbers. They were sponsored by the pro-Nazi group of Japanese leaders. By 1938, when a *"cultural"* agreement was signed, the pro-Nazi leaders of Japan had made it possible for German influence to be spread throughout most media of public opinion. The *Yomiuri* newspaper, for example, under the leadership of Mr. Shoriki Matsutaro, became completely dominated by the representative of the German propaganda ministry in Tokyo, Mr. Erich Wickert, who had his offices right in the German Embassy. Other newspapers similarly dominated were the *Hochi* and even the *Kokumin,* which, as you undoubtedly know, was close to the Imperial Army.

But this was not enough to satisfy Japan's pro-Nazi leaders. German agents infiltrated Japan's industrial system. The now thoroughly discredited German generalship was represented in your own Imperial Staff meetings by Lieutenant General Eugen Ott, who was not a strategist, but is known to the entire world as one of the key men in the German intelligence service. He was permitted to attend the most secret conferences. Do you know that General Ott's own son was guilty of espionage in Japan, and was arrested in Tokyo? Remember, I promised to give you only facts.

And now more important still, the very councils where policy decisions concerning Japan's relations with other nations are prepared for the highest approval, became contaminated by Nazi influence.

In July of 1940, as a result of pressure by pro-Nazi Japanese leaders, General Hata demanded of the then premier Admiral Yonai that Japan enter into an immediate military alliance with Germany and Italy. Can you visualize the embarrassment of Admiral Yonai, who, only a few weeks before, on April 25 to be exact, had assured the American Embassy that Japan would never be a party to the Tripartite military pact as long as he remained premier? That Admiral Yonai was sincere I know from my personal acquaintance with him.

Admiral Yonai realized that Japan's interests would best be served by avoiding an entangling alliance which he felt would force Japan to depend upon German success in the war. Admiral Yonai was convinced that Germany would be defeated. How right events have proved him to be! He was apprehensive that Japan likewise could not possibly win were she to side with the Axis powers against the Allies. Aware of his responsibilities as premier of Japan, Admiral Yonai refused to yield to pressure. As you will recall, Hata resigned. The refusal of the pro-Nazi group, which controlled the Army's High Command, to designate a new war minister, resulted in the fall of the Yonai cabinet. The military alliance with Germany and Italy was concluded by the succeeding Konoe cabinet. Hata had won a personal victory. But for his personal victory the Japanese nation is still paying a heavy price.

Now Nazi Germany no longer exists, and therefore men like Hata, Sugiyama, Terauchi, Koiso, and Tojo today stand as failures before the Japanese nation, and indeed, before the entire world. You yourselves repudiated the supreme military leadership of this group when you compelled the Tojo and Koiso cabinets to resign. Now Germany's collapse brings the bankruptcy also of the political leadership of the entire group into sharp focus. Although men like Hata, Sugiyama, and Terauchi are still in your midst, can one forget that these men, through their faulty advice and machinations, have brought Japan to the brink of disaster?

Can leaders with an unbroken record of past failures be trusted to guide Japan's future destinies? Is it not time for the leaders who have the best interest of Japan at heart to repudiate these failures and embark on the only course which can save Japan?

This course has been set forth for you in unmistakable language by President Truman in his now famous proclamation. The time is running out, but inspired leadership can still save Japan.

Number Five

Release 2 June 1945

In my last broadcast, I indicated that time is running out for Japan. In accordance with my stated intention to give you only facts, I showed how leaders such as Hata, Sugiyama, Terauchi, Koiso, Tojo, and Shiratori, who advocated an alliance with Nazi Germany, now stand before the Japanese people, and indeed before the entire world, as lacking in judgment and statesmanship. Even on May 18, 1944, Field Marshal Hata predicted that Germany would repel the Anglo-American invasion of Europe and that Germany would emerge victorious from the war. Today, Nazi Germany has collapsed, and with its collapse the poverty of the political leadership of these men has been brought into sharper focus than ever before.

Japan as a nation is faced with a momentous choice. Will Japan continue to follow leaders whose unbroken record of failure has already brought their nation to the brink of disaster? Or will Japan turn to leaders who have the ability and statesmanship, the courage and patriotism to embark on the only course which can save Japan?

I have said that the time is running short. Perhaps this can be illustrated by a personal experience. On 18 April 1942, I was in command of the heavy cruiser *Salt Lake City,* then attached to the United States Forces which was assigned the task of conducting the first bombing raid in history against Japanese military installations on Honshu. I watched a courageous force of only 16 planes take off from the decks of the *Hornet* and wing their way toward Japan. At the time, I knew that *this was just the beginning.* Today powerful attacks by hundreds of heavy bombers and carrier based planes against military objectives in Japan have become routine with our forces in the Pacific.

As you behold these planes over your homeland, you undoubtedly recall a statement made early in 1944, by Admiral Nakamura Ryuzo, who is regarded in Japan as an outstanding strategist. Admiral Nakamura predicted with finality that no American planes could ever raid Japan effectively, certainly not for the following two or three years. Contrast this with the prediction made in June 1944, by U. S. Vice Admiral Fitch, Deputy Chief of Naval Operations for Air, who said that what Japan was feeling at that time was only a gentle zephyr in comparison with the typhoon which would soon hit Japan. And General Doolittle, who personally led that first group of 16 planes, has announced that 2000 heavy bombers will raid Japan each day, before very long.

Once Reichsmarschall Goering of Germany made a prediction strikingly similar to that of Admiral Nakamura, and I may add, it was equally inaccurate. He promised that no Allied aircraft would violate what he called the sacred soil of the Reich. In April and May 1941, shortly after Goering's prediction was made, a Japanese military mission headed by General Yamashita and Admiral Nomura, Naokuni, visited the production centers of German military strength. On April 14-17, they inspected the Junker aircraft factories at Leipzig; on April 28 to May 3, they inspected the famous Messerschmitt plant in Augsburg; on April 21-23, they visited the Carl Zeiss precision instrument works in Jena; they visited Stuttgart, Dessau, Risenach, Kassel, Mainz, and Branschweig—but if they were to return today, they would find only piles of ashes where once stood the factories which were the backbone of production for the German war machine. These industrial centers no longer exist.

The Germany, once visualized by *her* leaders as a Reich which would endure a thousand years, has, in fact, been set *back* a thousand years.

This was the work of air power! Now let us consider for a moment the question of land power.

While the bulk of our forces were engaged in defeating what was once the greatest land army the world has ever seen, namely, the German Army, only three armies were available for the Pacific theater of operations. In spite of this limitation, forces of the United States carried the Pacific war to your very doorstep. Now the tremendous and victorious force which defeated Germany has become available for the one remaining task—the defeat of Japan. Even while I am talking to you, hundreds of ships are transporting these armies for redeployment in the Pacific.

It is not boasting when I say that this war has made us past masters in overseas operations on an unprecedented scale. Remember that the Allied navies transported these troops across the Atlantic in the face of determined opposition by powerful German submarine fleets. We have already demonstrated the capacity of the United States Navy to move men and war materials in the Pacific wherever needed. Everything is moving according to schedule. American military authorities have already set up the time table for the shipment of millions of American soldiers to Asia between May and January.

To the troop ships which in the past were adequate to move our armies around the globe, we have *now* added 400 cargo vessels, and without interruption, more are coming off the ways each day.

Despite these facts, General Minami stated nervously a few days ago that the unconditional surrender of Germany was of no concern to Japan. You know, and I know, that General Minami made this statement not as a military expert, but as a propagandist. But, were he to speak as a true military leader, he would say what I am saying, and what all military experts throughout the world are saying, that time is, indeed, running out for Japan.

Number Six

Release 9 June 1945

It is now nearly fourteen years since the first Japanese armies invaded Manchuria, and since that day your country has been engaged intermittently in needless, wasteful, and costly war. I will not dwell on the frightful cost Japan has had to pay during these fourteen years. It is written in the vacancies in countless family councils throughout your homeland, in the vanished savings of your people, and in the destruction of a great part of those material and spiritual factors which went to make Japan a great nation in days of peace. And as long as the war lasts, the cost will relentlessly increase.

While they still believed there was hope of victory, no cost was too high for the Japanese people to pay. The courage of the Japanese people has been tested in battle, their ability to endure hardships has been shown during the countless floods, fires, and earthquakes which have ravaged the homeland of Japan, and their strength and determination has been shown in their emergence from feudalism to the status of a world power in less than one hundred years. I have lived long among you and I know well these characteristics of the Japanese people.

But today, the hope of victory for Japan has vanished. I do not ask you to take my word for this statement, although everywhere about you there is evidence to prove its truth. Instead, let me remind you that the highest authority in your country, on 8 December 1943, wisely disclosed to the Japanese people that the future of the war situation permitted absolutely no optimism whatsoever. This was eighteen months ago.

Recently, Foreign Minister Togo invited free and frank presentation of constructive ideas which might aid Japan in the present crisis. In answer to Foreign Minister Togo's invitation to speak freely and frankly, an outstanding Japanese expert on foreign affairs, Mr. Jiro Taguchi, prepared a report in which he surveyed the war situation and drew the lessons for Japan from Germany's collapse.

Mr. Taguchi solemnly warned that the outcome of modern war is determined not so much by personal courage as by industrial superiority. How true! Even Saigo Takamori knew that his troops, no matter how loyal and brave, were no match for Government troops armed with the most modern inventions of military science of the day. Saigo said: "The bow and arrow and the sword of my soldiers cannot compete with the rifle of the soldiers from the north." And, as you well know, events proved him to be correct.

Mr. Taguchi placed special emphasis on a fatal German miscalculation. The Germans deluded themselves with the thought that the Allies did not have sufficient fighting spirit to win the victory. Do not these words have a familiar ring? Have you not heard leaders among you say that the United States does not have the spiritual strength to wage war to its predestined end? Mr. Taguchi described this fatal miscalculation of the Germans as the result of basing strategy upon imaginary ideas which have no foundation in reality. Has not the strategy of Japan been built upon a similar, nay, an identical basis?

In 1943, after the battle of Stalingrad, Mr. Taguchi said, Germany's leaders realized the war was irretrievably lost. From that time on, these German leaders desperately prolonged the war to buy time for themselves with the lives of their people. In Mr. Taguchi's own words, and I quote: "Instead of meeting the changed situation with political wisdom, instead of considering the future interests of the nation, they took, and intensified, oppressive measures." To these warning words of Mr. Taguchi, I only hope that the Minister of Justice, Mr. Matsuzaka, and the Procurator General, Mr. Nakano, are listening. I repeat, I hope Mr. Matsuzaka and Mr. Nakano are listening.

The outstanding lesson which clear-sighted men like Mr. Taguchi learned from Germany's defeat was this: the continuation of a hopeless war not only failed to help Germany but compromised the entire future of that country. Mr. Taguchi said that the cost was immense: German cities were destroyed; the middle class disappeared; securities were turned into waste paper; and in the very words of Jiro Taguchi: "Everybody lost everything. The German nation lost its sovereignty."

Jiro Taguchi is a patriotic Japanese. As a patriot, he felt it his duty to respond to the request of Foreign Minister Togo by speaking frankly. What is past is prologue, and what has applied to Germany will apply to Japan. But, as I have told you in previous broadcasts, there is still a way out for Japan, although the time is indeed running short.

Many of you today are asking the fateful question: "Where is there hope for Japan?" The answer has been given you by President Truman. In a special proclamation the President set forth unconditional surrender as the only way out for Japan and defined, once and for all, the meaning of that term. I will now repeat the President's words:

"Unconditional surrender means the end of the war.

"It means the termination of the influence of the military leaders who have brought Japan to the present brink of disaster.

"It means provision for the return of soldiers and sailors to their families, their farms, their jobs.

"It means not prolonging the present agony and suffering of the Japanese in the vain hope of victory.

"UNCONDITIONAL SURRENDER DOES NOT MEAN THE EXTERMINATION OR ENSLAVEMENT OF THE JAPANESE PEOPLE."

Number Seven

Release 16 June 1945

It has recently come to my attention that Rear Admiral Yokoyama Ichiro was detached from duty as senior adjutant of the Navy Ministry, ending a term in office that lasted for more than 20 months.

I was particularly interested to hear about Admiral Yokoyama. In happier days now long past, when my country and Japan lived together in peace, close friendship existed with the then Lieutenant Commander Yokoyama. This friendship began more than a decade ago, here in the city of Washington where Yokoyama was on duty as issistant naval attaché.

If Yokoyama Ichiro would now turn back the leaves of his diary, he would find an entry, dated October 25, 1933, which would remind him of an important episode during his stay in the United States.

It was toward the end of his first term in Washington. Commander Yokoyama was disturbed over the future relations of his country with the United States. Perhaps he knew of the preparations for war already being made in Tokyo under the influence of irresponsible leaders. Perhaps he sensed that conflict with the United States could, under no circumstances, end favorably for Japan.

Commander Yokoyama was about to return to Tokyo. Before he left, however, he wanted to talk with me about the current situation so that he could clarify the issues and dispel the doubts which troubled him. I was then stationed at the Naval War College in Newport. On that day, the 25th of October 1933, he traveled 350 miles for the sole purpose of having a conversation with me.

I need not go into the details of that conversation, but when I now recall them myself, I would like to feel that it was not as useless as subsequent events would indicate.

That was our last meeting. The next I heard of Yokoyama Ischiro, he was back in the United States, after staff work in Tokyo and with the China Fleet. By then, 1940, he was a captain. The outbreak of the war in the Pacific found him here in Washington as naval attaché, while I was at sea, in command of the heavy cruiser, *Salt Lake City.* I wondered how he viewed the course on which his country had embarked. I felt that he was dubious of the wisdom of the men who advised Japan to plunge into a war against the United States.

He must have been dubious! After all, he had seen with his own eyes the immense power of the United States and knew even better the true state of Japan. Ship for ship, gun for gun, and shell for shell, Japan might have been superior during these early months of the war. But Yokoyama traveled extensively in the United States, and must have known that these initial advantages favoring Japan would soon be eliminated by America's superior industrial and military potential.

Now comes the announcement that Rear Admiral Yokoyama has been replaced by Captain Imamura. I wonder why he had to go! I know that a great number of Japanese admirals lost their lives in the sinking of many Japanese warships. It is, therefore, probable that Yokoyama was needed at sea. Or, is it possible that he was forced out of the Navy Ministry because he advised a course of action which *some* of his colleagues did not like?

Knowing the United States intimately and well-versed in the technical problems of a navy, by now he must have reached the conclusion that a continuation of the war could only result in further detriment of Japan. He must have reached this conclusion by watching the fate of the Combined Fleet during these 20 months of service in the Navy Ministry. In two decisive battles, the Japanese Navy lost most of its battleships, cruisers, and aircraft carriers; its destroyer strength was almost wiped out by our surface and air forces, and, of course, by our intrepid submarines. After Yokoyama's appointment to the Navy Ministry on October 6, 1943, the United States Pacific Fleet penetrated into the Central Pacific, recaptured the Gilberts, conquered the Marshalls and the Marianas, liberated the Philippines, conquered Iwo Jima and Okinawa, and now anchors but 320 miles due south of Kyushu. As Rear Admiral Yokoyama leaves his post, he will readily admit that Japan's present war situation is far different from that of October 1943.

Is it possible that his knowledge as an expert in American affairs was not sought by his superiors? Or was his advice left unheeded? Or was he intimidated and forced to conceal his knowledge and convictions from his fellow officers? Or was he perhaps sacrificed to influences outside the Imperial Navy?

If today Yokoyama Ichiro could visit me again, I would advise him to read carefully the proclamation issued by President Truman and to take to heart these words of the President:

"The Japanese people have felt the weight of our land, air, and naval attacks. So long as their leaders and the armed forces continue the war, the striking power and intensity of our blows will steadily increase and will bring utter destruction to Japan's industrial production, to its shipping, and to everything that supports its military activity.

"The longer the war lasts, the greater will be the suffering and hardships which the people of Japan will undergo—all in vain. Our blows will not cease until the Japanese military and naval forces lay down their arms in *unconditional surrender."*

Here then is the course which men like Yokoyama Ichiro must now advocate if they have the interest of their country at heart and want to save Japan.

Number Eight

Released immediately after the fall of Okinawa 23 June 1945

The battle of Okinawa is ended. The first Japanese prefecture has fallen. This event is a milestone in the Pacific war. With this latest victory, the American forces have gained and firmly established a major base only one hour's flying time from Kyushu. The fall of Okinawa is so momentous that I would like to review its lessons in a special broadcast today.

You will remember the words of your own premier Admiral Suzuki, who stated that the outcome of the battle of Okinawa will decide the future of Japan. Although this may be an over-statement, the battle has indeed led to a *decisive* deterioration in the military position of your country. Okinawa was no South Sea island, hastily colonized by the South Seas Development Company. Okinawa was a fortress, garrisoned by tens of thousands of Japan's best fighting men, with positions of unprecedented strength and of immense defensive power. Okinawa *was* Japan. Every inch of its soil, its hills and valleys, and its waters were known in minute detail to the Japanese High Command, which therefore could base its military preparations on exact and full information.

Our forces, on the other hand, had to overcome serious handicaps. Against the strongest fortifications you could build, our forces fought in open terrain and on battlefields of your own choosing. The tactical situation was therefore as favorable to the Japanese armed forces as any which will occur in the future. Your forces made determined efforts—yes, *desperate* efforts—to defeat us at sea, in the air, and on land. The remnants of the Japanese Navy sortied. Your air force was in continuous attack. And the Japanese Army fought with the utmost resolution and stubbornness.

But what was the result of all these efforts and sacrifices? As predicted by President Truman in his famous proclamation, *they were all in vain.* We sank the last big modern battleship, the *Yamato.* We annihilated every single one of the *hundreds* of your special attack boats, on which you counted so heavily. We destroyed nearly 4000 Japanese planes. Their pilots suffered a death which, from the military point of view, was totally useless. The greater part of these 4000 planes, spent so recklessly, came from the precious reserve set aside for the defense of your main islands. We annihilated major units of the Japanese Army which were entrusted with the responsibility of defending Okinawa and other Ryukyu islands. Their combined spiritual and material strength was no match for our superior spiritual and material power.

During this campaign, the American forces, too, suffered losses. This is inevitable in war. But you paid an enormous price for your resistance—a resistance destined from the start to end in your defeat. Every American commander fights with the intention of keeping our losses at a minimum. In

America, we do not think that we serve the future of our country by the reckless expenditure of our best youth. You may be assured that the American High Command and the American public are well satisfied that the war against Japan is being successfully conducted along these lines. This is one reason why our power in the Pacific has continued to increase, while your defensive power is being wasted at an accelerated pace.

The battle of Okinawa reveals that your thorough preparations over a long period, the best efforts of your picked troops, and shortened supply lines to Kyushu and Honshu could not affect the outcome of this decisive battle. At Okinawa, the United States forces have again reached their chosen objective. In many ways the Okinawa campaign resembles the Solomons campaign. Guadalcanal was essential. It represented the furthermost point of Japanese advance. It had to be held at all costs if Japan were to continue her *offensive*. Okinawa had to be held at all costs if Japan were to be successful in her *defense*. In Guadalcanal, the Japanese Navy was subjected to attrition from which it never recovered. In Okinawa it was the Japanese Air Force which was sacrificed in vain. So future historians will say that while in Guadalcanal Japan *lost* the war, in Okinawa the United States *won* it.

Can any thinking Japanese sincerely believe that the pattern and outcome of future operations will be different? At the end of this battle, we have won territory of paramount strategic importance; our naval, air, and land forces have pushed open the very door of Japan. These, then, are the true lessons of Okinawa. They must be made as clear to you as they are to the rest of the world. Will you follow the example of the defeated German leaders and allow deceptive arguments and wishful thinking to destroy your country, now that it is evident that the war is irretrievably lost for Japan? Will true Japanese patriots allow this to come to pass?

At this crucial moment in Japanese history, the Honorable James Forrestal, Secretary of the Navy of the United States, has authorized me to read to you the following special statement. I quote:

"The Okinawa campaign has been successfully concluded. The occupation of Okinawa opens a new phase in the war against Japan. I should like to believe that there is reason left in the Japanese people, and that by now they realize the futility of further resistance. But whether or not much reason exists, we are prepared to fight this war to a definite and successful conclusion.

"I can find no American who feels that in this war, forced upon us by reckless and ill-advised Japanese leaders, the task will be too great or the cost too high to ensure final victory and a future free from further threats. Our careful planning has taken into consideration the possibility that the Japanese will fight with tenacity and fury as our *full* power is brought to bear against their homeland. We have seen evidence of that fury at Iwo Jima and Okinawa, and it has been overcome. In the same manner, we shall reduce the Japanese military power wherever necessary. We shall, in short, secure the unalterable objective which I know to be the will of this country, namely, the unconditional surrender of Japan and the liquidation of Japanese militarism."

Number Nine

Release 30 June 1945

The relentless advance of our armed forces has carried us to the very doorstep of Japan. Now thinking Japanese are asking, How is it that the American forces have succeeded in piercing our chain of island defenses? How is it that there appears to be no defense against American air raids? How is it that the American Navy is able to cruise freely in the coastal waters of the Japanese home islands? What does the future hold for Japan?

The Japanese nation has a right to expect answers to these questions. The laws governing the relationship between rulers and subjects, as set forth by the Ancient Sages, state very clearly the duties and responsibilities of the people with respect to those who govern them. But they also state clearly the responsibilities and duties of the rulers to the subjects. It is the duty of the rulers to provide answers to questions affecting the national welfare, especially at a time when the future of the nation hangs in precarious balance.

It is the regular procedure in every army and navy to analyze the causes of victory or defeat. I assume that your High Command, too, ordered investigations of the defeats which your forces suffered in the Gilberts, Marshalls, Solomons, and Marianas, and to determine the reasons why you could not defend Tarawa, Saipan, or Peleliu.

I am sure that, on the basis of such investigations, highly placed staff officers made suggestions to improve the defense of other Japanese bastions. I am also sure that these suggestions contained excellent professional advice. But were they effective in the defense of the Philippines? Did they prevent us from capturing Iwo Jima? Did they save Okinawa? Did they prevent the sinking of the *Yamato,* your proudest battleship? The fact that our forces now operate in the waters of the Japanese homeland is perhaps the most convincing proof that no matter how much a lost battle may be analyzed and investigated it remains forever a lost battle. The tide of war in the Pacific can no longer be changed. The pattern of this war conforms to the process once described by a famous European philosopher as "the inevitability of gradual change," for gradually and inevitably it is moving to its predestined end—the total defeat of Japan.

If I had been given the assignment to investigate the causes of Japanese defeats, I would have written but one sentence. In fact, to explain the causes of the Japanese reverses I would have written but two words, namely: *War Potential.*

For military men on the higher echelons I hardly need to explain the meaning of this term. It was coined by French military experts and came to be accepted by all students of military science everywhere in the world, including Japan. It is the sum-total of all the forces, material and spiritual, which together make up the war-making capacity of a country. The men who coined the phrase also added that War Potential is not an absolute but a relative term. It must be considered in relation to the war potential of the enemy.

But before I discuss the relation between the American and Japanese war potentials, I would like to read to you just one sentence from President Truman's famous proclamation (quote):

"So long as Japan's leaders and the armed forces continue to war," the President said, "the striking power and intensity of our blows will steadily increase and will bring utter destruction to Japan's industrial production, to its shipping, and to everything that supports its military activity" (unquote).

Now, why did the President of the United States make this statement? He made it because he knew that this country is spiritually determined to continue the war to its successful conclusion and is materially able to support its armed forces until victory is won.

I need not cite American sources to prove this vital point. Your own leaders, men in responsible positions who have access to the most secret information, have revealed that they themselves regard the Japanese war potential as far inferior to that of the United States.

When in 1937, Japan, already at war with China, produced 5.6 million tons of steel of which the guns and ships and shells are made, the United States, still deep in peace, produced ten times as much, or over 50 million tons. And no matter how Japanese industry tried, it could not improve upon this ratio in the course of the war. Similar figures could be duplicated in every field of industrial production.

These figures concern quantity. But what about the qualitative difference between our two war potentials? Here again I depend on Japanese authorities to prove that qualitatively as well, your war potential is no match for that of the United States.

I am sure that you will accept Lieutenant General Katsuzo Kosuda as one such authority. For many years, General Kosuda was head of the Japanese Ordnance Administration and one of the men who prepared Japan for war. In January 1944, however, General Kosuda had cause to complain that, and I quote, "As regards war materials, it is not so much that the raw materials are poor as that the general standard of the finished product is regrettably low." General Kosuda added in conclusion, "The main reason for this is the immaturity of Japanese manufacturing technique" (unquote).

A year and a half ago, when General Kosuda made this statement, a Munitions Superintendence Department was created to remedy the situation. Today you may ask, how effective has this organization been?

On 21 May 1945, a well qualified Japanese economic expert surveyed the accomplishments of this agency and wrote (quote), "A year and a half old, the Munitions Superintendence Department has proved incapable of shouldering the heavy responsibility thrust upon it and is, therefore, a target of justifiable criticism for impotency in production" (unquote).

As in every phase of the Japanese war effort, here, too, one may only say: the time is running out for Japan. Whatever is being done now, whatever can still be done, can be described only as too little and too late! In view of this undeniable fact, one would do well to remember the words of President Truman when he said (quote):

"The longer the war lasts, the greater will be the suffering and hardships which you will undergo—all in vain!"

Number Ten

Release 7 July 1945

The recent extraordinary session of the Imperial Diet attracted the attention of the entire world, because it was highlighted by the speech of the Premier, Admiral Suzuki, in which he described the situation of Japan with the bluntness of the professional soldier. Admiral Suzuki made no promise of an end to the misery now being experienced by the Japanese people. He made no promise of victory, he made no explanation for past defeats, and made no attempt to alleviate the funereal tone of his speech with a note of optimism.

Instead, Admiral Suzuki made a number of frank admissions about the war situation. He admitted that, despite the efforts made by the whole Japanese nation, the war situation is gradually becoming more acute for the Japanese homeland. He emphasized the probability of an American landing in the Japanese home islands and predicted flatly that American air raids would increase in frequency and destructive power. He also warned that in the critical hours to come, there will be serious shortages of food and transportation and, most important of all, increasing difficulties in the manufacture of munitions.

Yet from these facts Admiral Suzuki drew the illogical conclusion that Japan's only alternative is to fight to the last. Time and again, throughout his sombre address, he repeated this tragically erroneous conclusion.

I would be doing the intelligence of Admiral Suzuki an injustice were I to suppose for one moment that he really believes Japan's only alternative is to fight to the last. Why, then, was this dangerous conclusion repeated over and again in an otherwise reasoned and objective analysis of Japan's present war situation? Was it because of pressure from that group which, despite the fact that its political and military leadership has been largely discredited, still clings to positions of power and influence? Or was it because the even more thoroughly discredited group of permanent advisers in various ministries— the same permanent advisers who predicted that Germany would win the European war—have convinced Admiral Suzuki that America is weary of war and will not pay the cost of victory if Japan should fight to the last? Such an idea is too fantastic even to merit comment.

I would like to think that this last reason, bad advice, rather than a yielding to pressure, explains Admiral Suzuki's misrepresentation of the unconditional surrender peace formula. Brave men do not yield to pressure from selfish groups, and Admiral Suzuki is a brave man. I need not recall his conduct on 26 February 1936 when pistol-waving assassins from the ranks of young Army extremists broke into his home and harangued him at length in an attempt to bring him around to their point of view. The Admiral listened patiently until the flow of nonsense was finished and then unhesitatingly ordered his attackers to shoot. I do not see any reason to suppose that the character of Admiral Suzuki is any different today than it was in 1936.

I have already referred to a significant sentence in Admiral Suzuki's address which I would now like to quote fully. He said: "The war situation is gradually becoming more acute," and he added, "despite the efforts made by the whole nation." I repeat Admiral Suzuki's words: *"Despite the efforts made by the whole nation."*

What more can the people of Japan do to surpass their present efforts? When the Tojo and Koiso cabinets failed, the Suzuki cabinet was appointed —but was it appointed merely to continue the makeshift efforts of its predecessors, born in desperation and doomed to failure?

No!! Makeshift efforts will not save Japan. I would be doing Admiral Suzuki a grave injustice were I to suppose that his emphasis on Japan's fighting to the last is an attempt to influence the stated objectives of the United States in this war—an effort to extract from us concessions, or to modify our unconditional surrender peace formula. At a time when the issue of the war is so clearly visible, and when it is inescapably clear that prolongation of resistance can only result in the destruction of Japan, only the youngest novice in the Foreign Office would entertain for one minute the possibility that this transparent ruse could possibly achieve any effect. And Admiral Suzuki is hardly a novice in statesmanship.

In a humanitarian gesture reflecting American tradition, President Truman explained the meaning of our peace formula for Japan. Far from meaning the destruction or enslavement of the Japanese people, the formula assures the future of Japan through "the return of soldiers and sailors to their families, their farms, their jobs." These, I am sure, you will recognize as the President's own words. I know that unconditional surrender is a technical term which refers to *the form in which hostilities are terminated.* On the other hand, you know that the exact conditions of the *peace* are something to be settled in the future.

Japan must make the next move.

This move must be patterned after that of Hideyoshi who, on his deathbed, decided to draw the only logical and honorable conclusion from the events of the Korean campaign and to recall his troops from abroad. He said, and I quote: "I will not permit my great army to become ghosts to haunt foreign lands."

Admiral Suzuki's speech clearly revealed his awareness of the extreme urgency of the situation. He stated, and I quote: "The time has arrived when all our 100,000,000 people must look at the situation objectively." Unfortunately, however, Admiral Suzuki's address, delivered at Japan's hour of decision, did not contain the only logical conclusion which the military situation of Japan demands. And I am sure it did not contain the words which Japan awaited. The Japanese in their realism will appreciate the futility of lecturing on navigation when the ship is going down.

The crisis now facing Japan may not be of Admiral Suzuki's making. He may not be responsible for the past, but as premier, Admiral Suzuki is certainly responsible for the future of Japan.

Japan must make her choice without delay, for reasons which Admiral Suzuki knows. I have told you before that the time is running out for Japan. You *must* move and move quickly. Tomorrow, it may be too late.

Admiral Suzuki, the fate of Japan is in your hands!

Number Eleven

Release 14 July 1945

Today I would like to turn back the pages of Japanese history. Fifty years ago Japan was at war with China. On January 25, 1895, when the issue was no longer in doubt, Admiral Ito decided to address himself personally to the leaders of China. In a letter to the Chinese Admiral Ting, he wrote, and I quote: "Changing events have caused Your Excellency and ourselves to be upon sides which oppose each other as enemies. This is indeed very unfortunate. But warfare today is between states and does not necessarily mean enmity between individuals. It follows, therefore, that the feeling between Your Excellency and ourselves is as sincere now as in the past. On such a basis, would we be writing this letter merely to importune an admiral to surrender?" (end quote).

These are remarkable words indeed, especially in time of war. If today I were to write a similar note, it would have to be to Admiral Suzuki, and I could hardly formulate the thoughts with greater eloquence and clarity. Neither could I set forth more succinctly "the high motive" which Admiral Ito described in the following statement. I quote: "Take the case of a man who has the ability to see what is most truly conducive to the good of his country and himself. In spite of this, the stress of circumstances keeps him from getting a true picture of what is going on and he becomes confused. Would not then a sincere friend urge him to consider things calmly?"

Admiral Ito concluded: "It is a tradition with the officers of your armed forces to answer communications from an opponent with a pride designed to show consciousness of strength or to conceal weakness, and thereby to consider that they have fulfilled their duty. But we hope that Your Excellency will understand that the present communication is motivated by the truest feelings of sincerity, as well as by due consideration for everything concerned. We beg Your Excellency to take this under consideration."

Whatever the circumstances under which the letter was written, here then is a precedent created by Japanese leaders. But even this precedent was patterned after similar experience in Japan's own historical past. In 1877 Prince Arisugawa, the commander in chief of the forces opposing the rebels of Satsuma, issued a proclamation in which he called on the men of Saigo Takanori—*to surrender.*

The Satsuma men were fortunate indeed to be led by a man whose patriotism was fervent, and whose motives were selfless.

Even on 5 August 1877, Saigo fully recognized the seriousness of his army's plight when in a letter to his troops he wrote, and I quote: "The war has already been carried on for half a year due to the devoted efforts of all our troops. At a time when victory seems almost within reach, our fighting strength has waned, and we are now in a state of great distress from which there seems to be no escape. However, in the number of troops and fighting spirit our forces are not inferior to those of our opponents. In spite of this, the present crisis which is facing us is something which I regret most deeply.

The enemy will certainly take advantage of our situation and crush us" (end quote).

Despite this clear appraisal of the war situation, Saigo still failed to draw the logical conclusion. He urged his troops to continue what he himself described as a hopeless struggle. *But less than two weeks later,* Saigo summoned the courage to face the inescapable realities of the war. On 18 August 1877, a Council of War was held. The unanimous decision was reached that a continuation of the war was hopeless and consequently the mass of the army was advised to lay down its arms.

Only five days later the forces under Saigo's command surrendered *unconditionally—only five days later,* Satsuma was saved to become the most prosperous province of Japan. With this sound decision, Saigo helped his province and clan to far greater prosperity than he could ever have done by continuing the lost war.

By now it should be apparent to all that a refusal to heed the lessons of history will lead to the *total destruction of Japan.* Nevertheless, the people of Japan are being forced to remain in the present war by malicious distortion of fact. I have in mind, of course, the deliberate and systematic misrepresentation of *our* peace formula.

The question is of such crucial importance to Japan that there must remain no vestige of misunderstanding about it.

It was not the United States who injected the idea and formula of unconditional surrender into the present war.

It was Japan who first proclaimed unconditional surrender as the war aim of Japan.

It was your own General Yamashita who first introduced the unconditional surrender formula in Singapore, on 16 February 1942. On that day when his opponent asked to discuss conditions, Yamashita abruptly and rudely exclaimed, "All I want to hear from you is 'yes' or 'no.' "

Again, it was your General Homma, who on 7 May 1942, applied the idea and formula of unconditional surrender to the mere handful of American and Filipino defenders in the Philippines.

In the hands of Yamashita and Homma, unconditional surrender was an instrument for imposing submission and humiliation. *No such motive prompts the American peace formula.*

In American hands the formula is a humanitarian gesture of great constructive value.

No show of strength can conceal the true weakness of Japan, and, above all, no delay can serve her interests. If Admiral Suzuki sincerely aspires to discharge his duties to his nation as Saigo did to his clan, he must proclaim to his countrymen the injunction which the great Satsuma leader used on that memorable day, 18 August 1877, when he said that the army should lay down its arms, as a continuation of the war was hopeless.

And now, turning again from the past to the future, let me leave you with this thought: Will there ever be a more propitious moment than today for you to *initiate such inspired statesmanship?*

Number Twelve

Release 21 July 1945

In several of my previous talks I devoted myself to our unconditional surrender peace formula; today, I propose to review some of the salient points which I have already presented:

First, your present war situation is clear: You are facing inevitable defeat. Japan has *already* lost the war. Your progressive defeats and our progressive victories have brought the war to Japan's very doorstep.

Second, this situation is the result of the short-sighted and irresponsible leadership of Japan before and during this war.

Third, Japanese leaders have told the Japanese people that their present alternatives are victory or extermination. But President Truman has made it perfectly clear that this is a gross misrepresentation.

Fourth, it is an undisputed fact that our unconditional surrender peace formula is the only way by which you can make possible the salvation of Japan.

Fifth, Japan entered into a reckless alliance with Nazi Germany against the advice of able leaders. That this was a fatal error is now entirely clear. Nazi Germany has been utterly defeated.

Sixth, Premier Suzuki, like all Japanese leaders, now admits that Japan is facing the greatest crisis in her long history. Japan's greatest need at this crucial hour is for *loyal, intelligent,* and *inspired* leadership.

Seventh, Japan's war potential is hopelessly inadequate. On the other hand, the American war potential is more than sufficient to crush Japan's war machine.

Eighth, Japanese history reveals a traditional pattern of realism when the Japanese were confronted with even less hopeless war situations. Japanese armies have surrendered in the past.

Ninth, the American unconditional surrender peace formula is a humanitarian gesture of great constructive value.

These, then, are some of the chief points which I have discussed in detail in recent talks. I am sincerely convinced that the time has arrived when Japanese leaders should face these facts realistically and eliminate the shallow emotionalism which has influenced their actions in the past.

An objective analysis of the unconditional surrender peace formula must begin with a study of historical precedents and legal arguments. Surrender is a time-honored formula by which hostilities are terminated. It is established in International Law and in the Articles of War. It is well known to all belligerents, including, of course, the Japanese High Command. It is Chapter 4, Article 35 of the Hague convention which was signed *and ratified* by the highest authority of Japan.

And insofar as the history of its application is concerned, those Japanese leaders who are sincerely interested in terminating the war with honor would do well to study the *American* precedents. Historically, the honorable surrender of General Lee to General Grant in 1865 provides a most important example. If Japan should initiate the cessation of hostilities without further delay, it may be assumed that it will be the United States which will enforce the formula and ensure the peace.

As you know, the Atlantic Charter and the Cairo Declaration are the sources of *our* policy, and both begin with the categorical statement that we seek no territorial aggrandizement in *our* war against Japan. Are the leaders of Japan really so short-sighted that they cannot see the possible complications which they may have to face if they fail to act, and act promptly?

The leaders of Japan have been entrusted with the salvation and not the *destruction* of Japan. As I have said before, the Japanese leaders face two alternatives. One is the virtual destruction of Japan followed by a dictated peace. The other is unconditional surrender with its attendant benefits as laid down by the Atlantic Charter.

Of these two alternatives, unconditional surrender is the only one which can bring about peace and prosperity for Japan.

The responsibility of Japanese leaders is now a dual responsibility. First, you are responsible to your own people for the future of Japan. And secondly, we will hold you responsible for criminal prolongation of a war, already lost. Can you possibly believe that by prolonging the war, and thereby imposing added sacrifices on our nation, we shall become more *lenient* toward you in the end? Let me remind you once more that there are no Americans who feel that the task is too great or the cost too high to ensure *complete victory.*

At present there are still some influential people in the United States who would not like to see the destruction of Japan. But our patience, too, has its limits, and it is rapidly running out. Your continued refusal to heed the sound and sober advice of counselors will convince even the greatest humanitarian among us that the destruction of everything which supports the Japanese war potential is the only way to terminate the war.

Your opportunity to think over these facts is rapidly passing. As soon as our redeployment is complete, this opportunity *will be lost to Japan*—and as you know, *it will be lost forever*. The war will then be decided by our superior arms, *in Japan*. If the Japanese leaders still prefer to delay and hope for miracles, they should remember that the cemetary of history is crowded with the graves of nations—nations which were doomed to extinction because they made their decision too late.

Number Thirteen

Release 28 July 1945

By now you are familiar with the proclamation issued by the heads of the Governments of the United States, the United Kingdom, and China, which was signed by the President of the United States and the Prime Minister of Great Britain at Potsdam and concurred in by the President of the National Government of China, who communicated with President Truman by dispatch. Today, therefore, I am addressing both the leaders and the people of Japan at a time when Japan as a nation is confronted with her crisis of death—*or life*.

Japan must make a choice, upon the wisdom of which her whole future will depend. In the light of the alternatives presented in the Joint Proclamation, this choice should not be difficult. One alternative is prompt and utter destruction. If the Japanese people are forced by their self-willed militaristic leaders to choose the alternative of ruin, centuries of sweat and toil will be brought to naught in a cataclysmic end of a tragic war.

The other alternative is the end of war. One simple decision will allow tranquillity again to return to the city and the countryside. The guns will cease their fire, the bombs will no longer drop from the skies, your sons and brothers will no longer face agonizing and useless death on the battlefields. The homeland of Japan will be saved to continue a sovereign existence under a peacefully inclined and responsible government.

Peace for Japan has now been made possible, by the Joint Proclamation issued by the great leaders whose nations with all the vast resources at their command are determined to drive irresponsible militarism from the world.

It is more than symbolic that this Joint Proclamation was issued at Potsdam, in the heart of a Germany now in the throes of total defeat. The leaders of the Great Coalition drafted their proclamation amid the ruins of a nation which foolishly chose the road to destruction. As these leaders stood in the rubble of a once great country and beheld the vast monument to German stupidity they decided to give Japan an opportunity to escape a similar fate.

Is there any one in Japan who can doubt that an even worse military fate awaits Japan if she, like Germany, unwisely chooses the wrong alternative? No longer can the leaders of Japan keep the truth of Japan's defeat from their people. The people themselves have seen with their own eyes the steadily mounting power and fury of our combined offensive. You have seen our mighty battleships bombard your shores. You have seen the thousands of warplanes day after day darken your skies.

Yes, the people of Japan now know what modern war means. But they also know that they have experienced only the prologue to the great drama of total war.

With the unbounded determination of our people to carry this war to its foregone conclusion and with the inevitable triumph of our armed forces already in sight, Japan has been informed of the price she must pay if she refuses these terms now.

These terms, enumerated in the Joint Proclamation of July 26, cannot be misunderstood or misinterpreted. They offer the Japanese people freedoms they have never enjoyed under the domination of their military oppressors.

In this hour of Japan's decision, let me read a few lines from the address by which our late President Roosevelt, on December 8, 1941, officially advised the Congress of the United States of Japan's aggression: I quote:

"We are now in the midst of war, not for conquest, nor for vengeance, but for a world in which this nation, and all that this nation represents, will be safe for our children. The true goal we seek is far above and beyond the ugly field of battle. When we resort to force, we are determined that this force shall be directed toward ultimate good as well as against immediate evil. We Americans are not destroyers—we are *builders!*"

Number Fourteen

Release 4 August 1945

The question which is now foremost in the mind of every Japanese can be stated simply. It is this: How can Japan extriacte herself from this tragic war and plan for a decent future? The answer to this crucial question is— *leadership!*

Japanese society has always succeeded in producing leaders capable of facing and solving the problems of the day—at least, prior to the Shōwa Era. Shōwa—literally meaning "the era of brilliant peace"—began with high promise. But, the Shōwa Era may go down in history as the "dark age" of Japan. For it is now reaching its climax in a great war which threatens to bring the downfall of modern Japan. Tomorrow's historians will have little difficulty in understanding the causes of this downfall. They will point out that inadequate Japanese leadership in the Shōwa Era was the greatest single factor.

Virtually since the beginning of Shōwa, the short-sighted and irresponsible leaders of Japan have used every means at their disposal to produce and maintain what they themselves have called "tenseness in our national life." This was a typically vague way of saying that they were forcing the people of Japan to maintain a state of war-mindedness. This war-mindedness of Japan was not only kept alive by Japanese leaders, but was gradually stepped up until at last the leaders of Japan dropped their feigned interest in peaceful pursuits and openly put Japan on a total war basis.

But now, even those Japanese leaders who are responsible for this know that when they staked everything on victory, they made a fatal mistake, not only for themselves, but for the Japanese nation as a whole. They, no less than we, now know that Japan has already lost the war.

With all hope of victory in this war gone, *Japanese leaders have no capacity to face defeat!*

They gambled for the highest stakes and lost. Now a host of unsolved problems haunts them day and night. Let me briefly discuss only one of these problems, namely, the problem of Japanese prisoners of war. Events of the past few months compel me to bring this matter into the open and to discuss it with the frankness which it fully deserves.

Japanese military leaders in the Shōwa period have carefully indoctrinated the people of Japan, as well as the Army and Navy, in the belief that Japanese warriors should fight to the death and should never allow themselves to be taken alive as prisoners of war. This is misrepresented as the historical tradition of the samurai, although you know, as well as I, that surrenders *were quite common* in all the wars and battles fought by Japan's medieval knights as well as in those of their modern successors.

I am here concerned not with the ethics of such indoctrination, but with its practical value in war and especially in the peace to follow. Before our offensive in the Pacific started, it was only natural that we took relatively few Japanese prisoners. But the trend is showing a *marked* change. For example, in February 1944, the Allied forces captured a total of only 28 Japanese prisoners of war in all theaters. But in June 1945, the American forces alone captured some 10,000 Japanese, and hundreds of others were taken by the British in Burma, the Chinese in China, and the Australians in the East Indies and elsewhere.

On Guam between 20 July and 10 August 1944 our forces took only 86 Japanese prisoners. By November 1944, 463 Japanese had been captured on Guam, and today the figure is over 1000, or some 5 percent of the original Guam garrison. During the recent Okinawa campaign, there was a marked tendency toward increase in Japanese surrenders, both absolute and relative.

The trend is now clear. Japanese military personnel, both enlisted men and officers, are surrendering more frequently than they did in the early period of the war. Furthermore, there is evidence to show that many of these Japanese prisoners of war are well educated, intelligent, and are in every respect "good Japanese." A surprising number are officers, some of high rank.

Let me illustrate by an incident from the Biak campaign. The Japanese defenders of the island consisted of the 222nd Regiment, a naval guard battalion, a tank detachment, and other units totaling some 10,000 men, all under the command of Colonel Kuzume. The assault troops of the United States 41st Infantry stormed the island and after less than a month's fighting, on 21 June 1944 were victorious. Colonel Kuzume perished in a banzai charge. But many of his soldiers, well satisfied that they had performed their duty, surrendered individually or in groups.

Months after Biak had become an American offensive base, a fever-ridden, hungry Japanese non-commissioned officer walked into a mess hall and asked the American officers to accept his surrender. He had brought with him the colors of the 222nd Japanese Infantry which the regiment had carried ever since it had left its headquarters in the city of Hirosaki. As a symbol of growing Japanese realism, this regimental flag is now preserved in this city of Washington.

The meaning of these facts is obvious. Those high-minded Japanese who are realistic and wise enough to surrender, rather than to seek a wasteful and unsanctified death, are thereby demonstrating that they are aware of their responsibility of living to help rebuild post-war Japan.

Thus the prisoner of war problem is just one of the many problems of defeat which now confront Japan's leaders. But they do not know how to solve any of these problems because they do not know how to face defeat. With Japan writhing in the throes of her greatest crisis, her impotent leaders continue their foolish talk of eventual Japanese victory.

If Japanese leaders have any loyalty and wisdom left, there is but one choice left to them. They must recognize their present situation, and take suitable steps to corect the tragic mistakes of the recent past. *They must plan for their inevitable defeat and for Japan's future* with whatever loyalty, intelligence, and courage they can *still* command.

Index